BUG OUT TO BELIZE
Sustainable Living Guide to Escaping Politics, Consumerism, Big Brother and Nuclear War in Beautiful Belize

By Lan Sluder

BUG OUT TO BELIZE Sustainable Living Guide to Escaping Politics, Consumerism, Big Brother and Nuclear War in Beautiful Belize

By Lan Sluder

 quator

Published by Equator, Asheville, NC.
Printed in the United States.

ISBN: 978-0-9994348-4-0

Parts of this book have appeared in different forms in other works by Lan Sluder, including *Easy Belize, Lan Sluder's Guide to Belize, Lan Sluder's Guide to Mainland Belize and Lan Sluder's Guide to the Cayes, Coast and Beaches of Belize.*

Photos by Rose Lambert-Sluder, except where noted.
Cover photo by Black Day/Shutterstock.

Websites:
www.belizefirst.com
www.bugouttobelize.com
www.amazingasheville.net
www.lansluder.com

Notice: This work does not purport to give legal, medical, tax or other professional advice. Rules, regulations and other information changes frequently. Seek competent professional counsel and perform due diligence before acting on information contained herein.

Table of Contents

Photo by Gage Skidmore/Shutterstock

THE WORLD WE LIVE IN

An Introduction: Are You Worried?

Are you concerned about the direction your government is taking? Do you believe politicians are taking your country down the wrong road? Do you worry about your own future or that of your children? What about if the unimaginable happens? A deadly disease caused by a new or mutating virus sweeps the world? A severe drought, crop failures or other climate-change event that changes the familiar circumstances of where you now live? Religious wars? Or, heaven help us, political leaders overreact or make a mistake and unleash thermonuclear weapons?

Or, do you simply want to escape the ever-growing commercialism of so much of the world? Do you want to live a simple, satisfying, self-sufficient life, growing your own food, building your own home and living life the way you want it?

With things getting a little crazy in the United States, in parts of Europe and in Asia, not to mention some other parts of the world, maybe it makes sense to find a little place to hide out and hole up until the worst is over?

Or, are you simply a prudent person and want a little insurance against the worst-case scenarios actually happening? Perhaps nothing will happen, but just in case....

While no place is ever going to be 100% safe, and no place is 100% perfect, it's just possible that you can find a small, obscure corner that offers a better chance of escaping some of the potential problems of the modern world.

Could that place be Belize?

Here are a few of the reasons why you may want to consider Belize as a option to where you are living now, or at least as that insurance policy:

Belize is where most people aren't. With only around 385,000 people in an area the size of the state of Massachusetts (population about 7 million), Belize is one of the least densely populated countries in the Western Hemisphere. Outside the cities and towns, you can often drive for miles without seeing another human being. In that regard, Belize is like a little, subtropical Alaska. Or like Florida 75 to 100 years ago. Belize's low population density means that you can find a place away from other people and do your own thing. In case of some political, social or military calamity, Belize has little strategic importance to any of the world's powers. In the case of a nuclear accident or war, while prevailing winds at times do bring poisons down from the U.S., Belize has the most extensive cave systems in Central America for escaping radiation.

Belize is a place to escape frantic consumerist society. In Belize, you won't find Starbucks, McDonald's or Walmart. Global franchise businesses are almost unknown. That can be frustrating when you're trying to find a cheap home appliance or a quick meal, but on the plus side you don't need to spend your life accumulating stuff.

Belize has a low-voltage government. Big Brother won't make it here, if for no other reason than that the Belize government doesn't have the resources to create Big Brother. Belize has its share, some would say more than its share, of red tape and nosy bureaucrats. Yes, there are politicians with their hands out and government functionaries that want you to do this or don't do that, to get a permit or pay for a license. Only a few decades ago, it wasn't this way in Belize. You could do almost anything you wanted to, and nobody in the government would know or care. That has changed to some degree.

But here's the good thing, Belize is such a small country, with such a small population, and, to be frank, most Belizean pols and bureaucrats just want to go along and enjoy life, maybe getting a little piece of this or that, so as long as you stay under the radar you won't be much bothered. At the worst, you may have to grease someone's palm a little. And there's another plus to government in Belize: Along with Costa Rica, Belize has the most stable political system in the region, so things are unlikely to change much.

Belize is out of the nuclear zone. Belize is too small and insignificant to be a target for any country or terrorist's nuclear bomb. Thinking about the unthinkable, the worst that would happen is that an ICBM would veer off course and accidentally hit Belize or nearby. Or radiation might be brought by wind currents to Belize. But the good news is that Belize has natural bomb shelters, in one of the largest number of cave systems in the hemisphere. Also, it's relatively easy to quickly build an underground shelter to protect you, your family and your friends from most of the effects of nuclear blasts and radiation.

English is the official language of Belize. You don't have to learn a new language to live in Belize, because English is the official language. You don't have to struggle with grammar and syntax in an unfamiliar tongue. While Spanish and several other languages are widely spoken in Belize, and many Belizeans are bi- or trilingual, everything from street signs and newspapers to official government documents are in English. From your first day in Belize, you can shop, dine, chat and gossip without having to thumb through a dictionary or cast about for the right verb ending.

Belize has a warm, sunny, frost-free climate, perfect for self-sufficient living and off-the-grid survival. Belize has a sub-tropical climate year-round with no real need for furnaces or other things requiring lots of power or special equipment. You can live in an old tee shirt and a pair of shorts. It has 200 miles of shoreline on the Caribbean and hundreds of islands in the sea with all the fish, lobster, conch and other seafood you could possibly eat. Healthy food like mangoes, bananas, pineapples, papaya, avocados and other fruit grow everywhere. There's fertile land for farming, with little need for chemicals, and you can grow up to three crops a year.

As the Maya have shown, building materials such as thatch and limestone are readily at hand for simple houses. Yurts and similar tent-style accommodations are an option for some. You can put up a simple frame house or a pre-fab Mennonite house without insulation or other cold-weather construction.

It never frosts or snows in Belize. The climate is similar to that of South Florida. As long as you're comfortable with warm to hot temperatures, perhaps tempered by cooling breezes from the sea, you'll like Belize weather. You'll never have to pay for heating oil or natural gas again.

Newcomers are welcomed to Belize. Belize is not a Never-Never Land where everyone loves everybody in perfect harmony, but the fact is, by and large, Belizeans are as friendly a bunch of people as you'll ever find. Belizeans take people one at a time. Whether you're black, white, brown or green, short, tall, fat, ugly or beautiful, rich or poor, you'll find acceptance in Belize. Your neighbors will say hello to you on the street, check on you if you're sick and share a joke with you over a Belikin at the bar. Of course, they may try to hit you up for a loan. For the most part, Belizeans genuinely like Americans (and Canadians and Europeans). At the official level, the Belize government welcomes retirees and others, especially if they bring some resources to the country. The Qualified Retired Persons Incentive Program *(see the section on this and other options for living in Belize)* is administered not by a bureaucratic immigration department but by the Belize Tourism Board, which usually provides approvals quickly.

Belize is great for those who love an active outdoor lifestyle. Belize offers relatively little in the way of cultural activities — museums, art galleries, theatre, the arts. But it makes up for it with a wealth of options for those who love the outdoors. You can garden year-round. The saltwater fishing is some of the best in the world. Boating, diving, swimming and snorkeling can be as close as your back yard. For the more adventurous, there are caves and ancient ruins to explore, rivers to canoe and mountains to hike.

If you're bored in Belize, it's your own fault. Belize is a natural wonder. You could spend the rest of your life just learning about the flora and fauna of the country. Belize is home to thousands of species of trees and flowers, hundreds of kinds of birds and butterflies. The culture of Belize is wide and deep. The history of the Maya in Belize goes back thousands of years. You can take trips to the enchanting corners of the country, to the high hills of the Mountain Pine Ridge, to the endless caves of the Chiquibul wilderness, to the lush rainforest of Toledo, to the many islands in the Caribbean Sea and to the 190-mile long Belize Barrier Reef.

Belize isn't the cheapest place in the world, but if you're smart you can live in Belize for less. Belize is not the cheapest place to live, and in some areas of Belize an American lifestyle will cost U.S. prices or even higher. Overall, however, many expats in Belize say they can live larger than back home, enjoying some luxuries such as a housekeeper, a gardener or nice meals out. Investment income, pensions and Social Security checks seem to stretch a little farther in Belize. While some items such as gasoline, imported foods and electricity cost more in Belize, other things including medical care, housing, insurance and household help are significantly cheaper in Belize than in the U.S., Canada or Western Europe. Although Belize has a few million dollar houses and condos, you can rent a small house for US$250-$500 a month, set up a made-in-Belize Mennonite cabin for US$20,000, build an attractive new home for US$75,000 to $175,000 and buy a waterfront lot for as little as US$75,000 to $100,000, although you can pay much more. In this book we've concentrated on areas of Belize where living is cheaper, and we've avoided the areas, such as Ambergris Caye and Placencia, where real estate and rental costs are higher.

Belize offers the chance for a healthier lifestyle. As discussed in detail later in this book, Belize does not have the high-tech, state-of-the-art medical care available in the U.S. or even in countries like Mexico or Panama. But the Belizean lifestyle can be very healthful. You eat fresh fruit and unprocessed food. You walk more and ride less. You stay outside in the clean, unpolluted air rather than being cooped up in a climate-controlled box all day. You go home for lunch or take a nap at mid-day. In Belize's balmy climate, your arthritis and other aches and pains may fade away. Many people who move to Belize start feeling better within a few weeks. Quite a few lose weight. Blood pressure levels go down. Of course, you can also live an unhealthy life in Belize — watching cable TV all day, drinking all night and eating fried foods and lardy beans and rice.

Back-a-bush in Toledo, Belize with a traditional Maya house

Property rights are respected in Belize. Property rights are protected in Belize through the traditions of English Common Law. In some countries, if you leave your house or land unoccupied, squatters can move in, and it's almost impossible to get them out. Legal documents may be written in a language you don't understand. Powerful local interests can take your property through tricky legal — or illegal — means. In many parts of Latin America and Europe, the legal system is Civil Law based on the Napoleonic Code, very different from the system in the United States. But Belize shares with America, Canada and the United Kingdom a legal system based on English Common Law. In Belize, private property is respected and protected. Foreigners can own property virtually anywhere in Belize, with exactly the same rights and protections as exist for Belizeans. Squatters cannot take your property. The Belize legal system isn't perfect, and lawyers in Belize are almost as costly as those in the U.S., but it's a better system than, for example, in Honduras or Mexico.

The U.S. dollar is accepted everywhere in Belize. Belize has its own currency, the Belize dollar, so technically the American greenback is not the official monetary unit of the country. As a practical matter, though, the U.S.

9

dollar is accepted anywhere and everywhere in Belize, and the Belize dollar has been pegged for decades at the rate of 2 Belize to 1 U.S. dollar (though the rate may vary slightly if you exchange with money changers.) Anything of substantial value, such as real estate and hotel room rates, is priced in U.S. dollars. This means that prices in Belize are more stable for American dollar holders than they would be if the Belizean currency floated against the dollar. It also means that in periods when the value of the U.S. dollar declines sharply against the euro, yen and many other hard currencies, prices in Belize remained about the same as always for Americans. Of course, during periods of appreciation of the value of the U.S. dollar, prices in Belize do not become cheaper for U.S. dollar holders.

Belize has easy access by air, sea or land. For those in North America, Belize has the special advantage of having easy access by air, sea and land. If you need to bug out to Belize, you can get there quickly. From major cities in the U.S. and Canada, Belize is just a few hours away via a non-stop flight. By car, it's a two- to four-day drive from Texas, depending on how hard you push it. Driving nonstop (which we don't recommend), you could even make it in a single long day. By sea, Belize is a reasonably short sail from neighboring countries Mexico and Guatemala. Yacht owners can make the trip across the Gulf of Mexico and Caribbean by island hopping from Florida or elsewhere in the American Southeast and Texas. Numerous cruise ships call on Belize, mainly at Belize City and Harvest Caye off Placencia. Cargo ships make regular stops in Belize.

The Consumerist Society

Are you getting tired of the consumer society? Do you seem to be constantly accumulating more "stuff" that you don't really need and that brings you little happiness? Are you being bombarded with promotional messages that try to convince you to buy, buy, buy?

Consumerism, or the consumer society, is an economic and social concept that encourages the purchase and consumption of goods and services in ever-increasing amounts.

It came about in part because industrialization in the 18th and 19th century was so successful in producing goods at lower and lower costs. This success, however, had a downside. Companies produced goods in such large amounts that from time to time there was overproduction. The supply of goods grew beyond demand for them.

One solution was the development of sophisticated advertising to encourage people to buy more goods and services. The first full-service advertising agency, N. W. Ayer & Son, was established in 1869 in Philadelphia and continued in business until 2002. There had been advertising agents before then, in Europe and the U.S., but Ayer was considered the first full-service agency that not only brokered space in newspapers and magazines but also helped clients write ad copy and design eye-catching ads. A few years later, J. Walter Thompson expanded on this idea and created what became for many years the world's largest global ad agency. In the 20th century, ad agencies expanded into the creation of advertising and marketing campaigns in many other media, first radio and then television. They also used direct mail, standardized outdoor and point-of-sale materials, all often supported by public relations campaigns. In the late 20th and early 21st centuries, with the development of digital media and the internet, online advertising became an increasingly important component of the marketing mix.

Another solution to overproduction was what came to be called planned obsolescence. Instead of making a high-quality product that might last a lifetime, or even for generations, companies began making cheaper products that might last only a few years or a few decades. After that, consumers would have to buy a replacement.

Concurrent with the rise of a consumption-based economy was a change in how goods and services were distributed. Until the late 19th century, nearly all businesses were independently owned shops and stores. Most had just a single location. In larger cities, some stores had multiple locations.

The Great Atlantic & Pacific Tea Company, better known as A&P, was one of the first large national companies in the U.S. Founded in 1869 as a retail, tea and coffee store, it grew into America's first grocery chain. At its peak in 1930 A&P had nearly 1,600 stores in the U.S. and Canada. It remained the world's largest retailer in terms of sales until 1965. After a series of business and financial problems, it downsized and eventually filed bankruptcy and closed in 2015.

Sears, Roebuck & Co., later known as just Sears, was another early retail pioneer of consumer goods and services. It began as a mail order company, became a publicly owned company in 1906 and began opening retail stores in 1925 in

Indiana. By the mid-20th century, Sears had become an international conglomerate with interests in auto repair, insurance, financial services and real estate in several countries. Now, after joining with Kmart as a part of a public holding company with a large amount of the shares held by a billionaire investor, Sears Holdings is struggling to stay afloat in a changing marketplace.

Today, retailing is dominated by a handful of large multinational chains. Walmart is the largest retailer in the world, with annual sales of more than half a trillion U.S dollars and nearly 12,000 stores worldwide. Six of the world's 10 largest retail chains are based in the U.S.: Walmart, Costco, Kroger, Walgreen-Boots, Amazon, Home Depot. Amazon is the fastest growing, controlling more than 45% of online retail sales and about 5% of all retail sales. Its Chinese competitor, Alibaba, is also growing fast.

The top 250 retail companies in the world generate more than US$4.3 trillion in revenue annually, according to the National Retail Federation in the U.S. Each of the world's top retail companies have average annual sales of US$17.2 billion. That's about 10 times the annual GDP of the entire country of Belize! Just to be in the top 250, retailers need annual sales of about US$3.5 billion, twice the Belize GDP.

Interestingly, not a single one of the top 250 retail operations in the world has a location in Belize.

Franchising was another way in which capitalism found a way to expand and create new outlets for its goods and services. Although franchising dates back to at least the Middle Ages in Europe, when wealthy landowners made deals with tax collectors to receive a percentage of the taxes obtained from peasants. However, modern franchising didn't begin until the late 19th century. Coca-Cola was the first truly successful franchise, when an Atlanta druggist made deals with representatives to sell his drink, which initially was made from sugar, molasses, spices and cocaine. Another druggist, Louis Kroh Liggett, made another early franchise success, when he brought together a group of drugstore owners in a cooperative called Rexall.

The concept of franchising really took off after World War II, especially in the U.S. Some of the companies and brands still widely known today were developed to sell products and services to the growing middle class in America. Holiday Inn, founded by Kemmons Wilson in Memphis, opened its first motel in 1952. (A Holiday Inn was briefly in Belize City; it is now part of the Radisson Fort George.) That same year, Colonel Harland Sanders began franchising his Kentucky Fried Chicken restaurants. He had been selling his special recipe chicken in Corbin, Ky., since 1939. A KFC opened in Belize City in the 1970s but didn't last long.

About that same time, the McDonald brothers, Mac and Dick, tried to franchise their hamburger joint, which was successfully selling burgers, fries and milkshakes in San Bernardino, Calif. It took off when Ray Kroc, a salesman for a milkshake machine company, got the rights to franchise McDonald's. The McDonald brothers were to receive one-half of 1% of gross sales of all franchisees. Kroc opened his first restaurant in 1956 in Des Plaines near Chicago. By 1959, Kroc's franchisees had 102 restaurants. With the ad campaign "Look for the Golden Arches," growth exploded.

McDonald's Corporation went public in 1965 at $22.50 a share. A block of 100 shares purchased in 1965 for US$2,250, after more than a dozen splits, would now be worth more than US$10 million.

Today, there are some 34,500 McDonald's restaurants in 119 countries around the world. For years, there have been reports of a McDonald's planning to open in Belize, but to date that has not happened. The nearest McDonald's is in Chetumal, Mexico.

Subway, the world's largest franchise operation in terms of units, now has more than 44,600 locations. In 2003 a Subway opened in Belize City, but it later closed.

Branding is another aspect of consumerism. The use of brands dates back at least to the ancient Egyptians, who used hot branding irons to brand their cattle. This still goes on today in many parts of the world. In Belize, the law requires all cattle to be branded.

The term branding has been expanded and extended to mean a strategic personality for a product or company. Brand now suggests the values and promises that a consumer may perceive and appreciate. Branding is a set of advertising, marketing and communication methods that help to distinguish one company or one product from competitors. It aims to create a lasting impression in the minds of customers.

The proliferation of consumer brands is nothing short of amazing. In the U.S. alone, there are now almost 300 brands of hotel chains, 3,000 brands of craft beers, 600 brands of cereals and 30,000 different specialty coffee house brands. Got a sweet tooth? There are some 250 brands of chocolate bars alone sold worldwide.

Beginning sometime in the late 20th century, branding moved from companies and products to people and ideas. Today, many people try to develop, and monetize, their personal lifestyle or personality into a brand. Likewise, political and other intangible brands have developed.

Reaction to Consumerism

The great growth of consumerism, especially in highly developed countries such as those in Western Europe and in North America, has spawned many anti-consumerism movements and efforts.

Some of these anti-consumerism efforts are based on religious or moral beliefs. Others are based on a philosophical opposition to constantly accumulating more and more "stuff," or to keeping up with the Jones. Some, such as the conservation or green movements, are based on the belief that excessive consumerism is harmful to nature and the planet.

Some prefer to call the movements "postconsumerism." Whatever they are called, they have taken many forms over time.

Religious sects and groups have often been involved in anti-consumerist and anti-materialist efforts. Catholic priests and nuns, at least in theory, gave up worldly goods and worldly pleasures, to serve Christ. Similarly, Buddhist and Hindu monks take vows of poverty and live simply in communal situations. The United Society of Believers in Christ's Second Appearing, more commonly known as the Shakers, founded in 18th century England, established celibate, communal and pacific farms and communities in 19th century America. The Shakers were known for their belief in the equality of the sexes and in simplicity in life, architecture and furniture.

The hippies in the 1960s had a strong anti-consumerist philosophy, with some living in communes, sharing everything including their partners and their dope.

Today, the simple living movement, with its "small houses" and dedication to a small-footprint life, are an important niche component of the developed world. The green movement, with its emphasis on ecology and recycling, has become a political force in Western Europe, the U.S. and Canada and elsewhere.

The Situation in Belize

Belize has no Walmart. No Home Depot. No Circuit City. No McDonald's or Wendy's or Papa John's fast food restaurants.

It is not true that there are no international franchises in Belize. There are a few, mainly in the travel industry. Hertz, Avis, Budget, Alamo and National are among the car rental franchised agencies in Belize. There are a few hotels with international flags: a Radisson, Best Western and Ramada in Belize City and one of the Hilton brands in San Pedro. One or two others may open. As noted, in the past there was a Holiday Inn, a KFC and a Subway in Belize City, but these have all been closed or changed from those franchises.

Nearly all the businesses in Belize are independents, owned either by Belizeans or by foreigners, most of whom also have become Belize citizens or at least official permanent residents. A single giant retailer, Walmart, has annual sales that are some 300 times larger than entire yearly output of the Belize economy.

While this lack of homogenization and consumerism is a big plus for Belize, it also means that you can't go down to your neighborhood hyperstore and select from 40 kinds of dish soap, or 18 brands of underwear. Rum may be US$7 or $8 a bottle, but Cheetos may be US$5 a bag. Every computer, nearly every piece of plumbing and electrical equipment, every car and truck, every pair of scissors, is imported, and often transshipped thousands of miles from one port to another before it gets to the final destination in Belize. Then it's carried by truck or on a bus or in the luggage area of a Cessna somewhere else.

Some items simply aren't available in Belize, or supplies may be spotty. Bags of cement, for example, sometimes are in short supply, and the cost is higher than you'd pay back home. To get ordinary items such as building nails or a certain kind of auto part, you may have to call several different suppliers. Belize's small population is spread out over a relatively large area, served by a network of bad roads (though they are getting better), well-used planes and old boats. Although the government has shifted some of its focus from excise and import taxes to income and consumption taxes, much of government revenue still comes from import taxes, so the prices you pay may reflect a tax of from 20% to possibly as high as 80%.

In short, Belize is an inefficient market of low-paid consumers, a country of mom 'n pop stores, few of which could last long in a highly competitive marketplace such as the U.S. This is what gives Belize its unique flavor in an age of franchised sameness. But, you better Belize it, it also provides a lot of frustration and higher prices.

This is not to say that most Belizeans reject consumerism. Both locally originated and international programming on television run ads that invite Belizeans to try the latest products. Many Belizeans would like to be able to afford a new car, the latest big-screen TV or current fashions from leading designers. Most, however, cannot afford them. With average household and per capita incomes only one-tenth of that in the U.S. or Canada, Belizeans have to make do with less.

Quite a few expats in Belize decide to emulate their Belizean neighbors and also make do with less, even if they could afford to buy the latest, best and most improved. They learn they can do quite well with an older car or truck, and that they do not need to replace their smartphones every time a new version comes out.

Is Big Brother Watching?

Most of us greatly value our individual freedoms, such as the right to freely express our opinions, to practice any religion we choose, or none, to meet with our fellow citizens for any purpose including politics, to pursue our own choices personal relationships and about career and business, to enjoy the activities and interests we prefer in the privacy of our homes and other rights. In many countries, including the U.S., Canada, Britain and most countries in Western Europe those freedoms long have been protected by constitution or laws.

Unfortunately, in recent decades in much of the world these freedoms have been eroded. Governments have grown ever larger and ever more powerful. In the name of fighting a war on terrorism, or drugs, or whatever evil a particular government sees, the freedoms and rights of its citizens too often have been diminished. While government can do much good, it also has the power to do great harm.

In China, amidst unparalleled economic success, the ruling Communist Party has moved to establish control over even the most intimate and personal individual decisions. For a time, the party controlled how many children families could have, with the one-child policy that was in effect from 1979 until 2015, when it was phased out. More recently, the Chinese government, through partnerships with large Chinese technology companies such as Ten Cent, Baidu and Alibaba, is establishing one of the world's most comprehensive and absolute systems of control. In November 2017, the *Wall Street Journal* reported, "The Chinese government is building one of the world's most sophisticated, high-tech systems to keep watch over its citizens, including surveillance cameras, facial recognition technology and vast computers systems that comb through terabytes of data."

In mid-2017, a new cybersecurity law requires internet companies in China, including those based outside the country, to help ferret out content that "endangers national security, national honor and interests." Beijing has more surveillance cameras installed than any other city in the world. Three major U.S.-based internet companies, including Facebook, have been banned in China. Many international internet sites are blocked.

Russia, under the quasi-dictatorship of Vladimir Putin, may be less sophisticated than China in watching and controlling its citizens, but it is nonetheless quickly destroying individual rights. Freedom House, an independent watchdog of freedom around the world, has rated the Russian Federation as "Not Free." Freedom House in a 2016 report stated, "Although the constitution provides for freedom of speech, vague laws on extremism grant the authorities great discretion to crack down on any speech, organization, or activity that lacks official support. The government controls, directly or through state-owned companies and friendly business magnates, all of the national television networks and many radio and print outlets, as well as most of the media advertising market."

Transparency and accountability in the day-to-day workings of the Russian government barely exist. Decisions are adopted behind closed doors by a small group of individuals. Corruption in the government and business world is pervasive. Many experts argue that the political system is essentially a kleptocracy, in which ruling elites plunder public wealth to enrich themselves. The Putin regime has a tight grip on the media, using state-run media to saturate the country with government propaganda. Elections are held, but serious opposition candidates are unable to get their views out. One opposition leader, Boris Nemtsov, was murdered, and others have been imprisoned.

A number of countries, mainly in the Middle East and South Asia, operate as theocracies, with the state operating under religious law. The best known are Islamic countries with Sharia law such as Saudi Arabia, Iran, Sudan, Yemen, Afghanistan, Somalia and Pakistan. However, the second-most populous country in the world, India, has many laws that appear to discriminate in favor of Hindu beliefs, such as vegetarianism and against Muslims, Christians and others.

Even in Western and Northern Europe, the United States, Canada and in Central and South America, there is increased central government control, said to be necessary in "wars" on terrorism, drugs and crime. Britain, for example, has some 6 million CCTV cameras. This is about one security camera for every 11 people. London alone has about half a million surveillance cameras.

Wars in the Middle East, notably in Syria and Iraq, have created a flood of refugees coming to Europe. This has caused a backlash, marked by the rise of nationalist, populist and rightwing political groups. In turn, this leads to larger police forces, more surveillance of the population and less individual freedom.

Even the United States, long known as a bastion of personal freedom, enshrined in the U.S. Constitution and its Amendments, has tightened the screws on personal freedoms in the name of law and order, stemming illegal immigration and fighting terrorism. Among the provisions of these sweeping laws are the right of law enforcement officials to search a home or business without the knowledge of the owner, the indefinite detention of immigrants and the use of National Security Letters to allow the FBI and other government agencies to demand information from individuals and businesses without showing probably cause or having any judicial oversight. The government was given wide powers to tap the phones and collect huge amounts of data from cell phones, email and texts, even if involving U.S. citizens.

The Patriot Act, enacted in 2001, and the Freedom Act, passed into law in 2015, allows the government rights it seldom if ever had in the past, including what critics claim is warrantless searches of information about or from U.S. citizens and permanent residents The Foreign Intelligence Surveillance Act, first authorized by Congress in 2007, is aimed at non-Americans who are overseas, U.S. spy agencies sometimes collect communication to, from or mentioning U.S. citizens and permanent residents under the law's authority. The law was renewed for six years in early 2018.

Anyone who travels by air in or from the U.S. knows the power the government has to tell you what to do – take off your shoes, remove your belt, go through a body scan, take a pat-down, etc. Millions are inconvenienced in the name of protecting us from terrorists.

Use of surveillance cameras to watch Americans at work and play has surged. As of 2016, there were an estimated 62 million surveillance cameras in the U.S., or roughly one for every five Americans.

The Cato Institute, a conservative-leaning think tank, ranks the U.S. only 23rd in the world on its human freedom index.

The U.S. has the largest prison population in the world. More than 2.2 million people are in federal, state and local prisons. That's about 1 in every 110 Americans.

One of the latest developments is that U.S. citizens owing the Internal Revenue Service more than US$51,000 (in taxes, penalties and interest) may give those delinquent taxpayers' names to the U.S. State Department, which can refuse to issue a passport to them. Some observers are saying this is like keeping citizens locked in their own countries, not allowed to travel abroad.

Situation in Belize

Belize does not rank at the top of rankings of personal freedom, as do jurisdictions such as Hong Kong, Switzerland, New Zealand, Denmark and Canada. A great deal of this has to do with the little country's continued struggle with the negative effects of organized crime, gang violence, drug trafficking and corruption.

In Freedom House's latest analysis of countries, Belize gets a Free rating. It scores an overall 1.5, where 1 is best and 7 is worst. On political rights, it scores a 1 and on personal liberties a 2.

Many think tanks and institutes don't even include Belize in their rankings, because the country is so small.

Those that do, however, sometimes overlook the fact that while Belize has its problems with transparent governance, red tape and occasional overstepping of individual rights by government bureaucrats and police, the reality is that Belize is so small and so poor that it can barely run itself. It simply does not have the resources to become a police state. The entire Belize police force consists of only about 1,400 officers. Its active Defence Force (military) has about 1,300 personnel. Accurate estimates of the number of surveillance cameras in Belize are not available, but it is likely only in the hundreds. In 2017, the Belize police finally installed 11 new surveillance cameras on the South Side of Belize City, the focal point of crime and gang activity in Belize, an effort that made the national news.

The fact is, if you want personal freedom in Belize, you just need to drive a few miles and then hike a ways into the bush. You'll be in a place where there are more critters than people. Surveillance cameras? Don't be ridiculous! Nobody will tell you what to think or what you can't say.

Belizeans say their mind. They say exactly what they think. If you're in Belize, you can, too.

Political Exhaustion

It's called many things: political exhaustion, chronic politics fatigue, voter fatigue. Whatever you call it, it stems from the political divisions we all face today. Conservatives versus liberals, populists versus progressives, pro-Trump versus anti-Trump, right wing versus left wing, traditionalists versus radicals, social conservatives versus fiscal conservatives, moderates versus extremists. The list goes on.

Wherever you live – in the U.S., Canada, the U.K., Europe, Hong Kong, Australia or elsewhere – the talking heads on television keep the political conversations, nay the shouting, going.

If you're sick and tired of it, maybe you're ready for a little Belize.

Of course there is plenty of politics in Belize, too. There's Blue (the People's United Party or PUP) and Red (the United Democratic Party or UDP). Also, there are splinter parties and a continuing attempt to start a viable third party.

Politics in Belize can be mean, vindictive and very personal. Supporting one party over another can mean a job for you and your relatives or a chance to buy land at low cost.

Some villages and towns in Belize are known as PUP villages or towns, and some are UDP. Because Belize is such a small country, where families may known each other for generations, and political rivalries run deep and strong. Even within political parties, there are factions that ebb and flow.

Having said that, as a foreigner in Belize, as a newcomer, you likely will not be involved in politics at all. In fact, it's best if you don't. It's like boating around the barrier reef: The clear waters hide tides and currents, the winds are tricky and you stand a chance of running aground.

As a non-citizen, you are pretty much outside the Belize political process. Politicians you speak with will be polite and may even seek your advice, or request your support, financial or otherwise, but the reality is you have no real place in the system, no juice and nobody really cares what you think.

If you're in Belize on visitor's permit, as a participant in Belize's Qualified Retired Persons program or even as a Permanent Resident, you won't be allowed to vote. (An exception exists for those from other British Commonwealth countries, who may be able to vote in local elections, although not in national ones.) If you stay long enough – at least five years after you obtain Permanent Residency status – and apply for Belizean citizenship, then of course you will be able to vote. You'll be a Belizean.

The good thing is that as an outsider in Belize, you can escape the political conflicts in Belize and the political maelstrom back home. Unless you seek it out, you don't have to follow the daily political news in the U.S. or wherever you're from. You don't have to watch the politicians posturing and the talking heads arguing. You may well find it a relief not to have take sides anymore. Who cares if your neighbor is a socialist or a raving Trumpanzee? You can go fishing or work in your garden or fruit orchard and forget about all that political nonsense.

It probably will lower your blood pressure and make your appreciate the more important things in life.

You, Nukes and Belize

An explosion of the H-Bomb during testing in the Marshall Island, 1952
Photo credit: Everett Historical/Shutterstock

Let's think about the unthinkable: thermonuclear catastrophe.

You don't want to think about it. We don't want to think about it. But, these days, perhaps more than even in the depths of the Cold War, it's a real possibility.

Cold War and MAD

For those who lived through, or have studied, the Cold War (late 1940s to 1991) between the then-Soviet Union with its satellite countries, and the United States and European and other Western democracies, we know what MAD stands for: Mutually Assured Destruction.

MAD was a theory, happily never tested, that with both sides controlling so many thermonuclear weapons neither side would risk launching a strike for fear that a retaliatory reaction would result in the mutual, total and assured destruction of both sides. The theory relied not only on the Soviets and the U.S. having huge numbers of nuclear weapons but also on the fact that it would be impossible to destroy all of them, even in a surprise preemptive strike, because they were hidden in protective bunkers, in submarines at sea and in aircraft that were perpetually in the air, all awaiting a launch order.

Anti-ballistic missile systems (ABM) were developed in an attempt to shield both sides from nuclear attack, but these were made untenable with existing ABM technology by the development of multiple independently targetable reentry vehicles (MIRV) with as many 10 warheads on each ballistic missile. Even today, shooting down an ICBM is problematical at best. Missile shields simply don't work very well. The American missile defense system designed to shield the U.S. from an intercontinental ballistic missile -- a network of sensors, radars and interceptor missiles based in Alaska and California -- failed three of its five tests through 2017.

Nuclear Club

After the collapse of the Soviet Union in the 1990s, Cold War tensions eased somewhat, but with the rise of Vladimir Putin, who has worked to make the Russian Federation once again a leading world military power, concerns about a nuclear exchange have reemerged. Mutually Assured Destruction again is being trotted out as a preventive, but even the MAD theory is of no help if an accident due to human or computer error were the cause of an attack. Russia is believed to have nearly 2,000 deployed nuclear weapons, with another 5,000 temporarily in storage. The U.S. has about 1,800 deployed warheads and another 6,000 available.

In addition, other countries, some with interests opposing the West, have joined the "nuclear club." China is believed to have around 300 nuclear weapons. Like the U.S. and Russia, China has the nuclear triad delivery capability – land-based ICBMs, submarines and strategic bombers.

The United Kingdom, France, India, Pakistan, Israel and North Korea also are known to have developed and tested atomic weapons. All except Pakistan and North Korea are known to have hydrogen bombs, and experts believe North Korea also has tested either hydrogen bombs or "boosted" atomic bombs with yields similar to smaller hydrogen bombs.

South Africa successfully developed nuclear weapons but dismantled them. Iran has had an advanced nuclear program and may well restart it, if the treaty between it and the U.S. falls apart.

Under NATO's weapon-sharing program, the U.S. also has provided nuclear weapons for Belgium, Germany, Italy, the Netherlands and Turkey to deploy and store

Altogether, it is believe there are at least 10,000 usable nuclear weapons worldwide, with as many as 5,000 actively deployed.

Types of Nuclear Weapons

There are two main types of nuclear weapons: atomic bombs and hydrogen bombs.

A-bombs, such as those dropped on two Japanese cities in World War II, rely on fission, or atom splitting, as nuclear power plants do. H-bombs, also called thermonuclear bombs, use both fission and fusion, atomic nuclei coming together, to produce explosive energy in the same way that our sun and other stars produce energy.

Hydrogen bombs can be up to 1,000 times more powerful than atomic bombs. H-bombs can be made small enough to be delivered by a missile. H-bombs delivered by submarine weigh only a little more than 700 pounds. Both types rely on processed radioactive materials such as plutonium and uranium.

The A-bombs dropped on Hiroshima and Nagasaki had relatively low explosive yields, in the range of 12 to 23 kilotons. Yet these bombs killed more than 200,000 people. The U.S. has successfully tested H-bombs with yields of 600 to 800 times that of either of the bombs dropped on Japan. The biggest H-bomb ever exploded was Tsar Bomba, tested by the Soviet Union in 1961. It had a yield of at least 50 megatons of TNT, 2,000 times more powerful than the "Fat Man" A-bomb dropped on Hiroshima.

Neutron bombs are a type of hydrogen bomb designed to maximize lethal radiation near the blast while minimizing the physical power of the blast. It could be used in tactical battlefield situations to kill enemy troops in, say, tanks.

Thermonuclear weapons exploded at a high altitude above a target can generate an electromagnetic pulse (EMP) that likely will fry all electronic devices, electric motors, telephone and power lines, power generation equipment and other things. Tests of high-altitude nuclear EMP explosions were conducted by the U.S. and the Soviet Union in the 1960s and 1970s. Some results are still classified, but one test by the Soviet Union using a 300 kiloton hydrogen bomb exploded at about 180 miles above Kazakhstan had an impact on even underground power lines across much of the country.

How Would a Nuclear Attack Take Place?

Rational actors, such as the leaders of the Soviet Union and the United States during the Cold War, were persuaded through the concept of Mutually Assured Destruction that it would be foolish to engage in a nuclear war. No one could win, and everyone would lose. Some called this the Doomsday Machine.

That may be true among the major powers today as well. However, with thousands of nuclear warheads deployed around the world, an accident due to human or machine error could start the chain of events that would lead to a massive world nuclear war. Perhaps more likely, a rogue state, a delusional world leader or a terrorist organization might use nuclear weapons.

Accident: Near nuclear war by accident has happened more often than you might think. For example, in 1980, computers at the National Military Command Center at the Pentagon and elsewhere received a warning that the Soviet Union had launched 220 ICBMs against the United States. Zbigniew Brzezinski, President Jimmy Carter's national-security advisor, was awakened with the news. Moments later, Brzezinski's military aide, General William Odom, called back to say it was not 220 missiles but 2,200. While Brzezinski was deciding what to do, General Odom called back, saying it was a false alarm, that a 46-cent computer chip had sent an error message. Similar situations that could have had horrendous results have happened before and could happen again.

If anything, it is becoming more likely, as the nuclear weapons held by the

U.S. and the former Soviet Union age. America has 440 Minuteman III missiles in silos across the Plains States, some of which are half a century old. Computers in the series include an IBM System 1, which was introduced in 1976.

Cyber warfare: Cyberattacks could also cause a pfished fake launch signal or other problems with nuclear weapons. In 2010, for instance, 50 Minuteman III missiles at F.E. Warren Air Force Base in Wyoming suddenly went offline. The U.S. military denied it was a cyberattack, but others were not so sure. Russia is known to have especially sophisticated cyberwar capabilities. China also has cyberwar capability, as do some smaller states including North Korea.

Human Error: Human error is also a concern. In 2013, a two-star general in charge of all Minuteman missiles was relieved of duty after going on a drunken binge while on a visit to Russia. A year later, nearly 100 Minuteman launch officers were caught cheating on their proficiency exams. In 2015, three launch officers at Malmstrom Air Force Base, Montana, were dismissed for using illegal drugs.

Delusional Leaders: No matter what people may think of President Donald Trump, many would agree that he is impulsive. In 2017 he threatened to bring "fire and fury" to North Korea and to "annihilate" the country. Trump also tweeted that he had a "bigger nuclear button" than did Kim Jong-on. The Republican chairman of the Senate Foreign Relations committee at the time, Senator Bob Corker, warned publicly that Trump's "volatility" could lead us into World War III. The U.S. president has the sole power to order the use of nuclear weapons without any obligation to consult Congress or the Joint Chiefs of Staff. Russia, too, has a new generation of populist, anti-American leaders who are not as conservative as the old men who ran the Soviet Union during the Cold War.

Rogue States: North Korea, led by the absolute dictator Kim, has advanced nuclear weapon and ICBM programs. Kim has threatened to hit U.S. territories and even the U.S. mainland with thermonuclear weapons.

Terrorists: Terrorists, especially al-Qaeda and ISIS, have long sought to get their hands on the ultimate terrorist weapon, a nuclear bomb. There is realistic concern that they might steal bomb components from Russia or Pakistan, or buy a bomb from North Korea or another country.

Impact of Nuclear Event on Belize

It is highly unlikely that any of these scenarios would impact Belize or even Central America directly. However, the indirect impact could be significant. In a nuclear war, a stray ICBM could strike in or near Belize.

While prevailing winds locally in Belize generally come from the east, the Caribbean Sea, depending on macro-conditions and the time of year fronts from Canada or the United States can sweep down from the north to Belize, potentially bringing radioactive fallout to the country. Worldwide, prevailing winds generally blow from west to east.

Effects of Nuclear Explosions

Hydrogen bombs release three different kinds of energy: heat and related energy, concussive blast and radiation.

More than one-third of the energy from an H-bomb is released in the form of heat, light and some types of radiation, including ultraviolet and X-rays. An H-bomb creates heat that is 6,300 times hotter than the surface of the sun, in the tens of millions of degrees. Depending on the size and the height of the explosion, anyone caught outside even 25 or 30 miles from the explosion could receive severe, third-degree burns and those within 15 miles of the explosion likely would be instantly incinerated by the heat and thermal radiation.

Up to about one-half of an H-bomb's energy is released in the form of the concussive blast. The heat from the fire causes a high-pressure wave to appear and move outward quickly, at speeds up to about 700 mph, more than four times the win speed of a Category 5 hurricane. Depending on the size of the bomb and its altitude when exploded, this instantly destroys most buildings and other things in a radius as large as 10 miles. Humans in the buildings would also be killed.

Approximately 15% of an H-bomb's energy takes the form of radiation. About one-third of that 15% is ionizing radiation, or highly charged electrons, neutrons and gamma rays and other particles and rays that are emitted as part of the fission and fusion chain reactions. The remaining two-thirds of radiation energy is nuclear fallout, waste byproducts and unspent fuel from the bomb.

Although it represents only 15% of the energy of an H-bomb, radiation is deadly, and it has an impact at far greater distances than the bomb's heat and concussion wave. The historian and investigative journalist Annie Jacobsen wrote in her 2015 book on the history of the Defense Advanced Research Projects Agency (DARPA) regarding the Castle Bravo test by the U.S. of a 15-megaton hydrogen bomb in the Pacific Ocean in 1954: "If ground zero had been Washington, D.C, every resident of the greater Washington-Baltimore area would now be dead. Without a Station 70–style bunker for protection [a sophisticated underground bunker with three-foot concrete walls], the entire population living there would have been killed by 5,000 roentgens of radiation exposure in mere minutes. Even in Philadelphia, 150 miles away, the majority of inhabitants would have been exposed to radiation levels that would have killed them within the hour. In New York City, 225 miles north, half of the population would have died by nightfall."

Longer term, the effects of radiation fallout include cancers, genetic damage and developmental and growth problems. The impact of fallout can range from a few days to thousands of years. Probably the most serious threat is cesium-137, a gamma emitter with a half-life of 30 years. It is a major source of radiation in nuclear fallout, and it is readily taken into the blood of humans and animals. Other hazards include strontium-90, with a half-life of 28 years, and iodine-131 with a half-life of only 8 days. Plutonium-239, which causes cancer, has a half-life of 24,000 years.

Protecting Yourself Against Nuclear Holocaust in Belize

As noted, a nuclear strike against Belize is highly unlikely. However, a nuclear missile could go off track and strike in or near Belize. Absent that, there would still be the risk of radiation, both immediately following a blast and from fallout over the longer term from unspent nuclear material. Some of this could last for years, even for thousands of years. If there is a good side to all of this, it is that it is possible to protect yourself from the worst of radiation and nuclear fallout.

It is beyond the scope of this book, and of the expertise of its author, to tell you how to protect yourself in case of a nuclear event. One excellent source of information is *Nuclear War Survival Skills,* published in 1979 by Cresson H. Kearny for the Oak Ridge National Laboratory. An updated 1987 edition is available as a free download in PDF format at www.oism.org/nwss and elsewhere. The original book, written for the U.S. Department of Energy, is free of copyright, but some companies have published paperback and ebook versions for which they make a charge.

Kearny states that shelter, preferably underground, is the best way to avoid deadly doses of radiation. Each 3.6 inches (9 cm) of packed earth halves the danger from gamma radiation. So 18 inches of packed earth, reduces the impact of gamma radiation on humans to 1/32th that of exposed human flesh. Approximately three feet of packed earth provides sufficient protection for most cases.

The danger from nuclear radiation falls over time, rapidly at first and then slower. For example, near ground zero, the dose rate from an above-ground explosion initially might be 1000 roentgens per hour (1000R). Within seven hours, it has fallen to 100R and within 48 hours to 10R and after two weeks it would be 1R. Two weeks after a nuclear attack, even if you were near areas where bombs hit, it likely would be safe to leave the fallout shelter, at least for periods of time, Kearny says.

This book provides examples of build-it-yourself fallout shelters. A fairly large small-pole underground shelter for families or small groups that provides a protection factor (PF) of PF1,000 against radiation – that is, person unprotected would received 1,000 times the gamma radiation of a person inside the shelter – would require all occupants to spend two days building it, working 12 hours a day, using hand tools such as saws, picks and shovels. It also provides good protection against blast and fire. Less protective shelters, using packed earth and doors from homes, can be built by as few as two persons working for a total of about 36 hours. Those with access to a backhoe or frontend loader could build these shelters in much less time.

Belize's Caves

If you'd rather not build your own bomb shelter, Belize comes ready-made with its own shelters: deep, cool limestone caves. Most of the caves are in Cayo and Toledo districts, but there also are caves in Stann Creek, Belize, Orange Walk and Corozal Districts. Many large caves are in national parks or other forest reserves, but quite a number are on private land.

The Chiquibul Cave System is the largest cave system in Central America. Two linked caves in the system, Actun Tun Kul and Cebada Cave, below Chiquibul National Park and following the path of the Chiquibul River, alone are more than 23 miles in length. The linked cave is the longest in Belize.

At least 10 known caves in Belize are at least 10,000 feet (nearly two miles) in length. Many of these caves are hundreds of feet deep, with large open chambers that can hold large numbers of people.

Photo: Shutterstock

QUICK LOOK AT BELIZE

This Is Belize

Keel-billed Toucan, the national bird of Belize
Photo: Adobe

There's a whole world out there. Why should you consider Belize? What's special about it? What's different or unique? Will you like it? Is it a place you should consider for an escape from the problems of your current world, from politics, war, Big Brother or, even, an apocalypse?

Maybe. Maybe not. But you'll never know unless you check it out. Read this and other books on Belize. First come as a visitor. Stay a while and get to know more about the country from your own personal experience. Then decide if Belize is for you.

Where Is Belize?

Belize is on the Caribbean Coast of Central America, bordered by Mexico to the north and Guatemala to the west and south. To the east is the Caribbean Sea. In Belize waters are as many as 1,000 islands, most unpopulated specks of sand, coral or mangrove. Belize is about the size of the U.S. state of Massachusetts or the country of Wales in the U.K. — 8,866 square miles. The population is around 385,000, about as many people as live in metro Savannah, Ga. From north to south Belize is less than 200 miles in length, and at its widest point it is only about 70 miles across.

Caribbean Beaches

Belize has nearly 200 miles of coastline on the Caribbean Sea, although in some stretches the coast is swampy with mangroves, not sandy beaches. And that doesn't count all the miles of beaches on the islands and atolls off the Belize mainland.

Are the beaches in Belize the best in the world? Candidly, no. The Belize Barrier Reef along the coast of Belize creates an ecology that's a nursery for marine life. This means that even the most pristine of beaches in Belize, despite the crystal clear Caribbean waters and white or khaki-colored sand, may have seagrass or may not be ideal for swimming.

Still, until you've relaxed under a cocopalm on a sandy beach, looking out over the emerald green, turquoise blue and deep purple Caribbean and see the white waves on the reef, you've never been on a Belize beach. And, you don't have to live all on the beach in Belize to enjoy the beaches – all beaches in Belize are public, up to the high-tide mark.

Belize Barrier Reef

The Belize Barrier Reef and Belize's atolls became a UNESCO World Heritage site in 1996. Belize's reef, part of the Mesoamerican Barrier Reef system, is the longest reef in the Western and Northern Hemispheres. Belize's reef is only a few hundred yards offshore in the north of Belize and 25 miles out in the far south.

Although it faces challenges from human pollution and global climate change, the Belize Barrier Reef and its related marine environments remain home to a stunning variety of sea life, from hammerhead sharks and eagle rays to permit, bonefish, tarpon and other game fish to beautiful living coral and tropical fish.

Belize's reef is one of the most diverse ecosystems in the world, with more than 500 species of fish, more than 100 types of hard and soft corals and hundreds of species of invertebrates.

The Belize Barrier Reef system, altogether covering a total of 370 square miles, offers visitors some of the world's best diving, snorkeling and fishing. Note that you'll see figures on the number of cayes ranging from around 400 to more than 1,000. The reason for the variance involves how you count islands. Is a tiny square yard of coral or sand that may not be there next year really an island?

Also good news is that Belize is taking positive steps to protect its reef system. Belize has established seven marine reserves and marine national parks. In 2010, Belize became the first country in the world to completely ban bottom trawling.

In early 2018, Donald Trump proposed allowing oil drilling off nearly all of the coastlines of the U.S., opening up 390 million square miles of oceans and seas to oil exploration. At about the same time, in late December 2017, the Belize government voted to implement an indefinite, and likely permanent, moratorium on all new oil exploration in its waters. "Today is a great day for Belize," said Nadia Bood, a reef scientist at the World Wildlife Fund.

Rainforests and Bush
Nearly 80% of mainland Belize is covered in forests. Within that huge canopy are tropical and semi-tropical rainforests, from lush rainforests that get up to 200 inches of rain a year to dry rainforests and bush and even piney woods.

Wherever you go in Belize, you're not far from a carpet of rich green life.

Outdoor Adventures
Belize is all about outdoor fun. Hard, soft and in-between. Cave tubing. Hiking. Birding. Canoeing and kayaking, rivers and sea. Horseback riding. Diving and snorkeling. Swimming in clear Caribbean waters. Exploring underground rivers and caves or clambering to the top of a Maya temple. Mountain biking. Climbing a mountain peak or surviving nights in the jungle. Ziplining and skywalking. Even skydiving and parasailing.

Of course it's easier if you're 23 and a triathlete, but even we who are not young and fit anymore can participate in many of the outdoor adventures Belize offers.

Wildlife Encounters
Ever been face to face with a black jaguar? Heard the incredible booming thunder of a troop of howler monkeys? Seen keel-billed toucans or scarlet macaws or a flock of parrots in the bush? Jumped in the water with sharks and stingrays? Watched a hunky manatee peep out of the sea or a green iguana hang out on a limb over a river? Seen the eyes of a crocodile in a lagoon or a red-rump tarantula scuttle back in its hole?

All of this and more are everyday sightings in Belize. Belize is home to more than 590 species of birds, 145 species of mammals, 140 species of reptiles and amphibians. And that's before you even get in the sea, with its 500 or more kinds of fish, 100 or more species of living coral and hundreds of kinds of invertebrates.

Sunny Warm Weather
Belize has weather similar to that of Central and South Florida, depending on where you are in Belize. The mean average temperature varies from 81°F along the coast to 69°F in the hills. The coolest month is January while the highest temperatures are during the month of May.

Inland areas tend to have more extreme temperatures than coastal areas where the sea breeze moderates the temperature. For example, average maximum and minimum temperatures near San Ignacio in Cayo District are both hotter and colder than those at the Philip Goldson International Airport in Ladyville near Belize City. Although cloud cover can be significant, especially in the summer, generally Belize has warm, sunny weather year round.

Island and Atoll Hopping

In Belize's Caribbean are hundreds of cayes and three atolls. The Northern Cayes, Ambergris Caye and Caye Caulker, have regular water taxi and air service. However, as of this writing service to Caye Caulker has been suspended, due to deterioration of the airstrip landing strip. A few other cayes, such as Tobacco, have boats going out regularly. It's not easy, or cheap, to get out to most other islands, or from one island to another. The atolls, 30 to 50 miles offshore, are even tougher. But the payoff for your time and money is the awesome beauty of these islands in the blue Caribbean. Few other places in the world have remote islands like these where you can swim, snorkel, dive, fish and just relax in total peace and calm.

Cultural Diversity

Belize is a tropical gumbo of cultures, races and ethnicities. Talk about diversity. There are Creoles, a mixture of African, European and indigenous genes, once the dominant culture in Belize and still so in Belize City and a few other places. The Bileez Kriol language (to use the proper spelling) still is a lingua franca in Belize. However, Mestizos from Mexico and elsewhere in Latin America, often referred to as "Spanish," are now the largest group, about one-half of the population. Some are long-time Belizeans who came to south to escape the Caste Wars in Mexico in the 19th century and others are recent migrants from Guatemala, El Salvador and Honduras. There are Maya – Mopan, Yucatec and other – and Garifuna, plus East Indians, Middle Easterners (often lumped together by Belizeans as "Lebanese"), Chinese from Hong Kong and Mainland China, Mennonites, old school and progressive, and a good number of expat U.S., Canadian, British and other folks from Europe, Africa, South America and elsewhere.

National Parks and Jungle Lodges

Roughly one-fourth of Belize's land and sea resources is protected in government-owned national parks, monuments, wildlife sanctuaries and archeological, forest and marine reserves. In addition, more land is protected in privately managed reserves.

One of the wonders of Belize is the jungle lodges. Some, such as Chaa Creek, Chan Chich and Blancaneaux are among the best jungle lodges in the world. Most are in Western Belize, around San Ignacio and in the Mountain Pine Ridge, but some are in the north, in rural Belize District and Orange Walk District, and a few are in Stann Creek and Toledo districts. Most of these lodges, frankly, cost an arm and a leg, but if you can find it in your budget they are a great experience. Some, however, are affordable, even cheap, so even the budget traveler need not miss out.

At these lodges, often located near or in some cases even in national parks, you're next door to adventure and to wildlife and bird spotting. As the slogans go, it's adventure by day and comfort and cold beer at night.

(See the Appendix for information on all the parks, reserves and other protected areas of Belize. See individual chapters on the main areas of Belize for information on jungle lodges.)

Maya Temples

Belize and neighboring Guatemala and Mexico were at the heart of the great Maya civilization that reached its peak about 900 to 1,500 years ago. The Maya had architectural, mathematical and other skills that rivaled those in Europe and Asia. Maya cities like Caracol in Belize and Tikal in Guatemala were among the 10 largest cities in the world at the time. Belize has many important Maya sites. Besides Caracol there are Lamanai, Altun Ha, Xunantunich, Cahal Pech, Cerros, Lubaantun, Nim Li Punit and others. Perhaps the greatest of all Maya sites, Tikal, is just a hop, skip and a jump from San Ignacio. There are enough other Maya sites in El Petén, Guatemala, to keep a Maya buff busy for months.

Good Food & Drink

You might have heard that Belizean food is nothing special. You heard wrong! Belize today has some wonderful food, from basic Belizean dishes like stew chicken with beans and rice or garnaches to amazing pork and delicious lobster, conch, snapper and other seafood. You can eat a filling meal for a few dollars in a local restaurant in Belize City, Belmopan, San Ignacio, Corozal Town or Punta Gorda, or enjoy a sophisticated dinner in San Ignacio, San Pedro, Placencia or Caye Caulker. Meals at jungle lodges seem pricey, but considering that you are miles from nowhere the meals, even if served by candlelight or kerosene lamp in an open-air palapa, are amazing. That special dinner won't be cheap, but it probably will cost two-thirds less than you'd pay in Miami, San Francisco, New Orleans or New York. In most cases, you'll enjoy the seaside or jungle ambiance even more.

Get a Friendly Welcome

Every country brags that it is friendly and welcoming. In Belize, they really mean it. Belizeans, by and large, are among the friendliest people you'll ever meet. A few are out to hustle you, but most are just interested in you, what you have to say and want to pass the time with you. Relax, keep your guard down (but use common sense), and you'll meet some wonderful people in Belize.

Save Money

Whoever told you Belize was expensive was right. And wrong.

Sure, you can drop US$400 a night, or more, at some fancy beach resorts and jungle lodges. One private island resort goes for over US$2,000 a night, although that rate includes everything from cocktails to your personal butler.

But you can also stay at a delightful seaside cabaña for under US$100 or stay in a charming guesthouse for under US$75 or in a hostel for US$15. You can get a filling lunch of stew chicken and beans and rice for US$5, drink local rum or beer in a nice bar for US$2 or $3 and have an amazing lobster dinner with all the trimmings for US$25.

What is true for the visitor is likewise true for the expat in Belize. You can spend a ton on a luxury home in a resort area like Ambergris Caye or Placencia, or you can buy tracts of rural land at prices that recall U.S. prices 50 years ago. Buy a Mennonite prefab house and have it put on your land, and you've got bargain-basement living.

Belize may be a more expensive than much of the rest of Central America, but in Belize you can drink the water, eat salads and wander about most places without fearing for your life. And, by comparison with the islands in the main Caribbean, Belize is a bargain.

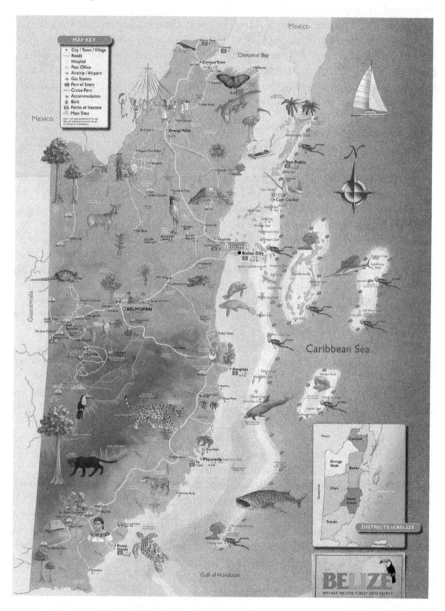

Speak English

English is the official language of Belize. Government documents and signs are in English. Police and immigration officials speak English. Tour guides, hotel employees and restaurant staffs speak English. It makes traveling and living in Belize really easy. You can have real discussions with Belizeans you meet.

On the other hand, if you want to practice your Spanish – or Kriol, Garifuna, German, one of the Maya languages or even Mandarin – you'll have a chance to do so in Belize. Many Belizeans are fluent in two, three or four languages.

Go for It!

Belize is only a few hours by air from many gateways in the U.S. and, now, Canada. Puddle jumpers provide daily nonstop from Mexico, Guatemala and Honduras. There are handy connecting flights from Europe, too. You can leave home in the morning and be on the beach or at a jungle lodge by the late afternoon. Come discover it. Check it out. What are you waiting for?

Overview of Places in Belize

Burns Avenue, the main street of San Ignacio in Western Belize   Photo Shutterstock

Here, in thumbnail sketches, are your main choices for living, retiring, investing and hiding out in Belize. In the chapters that follow, we'll explore in more detail the options in each of these areas, including a closer look at what each area offers, the cost of living, price and availability of real estate, examples of property for sale and rent and other practical matters. We'll also provide information on transportation, hotels, restaurants and sightseeing to help you make a scouting trip to Belize.

NORTHERN CAYES

The two largest of the Northern Cayes, and of all the islands in Belize, are Ambergris Caye (pronounced Am-BUR-griss Key) and Caye Caulker, sometimes known as Caye Corker.

Ambergris Caye

Ambergris Caye is the most popular place for tourists and also for retirees and other expats to live in Belize. It offers the beauty of the Caribbean in a fairly compact, accessible package. You can dive, snorkel, swim and fish to your heart's content. San Pedro, Ambergris Caye's only town, has Belize's biggest selection of restaurants and nightlife. By contrast with most of the rest of Belize, Ambergris Caye is highly developed ... and quite expensive.

Because the focus of this book on Belize as a place to escape from the problems of more developed countries, we are not going to cover Ambergris Caye in any detail here. If you think San Pedro and Ambergris Caye would be a good place for you, we recommend you get *Easy Belize* by Lan Sluder, *Lan Sluder's Guide to the Beaches, Cayes and Coast of Belize* or *Lan Sluder's Guide to Belize.*

Caye Caulker

Ambergris Caye's sister island is smaller and, if anything, even friendlier. It offers only a few choices for sustainable living, but it's a great spot for an island vacation, so we've included it in this book. Residents here have managed to maintain close ownership of land on the island, though some lots and houses are available on the open market. A few condos are going up. A few apartments are for rent, starting at around US$400 to $600 a month.

COROZAL IN NORTHERN BELIZE

Most visitors to Belize either never get to Corozal or pass through quickly en route somewhere else. But Corozal Town and nearby Consejo village and other small villages near Corozal Town, not to mention the Cerros area and Sarteneja village, offer a lot for those staying awhile: low prices, friendly people, a generally low-crime environment, the beautiful blue water of Corozal Bay and the extra plus of having Mexico next door for shopping. There's a modern mall, large supermarkets, fast food outlets and big box stores like Sam's Club and Staples in Chetumal, just across the border.

Corozal is one of the undiscovered jewels of Belize. There's not a lot to do, but it's a great place to do it.

The Sugar Coast – sugarcane is a main agricultural crop here as it is in the adjoining Orange Walk district – is a place to slow down, relax and enjoy life. The climate is appealing, with less rain than almost anywhere else in Belize, and fishing is excellent. The sunny disposition of residents – Mestizos, Creoles, Maya, Chinese, East Indians and even North Americans – is infectious. Real estate costs in Corozal are among the lowest in Belize. Modern North American-style homes with three or four bedrooms in Corozal Town or Consejo Shores go for US$100,000 to around US$350,000, and a few are even higher, but Belizean-style homes start at less than US$40,000. Waterfront lots are available for as little as US$75,000 to $125,000, and lots near the water are US$15,000-$30,000. Rentals are relatively inexpensive – US$200-$350 for a Belizean-style house or US$400-$1,000 for a modern American-style house.

Several sizeable real estate developments, including Orchid Bay, are building homes and condos and selling lots in areas along Chetumal Bay between Corozal Town and Sarteneja.

ORANGE WALK DISTRICT IN NORTHERN BELIZE

Orange Walk Town — the name came from the orange groves in the area — could be any number of towns in Mexico. There's a formal plaza, and the town hall is called the Palacio Municipal. The businesses and houses along the main drag, called Queen Victoria Avenue or the Belize-Corozal Road, have barred windows, and some of the hotels and bars are in fact brothels. In this setting, conservative Mennonites from Shipyard and Blue Creek who come to town to sell produce look strangely out of place. Except in Belize.

Not too many would want to live in Orange Walk Town itself. However, Orange Walk Town is a gateway to a magical area of Belize — the big sky, fertile land and unpeopled forests of Belize's northwest shoulder, where bush and jungle press against the Guatemala and Mexico border.

CAYO DISTRICT IN WESTERN BELIZE

Cayo has a lot going for it: wide open spaces, affordable land, not too many bugs and friendly people. This might be the place to buy a few acres and live off the land. The major towns are San Ignacio/Santa Elena, with a combined population of around 20,000, about 10 miles from the Guatemala border, and Belmopan City, the miniature capital of Belize, with a population of approaching 20,000. Agriculture, ranching and, increasingly, tourism are the major industries in Corozal District.

About 30 years ago, the first small jungle lodges began operation around San Ignacio. Now there is a flourishing mix of hotels, cottages and jungle lodges near San Ignacio and in the Mountain Pine Ridge, along with a lot of natural attractions and outdoor activities – canoeing, caving, hiking, horseback riding, to name a few.

The country's most accessible Maya ruins are here. Caracol, in its heyday a competitor city-state to Tikal, soon will be more accessible, as loans have been arranged to finish paving of the Caracol Road through the Mountain Pine Ridge and Chiquibul. Between Belize City and San Ignacio, Belmopan is the downsized capital of Belize, but the attractions are in the surrounding countryside. The Belize Zoo (in Belize, not Cayo, District) is nearby, as are several excellent jungle lodges. Along the scenic Hummingbird Highway are barely explored caves, wild rivers and national park areas.

Building lots start at around US$10,000, Belizean-style homes at US$25,000, and modern houses at around US$80,000 to US$100,000. Small farms are available for US$25,000-$150,000.

DANGRIGA AND HOPKINS ON THE SOUTHERN COAST

Follow the scenic Hummingbird Highway from Belmopan through the Maya Mountains and then citrus groves, and at the end of what is technically the Stann Creek Highway, you'll come to Dangriga, the largest center of Garifuna culture in Belize. Once called Stann Creek Town, Dangriga's run-down funkiness may be off putting to some, but the town can grow on you. It's a river and seafront down, and it's a jumping off place to some of the offshore cayes.

On the southern coast in Stann Creek District between Dangriga and Placencia, Hopkins today is what Placencia was like just a decade or so ago. Expatriates are moving to Hopkins, a friendly Garifuna village that got telephones only in the mid-1990s, and to real estate developments nearby. New small seaside resorts and luxury condo developments are going up in Hopkins and Sittee Point. Although at times the sand flies can eat you alive here, you can get in some excellent fishing and beach time, with day trips to the nearby Cockscomb Basin Wildlife Sanctuary or Mayflower/Bocawina parks and boat trips to the reef.

The controversial development, Sanctuary Belize, is located between Hopkins and its southern neighbor, Placencia.

PLACENCIA ON THE SOUTHERN COAST

The Placencia peninsula arguably has the best beaches on the mainland, and it's an appealing seaside alternative to the bustle of Ambergris Caye. The paving of the Placencia Road, which was completed in 2012, following the earlier paving of the entire Southern Highway, has made access to the peninsula much easier.

This peninsula in southern Belize has some 16 miles of beachfront along the Caribbean, a backside lagoon where manatees are frequently seen, two small villages, a few dozen hotels and restaurants and an increasing number of expatriates and foreign-owned homes. In recent years, the Placencia peninsula has been undergoing a boom, a boom that was slowed only temporarily by Hurricane Iris in 2001. Building lots by the score have been sold to foreigners who think they'd someday like to live by the sea.

Beginning around 2004-2005, condo development on the peninsula took off, and hundreds of condo units were built in condo zones in Placencia, San Pedro and elsewhere. However, construction screeched to a halt as the housing crunch and recession seized up markets in the U.S. and elsewhere, and a few condo projects on the peninsula shut down, while plans for others were shelved, at least temporarily. Now, with the world economy improving development projects are restarting, and for sale real estate signs are sprouting up anew.

Seafront real estate costs are higher in Placencia than anywhere else in Belize, except Ambergris Caye. Beachfront lots cost US$2,500 to $4,500 per front foot, making a seaside lot around US$125,000 to $225,000 or more. Lots on the lagoon or canal are less expensive. There is little North American-style housing available for sale or rent, and many expatriates are building their own homes, with building costs ranging upwards of US$100-$200 per square foot, depending on type of construction.

The Cocoplum project, spearheaded by Stewart Krohn, is a model for well-planned development in Belize. A new spa-oriented beach resort opened there in 2016.

The kicker here was the opening in early 2016 of the Norwegian Cruise Lines cruise port on an island just off Placencia. The impact so far has been relatively small, since the cruise ships really want their guests to stay on the island and spend their money there, but there has been an increase in cruise ship excursions in Southern Belize and some uptick in independent day travel.

Because in this book we focus on the more affordable areas of Belize, we are not including much on the Placencia area. If you think Placencia would be a good place for you, we recommend you get *Easy Belize* by Lan Sluder, *Lan Sluder's Guide to the Beaches, Cayes and Coast of Belize*, *Lan Sluder's Guide to Mainland Belize* or *Lan Sluder's Guide to Belize*.

PUNTA GORDA AREA IN SOUTHERN BELIZE

Rainy, beautiful and remote, Punta Gorda in far southern Belize is the jumping-off point for unspoiled Maya villages and for onward travel to Guatemala and Honduras. The completion of the Southern Highway, now the best major road in Belize, has made access to the far south a lot easier, and work recently has been completed on a new paved road connecting the Southern Highway to Guatemala. Improvements in transport should begin to pay off for Toledo, both in terms of tourism and as a place for expatriate living.

"PG," as it's known, is Toledo District's only population center, with about 6,000 people, mostly Garifuna, Maya and immigrants from Guatemala. Maya villages, hardly changed for centuries, are located around PG. Cayes and the south end of the barrier reef offer good snorkeling and fishing. Lumbering and fishing are about the only industries. Undeveloped land is inexpensive, with acreage beginning at a few hundred U.S. dollars an acre. Few North American-style homes are for sale. Quality rentals are fairly expensive due to demand from missionaries and lack of supply.

PRIVATE ISLANDS

The days of buying your own private island for a song are long gone, but if you have money to burn and the willingness to rebuild after the next hurricane, one of Belize's remote islands could be yours, beginning at about US$100,000 and going up to several million. In 2005, Leo DiCaprio bought Blackadore Caye, a 104-acre island near San Pedro, for a reported US$2.4 million, or about US$23,000 an acre. DiCaprio and partners are developing the island as a luxury retreat.

Developers have been selling lots on a few small cayes. Keep in mind that transporting materials to the island, building there and maintaining the property likely will be much, much higher than on the mainland.

Again, due to the high cost of purchasing and living on an offshore island, we do not cover them in this guide. For information on private islands, see *Lan Sluder's Guide to the Beaches, Cayes and Coast of Belize,*

Getting Along in Belize

Two kids and their Belizean pet, a boa constrictor   Photo Matt Jeppson Shutterstock

If you're looking for a place to live or to retire that's just like back home, only better, for a United States or a Canada on the cheap, for Florida with ruins, reefs and rum, you may get a rude awakening when you move to Belize. Because Belize isn't just like the U.S. or Canada. It does have cheap rum, awe-inspiring ruins, beautiful Caribbean seas and much more. But the rules are different. The people who make and enforce the rules are different. Sometimes there are no rules. Sometimes there is a set of rules for you, and a different one for everyone else. Just about every expat resident of Belize has some story to tell about problems he or she faced in adjusting to life in Belize -- or, in not adjusting. Let's look at some of the differences, and what they mean to you as a potential resident or retiree.

Population of a Small City

First, Belize is a country with a population hardly bigger than a small city in the U.S. Even including recent illegal and uncounted immigrants from El Salvador, Guatemala and Honduras, the population of the entire country is only about 385,000. Imagine the difficulties your hometown would have if it suddenly became a country. Belize has to maintain embassies, establish social, educational and medical systems, raise a little army, and conduct affairs of state and international diplomacy, all with the resources of a small city. You can see the difficulties Belize faces in just getting by in a world of mega states. It lacks the people resources, not to mention the tax base and financial resources, to get things done in the way North Americans expect. If you're a snap-to-it, get-it-done-right kind of person, you're going to wrestle with a lot of crocodiles in Belize.

No More Juice

Most expats seeking retirement or residency in Belize are white middle-class North Americans, from a society still run by white middle-class North Americans. Belize, on the other hand, is a truly multi-cultural society, with Creoles, Mestizos, Maya, Garifuna, Asians, and what in the rest of Latin America would be called Gringos, living together in complex and changing relationships, living together in probably more harmony than anyone has a right to expect. In several areas, such as Belize City, Creoles dominate; increasingly, in other areas Spanish-speaking Belizeans and immigrants dominate. One thing is for certain, though: In this mix, North Americans, Europeans and Asians have very limited power. Money talks in Belize, of course, as it does everywhere. Most of Belize's tourism industry is owned by foreign interests. Much of its industry and agriculture is controlled by multinational companies or by a few wealthy, well-connected Belizean families. Thus, to some extent, these wealthy foreigners do have some access to power and some actual power.

Politically, however, the typical expat resident of Belize is powerless. He or she has no vote and is truly outside the political process. That's the fate of expats everywhere, but some who come to Belize, seeing a country that is superficially much like back home, are shocked that they no longer have a political voice and are, in a political sense at least, truly powerless. The North American or European is not so much at the bottom rung of Belizean society, as off the ladder completely. If you like to pick up the phone and give your congressional representative a piece of your mind, you're going to miss this opportunity in Belize.

Culture Shock

Culture shock is what happens when everything looks about 20 degrees off kilter, when all the ways you learned were the right ways to deal with people turn out to be wrong. It is a state, someone said, of temporary madness. Usually it happens after about six months to a year in a new situation. At first, you're excited and thrilled by the new things you're seeing. Then, one day, you just can't stand one more dish of stew chicken and rice and beans.

In Belize, culture shock is sometimes masked by the surface familiarity. Most Belizeans speak English, albeit a different English. They watch American television. They drive big, old Buicks and Chevrolets or Japanese cars. They even accept U.S. currency. But, underneath the surface sameness, Belize is different, a collection of differences. Cases in point: The ancient Mayan view of time, cyclical and recurring, and even the Mayan view today, are grossly different from the linear way urban North Americans view time. The emerging Hispanic majority in Belize has social, religious and political views that are quite different from the views of the average American, or, even of the typical Belizean Creole.

A Belize Creole saying is *"If crab no walk 'e get fat, if 'e walk too much 'e lose claw."* In other words, don't be too lazy or too ambitious. Is that a cultural concept your community shares?

In many cases, family connections and relationships are more important in Belize than they are in the U.S. or Canada. Time is less important. Not wanting to disappoint, Belizeans may say "maybe" when "no" would be more accurate. Otherwise honest men may take money under the table for getting things moving. Values Americans take for granted, such as "work hard and get ahead," may not apply in Belize in the same way. Physical labor, especially agricultural work and service work, because of the heritage of slavery and colonialism, is viewed as demeaning among some Belize groups. A Belizean may work long hours for himself but be reluctant to do so for an employer.

Respect, Not Money

Respect is important in Belize. If you make a pass at a friend's girl, you may end up on the wrong end of a knife or machete. If you disrespect one of your employees or neighbors, you may find yourself in a bad situation on a dark night. Just when you least expect it, you may get jumped on a back street and beat nearly to death. If you say something bad about a politician or a business owner, it may come back and bite you years later. Belizeans have long memories, and they don't take well to criticism, especially not from outsiders.

On the other hand, Belizeans can be surprisingly rough and tumble in their personal relationships. They'll say the nastiest things to each other, just run the other guy down for being stupid and a total fool, and then the next day both parties forget about it and act like they've been friends or cousins all their lives, which they have been.

The best advice is to make as many friends in Belize as you can. Sooner or later, you'll need them.

Fruit stand near Belmopan – bananas 20 for US$1

What You Need to Know: Belize A to Z

Here are basic facts to get you up to speed on Belize, listed alphabetically:

Acclimatization: How long does it take the typical expat to acclimatize to Belize? The answer varies from immediately to never. In terms of the weather, it usually takes new residents about six months to a year to get used to the warm, humid subtropical climate, assuming they didn't come from a similar climate. Belize is superficially similar to the U.S. in many ways – from the use of English in official documents to the same standards of measurement – miles, feet, gallons and ounces rather than kilometers, meters, liters and milliliters. You drive on the right and cable TV offers HBO, CNN and other U.S. channels. But, below the surface, the differences are more subtle and significant *(see Getting Along in Belize chapter below.)*

Bargaining: In general, prices in Belize stores are fixed, and there is no bargaining. At street markets, you may do some light bargaining, but haggling is not a way of life in Belize as it is some other parts of the world. Hotels and other tourist services may offer discounts – it never hurts to ask. Of course, when buying real estate or other big-ticket items such as a vehicle, bargaining is the order of the day in Belize as most everywhere.

Business Hours: Most businesses open around 8 a.m. and close at 5 or 6 p.m. on weekdays. Some smaller shops close for lunch, usually from 1 to 2 p.m. Many stores are open on Saturday, or at least on Saturday mornings. On Sundays, many stores and other businesses are closed, except in tourist areas like San Pedro. Banks typically now have longer hours than in the past, usually open from around 9 a.m. until 3 p.m. or later Monday to Thursday and until 4 or 5 on Friday.

Capital: Belmopan, a small town (now technically a city) of around 20,000 people in the central part of the country, is Belize's capital and home to many government offices. The capital was moved from Belize City following the terrific destruction and loss of life caused by Hurricane Hattie in 1961. However, while Belmopan is growing fast, Belize City remains the cultural, social and commercial hub of the country, and many government offices remain in Belize's only sizeable city.

Churches and Religion: Although Belize was a British colony, the Catholic Church, not the Anglican Church, is dominant in Belize. Anglicans represent only about 6% of the population, while about 40% of Belizeans are at least nominally Catholic. Nearly 9% of Belizeans belong to Pentecostal Protestant churches. Other religious groups in Belize include Methodist, Church of Christ, Mennonite, Presbyterian, Jehovah's Witnesses, Assembly of God and Seventh Day Adventist. Belize has one small Muslim mosque. There is no temple, but Jews meet in local homes in Belize City.

Climate: Most of Belize has a sub-tropical climate similar to that of South Florida. Frost-free Belize usually enjoys lows in the 60s to 70s, with highs in the 80s to low 90s. More rain falls as you go south, with average annual rainfall in Corozal Town in the north being about 50 inches, similar to Atlanta, Georgia, but increasing to 160 inches or more in the far south. Generally the rainiest months are June through October, with the driest months being February through April. January sees the coolest temperatures of the year, while May has the hottest. In general, daytime temps are higher inland, due to the influence of prevailing winds from the sea on the cayes and coast. The humidity is high year round in all parts of the country.

Drugs: Despite its reputation as a transshipment point for cocaine and other drugs from South America, Belize has strict laws on the use of illegal drugs, with prison terms and fines for offenders.

Quite a few Belizeans smoke marijuana, and until recently possession of even small amounts of weed was a crime punishable by a fine and in some cases imprisonment. In late 2017, a new law was passed by the Belize House and Senate, with support from both major parties and the prime minister, and approved by the Governor-General, that decriminalized the possession by adults of up to 10 grams of marijuana. (Exceptions are in schools, where possession is still a criminal offense.) This was viewed by many Belizeans as a good move because it freed up police to concentrate on more serious crimes rather than wasting time on victimless crimes.

Unfortunately, crack, heroin, meth, opioids and other hard drugs are a fact of life in Belize, as they are in many countries. Much of the crime in Belize City and in other parts of the country is related to drugs.

Economy: The country of Belize **Gross Domestic Product** in 2017 was estimated at around US$1.9 billion, or around US$4,800 per capita. On a Purchasing Power Parity basis, the estimated Belize GDP in 2017 was US$3.2 billion and the per-capita GDP US$8,300. The PPP method involves the use of standardized international dollar price weights, which are applied to the quantities of final goods and services produced in a given economy. This method may be better for estimating economic power when comparing countries.

By comparison, U.S. GDP in 2017 was US$19 trillion, and per-capita GDP in the U.S. was US$58,600. Thus, U.S. GDP is about 1,000 times larger than Belize's. Per capita GDP in Belize is less than 10% of that in the U.S. Belize's GDP growth averaged nearly 4% annually between 1999 and 2007 but fell to 0% in 2009 and stayed low through the international recession. In 2014, GDP grew by 3.4%, about 1 percentage point higher than the U.S. in the same year. In 2015-2016 GDP growth turned slightly negative but rebounded to more than 1% in 2017.

Average income figures in Belize mask a huge income disparity between rich and poor. About 40% of the Belize population is below the poverty line.

Although the estimated population of Belize is now about 385,000, the entire Belize national economy is about the size of the economy of a U.S. town of around 30,000 to 40,000 people.

Tourism and agriculture/marine products are the two major industries, each representing about one-fifth of GDP. In terms of foreign currency earnings, tourism is number one. Due to recent growth, tourism is now the largest segment of the economy in most years. Ambergris Caye, Cayo and Placencia are the major areas developed for tourism, with Hopkins and Caye Caulker also having significant tourism development.

Belize got about 385,000 international overnight visitors in 2016, a record, with more than 60% coming from the U.S. About 296,000, or 77%, of the overnight visitor count arrived by air at Philip S.W. Goldson International Airport in Ladyville near Belize City, and most of the rest by land through Mexico or Guatemala. These figures do not include about a million day visitors annually on cruise ships, as of 2016, which mostly call on Belize City, coming in on tenders as large ships can't dock at the Belize City port.

In November 2016, Norwegian Cruise Line cruise ships began calling on the US$100 million **NCL cruise port** at Harvest Caye near Placencia village. How this will impact tourism and daily life in Southern Belize in the long run is as yet unclear.

The main **agricultural crops** are sugar cane, citrus, cacao, marine products, timber and bananas. Aquaculture, mainly shrimp and tilapia fish farming, has seen some growth in recent years.

Belize has a **labor force** of around 138,000. The unemployment rate in Belize averaged 11.7% from 1993 until 2016, reaching an all time high of 23.3% in 2010 and a record low of 8% in 2016.

The official unemployment rate in 2017 was around 9%, but in many rural areas of Belize it is much higher. Even so, there is a shortage of skilled workers in some areas, such as San Pedro.

Inflation in Belize has been low to moderate in recent years. It was 4.5% in 2007 but increased to over 6% in 2008, before dropping to just 0.5% in 2013 and 0.9% in 2014. In 2015, it was a negative 1%, and in 2016 it averaged under 1%.

The government runs a **budget deficit** most years. The budget deficit was 3.3% of GDP in 2016. **External debt** in 2016 was about US$1.2 billion. That is high given the small size of the Belizean economy, but relatively speaking the debt to GDP ratio in Belize is about 65%, a better ratio than that of the U.S., which has a gross external debt of around 93% of GDP.

In 2006, the government reached agreement with most international creditors to restructure its external debt, issuing new bonds at lower interest rates. Belize again renegotiated its external debt in 2013 but failed to come to terms on another renegotiation in 2016.

Economic concerns include a **balance-of-trade deficit** approaching US$300 million a year.

Key Economic Numbers:

(Figures are the latest available, in most cases for 2017):

GDP: US$1.9 billion

GDP Per Capita: US$4,800

GDP Growth: 1%+

Inflation Rate: 0.9%

Unemployment Rate: 9%

Education: Belize's educational system traditionally was based on the English system, where students move through forms, from first form in primary school to sixth form (a sort of post-high school final grade), although now many Belize schools, following U.S. and Caribbean Community practices, use the grade system -- grades K-12.

The Catholic Church, through an agreement with the government, operates many of Belize's public schools. About 35% of Belize's population is under age 15, so in every part of Belize you'll see school kids in their khaki, blue or other school uniforms. In Belize City and elsewhere, there are both Catholic and government-run high schools. A few private or parochial schools run by Protestant denominations also exist. The best schools are in Belize City and in larger towns, and many of the worst schools -- with some teachers without degrees or teacher training and few books or equipment -- are in the far south.

More than 100,000 students are enrolled in Belize schools at all levels, including 7,500 in preschools, 70,000 in primary schools, and more than 20,000 in high schools. Close to 5,000 students are in post-secondary schools called junior colleges in Belize. Belize has more than 5,000 teachers at all school levels. Around 6,000 students attend the University of Belize and other universities and community colleges in the country.

Primary education is free and compulsory through age 14. However, a sizable minority of Belizean children does not complete primary school. Only about six in 10 of teachers are professionally trained, but the number is growing. Even teachers with four-year college degrees earn around US$800 to US$1,000 or less per month. Secondary education, consisting of a four-year high school, is competitive, requiring passage of a comprehensive exam. The student's percentile ranking on the admissions test in part determines which school the student can attend. Charges for books and fees at secondary schools, while small by U.S. standards, are beyond the reach of many Belizean families.

The typical tuition and fees for public schools in Belize is around US$25 per month. The Belize government pays this tuition if the student is a child of a citizen or permanent resident and cannot afford the fee.

About 87% of primary school students do go on to secondary schools, though many do not graduate.

Some expats choose to do home schooling. Private schools are available in a few areas. The Island Academy, a primary school for Beginners through Standard 6 (Grade 8) on Ambergris Caye, as an example, charges around US$3,250 a year per student. This school has an excellent reputation. Belize Elementary School in Belize City is one of the best private elementary schools on the mainland. Saint Catherine Academy for girls, St. John's High School for boys and Belize High School, all in Belize City, are recognized as among the best high schools in the country. St. John's in Belize City traditionally has educated many of Belize's leaders.

Junior colleges, such as St. John's College Junior College in Belize City, Muffles Junior College near Orange Walk Town, Independence Junior College in Independence (Stann Creek District) and Corozal Junior College in Corozal Town offer post-high school training. In some ways, these junior colleges aren't like two-year colleges in the U.S., being generally more comparable with the junior and senior years of high school in the U.S.

Until the 1990s, Belize did not have a true four-year university system. However, in 2000, provisions were made for the development of the **University of Belize,** which combined five existing Belize educational facilities.

UB now has campuses in Belmopan, Belize City, Toledo and Cayo. UB offers associate, bachelor degrees, along with one master's degree in biodiversity management and sustainable development in cooperation with universities in Jamaica, Suriname, Guyana and Trinidad and Tobago. The faculty includes more than two dozen professors with PhD or other tertiary degrees, along with around 80 instructors with master's degrees. The University of Belize has around 4,000 students in about 50 different programs.

A small private college, **Galen University,** is in Cayo District near San Ignacio. It offers bachelor degrees plus master's degrees in four disciplines, including an MBA. In 2014, Galen opened a new campus center in Punta Gorda and offers BA degrees there. The **University of the West Indies** offers extension courses in Belize and works with the University of Belize on its master's degree.

In addition, there are several offshore medical schools in Belize. The best-known, **Central America Health Sciences University Belize Medical College** (www.cahsu.edu), founded in 1996, has a campus just north of Belize City. Another offshore med school, one that has been controversial at times, is **American Global University School of Medicine** (www.agusm.org). It is in Ladyville near Belize City. **Washington University of Health and Science** (www.wuhs.org) is in San Pedro. These offshore med schools typically are run on a for-profit basis. They accept foreign students who cannot get into med schools in the U.S. or other home country. Some offshore med schools don't require that entering students have an undergraduate degree, but they do require the completion of pre-med courses in the sciences and math. Most place students in medical rotations in association with hospitals in the U.S., Mexico and elsewhere.

Here is a sampling of education costs in Belize. All figures are in US dollars:

Primary School

Public schools (often run by the Catholic Church): Free except for uniforms, books and fees, which average US$20-$25 a month.

Island Academy, San Pedro -- private school: US$3,375+ a year.

High School

Saint Catherine's Academy, Belize City: US$4,500 a year (tuition and fees).

Mount Carmel High School, Benque Viejo: US$5,450 a year (tuition and fees.

Four-Year College

University of Belize, Belmopan and Belize City: US$1,350 (undergraduate tuition for 30 credit hours) per year for Belizean citizens and permanent residents; US$2,700 for students from developing countries; US$4,050 for students from developed countries such as the U.S.; all plus fees (around US$200 a year) and room and board, which can run several hundred dollars a month.

Offshore Medical School

Central America Health Sciences University Belize Medical College charges a US$2,200 "matriculation fee" for new students, then US$8,000 per trimester (US$24,000 a year) for the basic sciences program in Belize and US$9,500 per trimester in the U.S.; monthly expenses for books, food and housing in Belize are estimated at US$700 to $1,000.

Will Your Kids Adapt to Belize?

Belize is a country of young people, so your kids will probably have a lot of friends. Belizeans love kids, and kids are welcome almost everywhere. It's rare to find a restaurant or any other business that doesn't allow kids. In many respects, most of Belize is the way the U.S. was in the 1950s or earlier: Kids play outside all the time, walk or ride bikes to the store or school and hang out with friends. There are very few "soccer moms" in Belize spending their days driving their offspring here and there.

Whether your kids adapt well to Belize, or not, depends on what expectations they -- and you -- have. If their lives have revolved around going to the mall, seeing movies every weekend and eating fast food, they're probably facing a serious adaptation problem, as there are no malls or chain fast-food places in Belize, and only a couple of movie theaters in the country. On the other hand, if they like to be outdoors, and especially if they enjoy activities on the water (no place in Belize is more than a few miles from the sea, a lagoon or bay, or a river) they'll be in heaven.

Young kids do have to be watched, as they may not know the dangers from scorpions, snakes, Africanized bees and other wild creatures. In Belize City, in some neighborhoods, kids are in danger from gangs and drugs. Finding toys, children's books and children's clothes may be a challenge in Belize, especially in rural areas. Libraries are few and far between, and none is large.

Schooling obviously is an issue for expats with children. Schools vary widely in quality of teachers, equipment, and facilities. In rural Toledo, your local school may have few textbooks, no library and perhaps not even electricity or running water. In Belize City, the best schools are quite good indeed, and motivated students will be well prepared for a rigorous college. Most Belizean schools do teach religion as part of their daily curriculum, and that may be an issue for some families. Some expats home school their kids.

Electricity: 110 volts AC/60 cycles, same as in the U.S., and outlets are like those in the U.S. and Canada. However, electricity is at least twice as expensive in Belize as in the U.S. Rates vary slightly by amount of kilowatt hours used, but most residential users pay round 24 U.S. cents per kilowatt-hour. Service is provided by Belize Electricity Ltd. (www.bel.com.bz), with rates regulated by the Belize Public Utilities Commission. New service requires a US$100 connection charge, plus a US$50 deposit in most cases. Commercial and industrial rates and deposits are different from residential rates.

Embassies: The U.S. Embassy in Belize moved from Belize City to Floral Park Road in Belmopan in 2006. The new embassy is a compound constructed at a cost of US$50 million. The U.S. ambassador to Belize appointed by President Obama in 2014 was Carlos R. Moreno, a retired judge on the California Supreme Court who was once considered as a possible candidate for a U.S. Supreme Court vacancy. As of this writing, more than a year after his taking office, Donald Trump still has not nominated an ambassador to Belize.

The embassy's telephone number is 501-822-4011, fax 501-822-4012 and the website is www.belize.usembassy.gov. The U.K., Mexico, Guatemala, Costa Rica, Taiwan and about a dozen other countries have ambassadors, consuls or other representatives either in Belize City or Belmopan. Canada only has an honorary consul in Belize City; its Guatemala embassy in Guatemala City handles Belize affairs.

Family Life: With so many different ethnic groups in Belize, you can't generalize about family life. However, as in many countries, Belize faces social problems relating to the disintegration of traditional family life. Especially in Belize City and other urbanized areas, a large percentage of babies are born out of wedlock and the traditional nuclear family is becoming less the norm.

Government: Formerly a British colony, and known as British Honduras from 1862 to 1973, Belize became independent from Britain in 1981. It is now a democratic member of the British Commonwealth, with a Westminster-style government system with a prime minister, an elected house of representatives and an appointed senate. The current prime minister is Dean Barrow, a Jamaica- and

U.S.-educated lawyer. He heads the United Democratic Party (UDP), which swept national elections in 2008 and retained control of the government in March 2012 and November 2015 elections. The opposition party is the People's United Party (PUP). Both parties are generally centrist. The "George Washington of Belize" was George Cadle Price, an ascetic Creole who helped found the PUP and was Belize's first prime minister. George Price died in 2011. Politics in Belize is a freewheeling affair and often intensely personal. Belize has strong ties with the United States and Britain, but it also has cultivated ties with Taiwan, Cuba, Venezuela, Jamaica, Japan, Mexico and other countries, often out of the need to seek foreign aid or development funding.

GPS in Belize: Our experience with GPS in Belize has been mixed at best. We usually use our Garmin GPS for vehicles when in Belize. Garmin, a leading GPS provider, offers a Belize map at www.gpstravelmaps.com/gps-maps/central-america/belize.phpas as an add-on for US$29.95. It is helpful, but it does have limitations and some inaccuracies. You'll have some of the same issues with smartphone GPS maps, along with sometimes spotty cell service.

History: The human history of Belize can be divided into four broad periods: the ancient Maya period, the Spanish conquest, the British colonial period and modern Belize.

The **ancient Maya,** whose ancestors likely came originally from Asia, settled in what is now Mexico at least 2,000 years before the birth of Christ. The Maya civilization was influenced by and grew out of the Olmec culture farther north. The Maya migrated to what is now Belize about 3,000 years ago. During the height of the Maya empire, called the Classic Period, roughly 300 BC to 900 (CE, or if you prefer, AD), the area that is now Belize had a civilization that included large-scale agriculture, sizeable cities of up to several hundred thousand people, formalized religion and a sophisticated knowledge of architecture, art, science and mathematics. As many as a million people lived in Belize during the late Classic period, compared to less than one-third that number today. Caracol likely was the largest city-state in Belize, with a population perhaps several times larger than that of Belize City today. Then, rather quickly, in a matter of at most a few hundred years, most of the great Maya cities were depopulated and the Maya civilization went into decline. There are many theories as to why this happened, among them that there was a change in weather patterns that disrupted agricultural, that epidemic diseases swept the region, or that social changes – perhaps revolutions – transformed the society. It could have been a combination of reasons. Whatever the reasons, by around 1000 CE most of the major cities in Belize had been at least partially abandoned, though a few settlements, such as Lamanai in northern Belize, lasted for many more centuries.

The **Spanish Conquest** of Mexico and Central America began in the first quarter of the 16th Century. Spanish troops and missionaries destroyed much of what was left of the Maya civilization, including burning nearly all of the Maya books they found. Soldiers killed many, and the European diseases they brought such as smallpox killed even more. Belize offered little to the Spanish in the way of gold or other riches, so Spain never paid much attention to it.

By the early 17th century, Belize drew the attention of a motley group of **British loggers and adventurers.** The original Brits in Belize sought logwood, a valuable hardwood used to make dyes. These Brits also did a little buccaneering on the side. One of the most fearsome was Edward Teach, called Blackbeard for his huge black beard. According to legend, Blackbeard used Ambergris Caye for his hideout, continuing to terrorize ships of all nations, until he was finally killed off the coast of North Carolina. By around 1700, several hundred British loggers and hangers-on had settled around the mouth of the Belize River, near the bay of what is now Belize City. The Brits were known as Baymen. British logging settlements grew over the course of the next 100 years or so. The loggers imported slaves from Jamaica to help cut logwood and mahogany.

There was continuing conflict between the British and the Spanish. Finally, in early September 1798, a Spanish fleet of 32 ships with about 2,000 men came to settle the score and wipe out the British once and for all. But it didn't work out that way. A ragtag band of Baymen assisted by a Royal Navy battleship on September 10, 1798, defeated the larger Spanish force in the Battle of St. George's Caye. That event helped end Spain's claims to Belize once and for all and is now celebrated as National Day. Spain acknowledged British sovereignty in Belize in the Treaty of Amiens in 1802.

Thus began the **British era** in Belize, which lasted until the mid-20th Century. British Honduras, as it was then known, officially became a British colony in 1862, at the time of the U.S. Civil War. Following the Civil War, about 1,500 Confederate supporters came to British Honduras and established the town of New Richmond. Much of the British period was marked by the traditional colonial approach of exploiting the natural resources of the colony. Though slavery was abolished in Belize in 1838, almost three decades before it was abolished in the United States, English and Scottish companies employing hard-working Belizean blacks continued to log the native forests, exporting the timber back to Europe.

During this time, Belize began to become a melting pot of races and ethnic backgrounds. The old Baymen families, with names like Usher and Fairweather, married former slaves, creating a kind of provincial Creole aristocracy in Belize City. Some Mayas, fleeing the Caste Wars of mid-19th century Mexico, intermarried with the Spanish, and were then called Mestizos. Hundreds of Garifuna from Honduras, with African and Caribbean Indian heritage, settled in southern Belize. As the 20th century dawned, British Honduras was a sleepy backwater of the British Empire. But underneath the sleepiness, things were stirring. Jamaican-born Marcus Garvey helped raise racial consciousness in Belize, as he did elsewhere in the Caribbean.

The worldwide Great Depression and a terrible hurricane in 1931, which killed some 2,000 people in and around Belize City, both had a great impact on Belize. The country was only tangentially involved in World War II, though many Belizeans served in British or other armed forces.

The end of World War II sparked anti-colonial feelings and marked the beginning of **modern Belize history.** The first major political movements favoring independence from Britain arose. Of these, the People's United Party (PUP) under George Price, an ascetic Creole educated at St. John's College in Belize City, was the most important. In 1954, a new constitution for the colony was introduced, for the first time giving all literate adults the right to vote (until then only about 3 in 100 Belizeans were allowed to vote.) In 1964, George Price negotiated a new constitution, which granted British Honduras full internal self-government, although it remained a British colony.

In 1973, the country's name officially was changed to Belize. On September 21, 1981, Belize became an independent nation, with George Price as prime minister. Small by international standards, unpopulated and undeveloped, modern Belize has struggled to create a viable economy and infrastructure. The country several times faced off with Guatemala, which had long maintained that Belize was simply a province of Guatemala. It was not until 1991 that Guatemala finally recognized Belize as a sovereign state, although even up until today populist flag-wavers in Guatemala occasionally threaten to invade *Belice* (as it is known in Spanish).

In the 20th century, agriculture, especially citrus, bananas and sugar, replaced logging as the country's main industry. More recently, tourism has supplanted agriculture as the primary industry.

Democracy found fertile roots in Belize, and the little country has a dynamic two-party system. Occasionally, groups attempt to start a third party, but in recent times that's proved unsuccessful. The United Democratic Party (UDP), under the former schoolteacher Manuel Esquivel, first defeated the PUP in the 1984 national elections, and again in 1993, but the PUP under Said Musa regained power in 1998 and held it until 2008. The current UDP prime minister, Dean Barrow, elected in 2008 and reelected in 2012 and 2015, is the first black to hold the office.

Prime Minister Dean Barrow – photo courtesy Government of Belize

Holidays: The following are legal public holidays in Belize:

51

New Year's Day - January 1
Baron Bliss Day - March 9 (date of celebration varies)
Good Friday, Holy Saturday, Easter Sunday, Easter Monday
Labour Day - May 1
Commonwealth Day - May 24
St. George's Caye Day - September 10
Independence Day - September 21
Columbus Day (also called Pan-American Day) - October 12
Garifuna Settlement Day - November 19
Christmas Day - December 25
Boxing Day - December 26

Hurricanes and Other Natural Disasters: June through November technically is hurricane season in the Western Caribbean, but the September and October period is the most likely time for tropical storms and hurricanes. The worst hurricane in modern Belize history struck in September 1931, killing as many as 2,000 people in and around Belize City. About two-thirds of all tropical storms that have visited Belize in modern times have struck during the months of September and October.

Since 1889, some 55 tropical storms and hurricanes have made landfall in Belize, an average of about once every 2.3 years. During the last half of the 20th century, only five serious hurricanes struck Belize, with the worst being Hattie in 1961. Hurricane Keith hit Ambergris Caye in late September 2000, killing five and doing some US$150 million in damage, mainly on the backside of the island. Hurricane Iris in early October 2001 devastated the Placencia peninsula and rural Toledo District in southern Belize, killing 21 people, all in a live aboard dive boat. Hurricane Dean, in August 2007 hit Northern Belize, destroying some crops and homes.

In recent years including in 2016 and 2017, Belize has managed to avoid hurricanes completely, even while the U.S. and much of the main Caribbean was severely damaged by storms.

Even without hurricanes and tropical storms, flooding frequently does occur in low-lying areas, especially at the beginning of the rainy season, typically in June or July. Heavy rains from June through September in southern Belize can also cause flooding at any time during this period.

Belize is not much subject to that other scourge of Central America – earthquakes. While earthquakes have occurred in Belize, notably in southern Belize – there were several tremors felt in Belize from 2009 to 2018 -- no severe *terremotos* have occurred in Belize in modern times. In January 2018, a 7.6 earthquake in the Caribbean due east of Belize City created tremors felt around the country, and for a while there was tsunami warning, although a tsunami wave did not materialize.

There are no active volcanoes in Belize. Forest fires are a risk at the end of the dry season, typically April and May.

Internet: There are about 100,000 internet users in Belize (2018 estimate), or nearly one-fourth of the total population. Internet access in Belize has been greatly improved over the past few years. Belize Telemedia Ltd. offers DSL in most of the country, for either PC or Mac. It also offers wireless internet via line-of-sight towers. However, costs are m u c h higher than in the U.S. or most other countries, and speeds, while increasing, are lower than in other countries in the region. In 2017, the fastest rate for BTL DSL was only 16 MB per second down and 1 MBps up. That cost an amazing US$350 a month. A DSL speed sufficient for email (2 MBps down) is US$70 a month. By comparison, TelMex in neighboring Mexico offers 10 MBps down for around US$18 a month.

DSL internet combined with home phone services provides a small break on internet rates. In addition, there is an installation charge of US$50 (there's a larger deposit for non-residents) and a monthly modem rental fee of US$5 (or you can buy a modem for around US$75.)

DSL is currently available in the Belize City area, San Pedro, Caye Caulker, Corozal Town, Belmopan, San Ignacio, Benque Viejo, Orange Walk Town, Punta Gorda and Placencia areas, plus in a number of outlying areas. Check www.belizetelemedia.net for current DSL coverage.

BTL also offers wireless internet starting at US$125 a month for 1 MBps down. Smart/Speednet, another cell provider in Belize but operating on the CDMA system, offers cell internet starting at US$110 a month for 1 MBps down and up. Prices at Smart currently go to US$420 for 16 MBps down/8MPps up.

BTL in 2017 announced a new fiber optics landline and internet service for Belize that over the next three years is supposed to replace copper wiring by fiber optics to some 90,000 households. However, that will not be available in remote rural areas.

Internet via digital cable is available in Belize City, San Pedro, Placencia and elsewhere starting at around US$50 a month.

Some internet users in Belize, especially those in remote areas, go with a satellite service, mainly DirecTV/HughesNet. Setup, installation (usually a larger antenna than in the U.S. is necessary), deposits and activation fees vary but currently are in the US$1,000 range. Monthly fees for unlimited service are around US$60 to $100. In some cases, you may need a billing address in the U.S. or Canada. You can add satellite TV service, but it is expensive compared with local cable service. Satellite Internet tends to be slower than DSL and there can be a latency issue or service disruptions during heavy rains.

Most businesses and nearly all hotels in Belize have internet access. In most cases, internet service for hotel guests is now free. Internet access is also available at cybercafés in San Pedro, Caye Caulker, Placencia, San Ignacio, Punta Gorda, Belize City, Corozal Town and elsewhere. BTL also has internet kiosks for public access in several locations around the country, including some BTL offices.

Language: The official language of Belize is English, and English speakers have little or no trouble communicating anywhere in the country. However, Creole, a combination of mostly English-based vocabulary with West African grammar, syntax and word endings, is used daily by many Belizeans of all backgrounds. Spanish is widely spoken as well, and tends to be the dominant language in areas bordering Mexico and Guatemala. The Belize government has called on all Belizeans to learn both Spanish and English. Garifuna and t h r e e Maya languages also are spoken, and some Mennonites speak a German dialect. As many as two-thirds of Belizeans are bi- or tri-lingual.

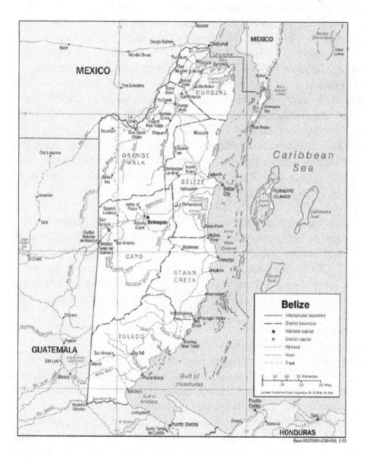

Largest Cities and Towns: Populated areas in Belize are officially designated as a city, town or village. The country's urbanized areas, in order of population from largest to smallest, as of the 2015 estimates by the Statistical Institute of Belize (more or less the equivalent of the U.S. Census Bureau), are:

Urbanized Areas Population, Belize
2016 Estimates
From Statistical Institute of Belize:

Belize City	60,963
San Ignacio/Santa Elena	20,582
Belmopan City	19,458
San Pedro Town	16,444

Orange Walk Town	13,687
Corozal Town	11,722
Dangriga Town	10,108
Benque Viejo Town	6,589
Punta Gorda Town	5,910
Country Total:	**380,010**

(This is the 2016 estimate – the 2017 estimate is 385,000)

Belize is divided into six political districts, which function a little like U.S. states in some ways and as counties in others.

The six districts, from north to south, are Corozal (population 40,400 in 2010, 45,530 in 2015, a five-year growth rate of 12,7%), Orange Walk (45,400 in 2010, 49,466 in 2015, a five-year growth rate of 9%), Belize (89,200 in 2010, 110,644 in 2015, a five-year growth rate of 24%), Cayo (72,900 in 2010, 87,876 in 2015, a five-year growth rate of 20.5%), Stann Creek (32,200 in 2010, 39,865 in 2015, a five-year growth rate of 23.8%) and Toledo (30,500 in 2010, 34,929 in 2015, a five-year growth rate of 7.3%).

According to the Belize Statistical Institute's estimates, about 45% of Belize's population lives in urban areas, so Belize remains predominantly rural.

Mail Service: Mail service to and from Belize is reasonably reliable and not too slow. Mail between the U.S. and Belize City usually takes less than a week. To outlying areas, however, it can take much longer – often several weeks. There are post offices in Belize City and in all towns and some villages. Many areas do not have home delivery. Unlike some of its Latin neighbors, Belize's postal service does not usually suffer from theft and lost mail. However, never send cash by mail. To mail an airmail letter from Belize to the U.S. costs US30 cents and US15 cents for a postcard. For fast, dependable but expensive international express delivery, DHL Worldwide Express is one choice. Federal Express is another.

Maps: The best maps of Belize are these:

Belize Traveller's Map from ITMB, at a scale 1:250,000, is still the best general map to Belize, but it was last updated as the 6th edition in 2005. Price is usually US$10.95. There is also an ITMB map, published in 2013, that incorporates the Belize map with the Tikal/Eastern Guatemala part of the ITMB Guatemala map (scale 1:300,000 and 1:470,000.) It's US$12.95. These maps are available from ITMB at www.itmb.com, from Amazon at www.amazon.com or at larger bookstores.

Other maps to consider:

Belize National Geographic Adventure Map, National Geographic Maps, 2009. Helpful, but it contains some errors.

Insight Fleximap Belize, American Map, 2003. It's sturdy and water-resistant but not fully up-to-date.

Laminated Belize Map, Borsch, 2012. German cartography company produced this handy, durable map. Scale 1:500,000. Would have been nice if the scale were a little larger. In English, Spanish, French and Italian.

Wall Map of Belize, Cubola Productions. This large 36 x 58 inch color map of Belize is suitable for hanging on your wall. Scale is 1:250,000.

Driver's Guide to Beautiful Belize, by Emory King, an American who was shipwrecked in Belize in the early 1950s and never left (or so the story goes) is a mile-by-mile guide to the main roads in Belize. The *Driver's Guide* also has maps of Belize City and major towns. It's really handy if you are traveling around the mainland. Rather than a folding map, it's 40-page booklet in 8½ x 11-inch format. Before Emory King's death in late 2007, it was updated annually, but as of this writing it is out of print. If you can find an old copy, the price is around US$15 in Belize and worth every penny.

Google Earth has satellite images of Belize. Some areas are in high resolution; others, not. **Google Maps** are available of Belize, but they often are out-of-date or contain errors, mainly in the location of hotels and restaurants. Mapquest also has Belize maps online.

Media: Belize has a half dozen **television stations,** several radio stations and a number of weekly and monthly newspapers. There is no daily newspaper in the country, although there was one in colonial times. Cable television companies operate in most populated areas, in some cases with pirated content. Most of the **weekly newspapers** in Belize are based in Belize City, but a few other towns have weekly or monthly newspapers. The two best national newspapers in Belize are *Amandala* and *The Reporter.* These two weekly tabloids are independent and outspoken, though coverage runs to strident political and crime news, and since they are based in Belize City both have a Creole, port city orientation that does not fully reflect the views of all of Belize's diverse society. Both have Web editions: www.reporter.bz and www.amandala.com.bz. *The Guardian* and the *Belize Times* are operated by the two leading political parties in Belize. The weekly *Belize Times* (www.belizetimes.bz) is the Peoples United Party paper, and *The Guardian* (www.guardian.bz) is the United Democratic Party's organ. *The National Perspective* (www.nationalperspectivebz.com) is a national weekly published in Belmopan.

Ambergris Caye has weekly print and online newspapers. The *San Pedro Sun* (501-226-2070, www.sanpedrosun.net) is operated by expats from the U.S. It has both a print and an online edition. *Ambergris Today* (501-226-3462, www.ambergristoday.com), operating since 1999, is now online only. *Ambergris Daily* (www.ambergrisdaily.com) isn't really daily, but it publishes occasional news blurbs.

There also are small newspapers in several outlying towns and villages: the monthly *Placencia Breeze* in Placencia and the quarterly *Toledo Howler* in Toledo and others. *The Star,* a weekly in Cayo, published from 2004 to 2016. The *Breeze, National Perspective* and *Howler* have had both print and on-line editions.

Two Belize City **TV stations,** Channel 5 and Channel 7, may also be picked up in a good part of the country and are carried on most cable systems. Channel 5 has an informative text version of its nightly news broadcast on-line at www.channel5belize.com. Channel 7 also has an on-line news summary at www.7newsbelize.com. Streaming video versions of the evening newscasts are now also available, though the quality can be spotty. Channel 3 in Orange Walk Town (www.ctv3belizenews.com), offers some news of Northern Belize and the nation. LOVE-FM radio also has a TV arm. While some of the equipment is primitive, it has some good locally produced programming. Plus TV and Open TV, both in Belmopan, cover capital news.

KREM-FM 96.5 and LOVE-FM 95.1 (frequencies vary around the country) are the two most popular **radio stations** in Belize. KREM-FM has a morning talk and call-in show from 6 to 8:30 a.m., with host Evan Hyde Jr. During the day it broadcasts an eclectic mix of local music, rap, soul and other music, along with Belize news. LOVE-FM offers "easy listening" music during the day, with a morning call-in and talk show hosted by station owner Rene Villanueva from 6 to 8 a.m. This station has three full newscasts at 6:45 a.m., 12:30 p.m. and 6 p.m., Monday to Saturday, and news updates frequently. Both stations offer internet broadcasts. Website for KREM is www.krem.bz, for LOVE www.lovefm.com. Another station, this one with a UDP slant, is WAVE-FM.

Belize First Magazine, a magazine about Belize founded by Lan Sluder, the author of this book, in the 1990s, is now only online at www.belizefirst.com. Among its free offerings are ebooks on Belize and a news archive going back more than ten years.

Most of these media can be accessed through links from www.belizenews.com. Cable TV, typically with some 50 or 60 channels from the U.S. and Mexico, is available in many areas of Belize, offered by local companies. You pay around US$20 to $40 monthly for cable service. Some Belize residents have satellite TV.

Medical Care: *See the chapter on Your Health in Belize.*

Money: The Belize currency is the Belize dollar, which for many years has been tied to the U.S. dollar at a fixed 2 Belize to 1 U.S. dollar rate. Moneychangers at the borders often give a slightly higher rate, sometimes as much as 2.1 or 2.2 to 1, depending on the current demand for American greenbacks. U.S. dollars (bills, not coins) are accepted everywhere in Belize, although you often will receive change in Belizean money, or in a mix of Belizean and U.S. money. There has been talk for years of dollarizing the Belize economy, but so far that move hasn't gotten traction.

The Belize dollar is difficult if not impossible to exchange anywhere outside of Belize (except at border areas of Guatemala and Mexico). Paper-money Belize denominations are the 100-, 50-, 20-, 10-, 5- and 2-dollar bills. Belize coins come in 1-dollar, 50, 25, 10, 5 and 1 Belizean cent units. The 25-cent piece is called a shilling.

People of Belize: Belize is truly a multicultural society. **Mestizos** make up about 50% of the 385,000 population (population estimate 2017). These are persons of mixed European and Maya heritage, typically speaking Spanish as a first language and having social values more closely associated with Latin America than with the Caribbean. Mestizos are concentrated in northern and western Belize. There is often a distinction made between Mestizos who came to Belize from the Yucatán during the Caste Wars of the mid-19th century and more recent immigrants from Central America. Mestizos are the fastest growing segment of the population.

Creoles, once the dominant ethnic group in the country, now make up only about 21% of the population. These are people usually but not always of African heritage, typically speaking Creole and English and often having a set of social values derived from England and the Caribbean. Creoles are concentrated in Belize City and Belize District, although there are predominantly Creole villages elsewhere, including the village of Placencia.

Mennonite school children near Little Belize in Corozal District

Maya constitute about 10% of the population. There are concentrations of Yucatec Maya in Corozal and Orange Walk districts, Mopan Maya in Toledo and Cayo districts, and Ket'chi Maya in about 30 villages in Toledo. **Garifuna** (also known as Garinagu or Black Caribs) make up about 5% of the Belizean population. They are of mixed African and Carib Indian heritage. Most came to then British Honduras from Honduras in 1830s. Dangriga and Punta Gorda are towns with large Garifuna populations, as are the villages of Seine Bight, Hopkins and Barranco.

The "Other" group, making up about 14% of the population, includes about 19,000 people, or 6% of the population, who say they are of mixed ethnic heritage. About 11,000 **Mennonites,** mostly of European original, originally came to Belize from Canada and Mexico in the 1950s. Divided into conservative and progressive groups, they farm large acreages in Belize. Conservatives live mostly in Shipyard, Barton Creek and Little Belize, avoid the use of modern farm equipment and speak German among themselves. Progressives live mostly in Blue Creek, Progresso and Spanish Lookout.

Belize also has sizable communities of **East Indians,** who live mainly around Belize City and in Toledo, **Chinese,** mostly from Taiwan, living in Belize City and elsewhere, **Lebanese** and **"Gringos,"** mostly expats from the U.S. and Canada concentrated in San Pedro, Placencia, Cayo and around Corozal Town. According to the 2010 Census, aside from the Mennonites only about 3,000 Europeans, Canadians and Americans considered themselves citizens or permanent residents of Belize. However, many expats in Belize are in the country for only part of the year or are on tourist permits.

Belize predominantly is a country of the young. About 56% of Belizeans are under 25 years of age, and the median average age is 22 years.

Pharmacies: There are drug stores in Belize City and in all towns. Many prescription drugs cost less in Belize than in the U.S., though pharmacies may not stock a wide selection of drugs. In general, in Belize prescriptions usually are not needed for antibiotics and some other drugs that require prescriptions in the U.S., although pharmacies owned by physicians or operated by hospitals (common in Belize) may require or suggest a consultation with the doctor.

Satellite Radio: Yes, satellite radio is available in Belize. Although Sirius and XM Radio have merged, and most of their programming is now shared, the two services use different satellites. Currently, Sirius can be picked up better than XM in most of Belize.

Telecommunications: Belize has one of the best telephone systems in the region, with a combination of fiber optic cable and microwave, plus cell service in most of the country. Mobile or cellular service now dominates telecom in Belize. There are some 173,000 cell phone users and only 23,000 landlines. You can dial to or from even remote areas of Belize and usually get a clear, clean line. That's the good news. The bad news is that telephone service in Belize is expensive, both for users and for Belizean taxpayers who are the footing part of the bill.

Belize Telemedia, Ltd. (BTL) is a company with a checkered history dating back to 1956, when a British firm, Cable & Wireless, set up the first telecommunications system in what was then British Honduras. After several changes, it became Belize Telecommunications, Ltd. in 1987. In 2001, majority ownership in BTL was purchased from the Belize government by Carlisle Holdings, Ltd., a U.K. company under the control of Michael Ashcroft, a British lord and Conservative politician. BTL retained a legal monopoly on all types of telecommunications services in Belize until the end of 2002, when its license to operate all forms of telecommunications in Belize expired.

BTL is no longer the monopoly it once was. Now it has competition, mainly from Smart Telcom, but it's still the 800-pound gorilla of Belize telecommunications. Lord Ashcroft's Carlisle Holdings sold its interest in BTL back to the Belize government in 2004. Later that same year, the Belize government sold BTL to Innovative Communications Corporation (ICC), an American company based in the U.S. Virgin Islands. ICC added 5,000 new landlines and claims to have brought on thousands of new cell users. Then, BTL/ICC and the Belize government got into a row, culminating in a lawsuit in

Miami.

In 2006, Lord Ashcroft, long a friend of some top Belizean officials, moved to repurchase some of BTL. However, in 2009 the Belize government under Prime Minister Dean Barrow renationalized Belize Telemedia Ltd. The government has taken over the operations of BTL, with a 90% ownership stake. The balance of the stock is owned by some 900 small investors. In 2017, on appeal to the Caribbean Court of Justice, the court order that the Government of Belize must pay US$78 million to corporate partners of the Ashcroft Group as compensation for the nationalization of BTL in 2009. At about the same time in late 2017, the Caribbean Court of Justice ruled in other case that the Government of Belize owed Belize Bank, another entity associated with Ashcroft, nearly US$45 million.

In spring 2005, a new wireless company, Smart, also known as Speednet, began offering digital cell service in Belize, with an interconnect to BTL. Smart offers wireless voice and Internet service in most of Belize on the CDMA platform only. It later was disclosed that Michael Ashcroft also had an interest in Smart. Today, Smart/Speednet claims it has 110,000 customers in Belize.

It costs about US$50 for BTL to install a landline telephone in your home, plus a US$100 refundable deposit. If you are not a citizen or official resident, the deposit jumps to US$500. Monthly residential service fees range from US$18 to $50. At the top tier, calls (up to one hour in length) to another landline within Belize are free. Otherwise calls in Belize are charged by the minute and vary depending on your service plan. Calls to cell phones are US7 ½ cents to 22 cents per minute, plus a US$5 a month add-on fee. Costs of direct-dialed long-distance calls to the U.S. currently are US21 ½ cents a minute for the first 5 minutes, then US17 ½ cents per minute, plus a monthly US$5 add-on fee for international calls. International calls are less at off-peak hours (6 pm to 6 am weekday and on weekends), and also less if you use BTL's 10-10-199 service.

A seven-digit dialing system was introduced in 2002. Formerly, telephone numbers in Belize had five digits, plus a two-digit local exchange. Now to reach any number in Belize you must dial all seven digits. All numbers begin with a district area code: 2 for Belize District, which includes Ambergris Caye and Caye Caulker, 3 for Orange Walk District, 4 for Corozal District, 5 for Stann Creek District, 6 for mobile phones, 7 for Toledo District and 8 for Cayo District. The second digit of the phone number is a service provider code: 0 for prepaid services, 1 for mobile services and 2 for regular telephone service. So a number like 22x-xxxx indicates that it is in Belize District and is a regular telephone, not a cell phone and not a prepaid service.

When dialing from outside Belize, you must also dial the country code and international calling prefix. **The country code for Belize is 501.** When dialing from the U.S., first dial 011, then the country code and then the seven-digit number in Belize.

Pay phones in Belize operate only with a prepaid BTL calling card. These cards are sold in many shops in denominations from US$1 to $37.50.

BTL provides a single **telephone directory** for Belize, published annually in the spring. Most numbers can be looked up on the online directory on BTL's web sites, www.belizetelemedia.net or www.belizeweb.com.

Cell service: Belize Telemedia Ltd. offers DigiCell, a digital service on the GSM dual band 850/1900 Mhz technology, including 4G. See www.digicell.bz for more information. BTL has more than 50 cell towers around Belize with good coverage in most urbanized areas. As with cell phone service nearly everywhere, cell plans in Belize are complex and change frequently. Currently BTL offers a basic DigiCell package for US$25 a month that includes 250 anytime minutes and text messages. The Premium Platinum plan is US$125 a month with 2,000 minutes a month, plus unlimited texts nights and weekends. You can also purchase pre-paid cell service at a higher minute rate – US30 cents per minute for the first 5 minutes, then US12 ½ cents per minute; pre-paid text messages are US12.5 cents each. BTL also offers a CDMA-based service in some areas. A BTL 4G cellular internet plan with download speeds of *up to* 1 megabyte for instant messaging, web surfing, sending emails and social networking costs around US$25 to $50 per month. The above plans do *not* include a phone. A non-Belize resident wishing to sign up for regular BTL/DigiCell service must have a valid passport and offer proof that he or she plans to stay in Belize for the next 12 months. A deposit may also be required.

Short-term visitors to Belize can buy a SIM card for any unlocked GSM 1900 cell phone for US$25, which includes US$5 of air time at per-minute rates for pre-paid cellular *(see above),* or rent a DigiCell phone from BTL for US$5 a day (not including outgoing call usage). With a pre-paid phone card, international calls are around BZ 65 cents a minute during the day and BZ 50 cents a minute off-peak (9 p.m. to 6 a.m.). Domestic outgoing calls within Belize are BZ 60 cents per minute for the first 5 minutes, then BZ 25 cents per minute for the rest of the call; pre-paid text messages are BZ 25 cents each.

Smart, also known as Speednet (www.smart-bz.com), is another digital cell service that began operating in 2005. It's on the CDMA system only, not GSM. It has monthly voice, text and cellular internet plans from US$15 to US$375 a month. The US$15-a-month Flex Jr. plan has a deposit of about US$34 and provides 125 domestic minutes and 750 SMS texts. Excess minutes cost about 28 US cents. The top-end US$375-a-month Enterprise plan includes 4,500 domestic minutes plus 200 SMS texts and 15 gigs of monthly data. This plan requires a deposit of nearly US850. All charges shown are plus 12.5% GST. International calls are extra. Short-term visitors can also get CDMA phone set up with Smart for a fee similar to BTL's so you can use it in Belize with a Belize number. *See also Internet above.*

Time: Local time is GMT-6 year-round, the same as U.S. Central Standard Time. Belize does not observe daylight savings time.

BELIZE: SOLUTIONS FOR YOU?

Self-Sufficient Living in Belize

Get fresh pineapples from your garden in Belize   Photo: Shutterstock

Want to live on the land? Here is information on edible fruits and vegetables that grow well in Belize. Here also are some of the important trees in Belize, and how they are used – for example, for making boats or building houses.

For more information on self-sufficient and sustainable living in Belize, see the sections on farming and ranching in Belize, on building your own home and on off-grid energy.

LOCAL FRUITS AND TREES
Fruits
If need be, you could live on fruits alone in Belize. More than 75 types of edible semi-tropical and tropical fruits are available in the country. Many grow wild, while some require cultivation. Fruits that require a dormant period with cold weather, such as apples, pears and peaches, are difficult to impossible to grow in Belize. However, some other temperate-climate fruits and berries, including blueberries, raspberries and mulberries, can produce well in Belize. Here are a few of the most popular, most delicious and most nutritious fruits that grow well in Belize:

Acerola *(Malpighia emarginata)*. Also known as Barbados Cherry and West Indian Cherry, this fruit, red when ripe, probably originated in the Yucatán and is native to Belize. Preferring dry, sandy soil and full sun, it grows on low shrubs to about 10 feet high. In Belize it ripens in May and June. The fruit, usually somewhat sour, is very high in Vitamin C and antioxidants.

Ackee *(Blighia sapida)*. A native of West Africa, ackee (also spelled akee) was introduced to Jamaica at the time of the African slave trade and has since become the national fruit of the island, often served with fish. It grows on evergreen trees,

63

which reach up to 30 feet tall. The pear-shaped fruit pods must be allowed to ripen completely (usually in August in Belize) to a yellow-orange color, and split open into three parts, as otherwise it can produce severe vomiting. The soft part of the fruit is boiled before used in cooking, and the seeds are dried.

Avocado *(Persea americana)*. Native to southern Mexico, which still produces more of this fruit than any other country, avocados are widespread across Belize. Avocados have been cultivated in Belize and elsewhere in the region, beginning with the early Maya, for as long as 5,000 years. They grow on attractive, moderate-sized trees of up to 60 feet or so in height. The trees prefer soil with a lot of moisture. While they can be grown from seed, in cultivation they are usually grafted. This delicious, healthful fruit is available in Belize from May to October. Avocados mature on the tree but ripen after falling or being picked. Agoutis love avocados.

Baboon Cap *(Couepia dodecandra)*. This medium-size tree, also called olasapo, is sometimes planted in gardens because of the sweet fruit it bears in April and May. It is a favorite of children. The hairy fruit looks a little like a green pickle, but it turns yellowish when ripe. It contains just one seed.

Banana (Genus *Musa*). Banana plants are not trees or shrubs but herbs, and the fruits are giant berries. The *Musa* genus is native to Southeast Asia and Australia. Commercial production of bananas began in Belize, then British Honduras, in the late 19th century. Belize's first and only "major" railroad line, the Stann Creek Railway, was built during 1911-1914 to transport bananas between United Fruit Co.'s Middlesex Estate and Stann Creek Town, now Dangriga. The railway roughly followed what is now the Hummingbird Highway. It operated until 1937. The industry was nearly put out of business in the 1920s and 1930s due to a fungal disease, Panama disease, and a leaf blight, both of which swept through Central America.

All Belize plantation-produced bananas, like those grown elsewhere for export, now are Cavendish, a variety originally from China. Nearly 99% of production for export world-wide is Cavendish, particularly the Grand Naine ("Big Dwarf") cultivar. The typical Cavendish plant produces around 200 bananas a year and lives for three or four years. Until the 1960s, Gros Michel was the variety grown in Belize and nearly everywhere else. Michel is a creamier, tastier, larger and less fragile variety than Cavendish. Its great weakness is its susceptibility to Panama disease. The Cavendish variety also is becoming more subject to disease, and scientists are working on a replacement.

Belize now has more than 6,000 acres in banana production, mainly in Stann Creek and Toledo districts. However, bananas will grow almost anywhere in the country. In most years, bananas are Belize's third largest agricultural export. Fyffes, originally an English company and a subsidiary of United Fruit, today called Chiquita Brands International and an Irish company, has dominated banana exports from Belize since United Fruit abandoned production in British Honduras in the 1930s. However, in 2015, Fyffes severed its agreement with one of Belize's largest banana growers, due to blacklisting by the U.S. of the alleged owner of the company for alleged drug connections. A variety of small banana called "apple banana" is preferred by many Belizeans for its superior taste, but it does not ship well so is not much grown commercially. There are other local varieties as well. Bananas grow year-round in Belize

Breadfruit *(Artocarpus altilis)*. Breadfruit, *masapan* in Spanish, is related to jackfruit It originated in the South Pacific but is now common in much of the Caribbean and Central America, including Belize. The legend is that Captain Bligh brought the fruit from Tahiti to the Caribbean in 1793. The grapefruit-size fruits grow on trees that reach more than 75 feet. The trees produce prolifically and thrive at all elevations in Belize, especially in alkaline soils such as those in Cayo and Toledo districts, but it is found in all districts. It is propagated by rooting cuttings. Breadfruits are roasted, baked, fried or boiled and can be made into a flour. When cooked, the taste is like a potato or, some think, like freshly baked bread. In Belize, breadfruits usually ripen in the summer months.

Cacao *(Theobroma cacao)*. Kakow, as it was known in several Maya languages, is a small tree of about 10 to 25 feet in height native to tropical areas of Mexico, Central America and South America. The cacao tree and its fruit, cacao beans or pods, which grow on the trunk and large branches of the tree, were actively cultivated by Maya, Aztec and other indigenous peoples. The chocolate processed from cacao seeds was widely used for eating, drinking and cooking.

In Belize, cacao now is grown mainly in Toledo District, which has the more tropical conditions best suited to cacao production. However, small cacao plantations are also present in most other districts of Belize, especially Cayo. The Toledo Cacao Growers Association (TCGA, www.tcgabelize.com) has a membership of some 1,100 small cacao farmers who together produce and sell more than 100,000 pounds of organic cacao.

A cacao tree begins to bear when it is four or five years old. A mature tree yields about 20 pods with about 600 seeds, which are the main ingredient of chocolate. The seeds of one tree will produce about a pound of cacao paste used to make high-quality chocolate. In Belize, cacao pods are ready to harvest late in the year, starting around November.

Cashew *(Anacardium occidentale)*. Most people are familiar with cashew nuts, but many don't know that the dwarf cashew tree also produces a delicious false fruit, the cashew apple. The cashew is native to Brazil but grows in most of Belize. It is best known in Crooked Tree village, in northern Belize District. In fact, the village, one of the oldest villages in the country, is named for the twisting, crooked cashew tree that only grows to about 20 feet in height, but its curvy branches reach out whichever way. The nut is the true fruit of the cashew tree, but the false fruit, cashew apple, *marañón* in Spanish, is usually a reddish yellow and has a strong, sweet smell that reminds some of the odor of grapes. Eaten raw, the fruit is sweet and delicious. The skin is delicate, and the cashew apple fruit doesn't last long after it ripens and can't be shipped. In Belize, it is ripe March through June. Belizeans also make a refreshing juice drink and a sweet wine from the cashew apple.

Craboo *(Byrsonima crassifolia.)* Native to Central and South America, the craboo tree grows wild in much of Belize, especially in savannah and pine forest areas. The tree rarely reaches more than 30 feet. The fruit, also called nance, is about the size of a cherry and yellow-orange in color. It has an unusual flavor that for many is an acquired taste. It is eaten raw or cooked with sugar in desserts. A

65

juice drink is made from it, as are a wine and liquor. In Belize, it ripens in summer, from June to August. People often sell small bags of it by the roadside.

Custard Apple *(Annona reticulate)*. This fruit (the name also refers to several other similar fruits) grows on a short tree, around 25 to 30 feet tall. It is related to the soursop. The fruit, round-, heart- or pear-shaped, ranges in size from that of a tennis ball to a baseball. It is brown or yellowish. In Belize, where it is native and grows wild, it ripens in March and April. The flesh of the fruit has a sweet custard-like flavor.

Dragon Fruit (Genus *Hylocereus*). Dragon fruit (also called pitahaya) is a cactus that bears a colorful red and green fruit with white flesh. It is indigenous to Central and South America. Until recently not well known in Belize, several species are now widely cultivated due to their bright colors and mildly sweet flavor are popular with chefs. The cactus can be grown from seed or by planting a stem from a plant in the ground. The flowers usually are pollinated at night, by moths or bats. Once mature, plants can produce several crops a year, although in Belize July and August are peak months.

Golden Plum *(Spondias dulcis)*. This is one of a number of plums in Belize, and it's a favorite with kids. The plums, also known as Arbarella, grow in clusters of about 12 oval fruits. On the small tree they are green or yellowish but when ripe (in July to September in Belize) they fall on the ground and turn a yellow gold. They are usually eaten raw with salt, pepper and hot sauce.

Grapefruit *(Citrus × paradise)*. The grapefruit was an accidental cross in the mid-18th century between the Jamaican sweet orange and the Indonesian polemo. It has since spread and now is cultivated throughout the Caribbean, Central and South America, the Southern U.S. and Asia. In Belize, it is a significant citrus crop but of far less commercial importance than the Valencia orange, which represents about 80% of citrus grown in Belize. It's estimated that about 6,000 acres of grapefruit groves are in cultivation in Belize. Grapefruits probably were first planted in Belize in the early 20th century in Stann Creek District but now also are grown in Cayo and Toledo. It matures in Belize in the fall, starting in late October. Grapefruit trees in Belize grow up to about 25 feet in height and start bearing fruit in five years. Each tree can produce up to 500 pounds of fruit. Many homeowners include a few grapefruit trees in their back yard.

Guava *(Psidium guajava)*. The guava originated in Mexico and Central America and is still cultivated in this region, including in Belize. If grown from seed, guavas can bear within two years and live up to 40 years. Due to the tree's small size, they are one of the few tropical fruits that can be grown indoors in pots. Guava fruits, from about 1½ to 5 inches long, can be eaten raw or made into a fruit juice. The fruits are high in pectin, so they easily can be made into preserves, marmalades and candies.

Lime. Several kinds of limes (*limónes* in Spanish) are widely used in Belize. The green Tahiti or Persian lime (*Citrus × latifolia*) that is commonly sold in the U.S. and elsewhere is available in Belize, too. Larger limes that look a little like a tangerine and are orange inside are locally called Jamaica limes. Markets and shops also carry a smaller greenish-yellow lime that is called a Key lime. By contrast, lemons are not much used in Belize and, if you can find them, are expensive. In

Belize Key and Jamaica limes generally ripen in the spring while Persian/Tahiti limes ripen earlier, January through March.

Lychee *(Litchi chinensis)*. A native of southern Chine, lychee is now grown in many tropical and sub-tropical areas of the world, including Belize. Lychee trees, which can reach 50 feet or more in height, grow best in well-drained, slightly acidic soil with a lot of organic nutrients. The fruit, about the size of a strawberry and pinkish-red with a rough skin, can be consumed raw or dried, or as a dessert dish. It is high in vitamin C. In Belize, some lychee trees are being cultivated in Cayo District. They ripen in the late spring, usually April and May.

Malay Apple *(Syzygium malaccense)*. Sometimes called Jamaica apple or mountain apple, the Malay apple is native to Indonesia and Malaysia. The fruit of the mid-size tree is small, red and oblong-shaped. It has a fairly bland taste. It grows well in most of Belize except the cayes, with the fruit ripening in December, January and February. If planted with coffee trees, it can divert the attention of birds from the coffee berries.

Mamey *(Pouteria sapota)*. Native to Central America and Mexico, the mamey, also known as Mamey Sapote or Mammee, is related to the sapodilla. It grows on a tall (some specimens reach 150 feet) and beautiful ornamental tree. The fruit is fairly large, as long as 10 inches, football-shaped, and the skin is brown and rough. However, the flesh is a lovely orange color when ripe and has a complex, hard-to-describe taste with tones of pumpkin, peach, apricot and cantaloupe. The fruit is high in several vitamins. It can be eaten raw or in milkshakes or smoothies. In Belize, the mamey begins ripening in May and stays in season through September.

Mango (Genus *Mangifera*). The mango, originally a native of South Asia, is one of the most common fruit trees in Belize and arguably the best loved. Many homes have a large mango tree or two in the yard, and they are also grown on plantations for export. Some trees reach up to 125 feet tall and can live for 300 years or more. Worldwide there are more than 400 varieties of mangos. There are at least a couple dozen varieties in Belize, diverse in size, color, taste and date of ripening. They have many local names, including Bellyfull, Blue, Sugars, Slipper, Apple, Julie, Tommy Atkins, Judgewig and Thundershock. Mangos of one type or another are available in Belize from May through September, with the height of the season around June and July. Most commonly they are eaten raw, but they also are used in smoothies, ice cream, juices, salads and many types of desserts.

Mangosteen *(Garcinia mangostana)*. A native of Indonesia, mangosteens grow in Belize, but they are not common. They usually are planted in plots as seedlings and transplanted to the field when they are about a foot tall, usually in the rainy season as they are susceptible to drought. You often find them growing beside a river. Mangosteen fruits, about the size of a tangerine, have a purple skin and white flesh. They are highly prized for their delicious, tangy yet sweet taste, unlike any other fruit. Trees usually take up to 10 years, or sometimes longer, to start bearing. This is one reason mangosteens are not usually seen in Belize markets. A mature, vigorous tree can produce hundreds or even thousands of fruit. Mangosteens are susceptible to the fruit fly so are not widely exported, so except where they grow they are expensive to buy. In Belize, they ripen in July and have a short season.

Noni *(Morinda citrifolia).* Related to the coffee tree, noni is native to South Asia and Australasia, but it is now grown in much of the tropics and semi-tropics, including Belize. It is a very easy fruit tree to grow. It tolerates all kinds of conditions, including saline seashore soils, forests and rocky open ground. The noni trees takes only 18 months to reach maturity and then produces 10 pounds of fruit, or more, every month of the year. The noni fruits are fairly large, up to 6 or 7 inches in length. They are green on the tree but turn yellow or whitish as they ripen. Some consider the noni to have important health and homeopathic benefits, and the fruit, cooked or raw or as a juice, is consumed in several cultures. However, the strong, pungent odor (it is sometimes called the "vomit fruit") puts off many people. Those in Belize who have noni trees usually do not have to worry about people tiefing their fruit.

Orange *(Citrus x sinensis).* The Valencia orange is a hybrid orange used mostly to produce juice and juice concentrate. Valencia is by far the most common orange grown in Belize, representing about 80% of juice and concentrate exports. It is commercially grown mostly in Stann River District but is also grown in other districts of Belize. The oranges produce from January through June. A few other varieties of oranges may be available from local nurseries in Belize. Besides oranges and grapefruits, a number of other citrus fruit grow in Belize, including **tangerines, tangelos, kumquats, loquats, Mandarin oranges** and others, but currently they have little commercial importance.

The citrus industry in Belize has been contracting in size for years. From a peak of about 1,000 small citrus producers, mainly along the Hummingbird Highway, the number of producers has fallen to around 400, perhaps fewer. There are two reasons for this. One is the lower prices received for citrus, due to worldwide competition. A second reason is Citrus Greening disease. The bacterial disease poses no threat to humans, but it has devastated millions of acres of citrus crops in the United States, mostly in Florida, where Valencia oranges also are a major citrus crop. Infected trees produce fruit that are misshapen, green and with a bitter taste. To attempt to control this disease, growers have to fertilize more and spray pesticides to control the vector, the Asian citrus psyllid. This of course is costly and is ineffective unless all the groves in an area are sprayed.

Papaya *(Carica papaya).* Papaya is one of the most important fruits in Belize, both commercially and as a fixture in Belizean diets. Worldwide it is the fourth most important tropical fruit, after bananas, oranges and mangos. It's common in Belize for a breakfast plate to include a few slices of ripe papaya, with a lime. The papaya is native to Central America and southern Mexico. It grows only in climates where there is no risk of freezing temperatures. The papaya plant, which likes sandy, well-drained soil, takes only two or three years to grow to maturity, at 15 to 30 feet, and to begin bearing fruit. Papaya plants can be either male, female or hermaphrodite; only female or hermaphrodite plants produce fruit.

The fruit is large, often nearly as big as a football, and oblong in shape. Once peeled, the flesh is orange, reddish or yellowish in color, depending on the variety. In Belize, Maradol, Sunrise and Caribbean Red varieties have been grown commercially for export. These varieties have a more reddish flesh and produce virtually year-round. However, in recent years, the largest commercial Belize operations have moved to Guatemala or elsewhere in search of lower labor costs. In 2016, Brooks Tropicals, the parent company of Fruta Bomba and Belize Packers, which had been operating in Belize for more than 20 years and was the largest commercial papaya producer and exporter, shut down, putting some 250 Belizeans out of work.

Passion Fruit *(Passiflora edulis).* Passion fruit grows on a vine. In Belize, there are two main varieties, yellow and purple. The fruit can be eaten raw, or juiced. Passion fruit juice is often added to other fruit juices or to cocktails due to its pleasant aroma. Passion fruit vines can be grown by seed, preferably in sandy loam soil with good drainage. The vines bear the first year and live up to about seven years. In Belize, the vines bear most June through August but often bear later in the year.

Pineapple *(Ananas comosus).* Pineapples are widely grown and consumed in Belize. Although there is little large-scale commercial production, many residents grow pineapples in their back yards, and fresh pineapples are available at fruit stands from May through October, prime time for pineapples in Belize. Pineapples can be cultivated from crown cuttings of the fruit with fruit available after about a year. As perennial, the plant will continue to bear for several years.

Plantain (Genus *Musa, Musa × paradisiaca*). This is the "cooking banana" that is widely used in Latin American cuisine. The term "plantain" is applied to any banana cultivar that is eaten after cooking. However, there is no real botanical distinction between bananas and plantains. Cooking bananas contain more starch and less sugar than dessert or eating bananas. In Belize as elsewhere plantains fruit year-round. They are used extensively in Mestizo, Creole and Garifuna cooking – fried, boiled or used in soups and stews. Plantains also can be dried and ground into flour or fried as potato-like chips and sold as snacks.

Rambutan *(Nephelium lappaceum).* Native to the Indonesia-Malaysia area, the rambutan is now grown in semi-tropical and tropical areas world wide, including in Belize, where it is most readily available in the rainy season starting in June or July to around September. The tree grows to 50 or 60 feet in height at lower elevations up to about 1,500 feet. It likes well-drained hillsides with clay or sandy loam. Rambutan trees can be started from seed, air layering or budding. After five or six years mature trees bear several thousand hairy green – red when ripe – fruit. When opened, the flesh is white and looks a little like an eyeball. It can be eaten raw or cooked and tastes somewhat like lychee.

Sapote. This is the name given to several different fruit-bearing plants in the genus *Pouteria* in Belize and elsewhere in Central America. *See Mamey above.*

Sea Grape *(Coccoloba uvifera).* Sea grapes aren't true grapes, although they look like them. Instead, they are a flowering plant in the buckwheat family. They grow from South Florida through the Caribbean to semi-tropical and tropical areas of Central America and of South America. Because they tolerate salty conditions and wind, they are commonly seen in coastal and beach areas, but they also will grow inland in frost-free areas. The fruit of the plant, hanging in grape-like clusters and green until it ripens to a red or purple color, are good to eat raw. The ripe grapes can also be used to make jelly or preserves and can be made into wine. Each grape has a large pit, a seed that can be planted (but it must be planted quickly and not allowed to dry out.)

Soursop *(Annona muricatga)*. The soursop, *guanábanaa* in Spanish, is a small tree – rarely over 12 or 13 feet tall – that bears a large fruit. The fruit is elongated, with prickly green skin, a little like a green durian but without the awful smell. It can be up to 10 or 12 inches in length and weigh as much as 10 to 15 pounds. The flesh is pulpy and white. It combines the flavors of pineapple and strawberry, with notes of citrus and banana. The soursop can be eaten raw as a snack or dessert, but it is often used in smoothies, juice drinks and ice cream. The soursop gelato at Tutti Frutti in Placencia is out of this world. In Belize, the soursop ripens from August to February.

Star Apple *(Chrysophyllum cainito)*. Native to the West Indies, the star apple, *caimito* or *cainito* in Spanish, is now widely grown in lowland areas of Central America, including Belize. The star apple is a fast-growing tree that can reach about 60 feet. It bears tennis ball-size fruit, usually purple but sometimes red or green. The rind of the star apple isn't edible, but the pulp is delicious, especially when served chilled. Star apple fruit is high in anti-oxidants. In Belize it ripens in March and April.

Starfruit *(Averrhoa carabola)*. Although not native to the Americas – it originated in Asia, possibly in Indonesia – the starfruit, *carambola* in Spanish, is now widely growth in semi-tropical and tropical areas in the Western Hemisphere, including in Belize. It grows on a medium-size tree, which begins to bear in four or five years. A vigorous, mature tree can produce 200 to 300 pounds of fruit a year. The fruit is a lovely light yellow color, with a waxy, edible skin. When cut into slices, the fruit, which is not overly sweet, resembles a five-sided star. Most eat it raw, such as in salads, but it can be made into relishes or used in juices. Some animals, especially horses, enjoy the fruit. It gets ripe in most of Belize in February and again in June. Starfruit is rich in antioxidants, vitamin C and potassium, but it should not be consumed by those with kidney failure or kidney disease. Like grapefruit it is counter-indicated for those taking statins and some other meds.

Surinam Cherry *(Eugenia uniflora)*. Native to the eastern coast of South and Central America, this large shrub, sometimes used as a hedge, is also found in some of the Caribbean, especially Haiti. The fruit, about the size of a regular cherry, ranges in color from yellow to red to almost black, and the flavors vary as well. It is primarily used as a flavoring in jellies and jams. In Belize, it isn't common, but if you look you can find it. In Belize, it typically ripens in March.

Tamarind *(Tamarindus indica)*. A native of Africa, the tamarind made its way to the Americas in the 16th century and eventually to Belize. The tamarind is a tall shrub, with fruits in hard, brown pods about 5 or 6 inches long. A well-established tamarind tree or shrub can produce 300 pounds or more of fruit. The ripe, edible pulp in the pod is used as a flavoring in relishes, curries and other dishes. It is also used in fruit drinks and in desserts. Medicinally it is used to relieve constipation. In Belize, the tamarind ripens in the dry season, mainly in April and May.

IMPORTANT TREES OF BELIZE

Several of these trees are important in building homes and other buildings in Belize. Others are notable for their beauty or for medicinal uses.

Cabbage Bark *(Andira inermis)*. This hardwood tree's bark is similar to that of the Cabbage Palm, hence the name. Its bright purple flowers only bloom once every two years. In Belize, the wood is used for framing and flooring in houses and for bridges.

Bukut *(Cassia grandis)*. This is a large deciduous native of Belize, growing to nearly 100 feet. Howler monkeys love to eat its leaves. In the early part of the dry season, it puts on a stunning display of salmon-colored flowers. Its seedpods, when broken open, smell like an old sock. Hence, its local name, stinking toe tree.

Caribbean Pine *(Pinus Caribaea* var. *hondurensis)*. The Caribbean or Honduran Pine is the only true tropical pine in Belize, reaching over 90 feet in height. The pine covers about 80% of the Mountain Pine Ridge, and it also is common in the palmetto-oak-pine forests at lower elevations. In the Pine Ridge, thousands of acres of these pines have been devastated by the Southern Pine Bark Beetle, which bores into the tree and kills it. A government reforestation program has helped restore the pines in some areas of this forest reserve.

Cedar *(Cedrela mexicana)*. Cedar has been an important timber since ancient times, as its wood is durable and resistant to insects. These trees, which have fragrant scented wood, are widely distributed throughout Belize. It is still sometimes used today for cigar boxes.

Ceiba *(Ceiba pentranda)*. Also called **cotton tree** or **kapok tree,** the ceiba is the national tree of Guatemala, but it also is native to Belize. The ceiba, which the ancient Maya cultivated in their plazas, is a huge tree, growing up to 230 feet high with a trunk 10 feet in diameter. The trees produce several hundred large pods containing seeds surrounded by a fluffy, cotton-like fiber sometimes used as filling for pillows and mattresses. Ceiba trees can live for hundreds of years.

Coconut *(Cocos nucifera)*. The original coconut palm was probably native to India and Indonesia, but it dispersed around the world by floating on oceans and seas. The coconut is not a true nut but a drupe fruit, like a cherry, plum or olive. It is present in Belize in several varieties. In coastal and cayes areas, you'll see the tall Atlantic or Jamaica coconut, which grows to 80 feet or more in height, begins bearing in five or six years and when mature bears several hundred coconuts a year, each weighing about 3 pounds. Watch your head! The tree, which has a huge root structure that makes it resistant to hurricanes, can live up to 100 years. However, the Atlantic or Jamaica coconut is susceptible to a disease called Lethal Yellowing, and this has wiped out many of the coconuts on the Belize cayes. Coconut trees can be treated against the disease, but this is a costly and time-consuming process. A much smaller, faster bearing coconut, the Malaya dwarf, is sometimes planted as a replacement, but it doesn't do so well in salty cayes soils, so you see it more often on mainland Belize. A naturally occurring hybrid cross between the Jamaica and the Malaya called the MayJam can grow in saline soils and produces a lot of nuts, but some MayJams are also susceptible to Lethal Yellowing. Another hybrid cross, between the Panama tall and Malay dwarf coconuts, the MayPan, is more resistant to Lethal Yellowing but doesn't tolerate salty, windy conditions well so is better suited to mainland Belize. It is often sold by nurseries in Belize, including the one at Central Farm in Cayo. You'll pay around US$3 per seedling. Coconut trees provide a variety of products, including coconut oil (made from dried coconut meat call copra), coconut meat (often grated), green coconut water and coconut milk, which is produced from the coconut meat. If you have fresh coconuts pick them mature but still green, just before they ripen to brown and fall. There's no need to husk them at this stage. Just split them open with a machete. The water is sweet, and the meat is soft and a bit like Jell-O in texture. Coconuts are high in potassium and have many medical as well as culinary uses.

Cohune Palm *(Attalea cohune).* This is one of many species of palms in Belize. The cohune palm was of great importance to the Maya and is sometimes a marker for Maya ruins hidden under earth and jungle. It is a dominant plant in parts of Belize. The **warree cohune** also is found in Belize.

The hard nuts of the cohune are a source of oil and a fuel for fires and the branches are used for thatch construction. Cohune palm hearts are a delicacy still eaten at Easter, and wine can be made from the heart of the palm.

There are many other palms in Belize, including the **coconut palm** found along the coast (it has been subject to Lethal Yellowing and is being replaced with other varieties), the stately **royal palm,** the distinctive fan-shaped **traveler's palm** (not a true palm, instead related to the banana) and the **xate palms,** three different small palms used for floral decorations that have been poached in the Mountain Pine Ridge and Chiquibul by *xateros* from Guatemala. The **bayleaf palm** (*Sabal mauritiiformis*) is the preferred material for making thatch roofs in Belize, because properly harvested and put together the palm makes a long-lasting, waterproof roof. It has been overharvested in Belize. Now the supply is limited, and the cost to do a bayleaf palm roof can run into many thousand U.S. dollars.

Copal *(Protium copal).* The Copal was a sacred tree to the Maya. It was mentioned in the *Popul Vuh,* the story of creation as told by the Maya priests. It can still be found growing around the ruins of Maya temples. The copal resin was burned as an incense in religious ceremonies and is still used today in Catholic churches in the region.

Flamboyant *(Delonix regia).* A native of Madagascar, the flamboyant is now widespread in the Caribbean and the Central American lowlands. It is a medium-size tree, growing to 50 feet, easily identified by its umbrella-like branches and from May to July by the brilliant blossoms, which vary in color from crimson to flaming orange. Parrots like the tree. When in bloom it is visited by leafcutter ants, carrying off the dropped blossoms. A flamboyant tree, now dead, is in the middle of Elvi's restaurant in San Pedro.

Guanacaste *(Enterolobium cyclocarpum).* This fast-growing tree can reach over 130 ft. Its timber is light and durable, making it desirable for dugout canoes. One of the local names for this tree is "Monkey's ear" due to the shape of the seedpod.

Gumbolimbo *(Bursera simaruba).* A medium-sized tree easily identified by its shaggy red bark that peels away leaving a smooth inner bark, like sunburned skin, earns it the nickname **tourist tree.** Its leaves have a turpentine smell. The gumbolimbo bark is boiled in water and applied as a soothing lotion to burning, itching skin from touching the sap of the **poisonwood** tree. The lotion is also good for sunburn. Gumbolimbo and poisonwood trees often grow near each other.

Jippi Joppa *(Sabal mexicana.)* This palm (the J is pronounced as an H) is only found in Toledo District. Maya women weave baskets by hand from the leaves. First, the leaves are boiled until just the straw-like spine is left, then dried and bleached in the sun. The baskets can be found in gift shops and in Maya villages of Toledo. The shoots of Jippi Joppa are a delicacy to eat.

Logwood *(Haematoxylon campechianum)*. The first of the three commercially important trees in Belize was the logwood. The other two were mahogany and sapodilla. By mashing and boiling the heartwood dye, ranging in color from yellow to black, can be produced. The dye was popular in the European clothing industry, and was also used for inks. By the 1700's, as synthetic dyes were developed, the logwood became less important as an export. The tree is still found in Belize.

Mahogany *(Swietenia macrophylla)*. This is the national tree of Belize. It appears on the Belize flag, along with the Latin motto *Sub Umbra Floreo* ("Under the Shade I Flourish"). Although many of the large Honduran mahogany trees in the country's virgin forests were logged and shipped overseas from the 18th to mid-20th century, there are still impressive specimens in remote high bush. The trees, considered endangered in Belize, can grow to 150 feet with a diameter of 6 feet or more. The wood is still used in Belize for kitchen cabinets and trim and for furniture. Harvesting mahogany trees require a government permit.

Mangroves in the littoral forest protect the coast from erosion. Unfortunately, although protected by law in Belize many mangroves have been removed by real estate developers and homeowners so their properties have better water views. Belize has several species of including **red mangrove** *(Rhizophora mangle)*, **black mangrove** *(Avicennia germinans)* and **white mangrove** *(Laguncularia racemosa)*.

Mayflower *(Tabebuia pentaphylla)*. This canopy species grows up to 100 feet and has a strong, durable wood much like English oak. The wood is valued for interior work, paneling and trim. From March to May, the Mayflower is leafless, with a mass of pink flowers.

Rosewood *(Dalbergia stevensonii)*. Rosewood is prized for its beautiful wood for furniture, cabinets and trim. It was used for interior trim in some Jaguar motorcars and in musical instruments. In Belize it grows in Toledo District, mainly around Monkey River. It is now illegal to cut a live rosewood tree in Belize, although there has been illegal logging of this endangered tree.

Santa Maria *(Calophyllum antillanum)*. The Santa Maria is a hardwood tree that is used for floors in homes in Belize and also for furniture and in boat building. It grows to 100 feet.

Sapodilla *(Manilkara zapota)*. The sapodilla, also known in Central American Spanish as *zapote* or *nisperio,* is a medium-size tree native to Belize and elsewhere in Central America, southern Mexico and the Caribbean. The tree can grow to 100 feet but more commonly is around 40 or 50 feet tall. It is famous in Belize as one of the trees that provided the latex chicle that in the 19th and early 20th century was collected by *chicleros* and exported for use in chewing gum. For chewing gum, it was mixed with latex from the mammee apple or mamey sapote. The Maya and Aztecs chewed chicle, and the name may have come from the Maya word *tsicte*. There must be millions of sapodilla trees in Belize, and the Sapodilla Cayes off Toledo are named after this tree. The fruit of the sapodilla is egg-shaped and egg-sized, with a brown skin and grainy yellow-orange flesh with black seeds. It is a favorite fruit not only of Belizeans but of many Belizean mammals including bats, howler monkeys, kinkajous, peccaries and tapirs. Several species of bats pollinate the flowers. The fruit has a very sweet, malty flavor. In Belize the fruit ripens in February and March.

Ziricote *(Cordia dodecandra).* This is a rare tropical hardwood that grows only in Belize and parts of Mexico and Guatemala. The heartwood of the ziricote is reddish-brown with black streaks. This contrasts with the blonde-or vanilla-colored sapwood, making striking furniture, musical instruments and wood carvings. The tree has vivid orange flowers that usually bloom in the hot, dry season during April and May.

FISHING AND HUNTING

Inland, Belize has 35 rivers plus many small streams and creeks. Many thousands of square miles of the Caribbean Sea are off the country's 200 miles of coastline. All of these waters team with fish and other marine creatures, many ready for the catching and eating.

Hunting is more limited, with only a few species legally permitted to be taken, but many Belizeans eat well on deer, turtle, iguana, game bird and other wild critters they catch or shoot.

From the Rivers and Sea

Belize offers inland fresh-water fishing, shallow-sea fishing inside the barrier reef and blue water fishing outside the reef.

Subsistence fishing has long been a way of life for many Belizeans. However, in 2009, the Fisheries Department, a part of the Ministry of Agriculture, Fisheries, Forestry, The Environment and Sustainable Development, issued regulations for sports fishing, and a requirement for fishing licenses. While focusing on three popular sports fish – tarpon, permit and bonefish, now catch-and-release only – the regulations spilled over into other kinds of fishing. Confusion developed over who needed a fishing license and for what kind of fishing the license was required. Even today, some confusion remains.

It is a good idea for visitors and expat residents of Belize to obtain a fishing license if you plan to do any fishing, even if you are fishing for food rather than sport. After all, you may accidentally hook a sports fish and confuse it with another type of fish.

Licenses can be obtained from the Coastal Zone Management Authority & Institute. The main office is on Princess Margaret Drive in Belize City, where daily (US$10), weekly (US$25) and annual (US$50) licenses can be purchased. Daily and weekly licenses, but not annual licenses, can be purchased online at www.coastalzonebelize.org.

Among the prize catches in the Caribbean Sea and rivers in Belize are:

Spiny Lobster *(Panulirus argus).* This is one of the most delicious of Belize's sea denizens. The season is June 15 to February 14. Cape length must be a minimum of 3 inches, and the tail weight 4 ounces minimum. Lobsters are usually caught in traps, or you can snorkel for them.

Queen Conch *(Strombus gigas).* Conch is wonderful fried, in soups, fritters, ceviche or in other preparations. The season usually runs from October 1 until June 30, but the season can close earlier if the conch quota is met before the end date.

The shell must be at least 7 inches in length. You can collect them when snorkeling or diving.

Red Snapper (*Lutjanus campechanus*). Snapper is frequently caught inside the reef. It is one of the best of the eating fishes.

Cuberra Snapper *(Lutjanus cyanopterus)*. Growing to over 100 pounds and usually found on or near reefs, this cousin of the Red Snapper also makes delicious eating.

Barracuda (genus *Sphyraena*). This is a ray-finned saltwater fish that is a favorite eating fish of Belizeans, despite the fact that it has a lot of bones. Open season year round.

Nassau Grouper *(Epinephelus striatus)*. Endangered in many areas due to overfishing, this grouper is protected in Belize. It can only be fished in two spawning areas near Lighthouse and Turneffe atolls from February through November. It is one of the largest fish on the outer barrier reef.

River Lobster (*Macrobrachium rosenbergii*). This is a large fresh-water shrimp that is usually caught in small lobster traps. Open season year-round.

Nile Talipia (*Oreochromis niloticus niloticus*). An invasive, non-native fish that has escaped from fish farms in Belize, talipia often appears on restaurant menus. Although its impact on local river ecology is negative, talipia, which can grow to be 2 feet long, make good eating.

Bay Snook *(Petinia splendida)*. Often caught in rivers and river mouths, snook is both a sports fish and a sought-after food fish.

Lion Fish (genus *Pterois*). This is an invasive predator from the Indo-Pacific. It is hurting local fishery populations and endangering the barrier reef. The Fisheries Department encourages catching these fast-reproducing fish, sometimes paying a bounty on them. Chefs are coming up with new ways to prepare them. Careful, though -- this fish may look beautiful, but it has poison spines with barbs that are painful if touched.

Hicatee (*Dermatemys mawii*). This is a river turtle that can grow to more than 40 pounds. The meat can be used in steaks or soup. The limit is three turtles per person or five per party, and Hicatees cannot be taken in the month of May.

Hunting

Deer, peccary, armadillo, iguana and some game birds are all popular game for hunting in Belize. In theory, hunting these game requires a license, available only to Belize citizens and official permanent residents, but in practice many rural Belizeans don't bother with a license. A local hunter's license is US$5 per day or US$100 a year. For a license visit a Forestry Department office (there's at least one in each district), or for information email wildlife.fd@ffsd.gov.bz or call 501-822-1524.

Game taken is for personal consumption only, and meat must not be sold without a valid game meat dealers license (US$1,000 per year).

White-Tailed Deer *(Odocoileus virginianus)*. This is the same deer found throughout most of the United States and south to northern South America. It is consumed as a substitute for beef. **Brocket Deer** (genus *Mazama)* is smaller than the White-Tailed but also offers tasty venison roasts and other cuts. The season for both types of deer in Belize is October through June for bucks and August through January for does.

Green Iguana *(Iguana iguana).* Locally called Bamboo Chicken or *Gallina de Palo* (Chicken of the Tree) in Spanish, as their flesh tastes like chicken, these lizards can grow up to 5 feet in length and 20 pounds in weight. They are favorite foods of many Belizeans. In some areas, over-hunting and the eating of their eggs have resulted in greatly reduced numbers. Open season is July through January.

Gibnut *(Cuniculus paca).* These large nocturnal rodents, which can weigh up to 25 pounds, are noisy and thus easy to hunt. Their meat tastes something like pork. The season is June through December. Hunting over time has greatly reduced their numbers in Belize.

Peccary *(Tayassu pecan).* This is a medium-sized new-world cousin of the pig. It can weigh up to 90 pounds. The meat is gamey but can be prepared similar to how pork is cooked. The open season is December through May.

Game Birds: Chachalaca (genus *Ortalis),* **Black-throated Bobwhite** *(Colinus nigrogularis),* **Blue-winged Teal** *(Anas discors)* and the **Lesser Scaup** *(Aythya affinis),* the latter two being types of ducks, are local game birds that provide tasty meals. They can be hunted from mid-July through January.

Farming and Ranching in Belize

An old Massey-Ferguson tractor on a farm near Punta Gorda

Considering farming or ranching Belize, or just growing your own vegetables? Besides information on vegetable crops that do well in Belize, here is information on some of the domesticated animals commonly raised in Belize.

Growing Vegetables

When it comes to growing your own vegetables in Belize, expect a mixed bag: You'll have some successes and failures. It also depends in part on where in Belize you live. On the coast and cayes, some vegetables simply do not do well with saline soils from the saltwater, and brisk winds from the water can also be a factor. Elsewhere, soil types (sandy, loam, clay, etc.), soil conditions (alkaline or acidic, for example) and depth of top soil obviously are factors, as are the type of terrain (hilly or flat) and of course how much or how little sun and water your vegetables get.

Remember that Belize, despite its small size, has a variety of microclimates. The Deep South has nearly a true tropical climate with lots of rain much of the year. Central and Northern Belize have a climate more like Florida, with not much more rain than many locations in the U.S. South, but there is usually a distinct hot, dry season from around March to May. The soil tends to be rocky with a lot of limestone, thus alkaline. The Mountain Pine Ridge, with its higher elevations and cooler, wet falls and winters, is more like Georgia or Alabama, with clay-like soil. Much of the coast and cayes, of course, have sandy soils, and unless you bring in "black dirt," (rich, loamy soil especially from parts of Toledo), it is difficult to get many vegetables to grow. Plants need to be salt- and wind-resistant.

Many backyard gardeners in Belize find that raised beds make vegetable growing easier, especially for plants that take up less space, such as herbs, lettuce and root crops like carrots and radishes. It is also important to be able to shade plants at times from the hot sun. You can use palm fronds to do this. Some vegetables do not produce much when soil temps at night stay above above 70 degrees, so that can be a factor in the warmer months, especially in the hot, dry season in the spring.

A lot of gardeners and farmers in Belize strive to grow organically. This is a challenge. Leaf-cutter ants can literally remove every leaf on a tree or plant overnight. Snails are a huge problem, especially with lettuce. White flies are hell on tomatoes, peppers, cabbages and cauliflower. Although there are challenges, it is usually cheaper to farm organically rather than using expensive, usually imported chemical insecticides, pesticides and fertilizer. At the end of this section is a listing of some organic farms, stores and co-ops in Belize.

Some gardeners in Belize build makeshift screened sheds to protect their sensitive plants from insects. A few gardeners are experimenting with hydroponic growing. You will find some hydroponic equipment at stores in Spanish Lookout and elsewhere.

Gardeners say their crops usually do better if they can use seeds or plants from Belize, or at least from neighboring countries, rather than from U.S. seeds imported to Belize, some of which may be out-of-date. Many Belizean gardeners save and dry seed from their neighbors' gardens, or in the case of crops such as Irish potatoes, let the local potatoes sit until they sprout eyes and then plant them. Of course, hybrid seeds and the increasing number of GMO seeds do not grow, or grow true, from seed.

Growing seasons in Belize vary from area to area, and the number of crops – one, two or continuous – that is possible in Belize depends on the type of vegetable. Generally, squash, zucchini, onions, sweet potatoes, eggplant and hot peppers, along with some herbs, can be grown nearly year-round. Other crops, especially those that are soil-temperature and water-dependent, may produce only one crop a year.

If you don't have your own kitchen garden, or if your crops fail, the local vegetable markets around the country have locally grown vegetables and fruits available at modest prices when in season, and sometimes some products not ordinarily available on Belize are brought in (legally or illegally) from Guatemala or Mexico. There are sizeable markets in Belize City, Orange Walk Town, Corozal Town, Dangriga, San Ignacio, Belmopan and Punta Gorda. In addition, there is a new Wholesale Farmer's Market in Corozal Town and a weekend Farmer's Market in at the Ag Tradeshow Center in Belmopan City. The main market in San Ignacio arguably is the best in the country because of the variety of crops that grow well in Cayo and also because of its proximity to Guatemala.

Because all these factors are so variable, it's impossible to state with assurance that such and such a vegetable will thrive in Belize, or not. However, here's an overview of vegetables, native and not, that can be grown successfully in large areas of the country.

Beans, Corn and Squash. The ancient Maya practiced what is known as companion planting, growing beans, corn (maize) and squash together. These "three sisters" of Native American agriculture were planted close together, usually on a mound about a foot high and two feet in width. The three plants help each other grow. The corn is planted first and after it reaches a few inches in height in height the beans and squash seeds are put in the ground. The beans climb the corn stalks and provide nitrogen to the soil. The squash vines cover the ground and reduce the amount of weeds and help keep moisture in the soil. Corn, beans, and squash contain complex carbohydrates, fatty acids and essential amino acids, and together the three vegetables provide a healthful, plant-based diet, especially when combined with fatty fruits such as avocado and greens such as chaya. Squash was likely domesticated first, about 10,000 years ago, followed by maize and beans.

The Maya and other Meso-American groups practiced what is called milpa agriculture. Milpa is from a Nahuatl word that means maize field. While milpa agriculture, with its slash-and-burn approach, is now frowned upon by many environmentalists, it actually made a lot of sense. It usually involved two years of growing the three sisters crops, then letting the land lay fallow for six or eight years. It provided significant yields of nutritious, complementary vegetables without the need for pesticides or fertilizers. The practice was self-sustaining as long as the population did not grow too large and as long as there was enough land to clear, by burning in the dry season.

Beets. Beets do not need rich soil, and they can be grown in many areas of Belize, even coastal and caye areas.

Cabbage. Cabbage is used in several Mestizo dishes, and it is locally grown in Belize as well as in Mexico and Guatemala.

Callaloo. This spinach-like plant, also called **Amaranth**, has been a staple of Maya diets for millennia and grows well in much of Belize. Callaloo has large green leaves that are good in salads (the stems also can be eaten), but many prefer it cooked as a vegetable, because the raw leaves are high in oxalic acid. If consumed in large quantities, oxalic acid can result in the formation of kidney stones. Callaloo grows wild in Belize, and some consider it a nuisance weed. From seed, callaloo grows quickly, even in poor soil. It reaches maturity in 30 or 40 days, reaching a height of about three feet. Callaloo is best harvested when plants are about 12 inches tall before seedpods ripen. It thrives in hot weather and flourishes in the dry season, but it can be grown virtually year-round in Belize.

Carrots. Carrots, which are related to weeds such as Queen Anne's lace, were first domesticated in the Middle East about 2,000 years ago. They can grow in Belize, but the soil has to be the right type. Carrots hate clay soil and love sand, and some growers even use all-sand soil. The sandy soil should be well drained. If your soil has a lot of clay, add 60%-80% sand mixed in with the clay. It's best to use raised beds, dug very deep. Do not add fertilizer or compost – that will just produce a lot of green carrot tops and no carrots. You'll want to plant them during the cooler winter months, as they do not do well in hot weather. Carrot seeds are difficult to germinate and must be kept moist after planting. If it doesn't rain, you may need to water the seeds twice a day. Do not transplant them. Plant them directly into the area in which they are to grow. Plant them very shallowly as carrot seeds are very small. After the carrots come up, mulch them well and thin them (smaller carrots and their tops can be used in salads.) It will take three months or more for carrots to be of a good size. **Radishes** are good as a companion plant, and the carrot and radish seeds can be mixed together with sand and planted. The radishes come up first. Thin them out and eat the baby radish greens.

Cauliflower. Cauliflower will grow in Belize, but some growers report that it does not head well in Belize's hot climate. Non-heading Asian varieties may perform better.

Celery. Although celery is more of a cool-weather plant, it can be grown in Belize, but results vary. Plant seeds in seed trays and transplant in about a month. It will do best when the soil temperature is not much over 70 degrees F. Space plants about six inches apart. Water and fertilize regularly. If you're lucky, you'll be able to harvest in about 16 to 18 weeks.

Chaya. There are many varieties of chaya, a spinach-like plant. One common variety is called tree spinach. Chaya is widely grown and eaten in Belize. It is both drought- and rain-tolerant. Tree chaya is usually propagated by cuttings and bears starting in the second year. It can be harvested continually as long as you don't strip the plant bare of leaves. Chaya should be cooked at least briefly before eating, due to the fact that it contains toxins that are killed by boiling briefly.

Cho-Cho. Sometimes called chayote, this pear-shaped and pear-sized vegetable, native to Belize and southern Mexico, is in the squash family. When ripe, it is a light green. It tastes like a combination of summer squash or zucchini and cucumber. It can be used a substitute for squash or zucchini in soups, stews and as a side vegetable. You don't need to cook it very long.

Cucumber. Cukes love sunshine and can be grown year-round in Belize. Plant seeds directly in mounded soil to provide better drainage. Feed with seaweed or manure regularly. Some people mulch them or, depending on the variety, provide trellises or stakes to let them climb. An Asian cucumber variety called Suyo Long seems to grow well in Belize, if you can find the seeds.

Eggplant. Aubergine, as the British and Canadians sometimes call eggplant, does very well in Belize's climate.

Lettuce. Heading varieties of lettuce, such as iceberg, do not do well at all in Belize. Stick with leaf varieties. Even some leaf lettuces will quickly bolt, so pick lettuce young. Sow arugula, mustard, kale, chard, endive and various other leaf lettuce seeds continuously, and, despite snails and bugs, you are likely to have fresh lettuce for salads year-round. There are some tropical varieties of lettuce, mostly from Asia, such as Ceylon spinach, ibika and salad mallow that you may want to try.

Herbs. Many herbs do very well in Belize. A number of restaurants and lodges have their own herb gardens to supply their kitchens, and thousands of Belizeans have kitchen herb gardens. Among the herbs that thrive in many areas of Belize are **cilantro, culantro** (a wild herb, *Eryngium foetidum,* sometimes confused with cilantro, but with a very different taste), **allspice** (*Pimenta dioica), **nutmeg, dill, cumin, parsley, fennel, mustard, ginger root, Thai basil, thyme, oregano, marjoram, chives** and **lemon grass.**

Onions. Onions are another crop that gets mixed results in Belize. They are grown commercially by Mennonites in North and Western Belize, but some years crops fail or do poorly. You may have more luck with **shallots** or **green onions** that mature quickly. Plant them in the winter and harvest before the hot, dry season.

Peas and Beans. Peas, mostly blackeyed-peas, are grown mostly on larger farms in Blue Creek. Beans, primarily red kidney beans used in typical Belizean dishes, are grown commercially on large farms in the Mennonite areas of Spanish Lookout and Blue Creek. Similarly, soybeans are grown commercially by Mennonites in those areas and elsewhere.

Peppers. Bell or sweet peppers generally do well in Belize. Hot peppers and chilies such as habanero do extremely well.

Irish Potatoes. While some Irish or Idaho potatoes are grown in Belize, they don't always do well. In other Central American countries, such as Panama and Guatemala, they are grown at higher elevations and mature in the summer months. Belize often prohibits the import of potatoes, along with onions and some other crops, to protect its domestic producers.

Rice. A little rice is grown in Orange Walk District, but commercial rice growing is mostly in low-lying flat areas of Toledo District.

Squash/Zucchini. You can grow both summer and winter squash in Belize. **Pumpkins** also will grow in Belize, although they are frequently attacked by beetles and various other insects.

Sweet Potatoes/Yams. All the starchy tubers that are staples in tropical countries grow well in the hot and humid summers of Belize. You can grow **yams** and **sweet potatoes** (they are two slightly different things), **taro** and **cassava.**

Tomatoes. You will find that gardeners in Belize have a mixed reaction to tomatoes. Some say they grow well; others say they have little or no luck. Tomatoes in Belize tend to do better in the winter and early dry season. You should look for heat-tolerant varieties. Cherry tomatoes are hardier in Belize than the full-size varieties. Most tomatoes grown in Belize are smaller and less well formed than those you would find in a grocery in the U.S.

Watermelon *(Citrullus lanatus).* Watermelons, annual vine plants, grow as well in Belize as they do in Georgia. They prefer sandy, low-lying soil. **Cantaloupes** also do well in Belize. As in the U.S., in Belize they are popular for eating at breakfast, as snacks, desserts and at picnics. The watermelon is believed to have originated in Africa, but it made its way to areas with mild climates around the world.

Free-range chickens in Belize   Photo: Shutterstock

Domesticated Animals in Belize

If you plan to farm or ranch in Belize, you'll want to focus, at least at first, on the kinds of animals that have proved themselves adaptable to the climate and geographic conditions of Belize. Here are some that do well.

Bees. Beekeeping in Belize and elsewhere in the region dates back to the ancient Maya who kept the native stingless bees to produce small amounts of honey as a sweetener. Modern beekeeping with the European honeybee, *Apis mellifera,* began in Corozal District in 1957. By the end of the decade there were some 1,000 hives in Corozal and Orange Walk districts.

Beekeeping continued to grow (by law beekeeping as a commercial enterprise was limited to Belizean citizens) until the late 1990s, when the widespread cultivation of marijuana reduced the natural sources of flower nectar. At about the same time, the arrival of Africanized bees, which are much more aggressive than the European honeybees, drove some beekeepers out of the business. However, Belizean beekeepers have adapted to the Africanized bees, hybrids of the African bee that escaped in Brazil in 1957, and the European honeybee. There is now a sizeable number of beekeepers in Belize. The Cayo Quality Honey Producers' Cooperative, for example, has about 30 members.

Still, keep in mind that Africanized bees, especially feral colonies, can be very dangerous. Many farm animals and pets have been stung to death in Belize by the bees, and several human deaths have been reported. In 2013, a 4-year-old Mennonite boy in Little Belize in Corozal District died from Africanize bees stings, and his 5-year-old brother was hospitalized. In 2017, a 60-year-old woman was stung to death in Cayo District when she went to pick up her grandchildren at school. Africanized bees are even present on the cayes. Also in 2017 a couple on North Ambergris Caye were badly stung from bees that had built a large nest in a coconut tree. Their dog died from the stings.

Cattle. The livestock industry in Belize is estimated to be worth about US$300 million. It is believed that there are around 90,000 to 100,000 head of beef cattle in Belize, plus about 4,000 head of dairy cattle. During a typical year, about 7,000 head of cattle are slaughtered in Belize for local consumption and around 8,000 to 10,000 head are exported.

The Belize Livestock Producers Association (www.belizelivestock.org) represents larger cattle ranchers in Belize. Altogether about 3,000 ranchers and farmers raise cattle in Belize. Nearly all are very small operations, most with just a few head. Among the larger ranch operations in Belize are John Carr's Banana Bank ranch near Belmopan, the Robertsons' Running W near San Ignacio and the Bowen family farm and ranch operation at Gallon Jug.

Not all breeds of cattle do well in the hot, humid conditions of Belize. Most commonly, Brahman and Brahman crosses are raised in Belize, as they can tolerate high temperatures. Zebu *(Bos indicus)* or humped cattle, which originated in Asia, are most commonly found in semi-tropical and tropical areas. Zebu have a fatty hump on their shoulders and often drooping ears. Brahman bulls are large, some weighing 2,000 pounds.

Among the crossbreeds that generally do well in the hot Belize climate are Beefmaster (Brahman-Shorthorn-Hereford cross), Braford (Brahman-Hereford cross), Brahmasin (Brahman-Limousin cross), Brangus (Brahman-Angus cross), Charbray (Brahman-Charolais cross), Gelbray (Brahman-Gelbvieh cross) and Santa Gertrudis (Brahman-Shorthorn cross).

Other breeds found in Belize include Red Angus, Black Angus, (due to the heat, Red Angus generally are preferred over the Black), Charolais, Red-Pol, Hereford, Nelore and Holstein. Holsteins, typically in a 7/8th Holstein 1/8th Brahman cross, are the dominant dairy cattle in Belize, but there are also some Brown Swiss.

Many ranchers believe that at least one acre of good pasturage is needed per head. Among the grasses that do well in Belize is cable grass, a kind of grass native to Belize. The blue stem variety of Bermuda grass, which comes from east Texas, also does well in Belize. This can be cut for hay. Hay is usually cut and baled in June and July. Brizantha and Mombasa grass work in Belize, too, as do other hot-climate varieties.

Under current Belize law, all cattle in the country must be branded before they reach 12 months of age. This helps prevent cattle rustling and provides proof of ownership. There is a fee of BZ$20 (US$10) to register your unique brand (payable to Belize Agricultural Health Authority or BAHA) with an annual fee of BZ$10 (US$5) to keep your brand registration active.

Goats and Sheep. Belize has around 10,000 sheep and perhaps 1,500 goats. Breeds of sheep in Belize include Dorper, Barbados Black Belly, Pelibuey and Katahdin. Anglo-Nubian and Boer are the main varieties of goats.

Hogs. There about 15,000 hogs in Belize, primarily Duroc, Landrace, Large White and PIC breeds. Nearly all are raised for domestic consumption.

Horses. Local horses in Belize, sometimes called potlickers, are mixed-breed horses that have become acclimated to the Belizean environment. Those providing horses for horseback riding trips, such as Banana Bank, Chaa Creek, Mountain

Equestrian Trails and Ian Anderson's Caves Branch Adventure Co., generally have quarter horses.

Poultry. Belize raises more than 30 million chickens a year. Most of these are produced on large commercial chicken farms run by Mennonites in Spanish Lookout and elsewhere and are consumed locally. Belize also raises around half a million turkeys in an average year. The country produces more than 4 million dozen eggs a year. Country Eggs, a co-op of about 85 mostly Mennonite chicken raisers in Spanish Lookout, produces about one-half of the eggs sold in Belize. Only brown-shell eggs are produced in Belize. You'll find Rhode Island Red, New Hampshire, Hyline Brown and Bovan Brown chickens producing brown eggs. Belize has an average per capita consumption of chicken meat of 109 pounds per person per year and approximately 141 eggs per person per year, one of the highest rates of chicken products consumption in the world. The Belize Poultry Association (www.belizepoultry.com) represents about 350 of the larger poultry and egg producers in the country. Many Belizeans keep a few "backyard chickens" for their own family use.

Belize Ag Report, a monthly magazine, is an excellent source of information on agriculture in Belize. Contact: *Belize Ag Report,* P.O. Box 150, San Ignacio, 501-663-6777, www.agreport.bz.

Plants, Agro, Farm and Garden Supplies
Agricultural Development & Service, Ltd., Mile 8, Stann Creek Valley Rd., Hope Creek Village (near Dangriga), 501-532-2113.

Agro Tech Supplies, 1 West St., San Ignacio, 501-824-3426.

Bamboo Belize, Rancho Delores Village, Belize District, 501-622-3184. Sells more than 10 types of bamboo seedlings.

Belize Agro-Enterprise Ltd., 18 Haulover St., Belmopan City, 501-822-3518.

Benny's Home Center, Mile 3, Philip Goldson Hwy., Belize City, 501-223-6236, www.bennysonline.com. Benny's, which also has locations at 33 Regent St. in downtown Belize City and a bargain center at 54 Freetown Rd., Belize City, is the largest building supply dealer in Belize, sort of like Belize's own Home Depot. While is mostly has building supplies, it stocks many items of interest to gardeners, farmers and ranchers.

Corozal Farmer's Supply, 99 5th Ave., Corozal Town, 501-422-2625.

Crossroad Farm Supplies, Center Rd., Spanish Lookout, Cayo District, 501-823-0366, www.crossroadfarmbz.com. Crossroad, based in Spanish Lookout, sells new New Holland and used Massey Ferguson tractors along with many farm tools such as chain saws and farm equipment and supplies.

Fresh Water Creek Farms, Ltd., Mile 10, Southern Hwy., Stann Creek District, 501-666-2051. Sells citrus plants. Rates vary by quantity – US$2 each in quantities of 1,000 or more.

The **Garden Center,** George Price Hwy. (across from Running W Central Farm, 501-824-0800.

Green Haven Nursery, Mile 68, George Price Hwy., San Ignacio, 501-804-2296

Habet & Habet, 107 Cemetery Rd., Belize City, 501-227-7459, www.habetandhabet.com. Although primarily a hardware and building supplies store, Habet & Habet has some garden supplies.

Hillbank Agricultural Co., Linda Vista, Blue Creek, Orange Walk District, 501-323-0600.

Midwest Steel & Agro Supplies, Center Rd., Spanish Lookout, Cayo District, 501-823-0131. This Mennonite-owned operation sells seeds, fertilizers and agricultural supplies.

O'Donoghue Landscapes, Mile 63, George Price Hwy., Benque Viejo del Carmen, Cayo District, 501-824-0800. This has one of Belize's largest selections of plants and garden supplies. It also provides landscaping services. It is associated with The Garden Center (see above.)

Our Heritage Seed, Spanish Lookout, Cayo District, 501-669-6756. David Johansen has a 35-acre farm in Spanish Lookout, and he has developed a specialty in saving and selling seeds that do well in Belize. He has a lot of bean seeds of different types, along with squash, kale, melons, eggplant, okra, basil and others. While he does not have a website, Johansen does have a Facebook page, Our Heritage Seed.

Reimer's Feed Mill, Center Rd., Spanish Lookout, Cayo District, 501-823-0105, www.reimersfeed.net. Reimer's Feed Mill sells vet supplies, feeds and some other farm and garden supplies.

River Walk Nursery, Mile 60 ½, George Price Hwy., San Ignacio, 501-824-2495.

Spice Farm & Botanical Garden, Golden Stream Village, Southern Hwy., Toledo District, 501-732-4014, www.belizespicefarm.com. Spice Farm, run by a physician and his wife from West Virginia who were originally from India, grows a number of herbs and spices including black pepper, vanilla, cardamom, cloves, cinnamon and nutmeg. It offers tours of the spice farm (US$15 per person) and also sells several dozen kinds of plants.

St. Thomas Plants Nursery, 5778 St. Thomas St., Belize City, 501-610-4415.

Westrac Ltd., Center Rd., Spanish Lookout, Cayo District, 501-823-0104, www.westracbelize.com. Westrac, with four locations in Belize (Spanish Lookout, Belize City, Orange Walk Town and Belmopan City), sells John Deere tractors and is the largest tractor parts, lawn and garden parts and automobile parts supplier in the country. It also has farm supplies and equipment and provides service on many types of equipment.

Selected Organic Farms, Gardens and Co-Ops

Here is a short, selected list of some of the organic farms, gardens, stores and co-ops in Belize. It is far from a comprehensive listing. Note that in addition to the jungle lodges listed here, a number of other lodges and hotels in Belize have organic gardens. These include Chan Chich Lodge, Blancaneaux Lodge, Belcampo Belize, Ka'ana Boutique Resort, Turtle Inn and Robert's Grove Beach Resort

Belize Botanic Garden: The Belize Botanic Garden was begun by the late Ken duPlooy and continued by wife Judy duPlooy, daughter Heather and other members of the duPlooy family who operate the adjoining duPlooy's Lodge on the Macal River. The 45-acre Belize Botanic Garden was officially established in 1997. Its specimen trees, shrubs, orchids and other plants were collected from various parts of Central America. Among other features the garden has a medicinal plants trail, a collection of most of the 40 palms native to Belize and a orchid house with hundreds of orchids native to Belize. The Botanic Garden also grows many tropical fruits including breadfruit, jackfruit, lychee, rambutan, mangosteen, mango, avocado, starfruit, jaboticaba, mammey apple, Malay apple, black sapote, sweetsop, soursop, Java apple, governor's plum, bilimbi and others. Self-guided tours of the Belize Botanic Garden are available daily starting at 7 am for US$7.50 per adult.

Belize Organic Family Farming: This Toledo-based group is committed to improving traditional farming systems and to helping poor families and children to generate sustainable methods to generate food and income through urban gardening and animal husbandry. It was started and is run by Nana Mensah. BOFF is partly funded by grants from the GO Campaign (www.gocampaign.org), which is an international organization devoted to helping orphans and poor children around the world, including in Belize.

Belize Perma-Kulchah Academy: The mission of this educational group is to create a sustain culture of interdependent living. It is based in Belize City at 55 Regent Street, 501-634-2233.

Chaa Creek Maya Organic Farm: Associated with Mick and Lucy Fleming's famed The Lodge at Chaa Creek, this 33-acre farm produces more than 20 organic fruits and vegetables for the lodge and for Mariposa restaurant in San Ignacio. The Lodge at Chaa Creek, www.chaacreek.com, 501-834-4010. Tours of the farm for those not staying at the lodge start at US$20.

Kuchil Balum Eco-Farm: This is a small organic farm and botanical garden in Red Bank village in Stann Creek District. It sells organic plants and flowers at retail and wholesale. Visit the farm on Farm Road in Red Bank, 501 624-1470.

Maya Mountain Research Farm: Located about 2 miles upriver from the Kekchi Maya village of San Pedro Columbia in Toledo District, the MMRF NGO is believed to be Central America's oldest working permaculture project. It has more than 500 species of plants In addition to its agroforestry system, it raises pigs and poultry and conduct training in permaculture, agroforestry and renewable energy. Contact: www.mmrfbz.org, 501-630-4386.

Pro-Organic Belize currently has a meeting weekly near Santa Elena, Cayo. For information, email proorganicbelize@gmail.com or call 501-677-9658. Pro-Organic Belize has a relationship with **San Antonio Cayo Organic Growers Association,** whose members sell organic produce at the San Ignacio Market.

Tropical Agro-Forestry, Ltd./Spanish Creek Rainforest Reserve is a 2,000-acre organic farm and nature reserve near Rancho Dolores in Belize District. It primarily grows bamboo. It has 75 acres of cleared land for organic production. Contact: See the farm's Facebook page or call 501-625-2837.

WWOOF has a number of participating organic farms in Belize. WWOOF is a "worldwide movement linking volunteers with organic farmers and growers to promote cultural and educational experiences based on trust and non-monetary exchange, thereby helping to build a sustainable, global community. Volunteer live with a host organic farfmer helping with daily tasks and experiencing life as a farmer. Usually they received food and board in exchange for work on the farm. To join WWOOF and to see what farms in Belize participate in the program, visit www.wwoof.net. There is a US$5 fee to become a member of WWOOF Belize.

Farm Equipment, Tractors and Vehicles
Farming and ranching in Belize requires the roughly the same type of farm equipment as needed for farming and ranching anywhere, with the exception that in some cases you will be doing more land clearing and working in semi-tropical and tropical areas where the bush grows and re-grows quickly.

Of course, the kind of equipment you need depends on the type of farming you plan to do, whether it's basic subsistence farms, cattle ranching, citrus growing, rice farming or whatever. Here are a few overall guidelines that apply virtually across the board:

• Choose brands and makes of equipment that are sold and serviced in Belize. You do not want to have to order expensive parts from the U.S. or Europe. In this section, we mention specific brands that are commonly sold and serviced in Belize.

• Keeping in mind that probably you'll be dealing with rough conditions – bad roads, rocky fields, thick bush and jungle, high temperatures – you'll want to buy the toughest equipment in the best condition you can afford.

• Because Belize is a small, inefficient market and some products carry high import tariffs, most vehicles, farm equipment and supplies will cost more in Belize than you likely paid back home. However, importing equipment also is costly.

National Ag Trade Show
The National Agriculture & Trade Show Grounds at the junction of the George Price and Hummingbird highways in Belmopan City is the venue for Belize's most important annual agriculture and trade exposition. It is usually held at the on a two-day weekend at the end of April. There are displays and demonstrations on livestock, fresh produce (both local and imported), arts and crafts, farm equipment, food and other.

Old-Fashioned Farming
Old-fashioned farming, using work animals and hand tools instead of diesel tractors and trucks and gas- or electric-powered tools, is possible in Belize, as it is anywhere. Old-school Mennonites in Little Belize, Barton Creek and elsewhere eschew modern mechanized vehicles and equipment and manage to produce a lot.

If this is your preferred style, our recommendation is to spend time in these conservative Mennonite communities in Belize and learn first-hand how they do it. You may even may be able to source some farm animals, such as mules, oxen and workhorses, along with animal-drawn equipment from the Mennonites.

It is beyond the scope of this book to cover this type of subsistence, basic farming. Get high-quality, comprehensive books on the subject, such as *Back to Basics, A Complete Guide to Traditional Skills,* edited by Abigail R. Gehring, Skyhorse Publishing, New York, 2008, 456 pp.

Tractors and Heavy Equipment
For clearing land and handling basic farming operations you'll want to look at buying a diesel tractor, preferably four-wheel drive along with equipment and attachments such as a bush hog, plows, harrows, front-end loader, scrape blades,

post-hole digger and other equipment. Specialized farming and ranch operations may require specialized equipment, such as fertilizer spreaders, sprayers and such.

Several makes of farm tractors are sold new in Belize, along with new or used equipment and attachments to go with them. Most commonly you'll see **John Deere, New Holland, Massey Ferguson** and **Ford.** Some Chinese and other Asian-made tractors are also on farms in Belize, including Jinma, Kubota, Mahindra and others, but parts may be difficult to find, and the Chinese-made tractors, although less expensive, do not have a particularly good reputation.

For land clearing and other heavy-duty users, Caterpillar is the world leader. Old D4, D5 and D6 series bulldozers, manufactured from the 1930s up to today, in various models, are often seen in Belize.

Among the farm tractor and heavy equipment dealers in Belize are:

Belize Diesel & Equipment Company, Ltd., 7142 Slaughterhouse Rd., Belize City, 501-223-2035, www.belizediesel.com. This well-known Belize company sells new Massey Ferguson tractors and attachments. It also has a branch outlet in Belmopan City and a diesel aftermarket store in Belize City. The company is the authorized dealer for Toyota trucks, vans and cars in Belize. It also is a dealer for Hino trucks.

Crossroad Farm Supplies, Center Rd., Spanish Lookout, Cayo District, 501-823-0366, www.crossroadfarmbz.com. Crossroad, based in Spanish Lookout, sells new New Holland and used Massey Ferguson tractors along with farming attachments, new and used.

Genrac, International Airport Rd., Ladyville, 501-225-2114, www.genracbelize.com. This company is a dealer for Caterpillar, including backhoes, excavators, dozers and other heavy equipment. It also sells used equipment and rents heavy equipment.

Westrac Ltd., Center Rd., Spanish Lookout, Cayo District, 501-823-0104, www.westracbelize.com. Westrac, with four locations in Belize (Spanish Lookout, Belize City, Orange Walk Town and Belmopan City), sells **John Deere** tractors and farming equipment. It also sells after-market equipment for Deere, New Holland and Massey Ferguson tractors.

Used Tractors and Farm Equipment

You'll see signs for used tractors and farm equipment for sale along the main highways in Belize. They occasionally are advertised in local weekly newspapers or in other publications, as well as online, but the best way to find used items is by word of mouth. Put out the word to everyone you can in farming areas such as Spanish Lookout, Shipyard, San Ignacio, Belmopan City and Punta Gorda what you are looking for, and you likely will get a lot of leads.

Quiet street in the village of Sarteneja

Homes and Land in Belize

The good news is that real estate generally costs less in Belize than it does in the U.S., Canada or Western Europe. To be sure, in a few prime areas you can spend hundreds of thousands of dollars, even millions, on a U.S.-style luxury home, or several hundred thousand dollars on a prime beachfront lot, but you can also buy raw land at prices not seen in the U.S. since the 1970s and in some areas find a simple but pleasant rental house for under US$400 a month. More good news: There are few restrictions on the purchase or use of real estate by foreigners, legal documents are in English and follow English common law traditions.

Shopping for Housing

Except for occasional ads in newspapers, few properties are advertised for sale, except on the internet. Real estate agencies maintain on-line listings. Most real estate brokers use the internet as the primary way of presenting listings and of getting prospective foreign buyers. See the real estate agent listings below for addresses of real estate websites in Belize. Note: because real estate listings on the internet are directed more to foreign buyers than to Belizeans, most properties tend to be the more expensive ones, and prices asked tend to be higher than fair market. Sellers and some agents take the view: "Why not ask a blue sky price? Some sucker out there may just pay it."

Even with the internet, however, you'll miss one-half or more of available properties. To find out what's really for sale, you'll have to spend time on the ground in Belize. Many properties are for sale by owner, rather than being listed with a broker. In many cases, you will see no sign or other indication that a property is for sale. Just start asking around, and before long you'll have more deals being offered you than you can even begin to consider. This goes as well for rentals. It is rare to see a house advertised for rent in a newspaper, except in San Pedro or Belize City, and brokers handle only the most expensive rentals.

About the only way to find a house or apartment to rent is to spend some time in the area where you wish to rent. Drive around and look for vacant homes, or ask foreign residents or Belizeans for tips on what's available. Several websites not affiliated with a real estate company have Belize real estate listings. Belize First maintains a section of free listings of Belize real estate for sale, wanted and trades. Visit www.belizefirst.com. Also on the site are some rental listings.

Real Estate Brokers

In Belize, despite rumblings about changing this, it is still the case that anyone can be a real estate broker. No license needed. No schooling, no bonding, no continuing education. All you need is enough money to print business cards, and, presto, you're a broker. Selling real estate is a popular first job for expats in Belize, and some do it on the side, illegally, without a work permit. Quite a few hoteliers, dive shop operators and taxi drivers peddle real estate to tourists on the side. One of the best-known real estate guys in Placencia, until he left to sail his boat around the Caribbean, was also the proprietor and barkeep of one of the most popular bars on the peninsula.

Efforts have been made to require some basic licensing of real estate brokers, but as of this writing this is still a work in progress. The Belize National Association of REALTORS® has been established – the group's web site is www.belizenar.org. Agent members, of which there are more than 100 in Belize, subscribe to a code of ethics and are supposed to follow other professional guidelines. Another group, the Association of Real Estate Brokers in Belize (www.arebb.com), was established in 2006 and has more than 80 agent members.

Not surprisingly, the quality of agents varies. Some are professional and honest. A few are out for a fast buck. Some are just not very knowledgeable. The ones we've listed here are among the best we know about, but even so your mileage may vary. Real estate commissions in Belize are similar to those in the U.S. Agents typically charge the seller 7% commission on residential property, and around 10% on raw land. Of course, rates are negotiable. Because many properties are in remote areas, brokers often charge prospective buyers expenses for travel and transportation incurred in connection with showing properties.

Selected Agents

These are some of the more frequently recommended real estate agents and companies in Belize (again, your mileage may vary). For more options, visit the real estate group websites mentioned above or see listings in individual destination chapters.

Belize North Real Estate, P.O. Box 226, Corozal Town, 501-422-0284, www.belizenorthrealestate.bz.

Caribbean Properties Consultants/CPC Real Estate Solutions, P.O. Box 149, Dangriga, 501-523-7299 or 669-9000, www.belizeproperty.com.

Ceiba Realty, 161 George Price Highway, Santa Elena Town, Cayo, 501-824-4050 or cell 501-610-4458, www.ceibarealtybelize.com.

Coldwell Banker Southern Belize, Point Placencia, Placencia, 501-523-3500 or 855-723-5493, www.coldwellbankerbelize.com.

Emerald Futures Real Estate, Mile 3½, George Price Highway, Belize City, 501-670-6818, www.emeraldfutures.com.

Keller Williams Rainforest Realty, P.O. Box 195, San Ignacio, Cayo, 501-670-4045, www.rainforestrealty.com. Macarena Rose is the founding president of the Belize National Association of REALTORS®.

REMAX San Ignacio, 30 Burns Avenue, San Ignacio, 501-824-0550, www.realestatepropertiesinbelize.com.

Tropic Real Estate, P.O. Box 453, Belmopan, Cayo, 501-610-1622, www.realestatebelize.com. This is one of the older real estate agencies in Cayo.

Few Restrictions on Ownership

Belize imposes few restrictions on ownership of land by non-nationals. Unlike Mexico, which prohibits the direct ownership of land by foreigners on or near the coast (though this can be gotten around through certain legal procedures), in Belize foreigners can buy and hold real estate, including beachfront property, in exactly the same way as Belizeans. Formerly an alien landholder's license was needed for purchases of 10 acres or more (or more than 1/2 acre within a town or city.) However, such a license is no longer needed.

The only limitations on ownership by foreign nationals are these: Government approval is required from the Ministry of Natural Resources before the purchase of any island, regardless of size. In a few coastal and caye areas such as Caye Caulker there are rules limiting purchases by non-locals, and approval by the local village council or board must be obtained in advance.

Real Estate Prices

Property prices vary greatly in Belize from one area to another. They generally are highest in Belize City, on Ambergris Caye and in Placencia, and lowest in remote rural areas.

In large tracts, raw land is available in Belize for under US$300 an acre, but for this price access may be poor and surveying costs may exceed the cost of the land itself. Agricultural land might range from US$500 to $3,000 an acre, or more, depending on quality and access.

Home prices range from under US$25,000 for a basic Belizean-style home in a small village to US$1 million or more for a luxury home on the beach in San Pedro. Finished, newer homes typically sell for from US$75 to $250 per square foot, though of course the location of the lot or land also is a major factor.

The condominium type of ownership is new to Belize, and most condos are on Ambergris Caye. There are a few condos in Placencia and Belize City and on

Caye Caulker, and a handful in Corozal Town. Prices start at around US$125,000 for a one-bedroom unit and go up to well over half a million dollars. On a square foot basis, you can expect to pay US$200 to $300 per square foot for a two-bedroom condo with sea views.

Belize has a few timeshares and "fractional ownership" properties, mostly on Ambergris Caye. These are generally not a good investment. They are a high-risk, low-reward way to use your money, in our opinion.

Property in Belize has appreciated over the past two decades, but by exactly how much is more difficult to say. Real estate agents say that some beachfront property in Placencia, San Pedro and elsewhere that was selling for a few hundred dollars a front foot in 1980 is now going for US$3,000 to $5,000 or more a front foot. Real estate agents naturally talk up the appreciation potential. Keep in mind that the Belize economy is closely tied to the economy in the U.S., and appreciation, or lack of it, in Belize tracks the economy in the U.S.

When the U.S. and world economies went into a tailspin in 2008-2009, real estate sales in Belize slowed. Condo sales in particular stalled. A few condo developments in Placencia and on Ambergris shut down, at least temporarily. Most have been resurrected, typically under new ownership. Former condo owners may have lost at least some of their investment. Several projects and hotels went into receivership. Others stopped or postponed construction. Lot sales also slowed significantly. "Very little is selling in Placencia," one agent said during the height of what has been called the Great Recession. However, even during that downturn interest in small tracts of rural land in inland areas such as Cayo continued.

Despite the slowdown, price levels seem to have held up in most areas. The big cuts in asking prices are on properties that were overpriced to begin with, real estate agents say.

As of this writing (early 2018), new condo and new home construction is going on again in formerly "hot" areas of Ambergris Caye, Hopkins, Placencia, Cayo and elsewhere.

Even with appreciation, real estate prices in Belize still are generally inexpensive by the standards of the U.S. or most of Western Europe. That's especially true of beachfront prices, on a relative basis. Waterfront lot prices on the Eastern seaboard of the U.S. or in Florida rarely are less than US$300,000 to $750,000, and in places like Hilton Head, S.C., or Ft. Lauderdale, Fla., can easily reach US$1 million or more, whereas beachfront building lots on Belize's Caribbean are still available for US$100,000 to $250,000, though in prime areas you can pay more.

Precautions and Pitfalls

Most of the same rules of thumb that apply when looking for a home, land or apartment in the United States or Canada also apply in Belize. But Belize also has its own special situations:

Be prepared to get out and hunt. You're not going to get a deal if you only go to a real estate agent. Many properties in Belize aren't listed with brokers, and the broker listings tend to be priced higher than those that are privately sold (though of course there are exceptions.) You'll need to go out and look for available properties. Just start asking around, and you'll soon have plenty of choices. In Belize, money talks, and if you have the cash some people who have never considered selling may decide it's time to cash in.

Understand that the Belize real estate market is small and inefficient. Someone asked us why a piece of property near Placencia was still on the market three years after he had first seen it advertised. "Is there something wrong with the property?" he asked. No, we told him, nothing wrong with the property. It's just Belize. The real estate marketplace in Belize is even more inefficient than it is elsewhere.

The pool of financially capable real estate buyers in Belize is small, leaving most sellers dependent on foreign buyers. There is little real estate classified advertising, and many properties are sold or rented by word of mouth. Multiple listing services are just in their infancy in Belize. There is no comprehensive computerized database of real estate sales with reliable selling prices. Thus, it's not easy to find out exactly what is on the market or what the prices are. There are relatively few well-trained real estate agents, appraisers and surveyors. Mortgage financing is not easily available for foreign buyers, further reducing the size of the buying pool and requiring cash sales or owner financing.

All this means that prices for similar properties can be all over the board. The time to sell a property may be measured in YEARS rather months. Which is something to think about as you buy real estate, which you may someday want to sell.

Negotiate. If you're a good horse trader, you'll likely get a better deal in Belize than the guy who isn't. Keep in mind that in most parts of Belize there is far more available real estate than buyers with cold cash, so don't jump at the first deal that comes your way. Remember, too, that in real estate you almost always make your money when you buy, not when you sell. The more you know, the better price you'll get. A common saying among expats in Belize is that the second house you buy or rent is twice as large as the first and costs one-half as much. The real estate market in Belize is so thin that many sellers just pull an asking price out of the air -- similar properties can vary widely in asking price. Unscrupulous real estate agents also sometimes change the asking price in mid-negotiation, in many cases without telling the owner. Spend as much time in Belize as you can before you put any money in real estate.

If at all possible, rent for a while before you buy. That's worth saying again: RENT BEFORE YOU BUY.

Caveat emptor. Buyer beware applies as much in Belize as anywhere else. Real estate agents in Belize still aren't licensed, although licensing efforts are under way, and a couple of real estate associations have been formed *(see above)*. That beachfront lot that looks wonderful in the dry season may be under two feet of water in the rainy season, and there are no laws in Belize that provide for you to get your money back if the real estate agent or seller didn't provide full disclosure. In addition, as soon as the word gets out that you're in the market for a place to live, everybody and his brother will tell you about this little piece of property owned by a cousin of theirs. It may be a good deal, but look before you leap.

In Belize, especially outside resort areas, there are sometimes two prices:

one price for locals and another price for foreigners. The difference may be relatively small, but sometimes the Belizean price may be one-half or less of the "rich foreigner" price. From the expat buyers' point of view, this is unfair. From the Belizean point of view, this is perfectly kosher and reflects the reality that Americans (or Canadians or Europeans) make far more money for the same work as Belizeans and can well afford to pay more. One way around this problem is to get a trusted Belizean friend to find out the "local price" for you. Another is spend enough time in the country to get a feel for the difference between the Belizean price and the non-Belizean price, so that at least you can bargain with your eyes open.

What You Get for Your Real Estate Dollar in Belize

Here's a sampler of what you can expect to get for your money in Belize in 2016:

Under US$10,000
Small building lot in some areas of Corozal, Toledo or Cayo districts

Under US$15,000
5 acres of land in Orange Walk or Toledo districts or other rural area
Building lot in or near towns such as Punta Gorda, Corozal and Benque Viejo

Under US$40,000
15-acre farm with small very basic dwelling in rural area
Belizean-style house in rural village

Under $70,000
Small cinderblock house in Belmopan or near San Ignacio
Lot on Caye Caulker north of the Split

Under US$100,000
Riverfront or seaview lot in some areas of Stann Creek, Corozal or Toledo districts
Small but modern concrete home in Belmopan, Corozal or Cayo
Mennonite "prefab" small house on lagoon or riverfront lot on southern coast (including lot)

Under US$150,000
50-acre farm with small dwelling and outbuildings in northern Belize, Cayo or Toledo
Modern 1,000 square-foot home, with river or other water view in Corozal or Hopkins area
One-bedroom house or condo on Caye Caulker

Under US$250,000
Deluxe 2,000 square-foot home on nice lot in San Ignacio or Corozal
150-acre farm with nice home, outbuildings and equipment in rural area

Under US$500,000
4,000 square-foot luxury home on small estate in Cayo
500-acre farm with home, outbuildings and equipment in rural area

Fees and Costs of Purchase
Besides the cost of the property, you are likely to incur charges associated with the purchase that total around 10% to 22% of the purchase price. These include the following:

Stamp Duty: This is a real estate transfer tax, generally paid by the buyer. Until 2006, the tax formerly was 15% for most foreign nationals. It was then reduced to 5% across the board, regardless of the nationality or residency status of the buyer. In 2017, the law was revised again, making the stamp duty for non-Belizeans 8% but keeping it at 5% for Belizeans. This tax is due at closing and is calculated on the gross sales price of the property, or, in the case of property being transferred at less than market value, of the actual value of the property. The government has the right to assess the property at a higher level than the sales price, if it believes the selling price does not accurately reflect the true market value. There is no stamp duty due on the first US$10,000/BZ$20,000 of the sale – so if a property is sold to a non-Belizean for US$50,000 there would be a transfer tax of 8% of US$40,000 or US$3,200.

GST: The GST of 12.5% applies to the FIRST-TIME sale of new or substantially renovated property. This applies, for example, to newly constructed condos and houses. Substantially renovated usually means that 60% or more of the property was renovated. It also applies in some cases to residential lots selling for the first time in a subdivision. It does NOT apply to the sale of other land or previously occupied homes. In many cases, the GST is rolled into the sales price so that the buyer may not even realize it is being paid.

Attorneys' fee: For around 2% of the purchase price, an attorney will draw up sales agreements, transfer documents and ascertain that the title is sound.

Thus, if you are buying a new condominium for US$200,000 at the time of closing you will pay the 8% stamp duty, 12.5% and 2% attorney's fee, for a total of 22.5% of the sales price, or US$39,000. Again, the GST is likely included in the sales price and the buyer doesn't see it as a separate charge. Clearly, though, the GST has the impact of increasing the cost of buying new homes, condos or lots in a subdivision. On the purchase of an existing home or tract of land, the total would be around 10% of the selling price.

In addition, there usually are nominal other fees and charges associated with transferring a title, such as for photocopying or filing.

Property taxes: Property taxes vary but typically are about 1.5% of the assigned value (NOT market value) of the undeveloped land, payable annually on April 1. In Belize, property taxes outside cities are based on land value rather than the developed value of the property, to encourage development. Property taxes on homes and other developed land even in cities are low, although the government has been increasing them in some areas. For example, the property tax on a nice four-bedroom North American-style home on a large lot would likely be in the range of US$200 to $400, but in some areas the tax might be under US$100. Some property owners pay as little as US$20 or $30 property tax annually.

Speculation tax: There is a 5% speculation tax on land of 300 acres or more, payable annually based on the value of the land.

Capital gains tax: There is no capital gains tax in Belize.

Registration and Title

There are three different real property title systems in Belize:

Registered Land Act system, in which application for transfer is made, and a new Land Certificate is issued to the purchaser. Belize is moving to this system throughout the country, but at present it is not yet available everywhere. However, it has now been implemented in many areas popular with foreign buyers. Under this system, an application is made for title transfer and a new Certificate of Title is issued to the grantee. Any existing "charges" will be shown on the Land Registry for that parcel of land. The owner holds a Certificate of Title, and this, together with the relevant Land Register entries is the proof of ownership.

Conveyance system, which involves the transfer of land by conveyance and registration. This is the system used in much of the United States. In order to assure that the seller actually owns the land, a title search must be made in the Lands Unit in Belmopan to unearth the chain of title and to un- cover any encumbrances such as uncanceled mortgages. This search usually is done by an attorney or a paralegal. Unfortunately, it is sometimes difficult or impossible to trace old conveyances with any degree of certainty of results, due to the condition of the index books.

Torrens system, which involves a First Certificate of Title followed by Transfer Certificates of Title. Unlike the Torrens system in use in parts of the U.S. and elsewhere, the Belize systems is not backed up by a fund, which guarantees title. Under this system, the uncanceled charges or encumbrances and the transfers from the title are shown on the relevant Certificate, so no further search is normally needed before the new Transfer Certificate of Title is issued, following the application for transfer. This system is now fairly rare in Belize.

Which system you use depends on where your property is located. You won't have a choice. If for example your property is located in an area of Belize where the Registered Land Act system is in place, such as around Belmopan, parts of Corozal, Stann Creek District and Belize District and elsewhere, or in a planned subdivision, your property will be registered under that system. Land in Belize is being put into this system area by area until eventually freehold land in the entire country will be included in it. Each year, more of Belize is converted to this system and within the next few years likely all or nearly all of Belize will be in this system.

Some property purchasers in Belize complain that it can take many months or even years for the Lands Department to provide them with their Certificate of Title.

Title insurance is available in Belize, though most buying property don't use it. RF&G Insurance and other insurance companies offer title insurance.

Typically, title insurance costs 1% of the purchase price. Stewart Title, a U.S.-based title insurance firm, does not have an office in Belize but provides title insurance for some properties through Belizean firms.

Need for a Lawyer

In Belize, attorneys remain trusted advisors. They're usually well-connected and well-paid pillars of the community who wield real power. Fees are not all that different from what you would pay in a small or mid-size city in the U.S.

An attorney, or other trained person, will research the title in the Lands Registry, or in the Companies Registry if the land is held by a corporation. A title opinion for land that is not in the new Title Registration system takes longer to research as an abstract of title must first be prepared that goes back at least 30 years. (The statute of limitations on land claims in Belize generally is 30 years.) Liens, judgments and other encumbrances are valid only if properly lodged. An opinion of good and clear title will be issued once the attorney has satisfactorily examined the abstract.

A roster of attorneys in Belize *(see Appendix)* reveals the surnames of prominent families with histories in Belize going well back into colonial times along with those of today's political leaders including Barrow, Young, Shoman, Musa, Courtenay and Godfrey. In any real estate transaction, you should have your own Belize attorney. Your attorney back home likely will be unfamiliar with Belize law and will not be licensed in Belize.

Caution about Buying Leased Land

Many Belizeans own property under a leasehold from the government. The Belize government provides building lots and other small pieces of land to Belizean citizens on a lease basis. After the Belizean clears the property and improves it with a building or some other structure, he or she can apply for a conversion to a fee simple title. However, some Belizean owners never get around to doing this or cannot afford the cost. Be sure that you are buying a fee simple, freehold property, not a leasehold property. Again, this is an area where a Belizean attorney can help you.

Financing

It is difficult for a non-resident to get a mortgage loan from a bank in Belize for buying or building, and if you can get a loan the interest rate will be high – typically 8% to 14% – so, if you can't get a mortgage in Belize or don't like the interest rate, you should be prepared to pay cash, arrange owner financing or get financing through a loan from a non-Belize financial institution on your assets back home.

Acreage and building lots in Belize are often purchased on terms under an Agreement for Sale or Contract for Deed whereby the seller keeps title to the property until it has been paid for in full. Terms vary but can range from 10% down with 10 years to pay at 10% simple interest per annum — about the best deal you can hope for — to 50% down and three years to pay at 10 to 14%, with perhaps a balloon at the end. Residential property may also have owner financing, although commonly the lowest price will be for all-cash deals.

For citizens and official permanent residents of Belize only, the Development Finance Corporation (DFC), a financial institution owned by the government of Belize, formerly made loans of US$2,500-$50,000 or more for building or buying housing. The DFC also developed housing subdivisions near Belmopan on Ambergris Caye, on the Northern Highway in Belize District, and in Corozal Town. These subdivisions offered new homes, such as a small, three-bedroom, concrete house near Belmopan for US$35,000 and a three-bedroom, two-bath home of 925 square feet at Ladyville for about US$47,000. Financing was at 12% for up to 25 years.

Belizeans did not seem to care much for most of these subdivisions, and some homes were never sold. Reportedly, some of the houses were poorly constructed and located in undesirable areas. In 2004, the DFC ran out of financial string and temporarily ceased active operations.

However, the DFC (www.dfcbelize.org, 501-822-2350) has been resurrected by the Belize government. It now makes loans for home purchases, home construction, home renovation, agricultural and tourism projects and even education. To qualify, the loan applicant must be a Belizean citizen, including citizens living abroad, or official permanent resident between 18 and 70 years of age and must meet the DFC's loan standards. Mortgage loans of up to US$100,000 currently are offered at interest rates beginning at 9.75% with repayment periods of up to 25 years. Loan origination fees start at 2%.

The DFC is based in Belmopan (P.O. Box 40, Bliss Parade, Belmopan City) and has offices in Belize City, San Pedro, Corozal Town, Orange Walk Town and Dangriga.

Real Estate Foreclosure Auctions

From time to time there are foreclosure auctions in Belize. Auctions sell property put up as security for bank or other financial institution loans. Usually these are advertised in the weekly newspapers in Belize. Some banks holding foreclosed property may put notices of property to be auctioned on their websites. Foreigners can participate in these auctions. Generally, at least 10% of the successful bid price must be tendered at the time of the auction.

There may be no particular problems in buying at a foreclosure auction, other than those ordinarily associated with auctions, such as the fact that among the savvy bidders may be local people who know more than you do about the property and its value. However, in Belize sometimes the owners of the property will still be in possession at the time of the auction. If so, you may face a real problem getting the owners out. Before putting up your money, you may want to consult with an attorney conversant with real estate property law and with foreclosure auctions *(see Appendix for a list of attorneys in Belize.)*

The DFC also occasionally offers foreclosed property for sell.

Rentals

Rental costs in Belize also vary widely, being highest on Ambergris Caye and in Belize City. In upscale areas of Belize City, you can expect to pay around US$.90 to $2 per square foot per month, or about US$900 to $2,000 a month for a 1,000 sq. ft. two-bedroom apartment in a fairly secure area. On Ambergris Caye, a one-bedroom apartment suitable for most expats goes for US$600 to $1,000 and a two-bedroom US$900 to $2,000.

Elsewhere, rentals are much lower. In rural areas and low-cost towns such as Corozal, you can find a small house in a safe area for under US$400 a month and sometimes for as little as one-half that amount. Modern three-bedroom homes near the water go for US$500 to $1,000 a month. We know of expats in Corozal who rent for under US$300 a month, and while their homes are not fancy they are comfortable, typically of concrete block construction with a couple of small bedrooms, bath, a living room and a kitchen with stove and refrigerator. In all areas, North American-style housing with air conditioning, modern appliances, and security systems will be several times more expensive than a traditional Belize rental, simple concrete or wood house, with only basic amenities and probably no appliances except for a butane stove and a small fridge.

Short-Term Rentals

If you're coming to Belize on a scouting expedition of a few weeks to a few months, consider a short-term rental. Staying in a house or apartment rather than in a hotel can help you decide if Belize is really for you. Unfortunately, there are not a lot of short-term vacation rentals in Belize. Most of them are concentrated on Ambergris Caye, but there are a few in other areas including Placencia and Corozal. In most areas, however, you can find a hotel with housekeeping facilities.

Free Land?

You may have heard about a program of homesteading or otherwise getting free land in Belize. Yes, there is such a program in place, but there are big catches: First, you must be a Belizean citizen or have lived in the country as an official permanent resident for at least three years. Second, land is only available in certain areas. Mainly it is small tracts or building lots. Third, you have to lease the land from the government, clear it and actually construct a home or make other improvements. At that point, for a nominal amount you can buy the property from the government, and you will get title. Given the time and red tape involved, and the low cost of land in Belize, it may not be worth it to get a small piece of land worth a few thousand dollars. Frankly, if the only reason you moved to Belize is to take advantage of such a scheme, it's unlikely you'll have the financial resources to make it in Belize long enough to qualify for the program.

Kitchen cabinets custom-made of Belizean mahogany

Building in Belize: On or Off the Grid

Building is usually cheaper than buying in Belize, as it is elsewhere, especially if you act as your own general contractor. As a rule, you will get more for your housing dollar in Belize by building rather than buying a completed home.

You'll usually get a lot more home. However, you'll also get a lot more headaches. If you can put up with construction hassles – which are many – you can build a house with details such as built-in furniture, exotic tropical hardwood floors and ceilings and custom-made mahogany cabinets that in the U.S. would be found only in the most upscale homes.

On or Off the Grid?

One of the first decisions you'll have to make about building in Belize is whether or not you want to be on or off the grid. Off-grid construction generally costs more up-front than on-grid, mainly due to the high initial cost and complexity of solar or wind or water power, or a combination. However, over the life of the house, the total cost is almost certainly to be lower if you're off the grid. Plus, and this is crucial for preppers and survivalists, you are independent of the existing infrastructure, so even in the case of a apocalyptic event you likely will be able to continue to live comfortably in your home.

Belize Electricity, Ltd. produces power from several sources, notably hydroelectric power from dams on the Macal River in Cayo District. It also uses some diesel and gas generation, especially for back-up power. But it buys a considerable portion of its electricity from Mexico. This means that Belize is not self-sufficient in electric power and is subject to supply and price changes by the government in power in Mexico. As noted elsewhere, electricity in Belize is roughly twice as expensive as in the United States, running around 24 US cents per kilowatt hour.

Power, Water, Sewage and Communications

Living off the grid essentially requires three basic elements: **power/electricity supply, water supply and waste (sewage) treatment.** The power supply involves the collection of electrical energy, most commonly through solar cells, and then the storage of it in batteries for use during the night and on days when there is little sunlight.

At its most basic, a **solar electric system** in Belize usually consists of four components: 1) solar panels 2) charge controller 3) direct current (DC) batteries for storage 4) an inverter to convert DC to AC to run your home. In the U.S. and elsewhere, many utilities allow net metering, allowing you to sell unneeded energy back to the utility. In this case, the solar panels often contain a micro-inverter and you don't necessarily need batteries. However, net metering is not currently (no pun intended) available in Belize, so you will need batteries and an inverter. Of course, if you want to be truly energy independent you don't want necessarily want to be hooked up to the grid.

Tesla and other companies are working on really remarkable home energy storage solutions. The company's Powerwall is a rechargeable lithium ion battery with liquid thermal control. It is paired with a home solar panel system. When your solar panels produce more electricity than you can use in your home, the excess is stored in the battery pack. Later, when your panels aren't producing enough electricity, you can use the electricity stored in your Powerwall. The second generation Powerwall (13.5 kWh, with 5KW steady and 7 kW peak) costs around US$5,500, plus another US$700 in hardware. This doesn't include installation, which can add another US$1,000 to $3,000 or more per unit. The Powerwall is about 45 inches high, 30 inches wide and 6 inches deep. It weighs about 270 pounds. There is a 10-year warranty. Powerwalls contain a built-in inverter to convert DC to AC, so a separate inverter is not required. A 1,200 sq. ft. home with air-conditioning and EV charging equipment might require three Tesla Powerwalls. The cost for three, with supporting hardware, would be around US$17,000. Installation, especially of multiple Powerwalls, can be complex and may require additional wiring and service panels. As many as 10 Powerwall units can be linked together to provide large amounts of storage. Powerwalls can be installed inside or outside, on the wall or on the floor, and up to 10 of the units can be stacked on top of each other. As Telsa's huge new Gigafactory in Nevada amps up productions, prices for home storage batteries are expected to fall.

One common complaint is that the Tesla batteries are noisy, in the 50-decible range. However, they are quieter than most generators.

Tesla also makes a Powerback unit designed for commercial use. With inverter a 200kWh system was introduced at around US$200,000.

A number of companies make home power storage batteries that compete with

Telsa. These include **LG Chem, Vivent** (which is partnering with Mercedes) and **Sonnen.** Sonnen's compact 4kWh battery costs a little over US$5,000.

Many in Belize use deep-cycle marine batteries. These batteries start at a little over US$100 each, and dozens can be linked together. Those work but do have to be replaced regularly, sometimes as often as every two or three years. They also require a battery charger manager or controller.

Another option is heavy-duty storage batteries, called "forklift" batteries because these batteries are used in electric forklifts and other equipment handling machines. These heavy units – 200 to 4,000 pounds or more each – also require a forklift to move them. These have longer lives and are more efficient than marine batteries. These start at around US$1,000 and range up to around US$5,000 or more. Again, forklift batteries can be linked together.

All batteries have a limited life. Typically it will range from three to 10 years, depending on the quality of the battery and how you use it. Batteries that are not completely discharged before recharging tend to last longer than batteries that are totally discharged and then charged. Clearly, in batteries as in everything else, there is a tradeoff between quality and cost.

To be safe, you will want to have a back-up generator for emergency use. This can be powered by gasoline, diesel or butane/propane. The cost for this could run anywhere from a few hundred U.S. dollars to several thousand. For example, a Westinghouse 7,500 running watt generator (9,500 peak watts) with 6-gallon gasoline tank that will run about 10 hours on a tank of gas costs around US$1,800; a Duramax 12,000 running watts dual-fuel generator (propane and gasoline) is about US$1,700; and a Generac 5,000 running watt diesel generator is around US$4,500.

There are a number of companies in Belize that do solar systems and solar consulting, including **Solar Energy Solutions Belize** in Belmopan City (501-666-1000), which has a Facebook page, and **Prosolar** (501-832-2217, www.prosolarltd.com), also in Belmopan. Another company you may want to consider is **Grupo Lumiere** in Chetumal, Mexico (www.grupolumiere.com, 00-52-983-833-1335). Some companies also do hydro and hybrid hydro-wind projects. You may also benefit by reading the catalogs and websites of U.S. and Canadian solar companies such as **Backwoods Solar** in Idaho (www.backwoodssolar.com) or **Energy Alternatives** (www.backwoodssolar.com).

How much power you need to generate and storage depends mostly on how you plan to use it. Do you want air-conditioning, and if so in your entire house or just in certain areas, such as your bedroom and office? What kitchen appliances will you have – large refrigerators and freezers, dishwashers, washer and dryer, or can you make do with less? What will be your peak load? Electric motors for air-conditioners, well pumps and other systems require a large charge to start.

How will you heat your water? On-demand hot water heaters are popular, but they can be undependable and some require butane to run, and you will have to depend on buying the gas. Solar hot water is usually a good way to go, either connected to your main electric system or in a separate system. You probably won't need as much hot water as back home. When it's 90 degrees, a cool shower is refreshing!

Import duty is waived on alternative energy products entering the country. However, the 12.5% GST is charged. As noted, BEL does not allow a buy-back or net metering of privately provided electricity. There is also no tax credit offered by the Belize government.

Some solar installers say the bring-even point for off-the-grid solar versus buying electricity from BEL is from three to five years. Other experts say it is longer. After that, except for periodic maintenance and battery replacement, your power is essentially free. Insurance companies in Belize do allow solar to be included on your homeowner's insurance.

Your **water supply** can come from a cistern, usually concrete or heavy plastic containers that collect water from roof run-off and other sources. This is the most common solution. If you are in an area where there are fresh water springs or clean creeks, that is an excellent solution, especially if you can get gravity to work for you to provide the water flow to your house and outbuildings. If you live near a stream with running water, you can build a simple water wheel to pump water to your home. A well, either a shallow dug well or a drilled well, is another option, although it is likely to be more expensive. In coastal areas, a reverse-osmosis system is a possible, albeit expensive, method of converting seawater to drinkable water. In any case, you'll want to have a system to check water purity and a way to control bacteria, mold and other build-up.

Sewage systems in Belize are usually septic tanks. If properly installed and sited, with a large concrete tank and a well-sited and prepared drainfield, septic systems can last for decades with essentially no maintenance. Of course, the type of soil and its ability to "percolate" and the topography are issues with septic systems. Aerobic bacteria that digest the sludge of the septic system more thoroughly than occurs in traditional systems can help. A dose of good bacteria needs to be added annually. Some systems also use a small pump to oxygenate the septic tank.

Alternatively, composting toilets and a gray water system for irrigating with dirty but ecologically safe water are options, especially for smaller homes.

For communications (telephone, television, internet) again it depends on your location. In many areas, cell telephone and mobile internet, available from BTL and Smart, is a good solution for reasonably fast internet and reliable phone communications. Satellite can provide internet (usually slow and weather-dependent) along with good television reception. **Computer Ranch** in Spanish Lookout (501-823-0373, www.spanishlookout.bz/business/computerranch) is a long-established and generally well-respected provider of computer parts and service along with satellite systems. **Tenchtronic Communications** in Belize City (501-227-2175) is another option. It has a presence on Facebook. In most areas, there are also freelance satellite installers, who may be cheaper. DirecTV and HughesNet are common in Belize.

Design of the House

Another key factor, more important in off-the-grid living but also important even if you are on the grid, is the design of your house. Generally, you want to have a house that is designed for the tropics. This means wide eave overhangs – five or six feet – for the roof, to provide shade from the sun. This prevents most of the sunlight hitting and warming the side of your house. It also prevents water coming into the house during heavy rains.

Good design for the hot climate also usually means high ceilings. Small cube-shaped rooms work well in cold climates but can be like ovens in semi-tropical and tropical climates.

The siting of your house is vital. It needs to take advantage of regular winds and to take in account where the sun is. You don't want the western sun shining directly into your main living area.

Self-Sufficient Communities

A few communities are being built in Belize that attempt to provide turn-key off-the-grid living. So far, these have had mixed results. One that is in its early stages is Carmelita Gardens (www.carmelitagardens.com) in the Bullet Tree area of Cayo District, on the Belize River near La Familiar village. It plans to be an off-the-grid gardening community. It was started by Phil Hahn, a Florida State grad who previously was associated with Orchid Bay and other development projects in Northern Belize. Carmelita Gardens offers turnkey "tiny houses" of 300 sq. ft., plus 225 sq. ft. porches on 50' x 100' lots starting at around US$60,000.

What Does It Cost?

Construction costs vary depending on such factors the cost of transportation of materials to the building site, the terrain and quality of work, and whether you are building totally or partially off the grid.

In Belize, construction costs are higher on the coast and cayes, because of the need to use hurricane resistant construction. In the case of the cayes, it costs extra to transport building materials out to the islands by boat. Building costs also are higher in southern than in northern Belize. Inexpensive building materials are more readily available in northern Belize since some can be imported from Chetumal or elsewhere in Mexico or are available at large home lumber and supply stores in Belize City such as Benny's.

Labor in Belize is much less expensive than in the U.S., with carpenters and masons typically getting around US$30 to $50 a day or less, depending on location. Unskilled construction workers may only get US$15 to $20 a day. At times when a lot of home building is going on, especially around Placencia and on Ambergris Caye, labor costs may rise.

While labor may be cheap, jobs usually take longer in Belize. Workers may be versed in construction techniques common in Belize but may lack knowledge about building in the American style. Outside of urban areas, it can be difficult to find well-qualified craftspeople such as electricians and plumbers. Building materials vary but are mostly no cheaper than in the U.S., except for locally produced items such as tropical hardwoods which run about US$1,000 for 1,000 board feet. Also, locally produced plywood is roughly one-half the cost in the U.S. (though plywood prices vary over time due to fluctuating demand.) Cement is more expensive than in the U.S. – a 50 lb. bag typically costs around US$6 to $8 – as are most bathroom and kitchen fixtures that have to be imported. Flooring materials such as salt tiles from Guatemala and Mexico are moderately priced and of high quality.

Overall, building costs in Belize range from around US$35 to $200 or more a square foot, not including the cost of land. At the bottom end, that would be a simple Belizean-style cinderblock house or frame construction, and at the top it would be high quality reinforced and poured concrete construction with hardwood floors and trim and with many custom details such as hand-made doors and windows. Most commonly, if you work with a builder you'd expect to pay about US$60 to $100 a square foot, so a 1,500 square foot home would cost US$90,000 to $150,000 to build, not including land. That's about one-third less than typical costs for construction in smaller cities and towns in the U.S.

Having said that, costs can vary tremendously from builder to builder. One resident said he got quotes for the construction of a five-bedroom reinforced concrete home that varied from US$90 to $250 a square foot.

Mennonite prefabricated houses can be much cheaper. *(See below.)*

Regardless of where or how you build, you need to be on-site to manage and oversee the construction, or pay someone you trust very well to do that for you. Expect that the process will take roughly twice as long as you expect – eight months to a year, or longer, to build a house is not uncommon.

Especially in rural areas or on the coast, a lot of the cost of building is underground – foundations, pilings, cisterns, septic tanks. You may need two or more septic tanks for a large house.

Of course, if you have a nose for saving money you can build for much less than that. We know one fellow who built a small house on a lagoon north of Corozal for about US$4,000. He collected building materials such as old planks and boards that were floating in the lagoon, scrounged others from old houses and did most of the actual construction work himself. The charity organization Habitat for Humanity has constructed a number of affordable homes in Belize. Habitat said that the cost around of a basic two-bedroom, one-bath 528 sq. ft. concrete blockhouse with a septic tank was about US$11,000, and US$15,000 for a 720 sq. ft. three-bedroom house. This does not include the cost of land. That was around US$21 a square foot. (The cost has increased slightly in the last several years.)

In areas at risk of hurricanes and tropical storms, you'll have to put in deep pilings and raise the first floor well above ground level to avoid water damage. Depending on the area and the depth and type of pilings, these can cost as much as US$3,000 to $5,000 each. Reinforced concrete is the preferred construction. Hurricane straps and rafter ties are inexpensive protection against having the roof blown away. Most insurance companies in Belize no longer will cover traditional thatch construction, and some also will not cover wood frame construction if the house is on the coast or cayes.

Off-Grid Costs
The upfront cost of providing power, water and sewage for off-grid living in Belize varies greatly depending on where you are building, the size of your house and especially how much power you expect to need.

Generally, due to shipping and taxes, solar systems in Belize are somewhat more expensive than in the U.S., and there are no tax incentives as there are in the U.S. and elsewhere.

Solar systems for a small house with little or no air-conditioning and only a few appliances start at under US$10,000. Those for a large home with full air-conditioning and many appliances could be US$50,000 to $75,000 or more. The cost will be lower if you can do most of the work yourself.

Cisterns for your drinking water cost roughly US$50 cents to $1 a gallon to construct. Septic systems cost many thousands of dollars, depending on the site and type of system. At a minimum, you're probably looking at US$3,000.

Insurance

Several types of home insurance are offered in Belize. These including fire insurance only; fire and peril insurance; fire and associated perils including catastrophic peril such as floods and hurricanes; and comprehensive householder's insurance for damage to personal property. Liability insurance also is available. Insurance costs also will vary with the construction: Wood frame construction in coastal or island areas will incur annual premiums of up to 2 to 4% of value, whereas steel construction will see premiums of around 1.25-1.50% of value and reinforced concrete about 2% or less. Insurance in inland areas is less, running around 1% of value per year or less.

Among the recommended home insurance companies in Belize are **RF&G,** based in Belize City (501-223-5734, www.rfginsurancebelize.com).

It is recommended that before deciding on the amount of insurance you get a reliable appraisal of the value of your home, focusing on the cost to replace it, along with any outbuildings or additions such as a garage, barn or swimming pool.

Building Codes and Permits

In the past, the only building codes in Belize have been those imposed by local municipalities. Many rural areas had no codes at all, and builders often ignored any existing codes. Those were, in some respects, the good old days.

Belize now has a building code calling for nation-wide standards of construction. The Central Building Authority (CBA) is taking a tougher stance to assure that builders follow the building code. Before construction for a house can be approved, at least three sets of drawings must be presented (including an electrical plan approved by the Public Utilities Commission) to the CBA, an application for construction made and the appropriate fees paid. Depending on the size of the building, the use of an architect and professional engineer may be required.

CBA application fee for homes under 1,000 square feet is US$25, and US$50 for homes over 1,000 square feet. Residential permit fees range from 5 to 7½ US cents per square foot, and there are other rates for decks, pools, fences, piers, etc. Builders now need approvals for zoning, fire safety, environmental issues and others from up to 15 different governmental regulatory authorities, including the National Fire Service, Public Utilities Commission, Fisheries Department and Department of the Environment depending on where and what you are building. What you've read in the past about the lack of construction red tape in Belize is to a great degree no longer true.

Check the CBA's website at www.cbabelize.org for more information.

The CBA has authority nationally, although it works with local building authorities. Varying local codes apply. For example, inside Belmopan City Limits only concrete new construction is permitted, not wood. More developed areas such as San Pedro and Belize City have the strictest building permit and code systems.

A licensed electrician must sign off on the electrical work before the building can be hooked up to Belize Electricity Ltd.

Trailers and Manufactured Homes in Belize

Trailer trash? Not in Belize. You won't find many mobile homes, trailers or "manufactured homes" *(except from the Mennonites – see below)*. There are several reasons for this: For one, trailers aren't known for durability or safety in hurricanes and tropical storms. The cost of shipping prefab units to Belize is high. Also, mobile homes and trailers don't stand up well to the hot, humid semitropical climate – rusting, abandoned RVs you see in the bush are proof of that. Perhaps most importantly, import duties make bringing in trailers an unattractive option compared with building locally. However, some expats do decide to import prefab buildings. The original owner of the old Nautical Inn beach resort in Seine Bight on the Placencia peninsula brought in pre-fab hexagonal buildings from North Carolina and had them set up on the beach by local laborers.

Living in an RV While You're Getting Settled

For the same reason that mobile homes are not good options in a humid semitropical climate with the potential for heavy rains and the occasional tropical storm or hurricane, living in an RV or travel trailer isn't a good long-term housing situation in Belize.

However, for some it can make sense to RV to Belize and then use your RV (we're employing the term RV to cover Class A, B and C class RVs and also travel trailers, campers and fifth-wheelers) temporarily as your living quarters while you are looking for a house to buy or are building your home.

There are only a handful of RV campgrounds in Belize *(see below),* but you can find someone to rent you a site. You can arrange with your temporary landlord for access to water and power, but you'll need a dumpsite for at least your black water. You can probably jury rig a temporary solution to this.

You'll likely be surprised about how much RV you can get for your money if you buy used. New RVs depreciate massively within just a few years. There are lots of RVs in good shape out there, less than 15 years old, that sell for a tenth of their original price. Many have very low mileage, as the average RV owner puts only about 3,500 miles a year on the RV. You can find plenty of Class A (the largest size) with slide outs, fully furnished, less than 15 years old and with under 30,000 miles on them, for US$15,000 to $30,000. If you buy shrewdly, you can recoup all or most of your money when you decide to sell, and you might even turn a small profit, although you may need to take your RV back to the U.S. to sell it quickly.

An excellent source of used RVs of all types is PPL Motorhomes in Houston. They sell about 4,000 units of all kinds every year. They maintain a list not only of current offerings but also the actual selling price of units sold in the past. For information, visit www.pplmotorhomes.com.

There are many good books on the full-time RV lifestyles. We like the ones by Jerry Minchey, whose books in paperback and Kindle formats such as *Secrets of RVing on Social Security* and *Motorhome and Retirement Living* are available on Amazon.com.

Camping/RV Campgrounds

Cayo District has more camping options than any other area of Belize. Here is a sampling. For other places that allow camping, ask locally. **Menzies** across from the bay in Corozal is one, and there is another near Altun Ha Maya site. A number of the hotels and lodges in Belize will permit overnight camping or RV parking.

Clarissa Falls. Mile 70½ George Price Hwy./Benque Rd. (P.O. Box 44, San Ignacio), 501-833-3116; www.clarissafalls.com. This popular Belizean-owned cabaña colony on the Mopan River also allows camping, at US7.50 per person. RVs and trailers are permitted, too.

Inglewood Camping Grounds. Mile 68 1/4, George Price Hwy., 501-824-3555; www.inglewoodcampinggrounds.com. A newer, more complete camping option with water and electric hook-ups and a dump station is on the George Price Highway just west of San Ignacio. Inglewood offers tent camping with hot and cold showers and hook-ups for RVs. US$15 to $20 for tent camping space, US$30 for RV camping with water, plus US$0.40 per kilowatt for electricity. Hot showers and sanitary dumping, no charge.

River Park Inn. 13 Branch Mouth Rd, San Ignacio, 501-824-2116; www.riverparkinnbelize.com. This place, a short distance from San Ignacio on the Mopan River, has tent and RV camping, plus cabins for rent.

Smith's Family Farm. 13 Branch Mouth Rd, San Ignacio, 501-604-2227. Camping here is US$7.50 per-person. Little cabins are US$25.

Mennonite Prefab: Cheap, Practical Alternative

An inexpensive alternative to building from scratch in Belize is to have a prefabricated Mennonite house set up on your lot. Mennonite builders in Spanish Lookout and elsewhere build and sell small frame buildings, which they will deliver and install on pilings on your site.

This is a quick way to get a home up in Belize, and even some small resorts use these buildings. The prefab buildings typically are made of local hardwoods (typically Santa Maria, Nargusta and My Lady). It is untreated but is insect-resistant. Local pine wood houses are somewhat cheaper. Most Mennonite prefab shells come with glass-louvered lockable windows, screens, two mahogany doors and two stairs. You can get them as unfinished shells or complete down to electrical wiring and plumbing. Interior finishing including doors, shower and tub, toilets, sinks, electrical, interior ceiling and wall finishing, etc. plus GST typically will add about 80% to the cost of the raw shell shown below. Usually there is a choice of roofing materials – zinc, tin (painted or unpainted) or asphalt shingles. The cabins are set up on 6"x 6" hardwood posts typically 8 to 10 feet apart and about 3 feet off the ground. You may want to upgrade the specs to your own standards -- for example using 2"x4" framing rather than smaller studs. You can buy these prefab houses from standardized plans or custom order, depending on the builder.

Prices vary, but here are typical prices for the shell (interior unfinished), including transportation to your mainland lot in the San Ignacio and Belmopan area and set-up on your mainland lot. Transportation and set-up in Corozal, Belize City or Toledo will be up to about 5% to 10% more.

20 ft. x 24 ft. (480 sq. ft.) US$11,000-$12,000
20 ft. x 30 ft. (600 sq. ft.) US$13,000-$14,000
20 ft. x 40 ft. (800 sq. ft.) US$18,000-$19,000

Delivery and set up and transportation to the cayes and to remote areas on the mainland could increase the price substantially. Also, septic systems, cistern, electrical hook-ups, kitchen appliances, permits and other charges will increase the cost.

Typical Cost of 800 Sq. Ft. Prefab Home Finished Inside and Out

Here's a typical breakdown of costs in BELIZE dollars as of 2017 for a 20'x40' (800 square feet) house with finished interior in prefabricated in Spanish Lookout (prices subject to change):

Basic price for 3 BR/2 BA 20x40 hardwood house	BZ$28,800
15 6"x6" hardwood posts installed to 3 ft. floor level	BZ$750
Transportation to Dangriga area	BZ$2,857
5 additional interior doors	BZ$1,125
Plywood interior partitioning of rooms	BZ$3,825
Interior ceilings	BZ$1,875
Walls cased with plywood	BZ$2,250
Electrical breaker box	BZ$200
Light switches and bulbs	BZ$500
28 electrical outlets	BZ$1,400
2 sets of 3-foot exterior stairs	BZ$300
Shower tub	BZ$1,800
1 shower stall, 2 toilets, 2 washbasins	BZ$1,825
12.5% GST	BZ$6,190
Total	BZ$55,711 (US$27,855)

Terms are typically 50% with order and 50% when prefabrication is completed, prior to set-up on your lot.

Sources of prefab Mennonite houses include:

Linda Vista Lumber & Houses, Route 40, Spanish Lookout, Cayo, 501-823-0257; www.lindavistabelize.com

Midwest Lumber Mill, Spanish Lookout, Cayo, 501-823-8000

Plett's Home Builders, Spanish Lookout, Cayo, 501-823-0398; www.plettshomebuilders.com

Tobar's Home Construction, Mile ½ Iguana Bridge, Spanish Lookout, Cayo, 501-824-2660; www.tobar-construction.com.

Household Expenses

You'll get some good – and some bad – surprises when you open your household bills in Belize. On the positive side, you won't be getting a bill for fuel oil or gas to heat your home. Very few houses in Belize even have a furnace or heater, since winter temperatures rarely fall even into the 50s. If a cold front comes through, just put a blanket on the bed or pull on a cotton sweater.

However, electricity (it's often called "current" in Belize) is much pricier than in the U.S. or Canada. Figure about US24 cents per kilowatt-hour, which is a little over twice the average in the U.S. High electric rates are why most Belizeans don't have air conditioning, or if they do have A/C, it's only in the bedrooms. Belize Electricity, Ltd., is the sole provider in Belize. About 40% of the electricity used in Belize is purchased from Mexico.

The Chalillo Dam in Cayo, along with three other dams, are supposed to help Belize become energy-independent, but arguably at the cost of wildlife habitat. So far, the dams have not lowered electrical costs in Belize, nor have they made the grid significantly more reliable. Outages and surges still occur – occasionally to frequently, depending on your perspective and need for 24/7 power. If you're off the grid, as many still are in remote rural areas, either you do without power or run a diesel generator. Wind, hydro and solar energy are making some headway in Belize, although despite recent declines in the price of solar systems, initial set-up costs in Belize are high. A small community of some 20 homes on Caye Caulker, for example, generates all its power from alternate sources, mainly wind turbines. Due to the cost of batteries and other materials, they say that their long-term costs are about US$1 a kilowatt.

Water and sewerage bills vary around the country, but a typical monthly cost per household is about US$10-$20. "Pipe water," as it's known in Belize, is costlier on Ambergris Caye and Caye Caulker. If you live in a rural area, you'll probably have your own water system, either a well or a cistern to collect rainwater, and a septic tank for wastes. Thus, your only expenses will be the initial cost of the systems, plus any electricity you use.

Most households in Belize run stoves and hot water showers on butane. Butane is sold in Belize instead of propane, since there's not an issue with butane freezing. Rates vary according to energy prices, but on average, a small household may use US$30-$80 worth of butane a month. Trucks deliver butane tanks to your home, or at least to the road in front of your home. In early 2018, butane in 100 pound cylinders was selling for around US$52, with a variation of a dollar or two around the country.

Aside from your telephone, electric and butane bills, the only other utility expense you may face is garbage pickup. Belizeans refer to it as "dirt." Your dirt bill will probably not run more than US$10, and pickup is free in some areas. Also, cable television bills generally are in Belize than you're used to back home. Typical monthly rates are US$25-30 but are increasing in some areas.

Working for Pay or Running a Business

Imagine you're living near the blue Caribbean Sea. You spend your days snorkeling, diving and fishing. Now imagine you get paid to do this. You pay your way through paradise by working as a dive master, or guiding tourists, or tending bar in a little thatch hut. Or you run a little hotel by the sea, welcoming guests and raking in the dough.

Sorry, but a reality check is required. About one in ten Belizeans is out of work, and those with jobs often don't make enough to live above the poverty level. The few good jobs that are available in Belize are mostly reserved for Belizeans. Many occupations, including tour guiding and waiting tables and bartending, are reserved for Belize citizens only. Residents under the Qualified Retired Persons Incentive Act can't work for pay at all. Even if you were able to legally get a job, salaries in Belize are far below those in the U.S., Canada or Western Europe, and even physicians, college teachers and other professionals may earn under US$15,000 or $20,000 a year. While some hotel and resort owners and other expat business owners in Belize do pretty well, others barely eek out a living. Costs are higher than they planned for, and the frustrations of doing business in Belize are far more numerous than they expected.

We know expatriates who have carved out a comfortable niche for themselves in Belize, either working for an established Belizean company or running their own business. It is possible to do so, but it's not easy. After all, it's the United States that is a land of opportunity for job seekers and entrepreneurs. Millions of people around the world vie to get a green card to let them live and work in the States. More than 100,000 Belizeans have left Belize to work and find their fortunes, legally or illegally, in the U.S. You're going to leave the U.S. with all its opportunity, resources and huge base of consumers and set up shop or find a job in poor little Belize, with its tiny population and economic resources of a small American town? If you can't make it in the U.S., how do you expect to make it in Belize?

There are good reasons why someone might decide to move to Belize and work or invest there, mostly having to do with quality of life, but economic rewards and an easy road to fortune are not among them.

The Reality of Investing in Belize

The late John Lankford, a New Orleans lawyer who lived for several years in San Pedro before selling his property and moving back to the U.S., put the situation bluntly: "As to investing, first realize that when Belize's government or general population speaks or thinks of foreigners 'investing in Belize' they mean bringing money and handing it over. They also contemplate a long-term, possibly permanent, commitment. They are not so solicitous of your expectations to realize a RETURN on your investment, and in some cases tend to think it craven of a 'rich' first-world person to try to make money off poor Belize. The approved motivation for investing in Belize is for the benefit of Belize. The investor's benefit is gratification at helping Belize advance, and any other motivation may be seen as exploiting rather than investing. As a general rule, don't even dream of investing in Belize unless you plan to be present with your eyes on your investment every day."

Starting and Running Your Own Business

With good-paying jobs few and far between, most foreigners who want to generate an income in Belize will be looking at operating a business. The Belize government says it welcomes investors who can contribute to the Belize economy and provide work for Belizeans, particularly in tourism, agriculture and manufacturing. But it's rarely simple or easy to do business in Belize. A timeworn saying in Belize, worth repeating again, is that if you want to make a small fortune in the country, better start with a big one. Belize's small domestic market, inefficient distribution and marketing systems, heavy-handed government red tape and other factors make it difficult for entrepreneurs to achieve great success in Belize.

What Type of Business?

Several types of businesses require special permits or licenses, and these may not be granted to non-Belizeans. The idea is to avoid permitting non-Belizeans to take jobs from Belizeans. The following businesses, in varying degrees, are not usually open to foreigners: commercial fishing, sugar cane cultivation, restaurants and bars (not associated with a resort), legal and accounting services, small retail shops, beekeeping, beauty shops, sightseeing tours and operation of bus, water taxi or domestic airlines.

Businesses that are most likely to succeed in Belize include export-oriented operations whose main markets are outside Belize. The Belize market itself is small and spread out, and average Belizeans don't have the income to buy much beyond the basic necessities of life. Niche export products such as specialty or organic agricultural products may have a future. Also workable are well-marketed resorts or lodges that target international visitors and, in addition, the companies that cater to them — for example, companies that provide specialty herbs, fruits and gourmet vegetables to larger resorts.

However, the difficulty of making a go in tourism in Belize is shown by the number of hotels that are actively on the market at any one time. In the San Ignacio area, for example, at any one time about one-fourth of the hotel properties are actively for sale, and other owners likely would quickly sell for the right offer. With hotel occupancies in Belize averaging only about 40% nationally, it is difficult to earn an adequate return. Only in San Pedro, which gets a regular flow of tourists year-round, do many hotels appear to be more consistently profitable. The typical small hotel in Belize can't afford to do the international advertising and marketing necessary to compete with larger, better-capitalized resorts in other parts of the Caribbean.

Quite a few expats gravitate to selling or developing real estate. Some have been successful; many have not.

Unemployment in Belize is stubbornly high, yet many of the best-trained and ambitious Belizean workers have moved to the U.S. This brain drain means that it's difficult to find skilled, motivated employees. In rural areas, many Belizeans have never held a regular job. Training must start with the basics like showing up on time and coming to work every day. Another problem is that the cost of labor in Belize, while low compared with the U.S., is relatively high compared with some other developing countries. The minimum wage in Belize is BZ$3.30 (US$1.65) an hour for manual workers, but that's several times the minimum wage of workers in Honduras or Nicaragua. The minimum wage in Mexico is around US$5 a day, less than one-half that of Belize. Most workers in Belize do earn more than the minimum wage.

Belizean workers also have comparatively strong workplace protections, including mandatory two weeks' paid vacation and participation in Belize's Social Security system, mostly funded by employer contributions of about 5% to 6.5% of wages (the percentage varies depending on the wage of the worker, and workers also contribute from 1.5% to about 3% of earnings), 13 paid holidays, 16 days of sick leave annually and a required two weeks' notice or pay in lieu of that notice should the employee be terminated after having been on the job at least a year. The workweek cannot exceed six days or 45 hours. Businesses in highly competitive export industries may be at a disadvantage if they are located in Belize.

Capital for Business
In Belize as in most countries it is difficult to borrow money to start a business. For successful, on-going businesses loans from Belize banks may be available but typically at higher interest rates than prevailing in the U.S. In recent years, 10 to 16% has been the usual rate for business loans. Business people in Belize complain that in some cases hidden fees and charges for business loans add to the overall cost. The Belize Development Finance Corporation, a government-owned entity whose mission is to help develop the Belize economy, did make loans for developing new tourism and agricultural projects, but the DFC, after reorganization, makes loans only to Belizean citizens or official permanent residents.

Steps Involved in Starting a Business in Belize
The following information is derived from Beltraide materials.
Business Name Registration
Complete an application form and submits the application to the Belize Companies Registry in Belmopan City. The applicant may also request a name search by telephone or fax for a fee.

A name search is conducted to check whether the name is unique or it is not similar to any existing business, and to ensure compliance with the rules set out in the legislation.

If business name is available, a Certificate of Business Name Registration will be issued. Note: Foreigners will need to apply with a Belizean partner or someone with a Permanent Residency to be able to register a business name.

Incorporation
Incorporation is usually done through an attorney, and requires the submission

of the company's Memorandum of Association and Articles of Association in order to be issued a Certificate of Incorporation. Attorney fees range from US$1,000 to US$2,000).

If the Share Capital is less than US$10,000, the processing fee is US$292; if it is more than US$10,000, the processing fee is calculated in accordance to the Companies Act, Chap. 250, Section 222, as amended.

Trade License

A business must obtain a trade license before the commencement of any type of operations in Belize. A trade license is required for each location that the trade will be carried on regardless as to whether it is the same business. The trade license must be renewed annually. This applies to companies, partnerships and sole traders including professionals.

Applications are submitted to the local city or town council and approved by the Trade Licensing Board of the municipality. The Licensing Board consists of the mayor, who is the chairman of the board, and four other members.

Annual license fees are calculated based on the annual rental value of the property and penalties are imposed for non-payment of fees. The police and Council Field Officers often go out to investigate whether there are businesses operating without a trade license. If the business does not have a trade license, it may be closed down. The Trade License must be displayed on the premises for the public viewing.

Business Tax Registration

All businesses must register at Income Tax Department to obtain a Taxpayer Identification to pay tax. These businesses include sole proprietorship, companies and partnerships.

The following persons/entities are subject to payment of Business Tax:

Persons carrying on a trade or business who earn BZ$75,000 or more per annum where such receipts are the only source of livelihood of the person;

Persons practicing a self-employed profession or vocation, earning BZ$20,000 or more per annum where such receipts are the only source of livelihood of the person;

Persons engaged in the business of investment or earnings from real or personal property;

Persons engaged in the provision of personal services.

Business Tax Rates

Note: The percentage of business tax paid is based on the gross receipts of the business before any deductions for expenses, losses or other costs.

Receipts from radio, television or newspaper business	0.75%
Receipts from domestic airline business	1.75%
Receipts from service stations (fuels and lubricants)	0.75%
Receipts from other trade or business	1.75%
Receipts from rents, royalties and other sources from real estate (except a real estate agency or business)	3%

Receipts from a profession, vocation or occupations	6%
Receipts from licensed insurance company	1.75%
Commissions and winnings from gaming	5 to 15%
Receipts of a bank/financial institution	8 to 15%
Management fees, rent of plant and equipment, technical services, paid to non-resident	25%
Receipts of telecommunications companies	19%
Gross earnings of casinos	15%
Gross earnings of real estate business/agency	15%

General Sales Tax Registration

General Sales Tax (GST), also sometimes known as the Goods and Services Tax, is a tax on consumer spending collected in stages on business transactions and imports when goods change hands or services are performed.

All persons engaged in a taxable activity with an annual turnover exceeding BZ$75,000 must register with the Department of General Sales Tax in accordance with the Sales Tax Act No. 49 of 2005. Note that it is not the business activity that is registered but the person conducting those activities. This person can be a company, partnership, sole proprietor, trustee or estate. Persons must register within one month of the day on which the person first becomes eligible.

Social Security Registration

All persons or entities employing one or more persons must register for Social Security with the Belize Social Security Board. The application must be made within seven days of employing an employee.

Employers pay 5.02% to 6.5% of the employee wages into the Belize Social Security system, based on the wages of the employee (the percentage is highest for employees with the lowest wages). Employees contribute from 1.5% to 2.98% (the percentage is lowest for employees earning the lowest wages.)

Opening a Local Bank Account

Belizeans and Permanent Residents

Customer must bring a valid identification (Social Security card and/or passport), along with a recent utility bill (not older than three months) to confirm place of residence. A minimum deposit will be required to open the account, and this may vary among banking institutions.

To open a checking account, the bank would require a Bankers' Reference from an established banking institution, or that the customer maintains a savings account prior to opening a checking account.

Non-Belizeans

Customer must bring in two Bankers' References from established institutions, along with his/her passport or a notarized copy, and one other form of identification. The customer also must bring in a recent utility bill (not older than three months).

Companies

For a company to open an account, identification is required for each beneficial owner and authorized signatory. Authorized signatories must each submit two

Bankers' References from established institutions. Certified copies of the company's Certificate of Incorporation and Memorandum and Articles of Association also are required.

Incentive Programs

Belize has several incentive schemes designed to encourage investment in the country, including the Fiscal Incentives Act, the International Business and Public Companies Act, Export Processing Zone Act and Commercial Free Zone Act. However, a U.S. Commerce Department advisory notes, "many foreign investors have complained that these investment promotion tools are rarely as open and effective as they are portrayed." The programs of most interest to those thinking of starting a business in Belize are the Export Processing Zone Act, the Commercial Free Zone Act and the Fiscal Incentives Act. For more information on these programs, contact **Belize Trade & Development Service (BELTRAIDE),** 14 Orchid Garden Street, Belmopan, 501-822-3737, www.belizeinvest.org.bz.

The International Business Companies Act (IBC) makes it possible for foreign companies to get tax exemptions on all income of the IBC, all dividends paid by an IBC, all interest rents, royalties to non-Belizean residents and capital gains realized. There are several thousand companies registered as IBC's in Belize. However, IBCs are not available to citizens or official residents of Belize.

Working in Belize

In theory, unless you are a Belize citizen or a permanent resident under the regular permanent residency program (as a resident under the Qualified Retired Persons Incentive Act program you can't work for pay, though you can own a business or rental property in Belize) you cannot work in Belize without a work permit from the government. You also need a Belize Social Security card. In practice, we have heard about a few foreigners without work permits who have part-time jobs and take in-kind or cash payments. If you're caught working without a permit, however, both you and your employer could be in trouble. You could be deported, or even jailed, and fines are imposed on employers found with illegal workers. The government has cracked down on foreigners working in Belize, and on at least a couple of occasions senior management at resorts alleged to be working without a work permit were arrested and jailed.

There are two basic types of work permits. One is a work permit that is obtained by an employer in Belize for an employee. The employer has to prove that the company can't fill the job with a Belizean and has exhausted all avenues for finding a qualified Belizean applicant, including advertising the position for at least three weeks. Examples of jobs that may require a foreign applicant are hotel restaurant chef or a specialized computer software engineer. Application must be made by the employer to the Immigration Department with proof that the foreign employee is qualified, three passport photos, a valid passport and a small application fee.

Another type of work permit is the temporary self-employment certificate. This category applies to foreign investors and others seeking self-employment or who are starting a business in Belize, where it is assumed that the venture will lead to the creation of jobs for Belizeans. The applicant has to show proof of adequate funds for the proposed venture — for example, a bank statement. Also, the applicant has to have a reference from the relevant government Ministry or other organization showing that the venture is reasonable. If opening a tourist operation a reference from the Ministry of Tourism or the local village or town council where the operation is to be located may be required. For the temporary self-employment certificate the residency period is waived.

Work permit fees (subject to change):

Professional workers	US$1,500
Technical workers	US$1,000
Self-employed workers	US$1,000
Religious/voluntary workers	US$100
Entertainers, in groups	US$500 to $750
General workers in banana, citrus and sugar industries	US$100

Permits must be renewed annually and the above fees paid each year. With rare exceptions, work permits are not granted for waiters, domestic workers, farm hands and anyone involved in retail or other types of sales. For information and application forms, contact the Immigration and Nationality Department in Belmopan. If that sounds like a lot of red tape, it is. The Belize government is trying to discourage foreigners from working in jobs in Belize that Belizeans can perform. Belize is also trying to discourage illegal immigration from Guatemala and other Central American countries.

One American who moved to Ambergris Caye from Florida, said, "It was very hard for me to find work. My husband found work as a bartender the first week we were here, but he is Belizean, so he didn't have the problem of a work permit to deal with. I found that businesses are reluctant to hire you if you don't already have a permit in hand. The problem is, the price of work permits has gone up for professionals. None of the employers want to spend that amount of money when they don't know if you will stay or go."

Another American, Katie Valk, who was an executive in the music business in New York City before moving to Belize about 30 years ago, recalls the frustrations of trying to get a work permit: "It was not at all difficult adjusting. Belize was a perfect fit for me. Finding work wasn't a problem for me, either. Getting a work permit was, however, and it took a tremendous amount of stick-to-it-ness, patience and energy."

Typical Salaries in Belize

Salaries and wages in Belize vary widely, even for the same position, just as they do in the U.S. or Canada. Overall, wage levels in Belize are about one-fourth of those in the U.S., or lower, although a few business people and entrepreneurs in Belize make as much or more than their American counterparts. In general, wages are highest in Belize City and San Pedro and lowest in remote rural areas. All figures are in **U.S. dollars**:

Maid/Domestic Worker	$10-$20 per day
Day Laborer	$15-$30 per day
Skilled Carpenter or Mason	$30-$50 per day

Nurse	$8,000 per year
Doctor in Public Health Care	$20,000+ per year
Primary School Teacher	$8,000 a year
High School Teacher	$10,000+ a year
College Professor	$12,000-$20,000 a year
Shop Clerk	$90-$150 a week
Office/Clerical Worker	$100-$150 a week
Secretary	$125-$175 a week
Lodge/Resort Workers	$20-$40 a day
Minimum Hourly Wage	$1.65 a hour

Your Money and How to Hold On to It in Belize

Belize banknotes come in $2, $5, $10, $20, $50 and $100 denominations

Belize's official currency is the Belize dollar, which for many years has been pegged to the U.S. dollar at a rate of 2 Belize dollars to 1 U.S. dollar. However, moneychangers often give a slightly higher rate than 2 Belize for 1 U.S. dollar, sometimes as much as 2.1 or 2.2 to 1, or even higher, depending on the local demand for American greenbacks. Generally, though, the premium is only 2% to 3%.

That brings us to a key fact about Belize and your money: Hard currencies, like the U.S. dollar, euro and yen, are good. Soft currencies, and the Belize dollar is one of them, are not so good. The Belize dollar is difficult to exchange anywhere outside of Belize (except at border areas of Guatemala and Mexico).

For years there has been talk of dollarizing the Belize economy, making the U.S. dollar the official currency of Belize, similar to what El Salvador and Ecuador and, to a degree, Guatemala have done, but so far that talk hasn't translated into action. There are several possible reasons. For one, the Belize government is reluctant to do away with its Central Bank and surrender so much of its financial control to Uncle Sam. That's understandable. For another, Belize politicians may think that in a tough economic pinch it's a lot easier to just print money than to actually earn it. That's also understandable.

Technically, according to Belize law, only the Central Bank of Belize is permitted to deal in foreign currencies including the U.S. dollar. But this rule is widely, almost universally, flaunted in Belize, and businesses routinely take U.S. dollars in payment for goods and services and have been doing so for decades. In any event, U.S. dollars (bills, not coins) are accepted everywhere in Belize, although you often will receive change in Belizean money, or in a mix of Belizean and U.S. money.

Paper-money Belize denominations are the 100-, 50-, 20-, 10-, 5- and 2-dollar bills. Belize coins come in 1-dollar, 50, 25, 10, 5 and 1 Belizean cent units. The 25-cent piece is called a shilling.

Currency Exchange Regulations

The U.S. Embassy in Belize provided this summary of currency regulations in Belize:

Under the Exchange Control Regulations (Chapter 43 of the Laws of Belize - 1980), only the Central Bank of Belize and authorized dealers/depositories (i.e., commercial banks and Casas de Cambio, if permitted) may deal in foreign currencies. In order to pay for goods and services procured outside of Belize in a foreign currency, a foreign exchange permit must be obtained from an authorized dealer or directly from the Central Bank of Belize. The permission of the Central Bank of Belize is also required to secure a loan from outside Belize that involves a foreign currency, and also to service repayment of foreign debt. According to the Belize Investment Guide, "the necessary approvals can be easily secured in the case of genuine, approved enterprises." Foreign investors are required to register any investments made in Belize with the Central Bank in order to facilitate the repatriation of profits, dividends, etc. Officially, no person, other than authorized dealers and authorized depositories, may retain any foreign currency in their possession without the consent of the Central Bank of Belize. In practice, however, many local businesses accept payment in U.S. currency.

Foreign exchange controls can be summarized by the following rules and guidelines: Residents and non-residents need permission to buy foreign currency for whatever purpose; Authorized dealers (i.e., commercial banks) are allowed to sell foreign currency up to US$2,500 for private travel and up to US$10,000 for business travel per calendar year; requests in excess of these amounts must be approved by the Central Bank of Belize; Exporters are required to register their exports with the Central Bank, guaranteeing delivery of their foreign exchange earnings; Authorized dealers may authorize payments for imports, where goods are paid for through letters of credit or bank collection. They may also authorize payments for imports against copies of invoices and customs entries, where the documents show that the goods were obtained on credit; Belizean residents, who wish to borrow abroad and where debt service will be in hard currencies, must apply to the Central Bank of Belize for permission to do so.

Banks and Banking in Belize

Belize has five commercial banks, not including offshore banks.

All the banks based in Belize are fairly small, about the size of a small-city bank or savings bank in the U.S. The largest in terms of assets is Belize Bank. Belize also has several credit unions and small mortgage lending institutions.

Here are the basic facts, including contact information for the main offices, about each bank in Belize:

Atlantic Bank was founded in 1971. It is 55% owned by Sociedad Nacional de Inversiones, S.A., a Honduran company, along with individual stockholders in Belize and Honduras. Atlantic Bank has 15 offices and sub-offices in Belize — in Corozal, the Corozal Free Zone, Belize City (three offices), International Airport, Belmopan, Ladyville, Caye Caulker, Orange Walk (two offices), San Pedro (two offices), Placencia and San Ignacio. Atlantic Bank also has a subsidiary insurance company that offers life, property and auto insurance. Atlantic Bank has assets of more than US$450 million. Main office: Atlantic Building, Freetown Road at Cleghorn Street, Belize City, 501-223-4123, www.atlabank.com.

Belize Bank traces its history back to 1902 when it was founded as the Bank of British Honduras. Lord Michael Ashcroft, a British billionaire and Conservative party honcho who holds dual citizenship in the UK and Belize, has a large interest in the bank and formerly was chairman. Belize Bank has assets of around US$450 million in Belize, according to the Belize Central Bank. It has 12 offices around the country— in Corozal Town, the Corozal Free Zone, Orange Walk Town, Philip Goldson International Airport, Belize City (two offices), Belmopan, San Ignacio, San Pedro, Dangriga, Placencia and Punta Gorda. Main office: 60 Market Square, Belize City, 501-227-7132, www.belizebank.com.

Closest bank to Sarteneja village is about 2 hours away by car

Heritage Bank (formerly Alliance Bank) has nine offices -- in Belize City (two offices), Belmopan, Benque Viejo, San Pedro, Orange Walk Town, San

Ignacio, Independence (near Placencia) and Pomona (near Dangriga). In cooperation with several credit unions, it offers ATMS around Belize. In mid-2015, Heritage Bank bought First Caribbean International Bank's assets in Belize. The bank is owned by a group of mostly foreign investors from Mexico and the Caribbean. It has assets of around US$215 million. Main Office: 106 Princess Margaret Drive, Belize City, 501-223-6783, www.heritageeibt.com.

National Bank of Belize, the newest bank in Belize, currently has only two offices, one in Belmopan and one in Belize City. It has assets of about US$25 million. Main Office: Forest Drive, Belmopan City, 501-822-0957, www.nbbl.bz.

ScotiaBank, formerly Bank of Nova Scotia, is a large Canadian bank with operations in 50 countries and with worldwide assets of more than US$800 billion. It has been operating in Belize since 1968. In Belize, after closing two offices in 2018 it has nine offices -- in Corozal Town, San Pedro, Orange Walk Town, Belize City (two offices), Belmopan, San Ignacio, Punta Gorda and Dangriga. Its assets in Belize are around US$420 million. Main Belize office: 4A Albert Street, Belize City, 501-227-7027, www.scotiabank.com/bz.

Credit Unions: Belize also has more than a dozen credit unions. The largest is Holy Redeemer Credit Union, operated by the Catholic Church.

Offshore Banks

In addition to commercial banks in Belize serving local customers, Belize has developed a small community of offshore banks, or international banks as they like to be called. These offshore banks were authorized by the Banks and Financial Institutions Act, 1995, and the introduction of the Offshore Banking Act, 1996, and the Money Laundering (Prevention) Act, 1996.

These banks are regulated by the Belize Central Bank, have physical offices in Belize and offer various services including international bankcards and demand, savings and time deposit accounts. Accounts maintained with these banks are not subject to local taxes or exchange control restrictions and may be denominated in one of several major currencies, including U.S. dollars, euros, U.K. pounds, Swiss francs and others. International banks tout their privacy for their customers, although if the Belize courts find that funds in the banks are proceeds of crime the banks are required to release the identity of the account owner. Funds are transferred into and out of Belize in foreign currencies with no conversion to Belize dollars taking place.

These banks are prohibited from doing business with Belize citizens or legal residents. The offshore banks also comply with United Nations sanctions and don't accept deposits from citizens of Iran, North Korea, Somalia, Sudan and several other countries. Most customers of international banks first establish an International Business Company (IBC). Here's information on some of the offshore banks in Belize.

Atlantic International Bank Limited: This bank, which is now separated from Atlantic Bank, offers demand deposit accounts, savings accounts, corporate accounts, credit cards and investment/brokerage accounts to non-Belize residents. Other services include offshore trust services and establishing International Business Companies (IBCs). Main office: 1 Belcan Plaza, Belize City, 501-223-

3152, www.atlanticibl.com.

Belize Bank International Limited: A division of Belize Bank Group, and a subsidiary of Caribbean Investment Holdings Limited, Belize Bank International Ltd. was licensed in 2006. The offshore bank offers personal and corporate multi-currency accounts in U.S. dollars, British pounds and EU euros. It also offers CDs, credit cards, corporate accounts and loans, wire transfers and other services. Main office: Matalon Business Center, Coney Drive, Second Floor, Belize City, 501-227-0697, www.belizebankinternational.com.

Caye International Bank: Opened in 2003, Caye Bank is located in San Pedro. The bank offers a mix of deposit and loan services to non-residents of Belize, including demand (checking) deposits, savings deposits and CDs. The bank has accounts in U.S. dollars, Canadian dollars, Swiss francs, EU euros and British pounds. Main office: 601 Coconut Drive, San Pedro, Ambergris Caye, 501-226-2388, www.cayebank.bz.

Heritage International Bank & Trust Limited: Formerly called Provident Bank & Trust of Belize Ltd., this international bank adopted its present name in 2010. Demand deposits, savings accounts and time deposits are offered. The bank also offers on-line banking, credit cards and other services. Main office: 35 Barrack Road, Belize City, 501-223-56783, www.heritageibt.com.

FACTA and FBAR

For a long time, wealthy U.S. taxpayers were able to hide foreign assets in countries, such as Switzerland, where bank-secrecy laws fostered tax havens. But in 2009 and 2010, after U.S. authorities obtained information about the identities of clients of Swiss banks, they began a sweeping crackdown on hidden offshore accounts. This has impacted Belize and its international banks.

The spillover also has impacted ordinary not-so-wealthy people, especially U.S. citizens or official residents, and also banks, both domestic and offshore, in Belize.

A primary reason is the Foreign Account Tax Compliance Act, called FATCA (www.irs.gov). The U.S. Congress enacted it in 2010. Foreign financial firms, including those in Belize, now must report to the U.S. Internal Revenue Service investment income and balances above certain thresholds (typically US$50,000 for individuals, but the rules vary depending on circumstances) for accounts held by U.S. customers. Nearly 100,000 banks and other companies around the world have registered with the IRS. If they hadn't, all their customers would have 30% withheld from income received from U.S. sources, such as interest and dividends. Individual U.S. taxpayers must also file on FATCA, using Form 8938, when filing their 1040 tax return.

Another big factor is FBAR, Report of Foreign Bank and Financial Accounts, another U.S. reporting requirement. FBAR applies to any U.S. citizen or official resident who has signature authority over one or more financial accounts – bank account, brokerage account, mutual fund account, etc. -- outside the U.S. and if the aggregate value of such account or accounts totaled US$10,000 or more during any calendar year. U.S. persons falling under FBAR must report holdings to the U.S. Treasury Department (separately from any IRS filing) on Form 114 by April 15 of the year following the calendar year being reported. Penalties for willfully not reporting the foreign holdings are high – US$100,000 or 50% of the amount not reported, whichever is higher.

U.S. citizens and official U.S. resident aliens, including those with dual citizenship, who have lived or worked abroad during all or part of a calendar year, may have a U.S. tax liability and a filing requirement for both FBAR and FACTA.

Frankly, this is a pain in the butt for both U.S. taxpayers and for financial institutions inside and outside the U.S., including in Belize.

So far, more than 40,000 U.S. taxpayers have entered amnesty programs to avoid fines or prison sentences under these financial reporting laws. More than 100 people have been indicted by the U.S. One consequence is that the number of Americans renouncing their citizenship has hit records.

In Belize, as in other countries popular with expats, banks have become more reluctant to open accounts for U.S. citizens, some accounts have been closed, and even U.S.-based banks and brokerage firms also have restricted expats from using their services.

In 2014, the *Wall Street Journal* reported: "The reality on the ground is that overseas Americans are facing restrictions and lockouts from both U.S. and foreign financial firms," quoting Marylouise Serrato, the director of American Citizens Abroad, a leading group representing U.S. expatriates.

Belize Banking Differences

Most expats find that banking is a little different in Belize. In most cases, you can't just sashay in to your local bank office and open an account. You usually will be asked for references, including a letter from your former bank. There is no standard format for this reference letter, but it should state something along these lines: "Mr. Jones is currently a customer of our bank and has maintained a satisfactory banking relationship here since 1985. His savings, time and demand deposit accounts with us current total about US$xxx,xxx." The letter should be on the institution's letterhead and signed by an officer.

Commercial banks in some cases may also require that you have some reason before you can open a banking account in Belize, such as owning property, building a house, living in Belize part- or full-time, etc. The offshore banks in Belize are just the opposite – you can't be a citizen or official resident and bank of Belize.

All of which brings us to another key fact about your money and Belize: The accepted wisdom is to keep the bulk of your liquid assets out of Belize. You may want to open a checking account in Belize to have easy access to spending money and for handling routine local transactions, such as paying your Belize telephone or electric bill. If you are in Belize under the Qualified Retired Persons Incentive Program, you are required to deposit US$24,000 a year in a Belize bank, convert it to Belize dollars and show proof of that each year. But the savvy expat will maintain a banking relationship in the U.S. or similar country, with the bulk of your demand and deposit cash accounts there. You can then transfer funds by wire or other means to your account in Belize, as needed.

CAUTION: Deposits in Belize banks are not protected by deposit insurance, as they are in the U.S. under the FDIC, and in many other countries. All of your deposits are at risk in the unlikely but possible event of a bank failure.

Belize Bank has 28 ATMs on its countrywide network around Belize. These ATMs accept foreign-issued ATM cards on the Visa, MasterCard, Plus and Cirrus systems. Atlantic Bank has 11 ATMs that accept foreign-issued ATM cards on the Visa, MasterCard, Plus and Cirrus systems. ScotiaBank has 12 ATMs around the country accepting foreign-issued ATM Cards. Heritage Bank has ATMs at its nine branch locations, plus ATMs at seven credit unions. Most ATMs have a limit of BZ$500/US$250 per day, although some bank limits are higher. Belize Bank has a limit of BZ$1,000/US$500 a day.

You can use these ATMs to tap your bank accounts back home, although you will get cash in Belize in Belize dollars.

It's possible to have U.S. dollar accounts in Belize, but this requires Belize Central Bank approval. As of 2017, sending U.S. dollar wire transfers from Belize to another country requires a three-day delay for approval by the Belize banks.

Banking hours are shorter in Belize, typically 8 a.m. until 3 p.m. weekdays, slightly later on Fridays. Most bank offices have modern conveniences such as ATM machines.

While bank personnel in Belize are usually very friendly – this is Belize, after all – you can't always say the same about bank policies, especially for loans. Loan interest rates have gone down but are still high compared with the U.S. and some European countries.

In late 2017 Belize banks were charging an average of about 12% on personal loans and over 9% on commercial loans, according to the Belize Central Bank. Fees and charges can add extra costs to the loan interest. Home mortgage loan rates were 5.5% to 12%, depending on the financial institution and the mortgage terms. Visa and MasterCard credit cards issued by banks in Belize carried interest rates of 16 to 22%. Typically, credit cards that can be used internationally carry a higher interest rate than those that can be used only in Belize.

Rates paid on savings in Belize have fallen in recent years. In late 2017, for example, money in regular savings accounts at banks in Belize earned from 0.5% to 2%, depending on the bank. CD/fixed deposit rates were higher but well down from the attractive rates of past years. Consumer protection laws haven't all made it to Belize yet. Don't expect the rules back home necessarily apply in Belize.

ISSUES TO CONSIDER IN BELIZE

Taxes in Belize

The tax picture in Belize is mixed, with some big advantages for expats but also some disadvantages.

The biggest savings for those moving to Belize from the U.S. in particular is usually on **property taxes.** In the U.S. property taxes generally are locally set. They vary from state to state, city to city and even school district to school district. However, in many places, property taxes are extremely high. The 10 states with the highest property taxes on the typical home in the state are, in order from highest to lowest, as of 2015: New Jersey (where the median average house in the state is charged US$7,410 annually in property taxes), Connecticut (US$5,326), New Hampshire (US$5,100), New York (US$4,600), Illinois US$3,995), Massachusetts (US$3,989), Rhode Island (US$3,884), Vermont (US$3,795), Wisconsin (US$3,248), Maryland (US$3,142) and California (US$3,104). Even the state with the lowest annual tax bill for the average house, Alabama, has a property tax bill of US$543 for the typical home.

By contract, in most of Belize very few homeowners pay more than US$100 a year for property taxes. US$200 a year is considered high.

Property taxes vary but are about 1% to 1½% of the value of the *undeveloped* land, payable annually on April 1. In other words, the government taxes the land, not the house.

Many people with modest homes pay only US$10 or $20 property tax annually.

There is a 5% **real estate speculation tax** on the value of land of 300 acres or more, payable annually on April 1 based on the value of the land.

In the last decades or so there has been a move to make property taxes based on the market value of the property, but politicians argue that many Belizeans would not be able to pay higher real estate taxes. There has been some implementation of the law that when a property is sold, if the sales price does not accurately reflect the market value, the price can be adjusted by the government and the tax increased according.

The main other taxes you'll face in Belize are:

National Goods and Services Tax, also known as **General Sales Tax (GST)** of 12.5% on nearly all products and services. A few items are exempt: basic foodstuffs such as rice, flour, tortillas, eggs and beans; some medicines; school textbooks; transportation on buses and airplanes; items being exported and hotel stays taxed under the hotel tax system.

Like a value-added tax, the GST is supposed to be included in the final purchase price, rather than added on like a sales tax, but many businesses quote prices without the GST and just add it on at the cash register.

Very small businesses, such as street vendors and small retail shops, don't have to register for the GST and don't charge the tax. There are additional taxes on alcohol, cigarettes and a few other items. More than one-half the cost of gasoline is due to government tax.

Import duties of up to 80% on imported items, with some items such as computers and books having no duty (though you pay the GST) and most having

30% or less duty. The average duty on imported items is around 20%. Import duties are an important source of government revenue in Belize, so customs is careful to get the money you owe when importing goods into Belize. Motor vehicles are highly taxes, with total import and GST taxes on new cars totaling as much as 80% of the retail value of the vehicle. Pickup trucks are taxed at lower rates. Participants in the Qualified Retired Persons program can import a vehicle without tax, and the same may be true of those getting Permanent Residency.

Belize personal income tax rates range from 25% to up to 45%, with those making about US$10,000 or less per year effectively paying no tax. The 45% rate kicks in on an income of about US$47,500. Personal income tax is only on income derived in Belize; there is no Belize income tax on income generated outside Belize. Thus, for example, if you earn money from a job outside Belize, or if you work online and are paid in another country, you pay no income tax in Belize. If you do have to pay Belize income tax, it may be deductible against your U.S. taxes, or the income taxes of some other countries.

Belize corporate or business tax is on the *gross revenues* (without any deductions) and not on profits, as it is in the U.S. The percentage of the tax depends on the category of business. The rate for what is actually a turnover tax ranges from 0.75% to 25%. For most businesses it is 1.5% of gross revenue; for most professions it is 3% of gross revenue. Revenue taxes for several types of businesses change from occasionally.

Property transfer tax (sometimes called "stamp duty") is a tax on the property value if the property is sold, payable by the buyer at time of closing. Until 2017, it was 5%. In late 2017, it was changed to 8% for those who are not citizens of Belize or of CARICOM countries, for which it remains at 5%. This tax applies to existing homes, most lots and land. If you are buying a newly built, or substantially renovated (typically about 60% renovated, or more) home or condo, in addition to the 8% transfer tax you will also owe the 12.5% GST, for a total of 20.5% due on closing. However, as noted, sellers often roll the GST into the selling price, and the buyer may not be aware it is included.

This GST also applies, in some cases, to the first sale of lots in a subdivision, but not to their resale.

If the property value on which the tax is based seems low, the government can revalue the land based on comparable sales in the area, and the stamp duty will be charged on that higher property value.

In practice, most new home and condo sellers and residential developers fold these taxes into the price of the property, so the buyer may not even realize there is a tax charge.

Other taxes: There is **no Belize inheritance tax.**

Significantly, there also is **no Belize capital gains tax.** If you buy real estate property in Belize and it has increased in value since you bought it, you pay no tax in Belize on the gain. (You may owe capital gains tax if you are a U.S. citizen.)

The **Belize hotel tax** on hotel is 9%. An attempt to increase it to 12.5%, the same as the GST, failed.

Belize has signed **double taxation agreements** with many countries, including the United Kingdom, Bahamas, Barbados, St. Vincent and the

Grenadines, Dominica, Grenada, St. Kitts and Nevis, Suriname, Guyana, Jamaica, Trinidad and Tobago and St. Lucia. There is no such agreement with the U.S.

U.S. Tax Breaks for Expats

Note: In late 2017, the United States passed a sweeping tax bill. Not all of the impacts of the tax changes are yet clear, and some aspects of U.S. tax law may not be fully reflected here.

The U.S. in unusual in that it taxes the *worldwide* income of its citizens and resident aliens (Green Card holders) when calculating U.S. federal income taxes. So, generally, if you make US$50,000 in the U.S., the equivalent of US$25,000 in Mexico and of US$25,000 in England, as a U.S. citizen you are presumed to have total income of $100,000, on which you will pay federal income and Social Security/Medicare taxes.

For international corporations, not individuals, this was changed under the new tax law, to encourage repatriation of profits.

U.S. citizens living and earning income abroad get some tax breaks from Uncle Sam.

If you meet certain requirements, you may qualify for the foreign earned income and foreign housing exclusions and the foreign housing deduction.

You can use an IRS online tool to help determine whether income earned in a foreign country is eligible to be excluded from income reported on your U.S. federal income tax return (Form 1040). See www.irs.gov/individuals/international-taxpayers/foreign-earned-income-exclusion.

As noted, if you are a U.S. citizen or a resident alien of the United States and you live abroad, you are taxed by the U.S. on your worldwide income. However, you may qualify to exclude from income up to an amount of your foreign earnings that is adjusted annually for inflation (the exclusion amount for the 2017 tax year is US$102,100). This income could be from an employer or from self-employment income. However, you must still pay U.S. Social Security and Medicare taxes, if you owe them. In addition, in some cases you can exclude or deduct certain foreign housing allowance amounts.

(The new U.S. tax law permits the deduction of up to 20% of most pass-through business income for individuals, partnerships, LLCs and S-corporations that report on Schedule C of the 1040.)

To qualify for the foreign earned income exclusion, the foreign housing exclusion, or the foreign housing deduction, your tax home must be in a foreign country throughout your period of bona fide residence or physical presence abroad.

If you are a U.S. citizen or resident alien residing overseas, or are in the military on duty outside the U.S., on the regular due date of your return you are allowed an automatic two-month extension to file your return and pay any amount due without requesting an extension. For a calendar year return, the automatic two-month extension is to June 15. You must still pay any amount due by April 15 (unless April 15 falls on a holiday) to avoid interest charges, although penalties on unpaid amounts don't begin until June 15. You can also file for the standard six-month extension to October 15, with the usual rules.

If you are a U.S. citizen or resident alien and you live in a foreign country, mail your U.S. tax return to: Department of the Treasury Internal Revenue Service Center, Austin, TX 73301-0215 USA. Estimated tax payments should be mailed with form 1040-ES to: Internal Revenue Service, P.O. Box 1300, Charlotte, NC 28201-1300 USA. You may also be able to file electronically.

U.S. states have different tax rules, so you need to check any state, if any, in which you lived during any part of the tax year.

If you have deposits in a foreign bank or any other foreign financial account, including a bank in Belize, you must file the notorious FBAR, the Foreign Bank Account Report. It must be filed if you have an interest in, or signatory authority over, a foreign financial account, and if the aggregate value of those accounts exceeds US$10,000 at any time during the calendar year.

For tax years 2016 and onwards, the FBAR due date is April 15, but with a maximum extension for a six-month period ending October 15.

The FBAR form (FinCEN Form 114) is filed electronically using the BSA E-Filing System maintained by the U.S. Department of the Treasury's Financial Crimes Enforcement Network. Failure to file leads to very serious penalties – forfeiture of 50% of the amount in the account, even if no other crime except failing to file was committed.

Note: This very brief overview of Belize taxation should not be relied on for your actual situation, for which professional tax advice is recommended.

What Things Cost in Belize

San Ignacio market   Photo: Shutterstock

Belize doesn't have a cost of living. It has several costs of living. The traditional view is that Belize is the most expensive country in Central America, yet one of the least expensive in the Caribbean.

While there's truth to that, it really doesn't take into account that the actual cost of living in Belize can vary from almost nothing to very high. You can live in a luxury four-bedroom house on Ambergris Caye, with air conditioning, telephones, a dishwasher, microwave and cable TV, U.S. food in your pantry and imported booze in your glass, and you can spend thousands a month. Or you can live in a small Belizean-style house in Cayo, around Corozal Town or in rural Toledo, eat beans and rice and rice and beans, ride buses and drink local rum for a few hundred U.S. dollars a month.

Most expats in Belize choose somewhere in between. Some condos and houses in Belize go for more than US$1 million, but I know one expat who built and equipped his small house, using his own labor, with thatch from nature and scrounged lumber, for around US$4,000, and that included furniture and kitchen equipment.

After all, per capita income in Belize is a fraction of that in the U.S. A weekly wage of US$150 to $200 for six days of work is considered pretty good. Tens of thousands of Belizeans live, and in many cases live comfortably, on a few thousand dollars a year. You can, too.

Or you can compromise, forsaking those high-cost icons of civilization such as 80,000 BTU air conditioners, while keeping the family car, boat or other toys that you enjoy. Live partly on the Belizean style, partly in the U.S. style, and enjoy the benefits of both, and you'll get more for less. One American expat, who returned to Colorado after living in Belize for five years, said he was surprised at how much the cost of living in the U.S. had increased since he left. "Compared to Colorado Springs, ANYTHING in Belize is cheap. And I can't wait to get back — I just don't have enough money to live here in Colorado in anything but poverty!"

Price Sampler: What Things Cost in Belize

Here's a sampler of costs for common items in Belize, as of 2017-2018. *All prices are shown here in U.S. dollars.* As in other countries, prices for many items vary depending on where and when you buy them.

Transportation

Gallon of unleaded regular gas: $5.15 (the pump price varies slightly by area, and fluctuates frequently reflecting the international price of oil and government price controls)

Gallon of diesel fuel: $4.50

Bus fare from Belize City to San Ignacio: $4

Bus fare from Belize City to Corozal Town: $6

Water taxi from Belize City to San Pedro, Ambergris Caye: $12-$18 one-way

Water taxi from Corozal Town to San Pedro, Ambergris Caye: $25

One-way adult airfare from Sir Barry Bowen Municipal Airport in Belize City to Placencia: $118

Taxi from Belize international airport to Belize City: $25 for two persons, US$5 for each additional person

Taxi fare within Belize City: $3-$5

Utilities/Telecommunications

1-kilowatt hour of electricity: $0.24 (varies slightly by usage)

"Current" (electrical service) for 800 kW hours monthly: $192

Monthly charge for residential telephone: $50 for landline with unlimited calls to other landlines in Belize

DSL internet access: $150 a month for 4 MB (download speed)

Digital cellular service: $25 a month for 250 minutes/texts to $125 per month for 2,000 minutes/texts

Butane, 100-pound tank, delivered: $52 (varies by area)

Bottled water, delivered: $2.50/gallon (varies by area)

Pipe water and sewerage (where available): $25 a month, higher in some areas

"Dirt" (trash) pick-up: Free to $10 a month (varies by area)

Staples in Grocery Stores (Prices Vary by Store)

Red beans: $1 per pound

Milk: $1.70 (quart)

Ground steak (lean ground beef): $1.50 per pound

Pork chops: $2--$3 per pound

Chicken (whole): $1.25 per pound

Loaf of white bread: $1.50 (whole wheat $2.50--$3)

Corn tortillas, freshly made: $0.02--$0.04 each
Bananas: 10 to 20 for $1
Avocados: 6 for $1 (varies seasonally)
Valencia oranges: 10 for $1 (in season)
Flour, bulk, 1 lb.: $1
Morton salt: $1.50
Bottle of imported moderate-quality Chilean wine: $16-$18
Case of 24 Belikin beers (pick up from Bowen & Bowen distributor): $24 plus $6 bottle deposit
Case of 24 Coca-Cola, Sprite or Fanta soft drinks (pick up from Bowen & Bowen distributor): $9 plus $6 bottle deposit
Soft drink, Coca-Cola, 12 oz. (at grocery): $0.75 each
Local Mennonite cheese, 1 lb.: $4.50
Kraft pepperjack cheese, 8 oz.: $4.50
Philadelphia brand 8 oz. cream cheese: $4.50
Onions: $0.60 per pound (varies seasonally)
Local rum, liter: $7 - $14
Sugar: $0.30 per pound
Crackers (Premium Saltines): $4.80
Cigarettes, Independence local brand: $4 a pack
Cigarettes, Marlboro: $5.75 a pack
Canned soup (Campbell's Chicken Noodle): $1.80
Cereal (Raisin Bran): $5
Cooking oil (1-2-3 brand from Mexico), 1/2 liter: $1.75

Household Items
Mennonite-made wood dining table: $175
Whirlpool 12,000 BTU air-conditioner: $700
Mabe (Mexican-made) frost-free 16 cubic foot refrigerator: $675
Small home appliances at Mirab, Courts, Brodies, Hofius or other stores: about 25% to 50% more than prices in the U.S.

Entertainment
Fish and beans and rice at local restaurant, Hopkins: $5
Lobster dinner at nice restaurant, Placencia: $25--$35
Movie theater ticket, Ramada Princess, Belize City: $8.50
Rum drink at bar, Hopkins: $2--$4
Belikin beer at bar in Cayo: $2--$3.50

Shelter Costs
Rent for simple two-bedroom house in Corozal Town: $250--$400
Cost to build a reinforced concrete home: $50 to $190 per sq. ft., finished out in basic to high-moderate level
Small concrete house and lot in Belmopan, Corozal Town or Cayo: $40,000--$100,000
Modern three-bedroom house and beachview lot in Consejo: $145,000--$400,000

Medical Care
Office visit, private physician: $25--$70
Teeth cleaning, private dentist: $40
Root canal and crown, private dentist: $300--$500

Building Supplies
50# bag of cement: $6--$7
"Prefab" Mennonite House, 800 sq. ft., set up on your lot, $20,000+

Family Budgets in Belize
As noted, the cost of living varies greatly in Belize, depending on your lifestyle, preferences and place of residence. Here are several different budgets. **All amounts are in U.S. dollars.**

Monthly Budget for a Small Family in Rural Cayo District
This budget represents the typical cost for a couple with two small children in Cayo District. They bought 25 acres of land for US$40,000 and built a 1,200 sq. ft. house using a combination of a stick-built construction and a Mennonite prefab. They live off-the-grid with a small solar system, have a septic system and get their water from cisterns. The house construction, done partly with their own labor, cost US$90,000. They have fruit trees, a year-round garden and keep chickens for eggs and good and goats for milk. They home school their children and have a double-cab pickup for transportation.

Repair and upkeep cost on off-the-grid systems	US$150
Property taxes	10
Cell phone (voice and internet)	75
Groceries (beyond what they grow on their own)	125
Transportation (gas, maintenance and insurance for truck)	150
Farm costs (food and care for animals, equipment operating costs and related)	375
Health care	225
Home schooling costs	50
Entertainment and dining out	150
Clothing	100
Occasional travel in-country and to Guatemala	100
Other personal expenses	150
TOTAL	**$1,660**

Monthly Budget for Expat Couple in Toledo
This budget reflects the cost of living for an expat couple who own a small house on 10 acres in a rural area near Punta Gorda, for which they paid US$80,000. They bought the property for cash. Also assumed: Their SUV is paid for, and they choose to purchase health insurance. They are on the grid but use solar and wind backup. They have fruit trees and a small kitchen garden but buy most of their

staples and other groceries.

Repair and upkeep cost on off-the-grid systems	US$150
Property taxes	10
Cell phone (voice and internet)	125
Groceries (beyond what they grow on their own)	180
Transportation (gas, maintenance and insurance for SUV)	200
Gardening costs	50
Medical insurance	400
Health care (out of pocket)	100
Entertainment and dining out	200
Clothing	75
Occasional travel in-country and to Guatemala	100
Other personal expenses	200
TOTAL	**$1,790**

Monthly Budget for Couple in Corozal

This budget is for an older couple on U.S. Social Security in the Qualified Retired Persons living in a rental house in or just outside Corozal Town. They own their own vehicle, but rent a two-bedroom house. They get medical care in Chetumal.

Rent	$500
Transportation (gas, maintenance and insurance)	200
Cell telephone and cell internet	100
Groceries	225
Medical and dental care in Chetumal	200
Electricity (800 kWh)	192
Butane	50
Bottled war, trash pickup	50
Cable TV	30
Clothing	75
Travel in-country, in Mexico and occasionally to U.S.	300
Entertainment/dining out	220
Other personal expenses	150
TOTAL	**$2,392**

Monthly Barebones Budget for Single Person in Cayo

This budget is for a single 65-year-old permanent resident in a Belizean-style rented house near San Ignacio. Assumptions: The individual uses public transportation and takes advantage of the local public health care system.

Rent	$250
Transportation (local buses/taxis)	50
Cell telephone	50
Groceries	150
Medical and dental care	90
Electricity (400 kWh)	95

Butane	30
Bottled war, trash pickup	30
Cable TV	25
Clothing	50
Entertainment/dining out	75
Other personal expenses	75
TOTAL	**$970**

Colonial-era buildings in the Fort George area of Belize City are scenic, but the old capital is the crime hub of the country

Crime and Safety in Belize

We don't want to scare you, because things aren't as bad as they sound when you read about them from afar, but you need to know: The dark underbelly of life in Belize (and indeed in most developing countries) is crime, especially property crime.

On the positive side, most expats in Belize say that while they have to be mindful of the possibility of thefts and burglaries that they don't spend much time worrying about it.

Most of the violent crime, indeed most of the crime, occurs in and around Belize City. It is most serious on the South Side of Belize, with its slum areas and gangs.

When I meet homeowners in Placencia, Cayo or Corozal Town often the talk turns to the latest break-in at a neighbor's home. Residents and tourism operators in Placencia village, Cayo, Caye Caulker and Corozal are reporting increasing problems with burglaries and thefts, a trend that mirrors a similar situation taking place in San Pedro.

Burglaries and petty theft in Belize are disturbingly common. Of course, this isn't unique to Belize. There are about 2.2 million burglaries reported in the United States annually. When you add together burglaries, auto thefts and larcenies/thefts, the total for the U.S. is around 10.5 million. That's one theft-related crime for every 10 households. So, in the U.S., in a decade the chance of your household being a victim of theft or burglary is statistically 100%.

Here is a recent statement on crime and safety in Belize by the U.S. Embassy in Belize. It focuses mainly on U.S. tourists, but visitors and expats from any country may find value in it.

Pickpocketing, burglary, and hotel room theft are the most common types of non-violent crimes committed against U.S. citizens; they occur throughout Belize, and they have increased in recent years. Non-confrontational petty thieves are particularly active in tourist areas and on public transportation. Stay alert to pickpockets when in crowds and when taking public transportation, and be conscious of distractions created to target tourists. Make use of hotel safes when available.

Violent crime has remained low in the tourist areas, though reports of theft are on the rise and some notable murders have occurred, including the widely-publicized murder of a U.S. citizen in the Cayo District of western Belize in 2016.

Corruption, human smuggling/trafficking, the drug trade, money laundering (institutional and trade-based), and organized gang activity remain significant criminal problems exacerbated by the low conviction rate. Criminal organizations and individuals often operate beyond the ability of the police to effectively disrupt them.

There is some evidence to suggest that Salvadoran and Guatemalan-based transnational criminal organizations provide logistical support to international drug and human trafficking organizations and utilize Belize as a transit country along smuggling routes. Gang tags from 18th Street (*Barrio 18*) and MS-13 (*Mara Salvatrucha*) have been reported; although there is no indication that formal gang cliques have been established in Belize.

Due to the small population and high murder rate per capita, Belize City consistently ranks among the top 10 cities in the world for homicides, according to the United Nations Office on Drugs and Crime. The average runs just under 40 homicides per 100,000 residents. [Countrywide] the murder rate in 2016, the second highest ever recorded, surpassed that of 2015 from 119 to 138. The increase from 119 murders in 2016 is likely due to an increase in shootings and burglaries and potentially from the displacement of crime from the central hub of local gang activity in south Belize City... As a result, particular caution and situational awareness should be exercised when living in smaller communities. Domestic violence crimes are extremely high and account for a significant portion of the total murder rate. Five out of six districts experienced an increase in murders in 2016:

The Belize District, which includes Belize City, continues to have the highest number of murders due in large part to dozens of street gangs that operate in the city. Belmopan, the tiny capital ... and home to several diplomatic missions, including the U.S. Embassy, recorded 13 murders in 2016.

Sexual harassment and sexual assaults against visitors have occurred.

Belize is a source, transit, and destination country for those subjected to forced labor and sex trafficking. No human trafficking cases were prosecuted in 2016. Cases from previous years remain pending and limited resources are available to victims.

Crime is a worldwide phenomenon, but the crime situation is perhaps more acute in Belize, in part because often the police often are unable to do anything about the problem. This can be because they are incompetent, or lack the necessary training or, in some cases, they know the culprits or are related to them and decline to arrest them. Most often probably it is due to lack of resources. In many cases constables don't even have the basic tools to do their jobs. There have been reports about police cars that simply sat at the police station because there wasn't money to buy gas for them.

In many cases, the local authorities do have a good idea who is responsible, but in a society such as Belize where most people in a village are at least distantly related, police have to go along to get along, and this may mean turning their eye if they think a cousin is doing the stealing or drug dealing. One American expat in Placencia had to briefly leave the peninsula because drug dealers thought this person had found and kept a shipment of cocaine. Local constables probably knew who the drug dealers were but were reluctant to take any action. They felt powerless to offer protection, so they recommended this American go away on vacation until things cooled down.

What can you do to avoid being a burglary victim in Belize? Several things can help:

Put burglar bars on your windows and doors. These are available from local hardware stores and cost around US$75 per window. If your house is in a remote area, the bad guys may just attach a chain to the burglar bars and pull them off with a truck, but in most areas they offer a good first line of defense.

Get a dog. A dog is THE most effective deterrent to break-ins in Belize. It doesn't have to be a vicious dog, but it should sound vicious. A big, black dog is considered the best deterrent. Note, however, that bad guys have been known to poison guard dogs to gain entrance to the property.

Put a fence or wall around your property. This won't deter serious thieves, but it may slow them down.

Get to know your neighbors. Community watch programs can be highly effective in deterring crime. But even if you just get on good terms with your neighbors, they will help keep an eye on your property.

Be sure the exterior areas are well lit. Nightlights supplemented by motion-detector lights can help. Using LED bulbs can help reduce your electric power cost.

Hire a caretaker you can trust. Though there are irresponsible or crooked caretakers, there also are many who are dependable and will look out for your property when you are away. Ask around, especially among fellow expats and at local churches, for an honest individual or family. Remember, the mango doesn't fall far from the tree. You will usually have to provide living quarters at no cost and a monthly stipend, typically about US$100 to $400 a month, depending on what you require of the caretaker. There can also be issues related to your role as an employer, including the requirement to provide social security payments, severance pay, vacation time and other employment issues.

Install an alarm system with motion detectors. Belize has several security companies that install and monitor residential security systems. Check the Belize telephone directory for security companies, or ask neighbors about their expensive. Note, however, that security companies don't operate in all areas of Belize, and even if you have a system there is no guarantee that the local police will respond. There also are install-it-yourself wireless security systems. **SimpliSafe** (www.simplisafe.com) is the best known, with more than two million systems in use. A basic system monitoring doors, a couple of motion detectors and a security camera or two costs only a few hundred dollars. Although you won't be able to have it professionally monitored, and SimpliSafe doesn't ship internationally or provide support outside the U.S. as long as you have cell service you can control and monitor it yourself with your cell phone.

You are probably best off with a system that uses loud air horns and flashing lights – these may alert your neighbors to a break-in and perhaps even scare off the intruders.

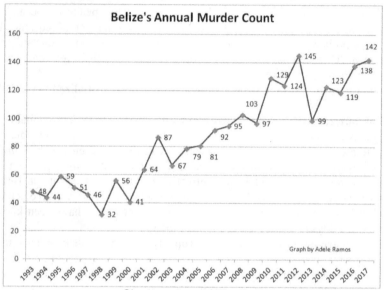

Chart courtesy of *The Reporter* and Adele Ramos

Personal Safety

The homicide and violent crime rate in Belize is higher than in most large urban areas of the United States. Typically, there are 90 to 145 murders a year in Belize. That's a murder rate about five to six times higher than the average in the U.S., which has an annual rate in the range of 6 murders per 100,000 population, which itself is very high compared to Canada (about 2 homicides per 100,000) or Western Europe. However, most of the murders are concentrated in Belize City, and much of the other violent crime involves a farm worker getting drunk on Saturday night and knifing or machete chopping somebody in a cool spot (bar.)

To put the Belize crime rate in perspective, Guatemala City sees about 100 murders a WEEK. Although there are gangs in Belize City, Belize does not have the severe youth gang problems that plague Guatemala, Honduras and El Salvador. In Central America alone, it is estimated there are 250,000 members of *maras,* Spanish slang for local gangs (*maras* are a species of swarming, aggressive ants) in those other countries in Central America. The situation in Belize is nothing like that in Honduras, where the number of gang members is higher than the total population of Belize City.

A recent report by non-governmental organizations in Central America puts the murder rate for Guatemala, Honduras and El Salvador as follows: El Salvador 56 homicides per 100,000 inhabitants; Honduras, 41; and Guatemala, 38. In 2016, Belize's rate was around 35 per 100,000.

While most expats are concerned about burglaries and thefts, despite a few high-profile murders of U.S. and Canadian expats in Belize in recent years, most retirees and foreign residents in Belize express relatively little concern about their personal safety. The author himself, who has traveled around Belize, even to the most remote corners, for more than 25 years, and has never once been felt personally threatened. The only minor crime experienced in a quarter century was an unsuccessful attempt to break into a car left parked on a rural road in Cayo, which resulted in a broke lock that cost about US$50 to repair.

Certainly, it's wise to use common sense: Don't walk on in unlit areas at night; don't pick up strangers in your car; put up exterior lighting around your home driveway and entrance and do the other things suggested in this chapter.

In January 2018, the United States State Department issued a travel advisory for Belize warning American citizens to exercise caution when in the country. The advisory states that violent crime, such as sexual assault, armed robbery, and murder are becoming more common in Belize and local police lack the resources to respond effectively to serious criminal incidents. Despite this warning, hotel operators and other members of the tourism industry continue to report good business. In the advisory, visitors were warned to always be aware of their surroundings, avoid walking at night, not to resist robbery attempts, and to be extra vigilant when visiting banks or ATM's. The State Department urged everyone to enroll in the Smart Traveller Enrollment Program prior to their trip. The program is a free service that allows U.S citizens traveling and living abroad to register their trip online or at the nearest U.S Embassy or Consulate.

Can You Own Guns in Belize?

Most of the world's countries have stricter gun control laws than the United States, and Belize is no exception.

The U.S. also has one of the highest rates of gun-related deaths in the world, with about 4 deaths per 100,000 population in a typical year. This is 30 times or more higher than Canada or than countries in Northern Europe such as Denmark and Sweden.

The Belize government imposes relatively strict controls on guns and ammunition, and licenses are required. Gun licenses must be renewed annually before the owner's birthday. Failure to renew the license, or possessing a gun without a license, will likely land you in jail, with no bond permitted for at least a month. However, if you follow the rules, and you are an official permanent resident or have acquired Belizean citizenship, you can obtain a license to possess a shotgun, rifle or handgun in Belize.

It is easiest to obtain a license for a firearm in Belize if you demonstrate a need for one. An example is a farmer who needs a gun, usually a shotgun, to protect domestic farm animals from wild animals. Another example is a business owner who needs a weapon for safety in a store or in making bank deposits. A business owner can get a Special Protection License to possess and carry a handgun. Sport hunters also can obtain a license for a gun used in hunting.

There also are rules on how much ammunition you can possess. Generally it is no more than 100 rounds, and the ammunition must be for the gun for which you have a permit.

How to Obtain a License

To get a license to own a firearm, first download the application from the Belize Police website at www.police.gov.bz. The two-page application asks for basic information such as your name, address, phone, date of birth, occupation, nationality; information on the type of license for which you are applying (Farmer, Sport Hunter, Special Protection, etc.); information on the firearm you wish to license including type, caliber, make and serial number; other firearms that you have licensed; your experience with firearms; and what security you have for the firearm. You will need to take a firearm certification course (US$150 if you are not a Belize citizen). The police will run a background check. Approval can take up to several months. If approved, you will pay your annual license fee *(see below)*.

Cost of Licenses

In late 2017, a significant increase in the cost of licenses for guns was proposed by the Belize government. (As of this writing, the proposed increases have not been implemented, but we're presenting the new rates here.)

The cost for licenses for non-citizens generally is much higher than for Belizean citizens.

Here are some examples of the cost of annual licenses:

Shotgun Holders License for Farmers: US$125 non-Belizean, US$12.50 Belizean

Special Protection License: US$750 non-Belizean, US$250 Belizean
Sport Hunters License: US$125 non-Belizean, US$75 Belizean
Security Guard License: US$12.50 non-Belizean, US$12.50 Belizean
Heirloom/Antique Gun License: US$150 non-Belizean, zero Belizean
Importation of Firearm: US$100 non-Belizean, US$100 Belizean
Bullet-Proof Vest License: US$50 non-Belizean, US$50 Belizean
Training and Certification for License Holder: US$150 non-Belizean, zero
Belizean

Firearms Prohibited in Belize
The following types of firearms are not permitted in Belize:

Rifles and Machine Guns
Assault rifles of any type
Rifles with a caliber larger than 7.62mm
Machine guns of any type
Rifles made to be fitted with bayonets
Sawed-off rifles
Rifles similar to those used by Belize Defence Forces

Shotguns
Shotguns with a barrel length of 21 inches or less
Shotguns with rifled barrels

Handguns
Handguns with calibers greater than 9mm or .38
Handguns that use magnum cartridges (except .22 or 5.6mm caliber)
Handguns altered to make them automatic or semi-automatic
.22 pen guns
Flare guns
Extended magazines for handguns

Others
Homemade firearms of any type
Firearms with sound suppressors (silencers)
Armor-piercing ammunitions
Bullet-proof vests
Equipment used to recharge expended ammunition

Penalties for Violating Belize Gun Laws
Penalties for violations of gun laws in Belize are severe. The Firearms Act, Chapter 143 of the Laws of Belize, 2000, as amended in 2003, 2008 and later, calls for imprisonment for a minimum of two years and up to five years for the first offense, and three to seven years for subsequent offenses.

Those who have a firearms license but inadvertently fail to renew it may be fined instead of imprisoned, with fines of no less than BZ$5,000 and no more than BZ$10,000.

Licensed Firearm Dealers

There are a number of licensed firearm dealers in Belize that sell rifles, shotguns and hunting gear. Here are a few.

Anchor Security Services, Forest Drive, Belmopan City, 501-822-0257, www.anchorsecurityservices.com. Anchor, which provides security guards and other security services, also is a license gun dealer and provides training

Apex Ammo, 695 Blue Creek, Orange Walk District, 501-323-0860, www.apexammo.bz. Sells hunting rifles, shotguns, handguns, ammo and hunting gear. A Stevens 12-gauge pump shotgun goes for around US$900.

Gillardo Services & Hardware, Mile 54, Hummingbird Hwy., Belmopan City, 501-822-2650. Supplies firearms, ammo and hunting gear.

Health Care in Belize

A major issue for expats, especially retirees, is health care. Health care in Belize is a mixed picture. As a developing country Belize's medical resources are not comparable to those offered in the United States, Canada and Western Europe. If you are older and especially if you face chronic health problems, you will have to look closely at the health care tradeoffs — a healthier way of living, lower medical costs and more personalized care in Belize versus the high-tech, low-touch, high cost of health care and health insurance back home. Plus, programs such as U.S. Medicare and Medicaid, and national health programs in Europe and Canada, generally are not available when you're in Belize.

Public Health Care System

There are eight public hospitals in Belize, with a total of about 600 beds.

Belize City is the center for medical care in Belize. It was here that the Belize National Insurance health care system was begun, and from Belize City the public health program, funded initially from Social Security funds and more recently from the government's general fund, was rolled out, beginning in 2007, to Southern Belize and to other parts of the country.

A number of private dentists and private medical clinics also are available in Belize City.

Many serious problems can be treated at the country's tertiary care center, **Karl Heusner Memorial Hospital** in Belize City (Princess Margaret Dr., 501-223-1548, www.khmh.bz). It is a modern public hospital albeit one plagued by occasional supply shortages and management issues. The KHMH has 134 beds, three surgical suites and two labor and delivery suits. The hospital has a 24/7 lab, weekend pharmacy services and more than 25 specialists on staff.

Rates are a fraction of the rates charges by U.S. hospitals – around US$250 per day for a private, air-conditioned hospital room, less for semi-private rooms, which may not have air-conditioning. Rates don't include physician fees, lab charges and other fees.

There are seven other public hospitals in Belize, including three regional hospitals: the Southern Regional Hospital in Dangriga, the Western Regional Hospital in Belmopan and the Northern Regional Hospital in Orange Walk Town. Altogether, there are about 600 public hospital beds in Belize.

The public hospitals provide the four basic medical specialties: internal medicine, surgery, pediatrics and OB-GYN. Karl Heusner Memorial also provides neuro, ENT, physiotherapy, orthopedic surgery and several other services.

The quality of these hospitals varies considerably. Karl Heusner Memorial -- named after a prominent Belize City physician -- opened in 1997 and has much modern equipment, such as a CAT-scan, though some Belizeans and expats complain that even this hospital has occasional shortage of supplies or certain medications. It has added new facilities and services including ones for neurosurgery and trauma care. The Southern Regional Hospital in Dangriga, which opened in 2000, is another modern facility, with much of the same medical technologies and equipment as you'd find in a small community hospital in an American town. However, other hospitals leave a lot to be desired.

The National Health System is divided into four regions:

The Central Health Region has the Karl Heusner Memorial Hospital, three polyclinics, 10 health centers and two mental health facilities, Rockview Mental Hospital and the Port Loyola Mental Acute Day Hospital.

The Northern Health Region is composed of two public health institutions (Northern Regional Hospital and Corozal Community Hospital), 11 health centers and 16 health clinics. The Regional Hospital has 57 beds and Corozal Community Hospital has 30 beds.

The Southern Health Region has two public hospitals, 14 health centers and 12 health clinics. The two public hospitals are Southern Regional Hospital (formerly Dangriga Hospital), which has 52 beds, and Punta Gorda Hospital/Community Hospital, which has 30 beds.

The Western Region has two hospitals (Western Regional in Belmopan and San Ignacio Hospital), four health centers and a number of health clinics.

Although this sounds good on paper, some of these hospitals, health clinics and health centers suffer from inadequate staffing, too many patients for their available resources and lack of equipment and medicines. Doctors may diagnose health problems accurately, but they may not be able to provide the proper medications or treatment modalities.

Private Health Care

In addition to these public hospitals, centers and clinics, Belize has **private hospitals** -- **La Loma Luz** (501-824-2087), a not-for-profit Seventh Day Adventist hospital in Santa Elena near San Ignacio with 20 beds, and **Belize Medical Associates** (5791 St. Thomas Street, 501-223-0302, www.belizemedical.com), a 25-bed for-profit facility in Belize City that is affiliated with Baptist Health Systems of South Florida. Altogether these private hospitals have around 50 hospital beds.

There also are a number of physicians and dentists in private practice, mostly in Belize City. **Belize Healthcare Partners Ltd.**, (Chancellor and Blue Marlin Avenues, 501-223-7870, www.belizehealthcare.com) is a health care facility with about 25 physicians on staff. Belize Healthcare Partners offers cardiology, vascular surgery, OB-GYN, radiology, kidney dialysis, laboratory and services for private patients. It also operates Belize Integral Health Centre at Gibnut and Curassow Streets, a primary and secondary care clinic serving about 12,000 patients under the National Health Care program.

Starting in the late 1990s, health care in Belize got a boost, thanks to the arrival of a group of several dozen medical volunteers from Cuba. Currently around 100 Cuban nurses and physicians are in Belize.

Most physicians and dentists in Belize are trained in the U.S., Guatemala, Mexico, Cuba or Great Britain. There are three so-called offshore medical schools in Belize, but their graduates are unlikely to practice in Belize. A nursing school, affiliated with the University of Belize, trains nurses for work in

Belize. While many expats do go to Guatemala, or to Chetumal or Mérida, Mexico, for specialized treatment, others who can afford it may go to Houston, Miami, New Orleans or elsewhere in the U.S.

In 2013, the Belize Medical Tourism Association was formed by tourism and medical officials, with the goal of increasing medical and dental tourism to Belize.

Medical Professionals

Government figures show Belize has fewer than one physician per 1,000 population, less than one-half the rate in the U.S. Belize has about 500 nurses, or one nurse per 735 population. Altogether there are perhaps 800 trained medical personnel in Belize. They are not distributed evenly around the country, however. More than one-half are in Belize City are, which has only about one-fourth of the population. About three-fourths of trained medical people work in the public sector, and the rest in the private sector.

Medical and dental volunteer teams from the U.S. and Canada regularly visit Belize to provide short-term care.

Medical care professionals in Belize earn very modest incomes compared with those in the U.S. Physicians employed by the government start at around US$15,000 to $20,000 a year, though they may supplement their income in private practice. Nursing salaries start at around US$8,000.

Most physicians and dentists in Belize are trained in the U.S., Guatemala, Mexico or Great Britain. There are several so-called offshore medical schools in Belize, but their graduates are unlikely to practice in Belize. A nursing school, affiliated with the University of Belize, trains nurses for work in Belize. Belize medical professionals, like Belizean society, come in every shape and flavor. "My dentist is Garifuna, my ear doc is Mayan, my eye doc Mestizo and my OB-GYN is Spanish," says one expat, a former New Yorker who now lives in Belize City.

The following regulatory bodies are established under the laws of Belize: The Medical Board responsible for the registration of medical practitioners, dentists, opticians and nursing homes. The Nurses and Midwives Council, responsible for the registration and regulation of nurses and midwives; and the Board of Examiners of Chemist and Druggists, responsible for the examining and registration of Chemist and Druggists and for carrying out other matters provided for in this Ordinance. The Nursing School participates in an accreditation program within the CARICOM countries.

What you won't find in Belize is topnotch emergency care, although Karl Heusner Memorial Hospital in Belize City has added a trauma care center. While there are ambulances, a helicopter transfer surface using Astrum Helicopters near Belize City and an emergency air transport service, Belize's spread-out population means it could take hours to get you to a hospital. In specialist care, such as for heart disease or cancer, Belize is behind the U.S. and Canada and even its larger Latin neighbors such as Mexico, Guatemala and Honduras.

"The big minus in Belize is that there is not adequate medical care for chronically ill people who need regular visits to specialists," said Judy duPlooy, who owns a lodge near San Ignacio. She said that for people in Western Belize,

Guatemala has "excellent care and is the quickest place to get to in an emergency."

While many expats do go to Guatemala, or to Chetumal or Mérida, Mexico, for specialized treatment, others who can afford it go to Houston, Miami, New Orleans or elsewhere in the U.S. For example, both Prime Minister Dean Barrow and his wife, First Lady Kim Simplis-Barrow, have journeyed to the U.S. for medical treatment during the PM's terms in office. Simplis-Barrow was treated for cancer in Miami, and Dean Barrow had surgery for chronic back pain in Newport, Calif.

Home Care

Some older expats like the idea that if they become disabled and can't take care of themselves they can hire local Belizeans to help them while staying in their homes, at relatively modest cost, especially compared with the cost of home care in the U.S. Full-time live in care by a Belizean, including meal preparation, light cleaning and health assistance, could cost US$200 a week or less, or around US$10,000 a year. That compares to US$25,000 to $60,000 a year for comparable assistance in the U.S., if available at all. This can allow elderly people to live at home rather than having to go to a nursing home.

We know of some families have moved to Belize specifically to have an elderly parent with dementia cared for at an affordable cost by an English-speaking home worker.

Pharmacies and Prescriptions

There are drug stores in Belize City, in all towns, and in some villages. Not all are licensed, however, and the Belize government is making an effort to inspect and license pharmacies.

Many prescription drugs cost less in Belize than in the U.S., though pharmacies may not stock a wide selection of drugs and some drugs cost more in Belize than in the U.S. or Canada. In general, in Belize prescriptions usually are not needed for antibiotics and some other drugs that require prescriptions in the U.S., even some painkillers containing codeine.

However, pharmacies owned by physicians or operated by hospitals, a common situation in Belize, may require or suggest a consultation with the doctor. In addition, especially if you are in Northern Belize, crossing the border to Chetumal is an option. Chetumal has large *farmacias* that have most medications at prices significantly lower than in the U.S., and often lower than in Belize.

If you are taking prescription medications, when you come to Belize you should be sure you have the generic name of the drug, as local pharmacies may not have the same brand names as back home.

Medical Records

If you have preexisting health conditions, you should bring a copy of your medical records with you when you move to Belize or come for an extended stay. It is also a good idea to have a letter from your physician outlining your conditions and past treatments.

148

Cost of Medical Care

Even if medical care isn't always up to snuff in Belize, at least it is cheap. The majority of health care is provided at little or no charge. Belizeans who can't afford to pay are treated in about the same way as those with more means. Only a tiny percentage of Belizeans have medical insurance. Private medical insurance coverage in Belize begins at US$150 to $200 a month, above what the average Belizean can pay. Rarely in the public health system in Belize will anyone be turned away for lack of cash or insurance, as thousands routinely are in the U.S. every day. Public hospitals and clinics may bill nominal amounts for tests and procedures -- for example, a woman's clinic in northern Belize charges US$10 to $20 for a Pap smear, cervical exam and breast exam and under US$15 for an ultrasound -- or they may ask for a donation. In some waiting rooms you will see a box where you can leave a donation. But even visitors are routinely treated for free. A British friend was injured in a boating accident off Dangriga. In great pain, he was taken to the hospital in Dangriga where he was he was diagnosed as having broken ribs. He was then transported by air to Belize City where he was hospitalized for several days. His total bill, including X-rays, hospital stay, transport and medications: Zero.

If you can accept long waits and less than state-of-the-art medical technology, you won't have to spend all of your pension income to afford care. "Medical, dental and eye care is a fraction of the cost of the U.S. I have my teeth checked and cleaned for US$40, pay U.S. $10 to $20 for an office visit to my physician, and medications are cheap," says one Californian who now lives in Belize full-time. Even if you opt for private care, office visits to a physician generally are just US$20 to $50, though in San Pedro, where docs cater to a lot of visitors and expats, it can be more. In 2013, I paid about US$90 for an office visit after a bad fall, but that included a couple of meds. A root canal with crown might cost US$300 to $500, although some Belize dentists charge more. Hospitalization runs under US$250 per day for a private room, a considerably less for a semi-private or ward room. Belize providers are trying to jump-start medical tourism in Belize, but so far such efforts have had but modest success, in part because of the lower costs and higher skill levels of providers in India, Thailand, Costa Rica and elsewhere.

Prescription drug costs vary but generally are less expensive than in the U.S. A few years ago, I paid just US$5 for a course of antibiotics. By the way, prescription drugs in Belize are usually dispensed in plastic baggies or envelopes rather than in bottles. While it is difficult to compare costs between Belize and the U.S., since the quality of care is different and the amount of medical tests done in Belize pales beside those routinely ordered in America, it's probably fair to say that even in the private sector overall costs for health care in Belize are one-fourth to one-third that in the U.S. and may be even less.

National Health Insurance

The medical care system in Belize is in a transitional period. A National Health Insurance scheme, proposed in the 1990s, is gradually being implemented. Under the scheme, through the Belize Social Security system all Belizeans and permanent residents would get medical care through a system somewhat similar to that in Britain. The scheme calls for individuals and businesses to pay into Social Security system for health care. The benefit, with the individual's Social Security card the identity card, would be comprehensive universal medical care. The system would pay for care, or at least part of it, at either public or private hospitals and clinics. Initially, a pilot project in Belize City, which started in the early 2000s, was funded by the government and was free to all residents of the Belize City South Side. Later, residents of the North Side were added. Then, in 2006-2007, the NHI was expanded to parts of southern Belize. It provided for care at a group of clinics, free drugs from participating pharmacies and free lab tests at participating clinics. Funding initially was through the Social Security system and then from the government general fund. Unfortunately, the Social Security system in Belize has been troubled for years, with charges flying back and forth about management and financial accountability of the system. The Belize government also usually runs a budget deficit. Together, these factors are hampering and delaying full expansion of the NHI.

Private Health Insurance

For routine primary care, most foreign residents in Belize make do with the low-cost public system, or they go to a private physician, dentist or clinic. Mostly they pay cash. They "self-insure," taking a calculated risk that what they save in medical insurance premiums will more than pay for their actual medical costs in Belize.

Health insurance policies for care in Belize are available on a referral basis through a few insurance companies in Belize, as agents for international health insurance companies and brokers, but these companies do not offer health insurance plans themselves:

RF&G Insurance, 81 N. Front Street, Belize City; 501-227-3744, www.rfginsurancebelize.com. RF&G, the largest firm in Belize, the result of a 2005 merger of Regent Insurance and F&G Insurance, is based in Belize City and has other offices around Belize, including branches in Corozal Town, Belmopan, San Pedro, Punta Gorda, Dangriga, Placencia and Orange Walk Town. It is part of the Roe Group, a diversified local company also with interests in tourism, tobacco and vehicle sales.

Belize Insurance Center. 212 North Front Street, Belize City; 501-227-7310, www.belizeinsurance.com. This group offers a variety of insurance products.

International Insurance Companies

Several international insurance companies and insurance brokers write health care policies for expatriates, with the premiums sometimes covering medical transportation back to the home country along with actual health care.

What rate you will pay for health care coverage as a resident of Belize depends on several factors. The most important factor is your age. Most insurers price their insurance coverage on age bands – for example, under 35, 35-39, 40-44, 45-49, 50-

54 and so on. Typically, the biggest jumps in cost occur for those over 50, especially those over age 60 or age 65. Those over 60 likely will pay four to 10 times as much as those under 30.

Other factors that impact the cost of insurance are your health condition including pre-existing illnesses, occupation, gender and lifestyle factors such as Body Mass Index and smoking. Also very important is the deductible level you choose, which might range from zero per year to US$10,000 a year. A zero deductible plan typically is about three times as expensive as a US$10,000 per year deductible. A deductible is the amount of health costs you pay out of pocket before the insurance kicks in.

Here are representative annual costs for a basic international major medical plan. A standard plan would include hospitalization, day-patient status at a hospital or clinic and emergency care. A more comprehensive plan that covers out-patient care, medical evacuation, maternity care and other extras could have annual costs twice as high as the figures shown. Most companies offer three or four, or more, levels of coverage, each with different co-pays, maximum lifetime limits and various extra features.

Keep in mind that these plans likely would include coverage not just in Belize but also in other countries, excepting the United States.

This is just an example to show how rates increase with age and is not meant to reflect actual costs for any particular individual in Belize. As a general rule, however, coverage outside the U.S. is much less expensive than in the U.S., under either the Affordable Care Act ("Obamacare") or other private insurance. In great part this is because the cost of hospitalization and other medical services in the U.S. is the highest in the world. Rates are per person and are in U.S. dollars.

Age	Annual Cost
30-34	US$1,800
35-39	US$1,900
40-44	US$2,200
45-49	US$2,400
50-54	US$3,000
55-60	US$3,900
61-65	US$5,400
65-69	US$8,000
70-74	US$9,000
75-79	US$11,500

Online quotes for healthcare plans are available from most of these companies. You will have to provide some information about you and others that you want to be covered, such as name, contact information, country of citizenship, country where you plan to live and whether or not you want coverage in the U.S. Most plans allow you to choose the country where you wish to have medical care. For example, residents in Belize might choose Mexico or Guatemala. Some plans provide coverage on a short-term basis in the U.S., if you are visiting the U.S. and experience a medical emergency. Note that countries served by the companies below change from time to time, so Belize coverage may not be offered by all companies.

Cigna Global Health, 877-539-6295 in the U.S., www.cignaglobal.com. Provides three basic levels of core coverage international and expat: Silver, Gold and Platinum. Cigna's core insurance policies provide you protection for hospital stays and treatment. Surgeon and consultation fees as well as hospital accommodation are covered. In-patient, outpatient and cancer treatments are also covered. A major difference among the plans are the total maximum coverage, ranging from US$1 million to $3 million.

Bupa Global (Victory House, Trafalgar Place, Brighton, BN1 4FY, United Kingdom; +44 (0) 1273 322074, www.bupa-intl.com). This company says it has more than 10 million policyholders around the world. It usually works through medical insurance brokers. Bupa took over Amedex, which had more than 1 million policyholders in Latin America. The Latin American Bupa website is www.bupalatinamerica.com. Most policies cover direct payment to hospitals, reimbursement for outpatient care and medical evacuation. Premium costs vary based on age, but an individual $1 million (annual limit) major medical policy with a US$500 to $1,000 deductible for a middle-aged individual could be around US$2,000-$8,000 annually, depending on the details of the policy, and assuming that you live most of the year outside the U.S. Most but not all policies exclude coverage in the U.S. Coverage in the U.S. typically doubles the premium cost. Bupa Global members have access to some 7,500 hospitals worldwide.

Aetna International (www.aetnainternational.com) is the international health care division of U.S.-based Aetna. Aetna has about 44 million participants in the U.S. and around 500,000 expat members internationally. Aetna International currently offers four levels of plans, from Basic to Exclusive. The Basic plan pays 100% of medical costs after US$2,500 coinsurance limit is reached, a maximum annual benefit of US$250,000 and medical evacuation.

Cigna International (www.cigna.com/international), a division of the U.S. insurance company, offers private international health insurance through a network of network of some 8,700 hospitals, 540,000 physicians and 167,000 dental offices.

Healthcare International (www.healthcareinternational.com) is a U.K-based provider that provides expat coverage worldwide with access to about 7,000 medical centers and 350,000 physicians. It currently has five levels of plans with varying costs and benefits.

My Matchmaker (www.mymatchmaker.com) is an international insurance broker that lets you compare plans from several different companies. To get an online quote for your particular situation, you have to put in your date of birth, gender, nationality and foreign place of residence, along with an indication of what kind of insurance coverage you desire.

Medicare
Medicare and Medicaid do not pay for medical care outside the U.S., except for some limited situations in Canada and Mexico. The U.S. Department of Veterans Affairs will pay for coverage outside the U.S. only if you are a veteran with a service-related disability.

For Americans, this is a major drawback of expat life in Belize, or indeed anywhere else outside the U.S. and its territories. For visitors and short-term residents, some private insurance policies including some Blue Cross policies do cover you regardless of where you become ill or have an accident. Also, some credit cards such as American Express Platinum pay for medical evacuations back to the cardholder's home country.

Health Issues in Belize

Bad water and poor sanitation are major causes of illness in much of the Third World. In Belize, happily these are less of a problem than in Belize's larger neighbors, Mexico and Guatemala. All residents of Belize City and nearly all towns have access to safe and adequate water supplies — "pipe water" as it's called in Belize — and close to 70% of rural residents do, according to the Pan American Health Care Organization.

Thanks to the plentiful rain in Belize — from 50 to 200 inches or more per year — drinking water literally falls from the sky, so even if you decide to live in an area without a community water system you can collect drinking water in a cistern. Concrete or plastic cisterns, with accompanying pipes and drains to gather rain from your roof, are sold in building supply stores or can be constructed by local workers, if your home does not already have one. To be safe, rain- water should be treated by filtering or with a disinfectant such as chlorine bleach. Overall, according to the Statistical Institute of Belize, **about 85% of Belizeans have access to potable water.** In short, in most areas of Belize, including nearly all areas of interest to expats, you can drink the water and not worry about getting sick. Increasingly, municipal water supplies in Belize are being privatized. In San Pedro, for example, the water system is run by a company based in the Cayman Islands.

In many areas, **sewage disposal** is less adequate. The Belize Water and Sewerage Authority (WASA), which was privatized in the early 2000s, with majority ownership by a European consortium, operates sewerage systems in Belize City, Belmopan and a few other areas. There is still a lack of facilities in rural areas, and even in urban areas more than one-third of houses do not have adequate sanitation, according to Belize government figures. In rural parts of Belize, refuse disposal is not organized at the community level; households are responsible for the disposal of their own solid wastes. While many homes have reasonably effective septic systems, or at least well-maintained pit latrines, in poorer areas Belizeans dump their household wastes into rivers or the Caribbean Sea.

Life expectancy at birth in Belize is about 70 years, only a little lower than that in the U.S. Heart disease is the leading cause of death from illness for both males and females, but Belizeans, as are Americans, are paying more attention to the causes of heart disease, such as smoking, lack of exercise and a diet high in saturated fats, and the incidence of death from heart disease is declining.

There are no reliable statistics on how many Belizeans **smoke tobacco.** Certainly, the antismoking crusade hasn't progressed as far as it has in the U.S. Few businesses, public buildings or restaurants are smoke free, and some Belizeans feel it is their right to light up anytime and anywhere. My own very unscientific survey of foreigners resident in Belize suggests that a large number, maybe as many as one-half, smoke. Perhaps some of these came to Belize just to be able to smoke without being harassed by the lifestyle police? However, with local brands of cigarettes costing US$25+ a carton and imported brands US$40 or more, the vast majority of Belizeans can't afford the habit.

The leading cause of death in Belize is not illness but traffic accidents. About one-fourth of all deaths in Belize are now due to traffic accidents, even though the vast majority of Belizeans don't own cars. Often the cause of accidents is alcohol-related. Such speed limits as there are in Belize, and most roads have no posted speed limit, don't mean much because Belize has very few traffic enforcement officers. The use of seat belts is now required in Belize, but this rule, too, is rarely enforced. Finally, many Belizeans simply aren't good drivers. Driver's education programs are virtually unknown. Normally you must pass a short written test to get a driver's license and have a medical exam. However, some residents say they have gotten one simply by showing up at your local Transport Department office with the necessary forms, including a certificate from a doctor that you are in good health and two passport-size photos, and paying US$10.

AIDS has become a serious epidemic in Belize, according to health officials. Although government figures are lower, AIDS workers estimate that as many as 7,000 people in Belize are HIV positive. Given Belize's small population of 385,000, this estimate means that about one in 55 Belizeans is HIV positive, thought to be the highest infection rate in Central America. Worldwide, about one in 120 persons is believed to be HIV positive. In Belize, nearly three-fourths of HIV infection is spread by heterosexual contact. The highest number of reported AIDS cases is in Belize and Stann Creek districts. All blood for transfusion in Belize is screened for HIV, with the cost absorbed by the government.

At one time, Belize had on a per capita basis one of the highest incidences of **malaria** in the world, and the highest in Central America. Thanks to a widespread program of spraying for mosquitoes, the incidence of malaria in Belize has been declining from its peak of more than 10,000 reported cases in 1994. In recent years, the number of reported cases has fallen to under 1,000 annually, mostly in remote bush areas and typically among recent immigrants from Guatemala or elsewhere in Central America. Another good thing is that more than 95% of the malaria cases in Belize are the *Plasmodium vivax* strain, which is less dangerous than *Plasmodium falciparum* and can be prevented with the use of chloroquine, a time-tested and fairly inexpensive drug.

Dengue fever is transmitted by another type of mosquito. It causes flu-like symptoms that are unpleasant but which in most cases are not life threatening. Dengue has become epidemic at the end of the rainy season in many countries of Central America, including Costa Rica and Honduras. Dengue exists in Belize, especially during the rainy season, but happily it is not very common. However, in 2009 there was an outbreak of dengue in western Belize. A vaccine has been developed for dengue, but some issues with it has slowed its implementation worldwide. Dengue symptoms can be treated effectively with Tylenol or its generic equivalent. Avoid taking aspirin if you think you have dengue, as aspirin can exacerbate internal bleeding sometimes associated with dengue.

Zika is a risk in Belize, as it is in much of the Caribbean, Central and South America, Mexico and elsewhere. Zika infection during pregnancy can cause serious birth defects and possibly other development issues for newborns.

Both **cholera** and **typhoid fever** are occasionally present in Belize, but only a handful of cases have been reported in recent years.

Insects and other pests can be a concern in Belize. **Mosquitos** are a nuisance in most areas of Belize. Cayo District has the fewest. Bug spray with 30% DEET works well. All **honeybees** in Belize are Africanized. Avoid them at all costs. **Sandflies** are an irritant in many beach and swampy areas. If infected, sandfly bites can lead to serious skin and other problems including Leishmaniasis. An oil lotion such as Avon Skin So Soft drowns the little buggers. In bush areas, a **botfly** or beefworm, with the assistance of a mosquito, may deposit an egg under your skin. The egg grows into a larva, which as it wiggles is unpleasant, not to mention painful. To rid yourself of your little pal, cover the larva's air hole with Vaseline. When it suffocates, remove it with a sterile blade or needle.

As noted elsewhere, there are **scorpions, tarantulas, crocodiles** and a variety of **poisonous snakes** in Belize, as in many other tropical and sub-tropical areas.

Probably the most common ailment of fair-skinned visitors and even residents in Belize is **sunburn.** If you persist in staying out in the sun unprotected, you have a significant risk of developing skin cancer.

The Healthy Belize Lifestyle

Belize could be good for your health. A positive side to the typical Belize lifestyle, especially outside urban areas, is that compared to the usual way of living in developed countries you tend to walk and exercise more, get more fresh air and eat simpler, healthier meals of complex carbohydrates and fresh fruits. One Canadian said that after a year in Belize he went for a health check-up. He found his blood pressure was down 15 points and his weight down 15 pounds. "But what do you expect?" he asks, smiling. "I live on the beach, walk 25 feet to work and eat almost nothing but fresh fish and fruit."

The use of herbal remedies also is common in Belize. Bush doctors or snake doctors often have an extensive knowledge of plants with healing properties. Don Elijio Panti was one of the best known of the herbal healers. He was a Guatemalan by birth but a long-time resident of Cayo in Western Belize who died in 1996 at over 100 years of age. His work was popularized by Rosita Arvigo (with Nadine Epstein and Marilyn Yaquinto) in the 1993 book, *Sastun, My Apprenticeship with a Maya Healer* and in other books. Dr. Arvigo today operates a herbal healing facility near San Ignacio. Many other herbal or snake doctors operate in Belize.

CHECK IT OUT

Belize visitor enjoys a cold Belikin and coconut shrimp

Check-It-Out Trip to Belize

Before you get very far along in thinking about Belize as a place to live, you MUST visit Belize and see it for yourself. Don't sit at your computer dreaming about this little English-speaking paradise – come see for yourself if it's for you.

Entry and Exit Requirements: You must have a valid passport to enter Belize, with at least six months before expiration, but visas are not required for citizens of the U.S., Canada, the U.K. and most Caribbean and European Union countries. You should also have an onward or return ticket. Immigration in Belize won't ask for it, but the airline you fly in on most likely will. Entry is granted for up to 30 days, with renewals of up to a total of six months permitted (renewals cost US$25 per month for the first six months, then US$50 a month.) When leaving Belize by air, there is a US$40 exit fee for those who are not citizens or official residents of Belize, who pay a lower rate. Many airlines include the fee in the ticket price. When leaving by land, at either the Benque Viejo border with Guatemala or Corozal border with Mexico, exit fees total US$20. The same US$20 exit fee applies when leaving Belize by water taxi/ferry – for example, when leaving Caye Caulker or San Pedro, Ambergris Caye, going to Chetumal, Mexico, by boat. Students with ID enjoy a lower rate, and children under 12 accompanied by parents are exempt.

What to Pack and Bring: Belize is a very casual country. You don't need evening clothes or even a coat and tie or other U.S.-style business dress. You'll live in tee shirts, shorts, loose-fitting slacks and casual shirts. A really dressy occasion for men might require a guayaberra or collared shirt and long pants; for women a simple skirt or dress. Leave all your fancy jewelry and Rolex watches at home. They will impress only thieves. Also leave your rain gear at home. It probably will rain, but most raincoats just make you sweat. At most, you could bring a light weight plastic poncho that folds up into a small package.

Here are ideas for your packing list:

Lightweight cotton clothes or quick-drying cotton/synthetic blends.

Comfortable walking shoes. Consider light boots or walking shoes for hiking and sandals for the beach.

Extra swimsuits.

Unlocked cell phone.

Maps, guidebooks and paperback books (if you prefer paper to digital versions). If available at all in Belize, books and maps will cost more than back home and may be out of date.

Cap or hat — be sure it's one that won't blow off in windy conditions on the water.

Sunglasses — the darker the better.

Small flashlight with extra batteries, baggies in various sizes, a roll of duct tape, a large garbage bag, pen and writing pad, and Swiss Army-style knife — with these you can go anywhere and do almost anything.

Replacement battery and memory stick (if needed) for your digital camera — you'll shoot many more photos in Belize than you think you will. Film is readily available in Belize, but it's expensive.

Health kit consisting of your prescription medicines and a copy of your eyeglass prescription, plus aspirin, insect spray with 30% DEET, sunscreen (more than you think you'll need), baby oil or Avon Skin-So-Soft for sandflies, Pepto-Bismol or other tummy medicine, antibiotic lotion, bandages, sun-burn lotion, toilet tissue, moist wipes, seasick pills and other over-the-counter medicines.

Optional:

Lightweight laptop or iPad or other tablet device, useful for getting on the internet at hotels and for storing books and other reading material. Some may prefer to substitute a smartphone.

Battery-operated radio if coming during peak tropical storm and hurricane season (July-November).

Snorkel mask — you can rent snorkel and dive gear in Belize, but rental masks often don't fit well.

Fishing gear.

Cotton sweater or light jacket may be needed in the winter, especially on the water or in the higher elevations of the Mountain Pine Ridge.

Frisbees, baseball-style caps with U.S. sports logos, tee shirts and boxes of crayons make good small gifts for kids. School supplies also make good gifts for children.

Money and Credit Cards: U.S. dollars (bills, not coins) are accepted everywhere in Belize, at a fixed rate of 2 Belize dollars to 1 U.S. dollar, although you often will receive change in Belizean money, or in a mix of Belizean and U.S. money. While there's no need to exchange U.S. dollars, sometimes you will get a better rate than 2 to 1 by exchanging at the border with moneychangers. At times when there's a shortage of U.S. dollars in Belize, you may be able to get up to 2.10 to 2.15 Belize for each U.S. dollar.

Canadian dollars, Euros and other currencies are not widely accepted. These should be exchanged at banks or moneychangers. The Atlantic Bank branch in the newer terminal at Goldson International Airport offers currency exchange. Traveler's checks in U.S. dollars are still accepted by most hotels and at some stores, restaurants and other businesses, but the use of traveler's checks is becoming less common due to the prevalence of ATM machines. You usually need to show your passport when paying with a traveler's check. Banks and some businesses only give about 1.96 Belize to 1 U.S. for traveler's checks.

Visa and MasterCard are widely accepted, except at small shops. American Express is accepted by some hotels and larger businesses. Discover and other cards are rarely accepted. Sometimes there is a surcharge for credit card use, usually 3 to 5% but occasionally more. Surcharges are becoming less common, due to complaints by consumers and moves by credit card issuers. Ask about surcharges before using your card.

In addition to a possible local surcharge, increasingly credit card companies are levying international currency conversion and foreign usage fees, from 1 to 3% or even higher. Most products and services in Belize will be charged in Belize dollars, so the currency conversion charges apply. Even if the charges are listed in U.S. dollars, some credit card companies charge an international exchange fee anytime a charge is made outside your home country. Some American Express, Capital One Visa/MC, Bank of America and other cards have no foreign transaction fees.

As explained elsewhere, most bank offices in Belize have modern ATM machines, and now most accept ATM cards issued outside Belize. If you can't tap your funds with your ATM card, most banks in Belize will issue an advance on your Visa or MasterCard. The fee for this is usually less than US$10, depending on the bank, plus whatever fees and interest your bankcard charges. Getting a cash advance may take a little time and paperwork.

Your bank back home may levy a foreign ATM fee of up to US$5 per ATM use, plus a foreign transaction fee of 1 to 3% of the money withdrawn, and the local bank in Belize may also hit you with a fee, so try to minimize the number of ATM withdrawals you make.

Savvy travelers bring a combination of cash in small U.S. currency denominations, an ATM card and credit cards, and perhaps a few traveler's checks, just in case your cards and cash are stolen or lost.

Clothing: Belize is a very casual place. You don't need evening clothes or a coat and tie or other U.S.-style business dress. Heavy winter clothes are unneeded, though a light cotton sweater will come in handy at times. Most of the year, you'll live in tee shirts and shorts or other casual clothes.

Best Times to Visit: Anytime is a good time to visit, but here are the "best times" for different reasons:

159

Best time to avoid tourists: September-October
Best time to avoid rain: February through April
Best time for lowest hotel prices: After Easter to U.S. Thanksgiving
Best time to visit Northern Belize: December-June
Best time to visit Southern Belize: February-May
Best time to visit Western Belize: November-March
Best time to avoid hurricanes and tropical storms: December-June

Air Travel to Belize: At present, eight international airlines fly to Belize:
Air Canada: seasonal weekly service from Toronto
American: daily flights from Miami, several flights a week from Dallas-Ft. Worth, weekly flights from Los Angeles and Charlotte
Avianca: daily flights from San Salvador, El Salvador
Copa: twice-weekly flights from Panama City, Panama
Delta: daily flights from Atlanta
Southwest: daily flights from Ft. Lauderdale and Houston and non-daily flights from Denver
United: daily flights from Houston, weekly from Chicago
WestJet: thrice-weekly flights from Toronto, weekly flights from Calgary
In addition, Belize-based **Tropic Air** has international flights, mostly less than daily, from Cancún and Mérida, Mexico; Flores and Guatemala City, Guatemala; and Roatán, Honduras.

The international airlines use Boeing 737, Airbus A320 or other smaller equipment to Belize, with the usual tight seating in coach and overpriced seating in first or business class, if there is any seating at all beyond coach.

Flights from Atlanta, Miami, Dallas, Charlotte and Houston take only about three hours of airtime.

One of the chief complaints from Belize travelers is the high cost of airfare. Tickets from the U.S. to Cancun or Cozumel often are one-half the cost of tickets to Belize City. From the chief gateways you can expect to pay US$500 to $900 round-trip. Airlines flying to Belize occasionally have internet specials with prices as low as US$300, but you have to act fast as the windows for purchase and travel are narrow.

Our advice: Sign up for internet fare notices on the airlines that fly to Belize. Keep checking the on-line reservation sites such as Expedia. Also check meta-reservation sites – they compare fares from a variety of sites – such as Kayak.com, Momondo.com and Priceline.com. A travel agent specializing in Belize, such as **Barb's Belize** in Stuarts Draft, Va. (540-337-1103 or toll-free **888-321-2272**, www.barbsbelize.com) may be able to find lower fares for you. The owner, **Barbara Kasak,** is very knowledgeable about Belize.

Another source of airfare deals and hotel and tour bookings in Belize is **Katie Valk,** an American who has lived in Belize for many years. Email her at **Belize Trips** in Belize at info@belize-trips.com or visit www.belize-trips.com. (Note the hypen.) Her U.S. telephone number is 561-210-7015.

Another idea is to fly into Cancún or Cozumel on a cheap scheduled or charter flight and bus it from there. There is now a first-class ADO bus service daily between Cancún and Belize City. Also, there is a water taxi from Chetumal, Mexico, to San Pedro and Caye Caulker. *See below for more information and travel tips.*

Arriving by Air -- What to Expect: The Belize International Airport (also known as the Philip S. W. Goldson International Airport, named after a long-time People's United Party politician) is about 9 miles north of the center of Belize City, off the Philip Goldson Highway (formerly Northern Highway) at Ladyville. The airport is small but fairly modern, having opened in 1990. It is believed to be the only "major" airport in the world with a mahogany ceiling in the original building. A new domestic terminal area opened in late 1998 and since then the runway has been extended. After your airplane taxis to the terminal building, you disembark the old-fashioned way, down a set of moveable stairs. You cross the tarmac and enter the immigration and customs area. Most days, you feel the humidity right away.

The immigration officer will look at your passport and usually ask the purpose of your visit and how long you are staying. You can be granted a visitor's entry permit of up to 30 days, but that's not automatic. If you say you are staying 10 days, the officer may grant only that period or two weeks at most. If you think there's any chance you may want to stay a little longer than your current reservations, be generous about estimating the time you'll stay. The officer will then stamp your passport and enter the arrival and departure date.

From here, you move to a small baggage claim area, where there is a small duty-free shop selling duty-free liquor and a few other items. (When entering Belize, you are permitted to bring in only one liter of alcohol, but you can buy an additional four bottles of booze at the airport arrival duty-free shop, where you need to pay in U.S. dollars.) You then go through customs. Belize has a Green/Red customs system. If you have nothing to declare, you can go through the Green line, though an officer may still ask to see inside your bags. On a typical flight, probably one-third of passengers have at least one bag inspected. Customs and immigrations officers generally are courteous and efficient, though like government officials in many countries they are not known for being overly friendly. Treat them with respect, and you'll be treated similarly. Do not even think of offering a bribe. That is not how things work in Belize, at least not at this level. The entire immigration and customs process usually takes from 15 minutes to half an hour.

After your bags pass customs, you can go into the main airport lobby or out to the taxi or rental car area. Porters are available to assist with bags, if necessary. A tip of US$1 per bag is standard, more if special services are provided. If you are continuing on a domestic flight, move quickly to the Maya Island Air or Tropic check-in area, as the domestic carriers use small airplanes, and they fill up quickly. The rectangular passenger lobby, which is usually bustling with people, has a Belize Bank ATM that provides Belize dollars only, a few tourist shops and airline ticket counters. Upstairs to your left are bathrooms (clean) and a decent restaurant, Global Spice, adjoining the "waving area" with views of the airstrip. There is another restaurant in the newer terminal section, along with a small Atlantic Bank office and ATM, and a bar in the international and domestic departure area.

Taxis are available right outside the passenger lobby door. The cabs at the airport – they have green license plates — are regulated and you shouldn't be ripped off. The fare is fixed at US$25 (BZ$50) to anywhere in Belize City — that's for two persons. Each additional person is US$5, and a small additional amount sometimes may be charged for extra luggage. In Belize, you do not need to tip taxi drivers unless they perform extra service such as carrying luggage, but a trip is always appreciated. There are no buses directly into Belize City from the airport. If you have the energy to carry your bags, you can walk almost 2 miles to the Philip Goldson Highway, or pay a taxi around US$6-7 to take you there, and flag down a bus to take you into Belize City (about US$1).

Rental car kiosks, including local offices of international franchised auto rental companies including Avis, Budget, Hertz and Thrifty, along with locals Crystal, Jabiru and others, are across the street on the other side of the airport parking area, a short distance. There is a small motel, Global Village Hotel, on the Philip Goldson Highway just south of the airport entrance road, and this hotel usually will provide a free shuttle from and to the airport.

Domestic Air: Belize has two domestic carriers, **Tropic Air** (800-442-3435 from the U.S. and Canada, or 501-226-2012 in Belize, www.tropicair.com), which services 11 airports/airstrips in Belize, plus four destinations in Mexico, Guatemala and Honduras; and **Maya Island Air** (501-223-1140, www.mayaislandair.com), which serves 10 airports/airstrips only in Belize.

Tropic Air operates 11 Cessna Grand Caravans (208B), two Gippsland Airvans and three Cessna 172/178s. These aircraft are configured for from three to 14 passengers. Maya Island operates eight Cessna Caravans, three Britten Norman Islanders, one Gippsland Airvan and one Cessna 182 Skylane.

As of 2018, Tropic has scheduled service at Belize City (both the Philip Goldson International Airport and Sir Barry Bowen Municipal Airport), Belmopan City, Caye Caulker, Corozal Town, Dangriga, Orange Walk Town, Placencia, Punta Gorda, San Ignacio/Benque Viejo and San Pedro. Internationally, it services Cancún in Mexico, Flores and Guatemala City in Guatemala and Roatán in Honduras. Maya Island Air has scheduled service at Belize City (both international and municipal airports), Caye Caulker, Corozal Town, Dangriga, Placencia, Punta Gorda, San Pedro and Savannah (across the Placencia Lagoon near Independence). Both airlines also offer charter flights and may offer non-scheduled stops at other airstrips in Belize such as Kanatik in Stann Creek District, Sarteneja in Corozal District or Caye Chapel near Caye Caulker.

Currently, Maya Island Air permits passengers to have one checked bag of up to 50 pounds, one carry-on (such as a computer, briefcase or purse) as a carry-on, all at no charge. Additional checked items are charged excess baggage fees ranging from BZ41 cents to BZ$1.13 per pound, depending on destination. On domestic flights, Tropic Air allows one small carry-on (such as a purse or computer bag, up to 15 pounds) and two free checked bags with size limit of 62 linear inches with a width limited to 30 inches and a height of 15 inches. On Tropic's international flights, the first checked bag up to 50 pounds is free, and additional bags or a bag weighing more than 50 pounds are charged US$35 each.

Domestic flights from the municipal airport, about a mile from the center of Belize City, are cheaper than from the international airport in Ladyville. For example, a Tropic flight to San Pedro on Ambergris Caye costs approximately US$90 one-way from international, and US$58 one-way from municipal. Savings to most other destinations are less significant. You have to pay a cab to transfer from one airport to the other – US$25 for two persons, US$5 for each additional person.

Usually there is little or no savings on roundtrip fares over two one-way fares, but there are exceptions so it's worth checking the airlines' websites. Except for occasional off-season specials, fares are about the same year-round, with no advance-purchase or other discounts. Sometimes you can get a 10% or larger discount by paying cash rather than paying by credit card. It pays to ask.

The airlines fly only during daylight hours, except at peak tourism periods when they have permission to continue flying into San Pedro until all waiting passengers are taken care of. Flights to other destinations in Belize are daytime only.

Which airline is better? In some ways, it's a toss-up. Tropic is larger, with 250 flights daily to 15 destinations in Belize and surrounding countries, but Maya Island, which operates about 100 flights daily, has added several new terminals, at Sir Barry Bowen Municipal in Belize City, Placencia and elsewhere. For most people, the decision comes down to which airline has the more convenient flight on a specific day and time. Fares are similar, although there are some small differences to specific locations.

Are advance air reservations necessary? Except at peak high-season travel periods, you can probably get on a convenient flight without advance reservations. Still, having a reservation gives you an extra edge, and we recommend you book ahead if possible. It's essential you do so at holiday periods such as Easter and Christmas.

Buses: Travel by bus in Belize is inexpensive. You can travel the whole length of the country from the Mexican border in the north to Punta Gorda in the far south for about US$25 or go from Belize City to San Ignacio in the west for US$5 to $6. It's also a good way to meet local people and to get a real feel for the country.

In Belize City, local and the Mexican-based ADO buses use the main bus terminal on West Collet Canal. It is still known as Novelo's, the name of a former bus company. Buses to and from Guatemala stop at the Marine Terminal near the Swing Bridge in Belize City. Other places have a bus terminal or a central point where buses stop.

There now is limited bus service within Belize City. Around half a dozen lines offer service in the downtown area and in the north and west parts of the city. Fares are around BZ$1 to $2.

Bus travel in Belize falls somewhere between the chicken bus experience in rural Guatemala and the deluxe coaches with comfortable reserved seats and videos in Mexico. Belize buses are usually recycled American school buses or old Greyhound diesel pushers. There are two types of buses in Belize – regular buses that pick up and let off passengers on demand, and express buses that are faster because they make stops only at a few places.

The country has a franchised bus system, with the government granting rights for certain companies to operate on specific routes. Belize City is the hub for bus service throughout Belize. Bus companies licensed to operate on the Philip Goldson Highway in the Northern Zone include BBOC, Cabrera's, Chell's, Morales, Tillett's, T-Line and Valencia. (Bus lines subject to change.) Northbound buses depart from Belize City about every half hour from around 5:30 a.m. to 7:30 p.m. Some of the northbound buses continue to Chetumal. Bus companies authorized to operate on the George Price Highway in the Western Zone include BBOC, D&E, Guerra's, Shaw and Westline, with lines changing frequently. Westbound buses depart Novelo's bus station roughly every half hour beginning at 5 a.m., with the last departure around 9:30 p.m. Bus companies operating in the Southern Zone – most running between Belize City and Punta Gorda via Belmopan and Dangriga -- are James Bus Line (the best bus company in the south), Cho, G-Line, Ritchie's and Usher. In addition, several lines are licensed to operate mainly in rural areas of the Southern Zone. These include A-Jay's, Chen, Martinez, Radiance Ritchie and Polanco. Keep in mind that many of these "bus lines" have just one or two buses. The small lines tend to come and go.

In some cases you can make advance reservations with the larger bus operations by calling the bus companies, although most people don't make reservations. If boarding at a terminal, you pay for your ticket at the window and get a reserved seat. If boarding elsewhere, you pay the driver's assistant.

Fuente del Norte (www.grupofuentedelnorte,com) and **Linea Dorado** (www.lineadorada.info) provide bus service between Flores, Guatemala, and Belize City. The fares are around US$25 one-way. In Belize, the buses pick up and drop off at the Marine Terminal near the Swing Bridge in Belize City. The Guatemalan buses are not supposed to pick up or drop off passengers anywhere else in Belize, but drivers sometimes will do so. Fuente del Norte buses also run daily between Flores and San Pedro Sula, Honduras, and San Salvador, El Salvador.

Mexican bus line **ADO** has two express services to Belize City – a daily one from Cancún and one from Mérida (where Belizeans often go for medical care) that runs three or four days a week. The ADO buses are much nicer than Belize buses, with 44 reserved reclining seats, videos, bathroom and air conditioning. From Cancún, the ADO bus leaves from the Cancún bus station in downtown Cancún City. In Belize City, ADO uses the main Belize City bus terminal (still known as Novelo's) located on West Collet Canal.

From Cancún to Belize City, the ADO bus currently departs from Cancún terminal daily at 10:15 p.m., with stops at Playa del Carmen, Tulum, Corozal Town and Orange Walk Town. It arrives in Belize City about 6 or 6:30 a.m. The current fare (subject to increase) is US$35 at current exchange rates. Trip time is about 8 hours.

Shuttles: Another option for traveling around Belize is to use a private shuttle service. There are around a dozen of these shuttle services, some based in Belize City and others in Corozal, San Ignacio and elsewhere. While the shuttles cost more than buses, because they use small vans they are more comfortable and less crowded than buses. In some cases, shuttles will make stops on demand, and some drop and pick up as far away as Cancún. Among the shuttle services in Belize are **Belize VIP Transfer Service** (www.belizetransfers.com) and **Moralez Travel**

Service (www.gettransfers.com), both based in Corozal Town; **William's Belize Shuttle** (www.williamshuttlebelize.com) in Cayo; and **Discounted Belize Shuttles and Tours** (www.discountedbelizeshuttlesandtours.com) and **Belize Shuttles and Transfers** (www.belizeshuttlesandtransfers.com), in Belize City.

Water Taxis: If you are going to San Pedro or Caye Caulker, you have the option of taking a water taxi. There are now two main water taxi companies, with boats that hold up to 50 to 110 passengers, connecting Belize City with San Pedro and Caye Caulker. From Belize City it's a 45-minute ride to Caulker and 75 minutes to San Pedro. Going between Caulker and San Pedro takes about 30 minutes. The water taxi business in Belize is in flux; schedules and rates are subject to change. **Ocean Ferry** (501-223-0033, www.oceanferrybelize.com) boats leave from the Marine Terminal in Belize City at 10 North Front Street near the Swing Bridge. On Caye Caulker, Ocean Ferry uses the front bridge and in San Pedro the pier on the seaside in front of Cholo's. **San Pedro Belize Express** (501-223-2225, www.belizewatertaxi.com) boats leave Belize City from the Brown Sugar dock at 111 North Front Street near the Tourism Village. In San Pedro the terminal is on the front side near the Tackle Box, and on Caye Caulker it is on the pier near Hicacao Street.

Ocean Ferry, which currently has five or six departures daily from each location, charges US$17 one-way or US$32 round-trip between Belize City and San Pedro and US$12 one-way and US$22 round-trip between Belize City and Caye Caulker and also US$12 one-way/US$22 round-trip between San Pedro and Caye Caulker. San Pedro Belize Express, which has around eight or nine departures from each location, charges US$28 one-way and US$38 round-trip between Belize City and San Pedro, and US$18 one-way and US$28 round-trip between Belize City and Caye Caulker or between San Pedro and Caye Caulker.

San Pedro Belize Express also has service every other day between the municipal pier in Chetumal, Mexico, and San Pedro and Caye Caulker, a trip of about 90 minutes to San Pedro, for US$50 one-way Chetumal-San Pedro and US$100 round-trip. To and from Caye Caulker the trip is nearer two hours and is US$55 one-way or US$110 round-trip. Another water taxi company, **Water Jets International** (501-226-2194, www.sanpedrowatertaxi.com) also has service, alternating every other day with San Pedro Belize Express, between Chetumal and San Pedro and Caye Caulker. One-way fares are US$50 between San Pedro and Chetumal and US$55 between Caye Caulker and Chetumal. Round-trip fares are US$100 and US$105 respectively. The fares usually do not exit fees of US$20 leaving Belize. If you have not already paid the fee to Mexico for the Mexican tourist card (FMM), you likely will have to pay this on arrival in Chetumal. The FMM fee currently is 533 Mexican pesos, about US$29 at current exchange rates.

Another company, **Thunderbolt,** has daily service between Corozal Town and San Pedro for US$25 one-way. The trip takes 90 minutes to two hours, and the boat will stop in Sarteneja on demand. In Corozal, the Thunderbolt leaves from the Reunion Pier in the center of town.

A local ferry company, **Coastal Xpress** (www.coastalxpress.com), provides scheduled boat transportation up and down Ambergris Caye, with rates from around US$5 to US$14 one-way.

There are several water taxis daily between Punta Gorda and Puerto Barrios, Guatemala (US$25 one-way). **Requeña** (www.belizenet.com/requena) is probably the best operator. A weekly boat, **D-Express,** (504-9991-0778 in Puerto Barrios) operates between Belize City and Puerto Cortes, Honduras, weekly on Fridays, with stops in Dangriga and Placencia.

From Dangriga to Tobacco Caye, you can arrange a boat (around US$20 one-way) but service is not scheduled. Ask at the Riverside Cafe in Dangriga

The **Hokey Pokey** operates about eight round-trips a day between Independence (Mango Creek) across the Placencia Lagoon, and Placencia (MnM Hardware). Cost is US$5.

Note: **Belize Bus and Travel Guide** (www.belizebus.wordpress.com) is an excellent source of information on bus and other travel options in Belize.

Health: The standards of health and hygiene in Belize are fairly high, similar to that in Costa Rica. Not many visitors become ill from traveler's diseases or from drinking the water. While malaria, dengue fever and other tropical diseases are present in Belize, they do rarely affect visitors in the more popular destinations of Belize. Most travelers to Ambergris Caye or Placencia and other popular areas don't get any special shots or take other precautions before they come. No shots are required for entry into Belize, except for yellow fever if you are coming from an infected area such as parts of Africa. However, it's always a good idea to keep tetanus-diphtheria, Hep A and B and other vaccinations up to date.

Malaria prophylaxis may be advised for mainland travel, especially to remote areas in southern Belize or in Guatemala. Chloroquine, taken once a week, starting two weeks before arrival, is usually all you need in most of the region. Better be safe than sorry. Check with your doctor or the U.S. Centers for Disease Control, tel. 404-332-4559 or visit www.cdc.gov for the latest information. The Zika virus, which can cause birth defects in unborn infants, is lightly present in Belize. Pregnant women should check with their physician before traveling to Belize or anywhere in the region.

The biggest trip-spoiler in Belize is probably sunburn. You're only 18 degrees of latitude north of the Equator, and the sub-tropical sun is much stronger than back home.

Accommodations -- What to Expect: Belize has some 600 hotels, guesthouses, lodges, B&Bs, inns and other lodging places, with about 5,000 total rooms. Most of these are small, owner-operated places; about 70% have 10 or fewer rooms. Only three hotels have more than 100 rooms: the 180-room Ramada Princess Hotel & Casino and the 102-room Radisson Fort George, both in Belize City, and the 106-room hotel at the Las Vegas casino in the Corozal Free Zone.

Travelers to Belize today can expect to find a variety of accommodations to fit almost any budget or preference. Among the uniquely Belizean accommodations are the so-called jungle lodges. These are mostly in remote areas, but despite the remote locations you don't have to forego life's little luxuries, such as cold beer, hot showers and comfortable mattresses. The best of these places, including Chaa Creek in Cayo, Hidden Valley Inn and Blancaneaux in the Mountain Pine Ridge and Chan Chich in rural Orange Walk, are as good as any jungle lodge in the world.

Usually, the birding and wildlife spotting around the lodges are excellent, and they offer all the amenities you enjoy after the day's adventures are done. Most, though not all, have bay thatch cabañas built with a nod to Maya-style construction, but done up in much more luxury and style than traditional Maya cottages. While the top places are first-class in every way, with rates to match — often US$200 to $400 or more a night in season — you don't have to pay much to get an authentic jungle lodge experience. Places like Clarissa Falls, Crystal Paradise and Parrot's Nest, all in Cayo, are bargains.

Another delightful type of lodging in Belize is the casual and small seaside resort. The best of these are sandy barefoot spots, with a friendly Belizean feel you won't find in other parts of the Caribbean. A couple can spend a night at the beach for US$50 to US$150.

All around Belize you can find small places with clean, safe rooms at budget prices. The Trek Stop, Aguada and Casa Blanca in Cayo, Sea Breeze in Corozal Town or Tipple Tree Beya Inn in Hopkins are examples. At these places you can get a nice little room for around US$50 or less.

At the other end of the scale, for those who demand luxury, a whole wave of upmarket hotels hit Belize starting in the 1990s. No longer is it necessary to stay in a hotel with linoleum floors and mismatched furniture. On Ambergris Caye and other cayes, places like Victoria House and The Phoenix have rooms that could earn a spot in *Architectural Digest,* with rates from US$200 to $500+ a night. On the mainland, Chaa Creek's newer digs are gorgeous. Blancaneaux's villas in the Mountain Pine Ridge are luxurious. In a few areas, mainly San Pedro, Caye Caulker and Placencia you can enjoy the extra space of a condo-style unit at a regular hotel-style price. Around the country are all shapes and sizes of personality inns, mostly run by their owners.

Many owners are struggling to earn a decent income, and they can't always afford to have the softest sheets or newest TVs in the rooms. But, whether the owners are Belizean, American, Canadian, British or from a galaxy far, far away, they're almost always friendly and helpful, willing to sit down with you and help you plan your day.

Can you wing it in Belize? Or do you need to book hotels in advance? The answer, except around busy holidays such as Christmas and Easter, used to be that you could just wing it. Average annual occupancy at Belize hotels was under 40%, and rooms in all price levels were plentiful most of the time. However, beginning in the late 1990s, tourism grew to record levels. Quite a few hotels, especially those offering the best value or top service and location, are heavily booked in-season. when visiting Belize in-season, roughly Christmas and March (the busiest month of the year for Belize tourism) through Easter, it's a good idea to book ahead for at least the first night or two. This doesn't mean that if you arrive without reservations you'll have to sleep on the beach with the sand flies — you'll be able to find a room somewhere — but your first choices may well be booked and you may have to spend valuable vacation time hunting for a room. Tours and dive trips can be booked after you arrive.

Belize is wired. Most hotels in Belize have websites and email. You can use their web sites (listings in this book include internet addresses) to help you choose your accommodations, but remember that these sites are advertising and naturally put the best face on things. Nearly all hotels in Belize are small, and though many won't admit it for fear of alienating travel agents and travel wholesalers, they would prefer you book direct, preferably via the internet. That saves them 10 to 25% in agent commissions, plus the cost and trouble of faxing, mailing brochures and telephoning back and forth. In many cases, booking direct also will save you money. Some, but not all, hotels offer discounts for direct bookings via the internet. Many don't advertise this, but it won't hurt to ask. Of course, many of the larger properties in Belize have tapped into the online reservations sites such as Expedia.com and Hotels.com.

The cheapest way to communicate with hotels in Belize is via email. Most hotels in Belize check their email regularly and respond to messages in a timely way, but a few, especially those in remote areas, may not. In addition, many hotels have to deal with spam email seeking bookings, with the scam coming in after the booker sends a credit card number. If you don't get a response to your email, try a phone call.

Eating Well in Belize: We don't know who started the rumor that you can't get a good meal in Belize. The fact is, you can eat gloriously well, at modest prices. Rice and beans is the quintessential Belizean dish, but this is not the rice and beans your momma used to fix — unless she's from Belize or perhaps New Orleans. Rice and beans (or beans and rice, which is slightly different) in Belize means spicy and smoky, with plenty of recado (also known as achiote) and other seasonings, perhaps flavored with salt pork and some onions and peppers and cooked in coconut milk. Usually these are served with a chunk of stew chicken, fish or pork. The whole thing might cost just US$5 or $6 in a pleasant restaurant. If you're not happy in Belize, you're probably not getting enough rice and beans.

Along the coast and on the cayes, seafood is as fresh as the salt air. In-season (mid-June to mid-February) spiny lobster — grilled, broiled, steamed, even fried — is fairly inexpensive and good. But a big filet of snapper or grouper, prepared over a grill with limejuice, is just as tasty and even cheaper. Conch, in season October to June, is delicious grilled or stewed in lime juice as ceviche, but we like it best in fritters, chopped and fried in a light batter.

Every ethnic group in multicultural Belize has its own taste treats. Among them: Sere and hoodut, the best-known Garifuna dishes, fish cooked in coconut milk with plantains. Boil-up is a Creole favorite, fish boiled with plantains, yams and potatoes, and served with a tomato sauce and boiled bread. The Maya dish most popular with tourists is pibil, pork and other meats seasoned, wrapped in banana leaf and cooked slowly in an underground oven. Of course, with Mexico next door, Belize has a wide variety of Mexican dishes, including tamales, burritos, garnaches (corn tortillas fried and topped with beans, salsa and cheese) and panades (deep-fried tortillas filled with fish). A few restaurants serve local game, including iguana, venison and gibnut, a rabbit-like rodent dubbed "the Royal Rat" because it was once served to Queen Elizabeth II.

We find most of the beef in Belize to be poor, although you can get a tasty steak if you look hard enough. But the pork — it's heavenly. The pork chops are tender and flavorful, the bacon a little different from most we've had, but delicious with fresh farm eggs. Only brown eggs are sold in Belize, by the way. For breakfast, fruit is the thing — fresh pineapple, mango, papaya, watermelon, orange. With fry jacks (a sort of fried biscuit, the Belizean version of beignets) and a cup of rich Guatemalan or Gallon Jug Estates Belizean coffee, you'll be set for the day.

For the most part, Belize dining isn't fancy, but even Belize is branching out in some of the newer worlds of cuisine – French, Thai, Vietnamese, Japanese, Italian and more. Extraordinary Italian gelato is delicious at Tutti-Frutti in Placencia.

To drink, there's nothing more refreshing than a fresh limejuice or watermelon juice. Belikin beer may not be up to the high standards of some of the beers of Mexico and Costa Rica, but it's good enough for us, and the Belikin stout will make you strong as an ox. Local rums such as One Barrel are cheap and flavorful.

Nightlife: Many visitors to Belize, after full days of hiking, caving, diving or snorkeling, are just too pooped to stay up late and party. At remote jungle lodges and dive resorts, often the lights go out by 10 p.m. Belize City and Ambergris Caye have the most clubs and bars. Visitors thinking about a tropical romance or a visit to one of the several brothels in Belize City, Orange Walk Town, Cayo or elsewhere should be aware that AIDS is a serious and growing problem in Belize. There are an estimated 8,000 people in Belize with HIV, a large number considering the country's small population of 385,000.

Gambling: A law passed in 1999 permitted gambling, and several casinos have opened in Belize; others are planned. Belize City has the Ramada Princess Hotel and Casino, with about 500 electronic machines plus live tables for poker, blackjack and other games. The Princess also has a branch in San Ignacio and in the Free Zone in Corozal. Two other casinos are in the Free Zone in northern Belize, including the large Las Vegas Casino, where a nice, new, 100+ room hotel associated with the casino opened in late 2015. San Pedro has a gaming spots at Captain Morgan's. In Placencia, there is The Placencia Casino and Sportsbar at The Placencia Hotel and Residences. It has 100 slot machines and six tables for blackjack and poker.

For each area of Belize *(see chapters below)*, we've sketched out the options for getting there, outlined what to see and do and selected our favorite hotels, restaurants and bars in all price ranges. In almost every case, the author has stayed at or eaten at these places (in a few cases we've relied on reports from trusted associates), so you're getting first-hand recommendations.

Of course, you can also use TripAdvisor and other social media sites to get further opinions. Yelp currently does not cover Belize.

Big, modern service station and convenience store near Belmopan

Driving in Belize: Road Update

The roads in Belize are getting better and better. Sure, there still are sections of wash-boarded dirt that will shake your fillings out, but more roads are now paved and even the gravel or limestone byways seem to be scraped more frequently.

A few roads, such as the Southern Highway, are very good indeed, among the best in all of Central America and the equal of many rural roads in the U.S. or Canada. Not too many years ago the Western Highway, now renamed the George Price Highway, was unpaved, the Hummingbird was a nightmare of potholes, the Old Northern Highway was a jungle of tire-stabbing asphalt chunks, the Southern Highway was a mud trap and not even Belize City had stop lights.

Signage, too, is improving, being better than in most of Mexico or the rest of Central America. Most critical turns and junctions are marked. Many roads have mile markers — although some markers on the Southern Highway and elsewhere are missing. Around Belize City, San Ignacio and elsewhere, new signage helps visitors and newcomers navigate to key destinations such as the international airport or the Mountain Pine Ridge.

Main Roads

PHILIP GOLDSON HIGHWAY (formerly Northern Highway). This 85-mile route is a good two-lane surfaced from Belize City to Corozal Town and then a few miles to the border with Mexico at Chetumal. The worst section is in the northern "suburbs" of Belize City. The only thing that will slow you down are a few "sleeping policemen" in villages and slow-moving trucks when the sugar cane harvest is going on in late winter through late spring, and a tollbooth at the bridge over New River (BZ75 cents). There is a handy paved by-pass around Orange Walk Town, which eliminates the need to fight clogged traffic through town. Your first glimpse of the azure waters of Corozal Bay is a highlight of the end of this route.

Overall Road Condition: Very Good (except sections near Belize City)

Paved Section: 100%

Gas Availability: Excellent — there are many gas stations including a few open 24 hours

GEORGE PRICE HIGHWAY (formerly Western Highway). The 78-mile road takes you from Belize City quickly past Hattieville (where there's a roundabout), the Belize Zoo, the capital city of Belmopan, the "twin towns" of San Ignacio and Santa Elena and then on the Benque Road to the Guatemala border. The George Price Highway is being rerouted at Santa Elena. Just past San Ignacio, you hit "cottage country," where a number of excellent lodges offer cold beer and a soft bed under quiet Central American skies. The George Price – usually the section from San Ignacio to Benque Viejo is called the Benque Road -- is still in pretty good condition, and some sections have been resurfaced. More topes (speed bumps) are popping up as the road passes villages. However, the shoulders are narrow, and the surfacing used on parts of this road can be very slick and dangerous after rains. There used to be a big sign warning of the number of deaths on this road in the past 10 years --"240 killed and 1,478 injured." In 2017 the government has announced plans to completely resurface this road.

Overall Road Condition: Good (but some sections very slick after rains)

Paved Section: 100%

Gas Availability: Good to Excellent

HUMMINGBIRD HIGHWAY This 56-mile highway stretches from the George Price Highway at Belmopan to Dangriga. The Hummingbird dips and swoops through some of the most beautiful territory in Belize. This was once a very bad road. Now it is in very good condition, with only a couple of bridges that are still one-lane. Take a break at the Blue Hole, where a swim in the truly blue water is refreshing. Technically, the road is called the Hummingbird for only about 33 miles from the Western Highway to the village of Middlesex, and then it is known as the Stann Creek Valley Road, but everybody calls it the Hummingbird all the way.

Overall Road Condition: Very Good

Paved Section: 100%

Gas Availability: Poor — best to gas up at Belmopan or near Dangriga

SOUTHERN HIGHWAY The Southern Highway, long known as the worst major road in Belize, is now the best major road in Belize. The 100-mile road is all paved. The scenery, save for views of the Maya Mountains at about the halfway point, is mostly unexceptional.

Overall Road Condition: Excellent

Paved Section: 100%

Gas Availability: Fair — best to gas up in Dangriga or near PG; in a pinch, there's gas in Independence and on the Placencia peninsula.

BELIZE CITY The roads and streets of Belize City confuse many visitors. Some streets are not signed, and some are little more than narrow, one-way alleys. Streets abruptly terminate at Haulover Creek, and you have to find a bridge to get from one side to the other. Taxis, bicycles and pedestrians dart in and out of traffic. However, things are getting better. New roundabouts on the Northern Highway have improved traffic flow, though the section of the Northern Highway near Belize City is still in need of resurfacing, and new signage has popped up on main routes. Most streets are paved. Starting in 2012 Belize City had a major road and street program, and many roads have been rebuilt or resurfaced. Belize City is so up-to-date these days it even has a rush hour and traffic jams.

Overall Road Condition: Fair to Good

Paved Section: 95%

Gas Availability: Excellent — modern gas stations have everything that U.S. stations have including convenience stores, except that you don't have to pump your own gas.

Other Important Roads

OLD NORTHERN HIGHWAY If you want to see Altun Ha ruins, you'll have to drive at least part of this 41-mile arc to the east of the Philip Goldson Highway. Under the British, this highway was paved, and at last the Belize government patched some of the remaining blacktop. The section south of Maskall village is better than the section north. Most sections are narrow and some are dirt. The 2-mile access road to Altun Ha is paved.

Overall Road Condition: Fair

Paved Section: 70% (but paved section is narrow, and some is badly potholed)

Gas Availability: Poor – gas up before leaving the Philip Goldson Highway

COASTAL HIGHWAY This 36-mile gravel road, connecting Democracia near Mile 30 of the George Price Highway with the Stann Creek Valley Road near Melinda, is also known as the Manatee Highway or the "Shortcut." Despite the name, you get no views of the water or of manatees from the road. It does save a little time on trips to Dangriga or Placencia from Belize City. However, the road is washboarded in places and is dusty in dry weather. During heavy rains, bridges occasionally wash out. It is far less scenic than the Hummingbird. It's easy to lose control of your vehicle on the gravel. In fact, some car rental companies forbid renters to drive the road, and others increase the amount you're liable for if you do have an accident. Visitors and even experienced residents are often advised to avoid this road and take the Hummingbird Highway instead.

Overall Road Condition: Fair to Poor

Paved Section: 0%

Gas Availability: Poor — gas up in Dangriga or on the George Price Highway

ROAD TO CONSEJO This level 8-mile stretch takes you from Corozal Town to the Chetumal Bay, where there is a Belize customs station (boats only).
Overall Road Condition: Fair
Paved Section: 0%
Gas Availability: Poor

ROAD TO SARTENEJA FROM ORANGE WALK TOWN Once past the paved section near Orange Walk Town, this road just goes on and on, over rough, wash-boarded limestone. It's about 40 miles to Sarteneja village and Shipstern, but it will seem like twice that. A redeeming feature of this road is Progresso Lagoon, the quintessential tropical lagoon. The Belize government has upgraded and paved part of this road, from near Orange Walk to San Estevan and then to Progresso. If you want to go to Cerros instead of Shipstern, you start the same way, but about 12 1/2 miles from Orange Walk Town, and 6 1/2 miles past the village of San Estevan, you go straight instead of turning right; this takes you to Progresso, Copper Bank and Cerros. The road can be tricky after heavy rains. From Corozal Town, take the hand-pulled ferry across the New River, and then a second ferry across Laguna Seca, saving you several hours of driving time.
Overall Road Condition: Fair to Poor (Poor after heavy rains)
Paved Section: 15%
Gas Availability: Fair – best gas up in Orange Walk or in Sarteneja

ROAD TO SARTENEJA FROM COROZAL TOWN From Corozal Town, take the Philip Goldson Highway south toward Orange Walk Town to just south of town (look for signs to the ferry). Turn east, and follow the road (and the power lines) for 2 1/2 miles to the ferry landing. The 90-foot-long, hand-pulled ferry, made from an old sugar barge, carries pedestrians and up to four vehicles on a nine-minute trip across the river. It operates from around 6 a.m. to 9 p.m. daily; there's no charge. When you disembark the ferry, you're about 2½ miles from Copper Bank village, and about 5½ miles from Progresso. Turn left and follow signs to Sarteneja. You'll have to take second ferry across the mouth of Laguna Seca. The road is unpaved and can be muddy after heavy rains.
Overall Road Condition: Fair to Poor (Poor after heavy rains)
Paved Section: 0%
Gas Availability: Fair – best gas up in Corozal Town or in Sarteneja

ROAD TO CHAN CHICH AND GALLON JUG From Orange Walk Town, it's about a three-hour, 68-mile drive to Chan Chich, the stupendous lodge built by the late Sir Barry Bowen. Along the way, on a road that varies from a poor rubble road to an excellent paved road at Gallon Jug, you'll pass a number of villages, some farms, the progressive Mennonite settlement of Blue Creek and plenty of jungle. As you cross the Programme for Belize preserve and Bowen land (you'll have to stop at two guard houses), you'll almost certainly see a variety of wildlife, including Belize's two species of deer and the oscellated turkeys. At San Felipe village, about 23 miles from Orange Walk Town, you can turn on a dirt road to the Lamanai ruins and Lamanai Outpost Lodge, about 13 miles from San Felipe. This road is now passable year-round. An alternate route for the first part of the road to

Lamanai and Chan Chich is the unpaved road from just south of Orange Walk Town through the Shipyard area.

Overall Road Condition: Mostly Fair to Poor, with a few Good to Very Good sections

Paved Section: 15%

Gas Availability: Fair (gas up at the Linda Vista "shopping center" at Blue Creek, run by Mennonites; closed Sunday)

BURRELL BOOM ROAD You have two choices to get to Boom, Bermudian Landing and the Baboon (Black Howler Monkey) Sanctuary: Either turn off the Philip Goldson Highway at about Mile 13, or off the George Price Highway at Mile 15½, at the roundabout. The road to the Boom also functions as a shortcut if going between points on the Philip Goldson and George Price highways, eliminating the need to drive through Belize City. The road is beautifully paved.

Overall Road Condition: Excellent

Paved Section: 100%

Gas Availability: Fair

Note: In mid-2017, plans for a new **Airport Link Road** were announced that would link the George Price Highway, at Mile 8, to the Airport Road near the Philip Goldson International Airport. This 5-mile long road has been funded with a US$12 million international loan.

ROUTE 30 ROAD TO SPANISH LOOKOUT AREA FROM NEAR GEORGEVILLE This part of Cayo will remind you a bit of the Midwest, with well-kept Mennonite farms and modern stores. The road from the George Price Highway near Georgeville to Spanish Lookout, signed as "Route 30" and sometimes called Iguana Creek Road, is a good paved road. Other roads are mostly gravel and better maintained than average, with a few paved sections, especially around Spanish Lookout. Baking Pot Road from Central Farm to Spanish Lookout is unpaved and requires crossing the Belize River on a hand-pulled ferry.

Overall Road Condition: Good (Central Farm route Fair)

Paved Section: 70%

Gas Availability: Good (modern stores and gas stations in Spanish Lookout, and gas often is cheaper here than elsewhere in Cayo)

ROAD TO CARACOL Note: In late 2017, the government announced it has secured loans to completely pave the road to the Caracol ruins. By the route from Georgeville, it is about 46 miles from the George Price Highway to the ruins of Caracol. From San Ignacio, via the Cristo Rey Road, the trip is a few miles longer — this route connects with the Mountain Pine Ridge Road near the village of San Antonio. Even in good weather in a good vehicle, don't expect to average more than about 25 mph on this road — it's a two-and-a-half hour ride to Caracol, even with recent improvements to the road in connection with the Chalillo Dam, including paving near Caracol. Currently you will be much better off going to the entrance to the Pine Ridge on the Cristo Rey Road, rather than the Georgeville

Road, as the Georgeville Road is extremely rough. A reward: the scenery in many spots is lovely. After a heavy rain, the limestone marl or red clay in unpaved sections can be very slick. En route, stop for a cold drink or a hot gourmet pizza at Francis Ford Copolla's lodge, Blancaneaux, about 15 miles in from Georgeville, or at the former Five Sisters Lodge, now Gaia Riverlodge.

Overall Road Condition: Good to Poor

Paved Section: 25% (plans announced to pave entire road)

Gas Availability: Almost none – gas up on the George Price Highway

ROAD TO PLACENCIA This used to be the road people loved to hate. It was a 25-mile mostly dirt and gravel road from the Southern Highway to the tip of the Placencia peninsula, passing Maya Beach and Seine Bight. After heavy rains, the road was occasionally impassable, even with four-wheel drive. Now, however, the road is completely paved and in excellent condition, although it's heavy with speed bumps. Except for the speed bumps (and some huge speed "humps") this road is a joy.

Overall Road Condition: Excellent

Paved Section: 100%

Gas Availability: Fair (stations in and near Placencia village)

SAN ANTONIO ROAD from the "Dump" about 14 miles north of PG at the Southern Highway to the Guatemala border near Jalacte was completed in 2016. It is an excellent and scenic two-lane paved road. A border inspection station has been completed, and a border crossing is planned, but the time of opening hasn't yet been established. Local people do cross here freely, but at present there is no way to have passports and other border documents stamped on either side of the border.

Overall Road Condition: Excellent

Paved Section: 100%

Gas Availability: Fair (best to gas up at the junction to the road to San Antonio)

ROADS TO MAYA VILLAGES IN TOLEDO A series of connected roads take you from the Southern Highway near PG to a number of Mayan villages (and one Garifuna village) north of PG. Except for the excellent new San Antonio Road (see above), these roads vary in quality. Most are unpaved, and some are very rough.

AMBERGRIS CAYE You can't rent a car on the island, although residents seem to be stocking up on pickups and cars, crowding out golf carts, bikes and pedestrians on the caye's roads. Front Street (Barrier Reef Drive), Middle Street (Pescador) and Coconut Drive south to Victoria House and sections of other streets, are now paved, mostly with concrete cobblestones.

The bridge over the river channel, now called the Sir Barry Bowen Bridge, takes golf carts, bikes and pedestrians, plus taxis and other vehicles.

In 2014-2016 part of the former dirt/gravel golf path north of the bridge was paved. It is surfaced some 8 miles north of the bridge. You can rent a golf cart and putt south to near the tip of the island, and also north 7 or 8 miles, and even farther, from the bridge at San Pedro, if you have the time and bug juice. After rains, the unpaved parts of these cart paths are rough and muddy.

Overall Road Condition (island wide): Good to Poor

Paved Section (island wide): +/- 40%

Gas Availability: Fair – there are now several gas stations in San Pedro

CAYE CAULKER Streets in Caye Caulker village are still hard-packed sand. The primary means of transportation are shank's mare, bicycles and golf carts, though a few cars have made their way to the island.

Overall Road Condition: Fair to Good

Paved Section: 0%

Gas Availability: Fair

PRACTICAL TIPS

Maps. The best general road map to Belize is from ITMB. A 6th edition was released in 2005. The color, 1:250,000-scale map retails for US$10.95. There is also a National Geographic Adventure Map to Belize (2012, US$11.95) and other maps, most available from Amazon.com. Also useful for most travelers is the mile-by-mile *Driver's Guide to Beautiful Belize,* formerly published annually by the famous Emory King but now out of print; you can occasionally find an old copy. Some car rental companies provide basic maps.

Gas Stations. Belize has Shell and Esso service stations, along with several private brands, including UNO (a Honduras-based brand with locations around Central America that took over 10 Texaco stations in Belize in 2012) and Jaguar. There are a total of around 80 stations in the country. Unleaded gas averages around US$5 to $6 a gallon, with ups and downs depending on world oil prices. Diesel is usually about 20% less. Skilled mechanics are available, though like mechanics everywhere not always trustworthy, but you can get a tire changed almost anywhere. Someone will come out and pump gas for you, and there's no need to tip, although tips are appreciated. Belize gas stations accept Belize or U.S. dollars, and sometimes credit cards.

Miles or Kilometers? Like the U.S., Belize has been slow to accept the metric system. Distances are given in miles, and gas is sold by the U.S. gallon. However, some Japanese-made rental cars have speed and distance shown in kilometers only, a source of slight confusion on Belize's mile-denominated roads.

Speed Limits. You occasionally see a speed limit sign in Belize, and technically the speed limit on highways is 50 to 55 mph, but there is little traffic law enforcement. Belize drivers, to be charitable, are not always the best in the world. Speeding is common, and road accidents are the leading cause for deaths in Belize.

Sleeping Policemen. Speed-breaker bumps are used to slow traffic coming into residential areas. In many cases, you'll get no advance warning about the bumps, but expect them as you enter any town or village and occasionally elsewhere.

Check Points. Check points are fairly common, but almost always in the same place, so everybody knows where they are. Unlike in some other countries in the region where shaking down gringos in rental cars is a small industry, in Belize you will not be pulled over for phony traffic offenses, and if you are stopped at a checkpoint, which often happens, no one will promote a bribe. Just answer the questions, if any, and you'll be on your way, perhaps with a smile and wave from the police officer. All cars must have insurance. If you don't have insurance, you'll face the consequences, including possibly some time in jail.

Safety. As noted, traffic accidents are the number one cause of death in Belize. Belize drivers are often not well trained, and driving after drinking is unfortunately common. Seatbelts are required, but many people don't use them. Watch carefully when passing stopped buses — people may suddenly dart around the bus to cross the road. Outside of settled areas, you may drive for a half hour or more and never see another car. Be prepared: Bring water, a flashlight and other basic supplies, and a cell phone, just in case. In a poor country like Belize, anyone driving a car is, *ipso facto,* wealthy. Don't leave valuables in your car, locked or unlocked. In Belize City and elsewhere, including in larger towns it's best to park in a secured lot, or at least in a well-lit area. Cars left overnight on deserted rural roads are ripe for the picking. Do not pick up hitchhikers, unless you know them or are sure they're okay.

Driving at Night. Driving at night in developing countries is seldom a good idea, but in Belize night driving is a little easier than elsewhere because there are fewer people on the roads after dark. Foxes, cattle, goats and snakes, yes; people, not so many. Still, after dark it's hard to see potholes and topes, and there are people in the streets in Belize City and on roads in the towns and villages. Animals such as goats and cow may wander on or sleep on rural roads.

Best Vehicles for Belize. Do you really need four-wheel drive in Belize? On the main thoroughfares such as the George Price and Philip Goldson highways, no. In the dry season, even back roads generally are passable without four-wheel drive if you have sufficient road clearance. But four-wheel drive is good insurance, just in case you hit a stretch of soft muck or sand. On long trips in Belize, usually there are a couple of occasions when four-wheel power comes in handy. After a period of heavy rains, some back roads become quagmires.

The vehicle of choice in Belize is a four-wheel drive diesel truck with crew cab. A lot of people swear by Toyota Hilux diesels. Larger vehicles such as the Toyota Prado offer a smoother ride on washboard roads, and the large petrol tank cuts down on the need to stop for gas so frequently. However, these are very expensive cars to buy, and rental rates on these large vehicles are high — US$80 to $110 day or more in most cases, plus taxes. Get a diesel if possible, as mileage is usually good and diesel fuel costs less than gas.

Tips on Rental Cars in Belize

When visiting Belize on a scouting trip or just for vacation, having a rental car is a real plus. You can go places not easily visited by bus, and while rental prices are not cheap, you may more than pay for the cost of the rental by avoiding high-priced tours. Here are questions to ask and things to check BEFORE driving off in your rental. Keep in mind that a breakdown on a deserted road in Belize is not like a breakdown in Suburbia, USA.

• **Check the mileage on the vehicle you've been assigned.** Even "name brand" renters often have high-mileage cars in their fleet, and local companies more often than not will provide a car with 50,000 to 100,000 miles on it, or more, (but usually in good mechanical condition.) If the mileage seems high, ask for another vehicle.

• **Check the tires.** High-quality radials or six-ply truck tires are best for Belize roads. At the very least, tires should have plenty of tread. Also, check the spare, and be sure you know how to locate and use the jack.

• **Agree on pre-existing dents and scratches.** Most car rental agencies will point out existing dents and mark them on your rental agreement form. Walk around the car with the agent to be sure major problems, such as a cracked windshield, is noted on the form. You might consider taking a photo of the vehicle. But don't stress about this, as the rental companies are almost always fair about this and in most cases aren't trying to rip you off.

• **Ask what will happen if you have a breakdown somewhere in the boondocks.** Major companies, such as Crystal, will send a mechanic out to repair the problem. Others may not.

• **Don't be shy about asking for discounts off published rates.** During busy times, discounts are probably not available, but in the off-season or during slow periods you may be able to negotiate a little on rates.

• **Determine in advance whether you need to accept Collision Damage Waiver/Loss Damage Waiver coverage.** CDW/LDW, which is a waiver, not an insurance product, runs about US$14 to $20+ per day in Belize, and often the basic plan does not cover the first US$500 to $1,000 in damage — so you have to cough up for a windshield broken by a flying rock, for example. American Express and some other credit cards DO provide primary CDW coverage in Belize, but you probably need to pay for a premium credit card plan to get coverage for off-road travel and for larger SUVs and trucks. Call your card issuer to confirm. Note that liability insurance, required in Belize, is provided on rental cars, but liability insurance does not cover damage to your rental vehicle.

Traffic in Belize City

Belize City

Note: *It's unlikely you will want to live in Belize City, unless you have work or a business there, but we're including it because it's the arrival point for most visitors to Belize, as well as being the commercial, transportation and cultural hub of the country.*

BUG OUT RATINGS

Ratings are on an A to F scale, just like your old high school report card. A is the top grade; F is failing. Grades are relative compared to other areas in Belize.

Popularity with Expats	D
Safety	D-
Overall Cost of Living	C-
Real Estate Bargains	C-
Investment Potential	B-
Leisure Activities	C+
Restaurants	B+
Cultural Activities	A-
Infrastructure	B+
Business Potential	B-
Medical Care	B+
Shopping	A-
Farming & Ranching	F
Safety in Nuclear War	D

179

Sustainable Living	D-
Overall Bug Out Rating	**D**

ADVANTAGES TO BELIZE CITY: • Access to good restaurants and social and cultural activities • Business and transportation hub of the country • Availability of stores and shopping, some with lower prices • Good medical care

Belize City has a bad rep among visitors and even among Belizeans from other areas, who sometimes dread visiting the "big city" with its rude layabouts and drug touts. In truth, the city is hardly more than an oversized town, with ramshackle buildings set close to the street in the central areas but also with its share of stately old colonial houses in the Fort George section and early 19th century landmarks such as St. John's Anglican Cathedral and the House of Culture, formerly Government House. And while crime is a considerable problem – hardly a weekend goes by without a murder or three – crime in Belize City is nothing like that you'd experience in the much bigger and meaner cities of the region such as Guatemala City and Tegucigalpa.

The city has an energy of its own. By day, Front, Queen and Albert streets swarm with shop clerks and shoppers. Restaurants are packed at lunchtime. On Regent Street you'll find lawyers and judges dressed in British-style robes. Day trippers from the cruise ships that now call on Belize City – nearly a million passengers make port here annually, much to the dismay of many resort and ecolodge owners who fear the impact of hordes of cruise tourists on environmentally sensitive ruins, caves and cayes – get on vans and boats for their shore excursions. (Some of the cruise tourists are being siphoned off to Southern Belize, with the debut of the Norwegian Cruise Lines cruise port on a caye off Placencia village.)

Everywhere you'll hear the sound of Creole being spoken, as local residents greet friends and lovers amid a happy Caribbean-style gumbo of sounds and smells. At night, despite the street crime, Belize City lights up with parties, gallery openings and political and professional meetings, as Belize City remains in all but name the true political, as well as cultural, commercial and social, capital of the country.

Belize City Practicalities

As the largest urban area and commercial hub of the country, Belize City offers most of the amenities of a town of similar size in the U.S. or Canada, although don't expect to find international big box stores like Home Depot or Best Buy.

Airlines: Belize City is the transportation hub of the country and offers more than 50 domestic flights a day by Maya Island Air (www.mayaislandair.com) and Tropic Air (www.tropicair.com) from two Belize City area airports to major destinations in Belize and to Guatemala, Honduras and Mexico. The international airport is served by major airlines including Air Canada, American, Avianca, Copa, Delta, Copa, Southwest, United and WestJet.

Goldson International Airport at Ladyville near Belize City

Buses: More than a dozen bus companies leave from the terminal in the Collet Canal area west of the city center. This terminal is still called Novelo's, though the original Novelo's bus line, for which it was named, no longer operates.

Taxis: Most taxi trips within the city cost US$5 or less. The rate to and from the city and the international airport is fixed at US$25 (for two people, each additional person US$5).

Banks: All five of Belize's domestic banks -- Atlantic Bank, Belize Bank, Heritage Bank, National Bank of Belize and ScotiaBank Belize -- have offices and ATMs in Belize City. The larger banks have multiple offices, in several cases along with their international banking (offshore) subsidiaries. Branches in the "suburbs" have drive-up windows.

Embassies: Some diplomatic missions to Belize maintain their offices in Belize City rather than Belmopan. However, the U.S. Embassy moved to a new US$50 million compound in Belmopan in 2006.

Groceries: The two largest supermarkets in the Belize City area — indeed in all of Belize — are Save-U (San Cas Plaza by Belcan Bridge, 501-223-1291) and Brodies (Mile 2½, Philip Goldson Hwy., 501-223-5587, www.brodiesbelize.com). Both are modern supermarkets with air-conditioning and free parking. Brodies was greatly expanded and redone in 2007. They both have pharmacies and sell liquor, beer and wine. Brodies also has a fairly extensive dry goods section. There is another, older Brodies downtown. Premium Wine & Spirits (166 Newtown Barracks, 501-223-4984) has a good selection of imported wines.

Restaurants: Belize City has many good restaurants in all price ranges.

Among the favorites are the Riverside Tavern, Celebrity Restaurant, Nerie's, Sahara Grill and Chon Saan Palace.

Other Stores: While there is no Walmart or Costco, Belize City does have a number of larger stores where you can buy appliances, hardware, home furnishings and construction supplies. Among them: Mirab Department Store (501-223-2933, www.mirabsbelize.com, for appliances, home furnishings and other items); Courts (501-223-0775, www.shopcourts.com/belize, for electronics and other goods); Benny's Home Center (501-227-3347, www.bennys.bz, for construction supplies); and Hofius (501-227-7231, www.hofiusbelize.com), a hardware store with a good reputation for appliances and kitchen equipment.

Car Dealers: Among the new car dealers in Belize City are those selling Ford, Toyota, Mitsubishi, Land Rover, Suzuki, Hyundai, Kia, Isuzu, Nissan, Dodge and Jeep.

Medical: Belize City is the medical center of Belize, with the largest hospital (Karl Heusner Memorial Hospital, Princess Margaret Dr., 501-223-1548, www.khmh.bz) and by far the largest number of physicians, dentists and other healthcare professionals. Belize Medical Associates (5791 St. Thomas St., Kings Park, tel. 501- 223-0302) is a 25-bed private hospital. (*See the Health chapter for other listings.*)

Among the several dozen physician practices in the city are Family Medical Center (3 Newtown Barracks, 501-223-2647, email b.e.bulwer@btl.net) and Caribbean Shores Medical Center (5756 Princess Margaret Dr., 501-224-4821, email fdsmith@btl.net). Among recommended dentists are Dr. Osbert O. Usher Dental Clinic (16 Magazine Road, 501-227-3415) and Heusner's Professional Dentistry (42 Albert Street, 501-272-2583).

Infrastructure: Belize City has the most advanced electrical, water, sewerage and internet/telecommunications systems in the country. Larger villages in rural Belize District also are generally well served, but more remote areas are exceptions.

Real Estate

Few expats will choose Belize City as a place to live, unless they need to be there for business reasons. Those that do likely will live in the suburbs north and west of the city, such as Bella Vista and Belama, or in the more upscale areas of town along Princess Margaret Street, King's Park and West Landivar. Homes in these areas are priced similarly to homes in nice areas of mid-sized U.S. cities, with prices of several hundred U.S. dollars for homes not being unusual.

Secure apartment rentals also are not cheap: You can expect to pay around US$1 to $3 per square foot per month, or about US$1,000 to $3,000+ a month for a 1,000 sq. ft. two-bedroom apartment, and more for luxury condos such as those in Renaissance Towers and Marina Towers.

Residential areas around Belize City range from upscale suburbs to poor villages. Ladyville near the international airport has subdivisions and a variety of businesses. Farther north in Belize District, Crooked Tree is a pleasant Creole village with a lagoon setting. To the west, Hattieville is a sprawling residential area that sprang up after Hurricane Hattie in 1961. To the south off the Coastal Highway, Gales Point, another Creole village, enjoys a beautiful setting between the sea and lagoons.

Properties Offered in and around Belize City

Here are some offerings, from individuals and real estate firms in 2018. Prices shown are asking prices:

• Small, two bedroom, one bath concrete block bungalow in Belama Phase 4 Extension, on 60' x 100' corner lot across from a small park, some repairs needed, US$40,000

• Three bedroom, two bath 2,400 sq. ft. split level concrete home in desirable Belama Phase 3 area, fully equipped kitchen, backyard and fenced parking, US$200,000

• New two bedroom, two bath condo with sea view in Northern suburbs of Belize City between international airport and city center, US$170,000, 40% down, balance bank financed

• 4,000 sq. ft., five bedroom, 3½ bath modern seafront home in exclusive Driftwood Bay area, with swimming pool, boat dock, garden and a separate 1,200 sq. ft. building for an office or staff. US$750,000

• Residential building lot in Belama Phase 3, 50'x90', river frontage, all utilities, US$32,000

• Restored Colonial building in the heart of downtown Belize City, 1,200 sq. ft., now used as offices, US$145,000

• 19 acres in rural Belize District near Altun Ha Maya site, US$35,000.

Real Estate Agents

Most of these real estate agencies have listing in other parts of Belize as well as in Belize City.

4 Realty Ltd. (Carlos Habet), 115 Barrack Rd., Belize City, 501-610-4186, www.4realtybelize.com

Belize Land Properties Ltd., 551 Buttonwood Bay Blvd., Belize City, 501-621-4754, www.belizelandproperties.com

Buy-Belize Real Estate, 2118 Guava St., Belama Phase 1, Belize City, 501-223-2121, Belize City, www.buy-belize.com

Century 21 BTAL, 1 Mapp St., Belize City, 501-224-5420, www.century21belize.com

Emerald Futures Real Estate, Mile 3 ½, Northern Hwy., Belize City, 501-670-6818, www.emeraldfutures.com

Vista Real Estate, 13 Cork St., Belize City, 501-223-2427, www.belizerealestate.bz.

Visiting Belize City

Coming into Belize you most likely will land in Belize City. Many Belize travelers will tell you the best way to see Belize City is through your rear view window. However, with an open mind to its peculiarities, and with a little caution (the city has drug, gang and crime problems, though this rarely affects visitors, and the areas usually frequented by visitors are watched by tourist police), you may decide Belize City has a raffish, atmospheric charm. You might even see the ghost of Aldous Huxley or Graham Greene at a hotel bar.

Getting to Belize City

Belize City is the hub of transportation in Belize. *For information on how to get to Belize City, see the chapter on Visiting Belize on a Check-It-Out Scouting Trip.*

What to See and Do in Belize City

Belize City, if nothing else, has character. It's full of interesting faces, streets full of color and charming old colonial houses. The city rewards the travelers with a surprising number of interesting sights and memorable places, among them the colonial-era buildings in the **Fort George** and **Southern Foreshore** sections. For the most part, the colonial buildings are wood with zinc roofs.

Belize is divided into the North Side and South Side, with the Swing Bridge effectively diving the two sides. The Fort George section on the North Side is bordering the Belize City Harbour, is Belize City's most photogenic area.

There are at least a half dozen buildings and sights especially worth seeing, including the Fort George Lighthouse, the Museum of Belize and the Swing Bridge, the Supreme Court Building and St. John's Anglican Cathedral House of Culture. These are described briefly below, roughly from north to south. The Fort George Lighthouse and Bliss Memorial and the Museum of Belize are on the North Side of the city. As noted, the Swing Bridge divides the North and South Sides. The Supreme Court, House of Culture and St. John's Cathedral are on the South Side.

All of these places are safe enough to visit during the day, but should be avoided after dark unless you are with people who know the area. At the very least, take a taxi to them.

Fort George Lighthouse and Bliss Memorial. Fort George Point, Fort George area, North Side. Admission free. The Fort George Lighthouse, on the tip of Fort George Point near the Radisson Fort George Hotel, was designed and funded by Belize's great benefactor, Baron Henry Edward Ernest Victor Bliss. The Edwardian nobleman never actually set foot on the Belizean mainland, but he sailed his yacht in the 1920s to the coast of British Honduras. For unknown reasons, in his will he bequeathed most of his fortune to the people of Belize. The date of his death in 1926, March 9, or on a weekend date close to it, is celebrated as a national holiday. Bliss is buried here, in a small mausoleum perched on the seawall.

Museum of Belize. 8 Gabourel Lane, North Side, 501-223-4524, www.museumofbelize.org, open Tuesday-Friday 9-4:30, Saturday, 9-4, admission US$10. This fascinating if small museum was the main Belize City jail from the 1850s to 1993. Displays on Belize history and culture include ancient Mayan artifacts, colorful Belize postage stamps, colonial-era bottles and an actual jail cell. Exhibitions change regularly.

Swing Bridge. The bridge spanning Haulover Creek actually swings, when needed to allow a boat through or by special request of visiting dignitaries. Four men hand-winch the bridge a quarter-revolution so waiting boats can continue upstream. The large creek over which it swings was so named because before the bridge lifestock were "hauled over" the stream, an inlet of the Belize River. The bridge, made in Liverpool, England, opened in 1923. It was upgraded in 1999. It's the only one of its kind left in Central America and one of the few in the world.

Near the Swing Bridge at 91 Front Street is the **Image Factory** (501-223-4093, www.imagefactorybelize.com, open 9-5 Monday-Friday, 9-noon Saturday), an art gallery and foundation that is the focus of Belize's contemporary art and cultural scene. The Image Factory also has a nice selection of books on Belize for sale.

Belize Supreme Court. Regent St., South Side. The 1926 Belize Supreme Court building was modeled after its wooden predecessor, which burned in 1918. The current building, of reinforced concrete painted white, has filigreed iron stair and balcony rails, similar to what you might see in New Orleans (the construction company was from Louisiana) and above the balcony a four-sided clock. Belize's Supreme Court for Belize and Cayo districts meets here four times a year (there are two other Supreme Court buildings, one in Corozal Town and one in Dangriga.) You can't enter the building, but you can admire it from the outside.

House of Culture. Regent St., South Side, 501-227-3050, www.nichbelize.org, open Monday-Friday 8:30-5 (until 4:30 p.m. Friday), admission US$5. Formerly Government House, the city's finest example of colonial architecture is said to have a design inspired by Sir Christopher Wren. Built in 1814, it was once the residence of the governor-general, the queen's representative in British Honduras. After Hurricane Hattie in 1961 the house became a place for tony social functions, weddings and a guesthouse for visiting VIPs. Queen Elizabeth stayed here. Now it's open to the public. It underwent a renovation in 2017. View art, silver, glassware, and furniture collections.

St. John's Cathedral. 8 Albert St. at Regent Street, South Side, daily 8-7, admission free. This cathedral, built staring in 1812, is the oldest Anglican church in Central America and the only one outside England where kings were crowned. Four kings of the Mosquito Coast (a British protectorate in Honduras and Nicaragua) were crowned here. The cathedral, built of brick brought to British Honduras as ballast on English ships, is thought to be the oldest building in Belize, other than Mayan structures. Its foundation stone was laid in 1812. The roof is constructed of local sapodilla wood, with mahogany beams.

Suburbs

Outside the downtown area to the west of the city, **Old Belize** (Mile 5, George Price Highway, 501-222-4129, www.oldbelize.com) has a cultural and historical museum (open daily 10-8:30, admission varies, a beach area, a zip line, waterslide and a marina.)

To the north of the city center, **Travellers Liquors Heritage Center** (Mile 2½, Philip Goldson Hwy., open Monday-Friday 8-5, 501-233-2855, www.onebarrelrum.com) is a small museum dedicated to the history of Traveller's brand rum, and rum in general, in Belize. You can enjoy free samples and watch rum being made in the back.

Belize City Lodging

The price level for lodging in all areas is as follows:

Inexpensive: Under US$75

Moderate: US$75-$150

Expensive: US$151-$300
Very Expensive: Over US$300
Prices are for a double room in high season (usually late November to Easter). Rates, which do not include taxes, service charges or meals (except in some cases breakfast), may be higher during holiday periods, especially Christmas and New Years. If specific prices are mentioned, they are plus 9% hotel tax and in some cases a service charge, usually 10%.

Lodging is listed alphabetically within each location.
City Centre Area
Great House, 13 Cork St., 501-223-3400, www.greathousebelize.com. The Great House offers spacious air-conditioned rooms with polished pine floors in a modernized and expanded colonial house, originally built in 1927. It is in the historic Fort George area, located a short stroll from the harbour and directly across the street from the Radisson Fort George. All 12 rooms, half on the second and half on the third floor (there's no elevator), have a balcony, private bath, mini-fridge, safe, TV and phone. There is also a pretty good, if somewhat pricey, restaurant in the courtyard, the Smoky Mermaid. **Expensive.**

Radisson Fort George Hotel and Marina, 2 Marine Parade, 501-223-3333 or toll-free from U.S./Canada, 800-333-3333, www.radisson.com/belize-city-hotel-bz/belize. This is the flagship of the city's international-style hotels, and the most expensive, though you may be able to get reductions from the rack rates. As the Fort George Hotel, it was the first major hotel built in the country, opened in 1953 with 36 rooms. Today, all rooms have cable TV, fridge and minibar, and those in the Club Wing, reached by the only glass elevator in Belize, have sea views. Most of the rooms, including those in the Villa Wing (once a Holiday Inn) across the street, have been remodeled. There are good restaurants, a bar, and the grounds are an oasis of calm on the edge of the sea. The hotel has two pools and a private dock. The marina can take large boats of up to 250 feet in length with a 10-foot draft. Management is solid, and the staff is friendly and helpful. **Expensive.**

Near International Airport and Between Airport and City Center:
Best Western Biltmore Plaza, Mile 3½ Philip Goldson Hwy., 501-223-2302, toll-free U.S./Canada 800-528-1234, www.belizebiltmore.com. If you want a U.S.-style motel, this is it. This Best Western franchise is between the international airport and downtown. It does have a pool and an okay bar, but the restaurant isn't much. Go to the Sahara Grill across the highway instead. Parking, while limited, is in a guarded and fenced lot. "Deluxe" rooms are worth the extra cost. **Moderate to Expensive.**

Black Orchid Resort, 2 Dawson Lane, Burrell Boom Village, 501-225-9158, www.blackorchidresort.com. This is a relaxing, if somewhat pricey, alternative to the crime and bustle of Belize City, and it's about the same distance from the international airport as the city center. The Belizean-owned resort is on the Belize River, and you can launch a canoe, kayak or other boat from the hotel's dock, or just laze about the riverside swimming pool and thatch palapa. Sipping a cold drink. There are gardenview and riverview rooms, which are more expensive. New luxury suites top out around US$300 with tax and service. The on-site restaurant serves Belizean food and gets quite a few locals. Tours are available. **Expensive.**

186

D'Nest Inn, 475 Cedar St., 501-223-5416, www.dnestinn.com. D'Nest Inn is a B&B run by Gaby and Oty Ake. Gaby is a retired Belize banker, and Oty is originally from Chetumal. The Caribbean-style house is on a canal 50 feet from the Belize River. It's in an area called Belama Phase 2, a generally safe, middle-class section between the international airport and downtown. Oty's gardens around the house are filled with hibiscus, roses and other blossoming plants. The four guest rooms – all on the second floor up a flight of stairs – are comfortable rather than deluxe, furnished with antiques such as a hand-carved, four-poster bed, but they also have modcons like free wi-fi, air-conditioning and cable TV. Some could use a little sprucing up. With a private entrance and your own key, you come and go as you like. Rates are US$82-92 double and include a delicious breakfast. Recommended, mainly due to the gracious hospitality by the owners. **Moderate.**

Global Village Hotel, Mile 8½, Philip Goldson Hwy., 501-225-2555, www.globalvillagehotel.com. If you have an early morning flight out or you're overnighting en route somewhere else, the Global Village Hotel (actually it's more of a motel than a hotel) is a decent choice near the international airport. The 40 rooms are clean and modern, at around US$55 double, including a basic continental breakfast and free airport shuttle. This Chinese-owned place is located just south of the turnoff to the international airport. **Inexpensive.**

Villa Boscardi, 6043 Manatee Dr., Buttonwood Bay, 501-223-1691, www.villaboscardi.com. This quiet and tasteful bed and breakfast is in an upscale part of Belize City north of the city centre, It's often rated the best B&B in the city. In fact, it's near the current prime minister's home. European-owned, Villa Boscardi has eight clean, attractive rooms, all with air conditioning, private bath, fan, desk, hair-drier, cable TV, wi-fi and phone. **Moderate.**

Dining in Belize City

In addition to the better choices listed below, greasy fried chicken is available as takeaway from small restaurants all over the city — a Belizean favorite known as "dollah chicken" whatever the price. The big hotels have their own restaurants, quite expensive but with varied menus and good service.

If you're shopping for groceries while in the city centre, **Brodies** is worth a look. It's on Albert Street, just past the park, and their selection of food is good if expensive, reflecting the fact that much is imported. Milk and dairy products, produced locally by Mennonite farmers, are delicious and good quality. Naturally enough, local fruit is cheap and plentiful, though highly seasonal — Belizean citrus fruits are among the best in the world. Fruits and vegetables are available at the Queen Square market near the Novelo's bus station. It has been renovated. Two modern supermarkets, a branch of **Brodies** and **Save-U**, are on the Northern Highway on the way to the international airport. This Brodies outpost has been remodeled and expanded, with dry goods as well as groceries, and is the largest and most modem supermarket in the country.

Most restaurants in Belize City are closed for lunch on Sunday, and many are closed all day. Some are also closed for lunch on Saturday.

The price level for restaurants in all areas is as follows:

Inexpensive: Under US$7
Moderate: US$8-$19

Expensive: US$20-$39
Very Expensive: Over US$40
Prices don't include tips or alcoholic drinks. If not otherwise stated, the price range is for one person for dinner.

Restaurants here are listed alphabetically.

Celebrity Restaurant, Volta Building, Marine Parade, 501-223-7272. The wallpaper in the main dining room takes a little getting used to, but the menu is extensive with lots of seafood, the staff is very friendly and the local buzz at this busy restaurant is a plus. Safe parking in a guarded lot. Recommended. **Moderate to Expensive.**

Hour Bar & Grill, 1 Princess Margaret Dr., Marine Parade, 501-223-3737. You don't go here so much for the food, which is mediocre, as for the view of the sea and for the happy hour atmosphere. Safe parking. **Moderate to Expensive.**

Neries and Neries II, Daily St., 501-224.5199, with another location at Douglas Jones St., 501-223-4028, www.neries.bz. Popular local joints, serving Creole favorites including cowfoot soup, barracuda, stew chicken and gibnut. Open for breakfast, lunch and dinner. **Inexpensive to Moderate.**

Riverside Tavern, 2 Mapp St. at North Front St., 501-223-5640. Opened in 2006, this Bowen family-owned restaurant is perhaps the best all-around dining and drinking spot in the city. It's still our favorite spot, too. Riverside Tavern has the biggest and best burgers in Belize City and arguably in all of Belize, with a variety of other well-prepared dishes, including steaks. You can dine outside overlooking Haulover Creek or inside in cold air-conditioning, with views of the large bar and its TV sets. Parking is safe, in a fenced, guarded lot right in front of the restaurant. Recommended. **Moderate to Expensive.**

Sahara Grill, Vista Plaza, Mile 3½, Philip Goldson Hwy., 501-203-3031, serves reasonably priced Lebanese/Middle Eastern food. Try the chicken kabobs, falafel or hummus. Popular lunch spot, but also open for dinner. Closed Sunday. **Inexpensive to Moderate.**

Bird's Isle, 90 Albert St., South Side, 501-207-2179, is an institution in Belize City. Its location on the water is still nice, and you'll be made welcome. If going after dark take a taxi. **Moderate.**

Where to Party in Belize City

Unless you know the city well, and go out with friends, it's best to do your drinking and partying at the bars of the city's main hotels, such as the Radisson Fort George and Ramada Princess Hotel & Casino, or in the more upscale restaurants, such as the Riverside Tavern. Don't venture out alone after dark in Belize City. If you need to go somewhere, take a taxi.

Rural Belize District Near Belize City
BABOON SANCTUARY

The **Community Baboon Sanctuary** (Burrell Boom village, 501-245-2009, open 8-5 daily, admission US$7) is a community organization of around 200 members in seven villages who banded together in 1985 to protect black howler monkeys, called baboons by local people. The effort was successful, and there are now about 3,000 monkeys in the sanctuary. Spend a few minutes in the small visitor center and then take a guided tour to see monkeys. **Black Orchid Resort** *(see above)* is nearby, as is **Belize River Lodge** (501-225-20002, www.belizeriverlodge.com), the oldest fishing lodge in Belize.

CROOKED TREE

Crooked Tree, a reference to the crooked cashew tree, is famous for the number and variety of birds that flock here, especially in the dry season (February to early June). The sanctuary and village are a little over 30 miles north of Belize City. You may see the jabiru stork, the largest bird in the Americas. It stands nearly as tall as a human, with a wingspan of up to 12 feet. Even if you're not a birder, you'll appreciate the beauty of the Crooked Tree lagoon. Coming from the Philip Goldson Highway across the causeway toward Crooked Tree village, an old and predominantly Creole settlement, you'll see cattle cooling themselves in the lagoon, with their egret pals. (Plans are underway to pave the causeway soon.) Check in at the visitor center at the end of the causeway. You'll get a map and can walk or drive around the village, nearby bush trails and the lagoon front. Or ask about a local guide. Canoes are available for rent, too. Admission: US$4.

Crooked Tree Lodge. Crooked Tree Wildlife Sanctuary, 501-626-3820; www.crookedtreelodgebelize.com. Formerly Paradise Lodge, this lodge on more than 11 acres was rebuilt and redone by a Belizean-English couple. It's now a fine place to stay in Crooked Tree. There are six nice cabañas on the shores of Crooked Tree Lagoon. A main lodge building houses a restaurant and bar. Camping also available. **Inexpensive to Moderate.**

Birds Eye View Lodge. Crooked Tree Wildlife Sanctuary, 501-203-2040, www.birdseyeviewlodge.com. Birds Eye View Lodge is a modern two-story concrete hotel, just a few steps from the lagoon, covered with climbing vines and flowers. The hotel's 20 renovated rooms are modest but clean – rooms on the second floor generally are larger and you have access to the patio with great views of the lagoon. The Belizean management and staff are friendly. The hotel's dining room serves tasty Creole fare. The hotel can arrange birding, local tours, canoe rentals and such. **Moderate.**

ALTUN HA

Altun Ha (off Old Northern Hwy. about 35 miles north of Belize City via the Philip Goldson Hwy., Old Northern Hwy. and Altun Ha access road, daily 9-5, admission US$5) is currently the most-visited Maya ruin in Belize, mainly because of day trippers from cruise ships and from Ambergris This Pre-Classic site was settled some 2,000 years ago. There's a visitor center, gift shop and craft sales area.

If you decide you want to stay overnight near Altun Ha, or just have a nice lunch, the main choice is **Maruba Resort Jungle Spa** (Mile 40.5, Old Northern Hwy., Maskall village, 501-713-799-2031 or 800-617-8227, www.maruba-spa.com). Overnight rates start at around US$200 and go up to several times that amount. **Expensive to Very Expensive.**

The border with Mexico

Corozal District

BUG OUT RATINGS

Ratings are on an A to F scale, just like your old high school report card. A is the top grade; F is failing. Grades are relative compared to other areas in Belize. Note: Ratings for Corozal reflect its proximity to Chetumal, Mexico.

Popularity with Expats	B
Safety	B-
Overall Cost of Living	B+
Real Estate Bargains	A-
Leisure Activities	B-

Restaurants	C+
Cultural Activities	C+
Infrastructure	B
Business Potential	C
Medical Care	B+ (Chetumal)
Shopping	A- (Chetumal)
Farming & Ranching	B
Safety During Nuclear War	B-
Sustainable Living	B
Overall Bug Out Rating	**B**

ADVANTAGES OF COROZAL TOWN AREA: • Low housing costs whether you're renting or buying • Proximity to Chetumal, Mexico, for medical care and shopping • Sizeable (several hundred) and growing expat community • Pleasant location on the Bay of Chetumal (sometimes called Corozal Bay) • Few sandflies and fewer noxious bugs than in some other areas of Belize • Pleasant sub-tropical climate with lower rainfall than Southern Belize • Generally safe, friendly area, though property theft is an issue and there were two high-profile murders of Canadian expats in 2017 • Easy access by car, bus, water taxi and air to Ambergris Caye and other areas of Belize and to the Yucatán

Few Belize casual visitors to Belize, except medical missionaries and tourists passing through from Mexico, pay much attention to Corozal District and its main population center, Corozal Town. Yet this part of Northern Belize is one of the friendliest, safest, least expensive and most interesting areas of the entire country.

For visitors, it's a place to slow down, relax and enjoy at least a few days of easy living by the beautiful turquoise waters of Corozal Bay and the Bay of Chetumal. True, there's not a whole lot to see here, not many tourist sites, no real beaches though nice swimming is yours in the bay and lagoons, and few memorable hotels or restaurants. But the climate is appealing, with less rain than almost anywhere else in Belize, and the sunny dispositions of residents are infectious. Corozal Town and environs is one of our top picks for expatriate living. It offers inexpensive rentals and affordable real estate. You'll want to be sure to visit here, if you are interesting in living or retiring in Belize.

Corozal District is 718 square miles in area, with a district population of 46,000, according to the Statistical Institute of Belize estimates for mid-2015. The largest town by far is Corozal, with 11,700 residents. Spanish is spoken more widely than English here, although you can get by in English at least in Corozal Town. The town is laid out on a small grid, with the most appealing part along the bayfront, with its colorful houses and parks.

Nearby on and near the Northern Highway are "suburbs" — the small villages of Ranchito, Xaibe, Calcutta, San Antonio and others. The Corozal Free Zone, just south of the Santa Elena border crossing from Mexico, is starting to make a name for itself as a place for businesses to set up free from many of the restrictions and high import duties of the rest of Belize. Mexicans come here for cheap gas. The Free Zone employs some 2,000 Belizeans. There are three casinos at the border, on the Belize side, including a branch of the Princess and a large casino, Las Vegas, which sports a new 106-room upscale hotel. These casinos, like the Free Zone, mostly depend on business from Mexico.

The district can be divided into two main sections. The west part is still sugar cane country, once anchored by Libertad, the now-closed sugar cane processing plant and farther north by Corozal Town on Corozal Bay. The main road artery of this hemisphere is the Northern Highway, a good two-lane paved road. From the southern edge of Corozal District near San Pablo village, it is about 28 miles to the Mexican border at Santa Elena. The border is about 9 miles from Corozal Town. The Consejo area about 7 miles north of Corozal Town on an all-weather unpaved road, on Corozal Bay, has attracted a small number of expats at Consejo Shores, Mayan Sands and other residential developments.

The eastern hemisphere consists of the Cerros/Copper Bank area and Sarteneja peninsula. This peninsula has far more trees than people. It is an area mostly of swamp and savannah, with the bulk of the peninsula's small population living in villages along the beautiful Progresso Lagoon and Chetumal Bay. Little Belize, a Mennonite area, is the largest population center, with around 2,000 residents. For visitors, a main reason to come here is the Shipstern Nature Preserve, a 22,000-acre park originally started and funded by a Swiss organization.

The fishing village of Sarteneja (pop. 1,800) is charming as well. An all-weather mostly unpaved road runs from Orange Walk Town to Sarteneja village, a distance of about 40 miles. You can also get to the peninsula from Corozal Town via a free, hand-pulled vehicular ferry across the New River and another hand-pulled ferry over the mouth of Laguna Seca. Several residential developments, including Cerros Sands and the aggressively marketed Orchid Bay, are on the bay, and Progresso Heights is on the Progresso Lagoon. While a number of lots have been sold at these developments, so far there are only a handful of homes built. Orchid Bay, despite its rather isolated location, is something of an exception, with a sizeable number of completed homes, condos and even a restaurant/bar and a bed and breakfast inn.

Corozal is one of the safer places in Belize. Even so, burglary and property theft are fairly common. One survey of expats in Corozal Town some years ago found that about 80% had been victims of theft, burglary and even home invasions over a period of four years. The town of Corozal and surrounding villages are on the power grid and generally have municipal water supplies with potable water. Sarteneja and other remote areas have less modern infrastructures.

One of Belize's two main land border crossing points is north of Corozal Town at Santa Elena (the other is at Benque Viejo del Carmen in Cayo, and a third is planned for Toledo District.) The Rio Honda marks the boundary between Belize and Mexico. Once across the border, some knowledge of Spanish is helpful. Chetumal has large supermarkets (San Francisco is one) and a modern mall with department stores, a multiplex cinema and food court. There are McDonalds and Burger King fast-food restaurants in Chetumal, along with a Sam's Club, Walmart and other big box stores.

Corozal Practicalities

Banks: Scotia Bank, Belize Bank, Heritage Bank and Atlantic Bank have branches in Corozal Town.

Groceries: Corozal Town has more than a dozen small groceries and tiendas and a market with fruits and vegetables. (No, despite the name, the author does not own Lan's grocery.) Large supermarkets are in Chetumal.

Restaurants: Among the best of the small bunch of restaurants in Corozal are Patty's Bistro, June's Kitchen and Corozo Blue's.

Other Stores: Corozal has a selection of small home furnishings, construction supplies and hardware stores, many run by Chinese immigrants. Chetumal across the border has larger stores of all kinds. There also are nearly 300 stores in the Free Zone, most of them selling cheap clothing and other items from Asia.

Medical: Corozal Town has a district hospital and several doctors and clinics. Nearby Chetumal offers low-cost and often high-quality dental and medical care.

Infrastructure: Corozal Town and surrounding villages are on the power grid and generally have municipal water supplies with potable water, along with sewerage. They also have DSL and cellular internet. If in doubt, ask locally. Sarteneja and other areas have less modern infrastructures. Remote areas depend on water from cisterns or wells, power from solar or wind and sewerage from septic systems, along with satellite internet. Some developments, such as Orchid Bay, have built their own sophisticated infrastructure.

Real Estate

Corozal Town and environs has some of the belter property bargains in Belize – whether you are renting or buying.

Corozal District, like the rest of Belize, has its share of blue-sky real estate peddlers, often operating via the internet. Watch out for sellers of lots in remote areas. Some are claiming that their lots on a part of a golf or hotel development. Such developments may be years or decades in the future, if they are ever built at all.

Properties in Corozal

Here are some of the property listings offered by individuals and brokers in 2018. Prices shown are asking prices.

• Seaview lot in Consejo Village, about 77 feet on road, depth 97 feet, US$55,000.

• Two-bedroom, two-bath modern house with a/c in Corozal Town, cistern plus town water, US$138,000.

• 60' x 90' lot in new development on north edge of Corozal Town, US$8,000.

• Three-bedroom, two-bath concrete home in Santa Rita Heights, about 2 miles north of center of Corozal Town, fenced, municipal water, cable TV, partially furnished, US$59,975.

• Waterfront lot in Consejo Village, 100 feet on the water, 90 feet deep and 100 feet frontage on village road, US$219,000.

• 100-acre farm less than 3 miles off Philip Goldson Highway, cleared and ready to farm or use as pasture, in two parcels, US$79,000.

• Fully fenced two-bedroom, one-bath concrete bungalow over more than 1,000 sq. ft., located in Finca Solana. The home on a 104' x 55' lot and was built in 2009. One block from the bay, US$109,500.

• Four bedroom, 2½ bath two-level home in Consejo Shores, with water view. About 3,200 total square footage. Swimming pool. US$260,000.

• Attractive three-unit guesthouse, with one-, two- and three-bedroom fully furnished units directly across the road from Corozal Bay, with views of the bay, in the upscale South End area, US$275,000.

Real Estate Agents
Belize North Real Estate Ltd. P.O. Box 226, Corozal Town, 501-422-0284, www.belizenorthrealestate.bz.

Corozal Belize Properties, 29 Consejo Beach Trail, P.O. Box 346, Corozal Town, 501-636-8400, www.corozalbelizeproperties.com.

Real Estate Developments
Here are selected real estate developments in Corozal District. Most market primarily to foreign buyers. Keep in mind that Cerros Sands, Orchid Bay and Progresso Heights are all a 30 to 60-minute drive on unpaved roads from Corozal Town, depending on road conditions and ferry wait times. Consejo Shores, Mayan Seaside and other developments around Consejo are about a 10- to 15-minute drive on an unpaved road from Corozal Town.

Cerros Sands, near Cerros Maya, 501-402-0297; www.cerrossands.com. Cerros Sands is a 92-acre development near the Cerros ruins, across the bay from Corozal Town. Lots start at around US$18,000, with some bayfront lots starting around US$99,000. There are no public utilities at the development. While lots have been sold, only a few homes have been built in the development. A beach bar/restaurant is open.

Consejo Shores, Consejo, 501-423-1005; www.consejoshores.com. Consejo Shores, with 350 acres and 7,000 ft. of bayfront, was one of the first and remains a top residential developments in Northern Belize. Around 150 homes have been built in the community. Open parkland allows access to the bay, and there is a small 9-hole golf course. Bayfront building lots with around 80 feet of waterfront have risen in price and are now selling by the developer for $165,000, though occasionally resales may be lower. Seaview lots back a row or two from the bay are US$29,000 to $39,000, while other residential lots start at around US$17,000. Modern three- and four-bedroom homes have sold for as little as US$100,000, and US$300,000-$400,000 gets you close to the top end of the market.

Mayan Seaside, Consejo, www.mayanseaside.com. This development near Consejo village has about 105 lots, most of which have been sold. About 30 homes have been built or are under construction. Lot owners in the development pay a US$250 per year maintenance fee.

Orchid Bay, between Copper Bank and Sarteneja, U.S. phone 470-223-5493;

www.orchidbaybelize.com. The 114-acre **Orchid Bay** on the Bay of Chetumal is being developed by Great Land Holdings, Ltd., which has some 4,000 acres in the area. Beachfront condos at Orchid Bay are now selling in the US$300,000+ range. Waterway villas, starting around US$250,000, and various casitas are also offered. Lot prices range from around US$100,000 to over US$200,000. There is a B&B inn on the property, Crimson Orchid Inn, and a restaurant/beach club with swimming pool. The development has an ambitious sales program and promotes popular group tours of the property from the U.S. and Canada.

Progresso Heights, on Progresso Lagoon near Progresso Village, 888-235-4934 or 561-859-1433; www.progressoheights.com. Hundreds of lots, mostly around ¼-acre in size, are included in the master plan, and more than 300 lots reportedly have been sold. Lot prices start at around US$16,000 for cash, or US$20,000 with financing (at up to 15 years at 6.99%, with 20% down). Lot owners in the development pay a US$250 per year maintenance fee. A clubhouse with swimming pool, a community pier and dirt and marl roads have been constructed but only a dozen or so homes have been built or are under construction in the development, though on a recent visit the entire development looked virtually deserted.

Rentals

Rentals in Corozal Town start at under US$300 a month, and for US$300 to $500 you can get a comfortable house in town. For rentals in the Corozal Town area, check with **Belize North Real Estate Ltd. or Corozal Belize Properties.** In **Consejo Shores,** a nice development on the Bay of Chetumal about 7 miles from Corozal Town, U.S.-style three- and four-bedroom homes rent for US$500 to $1,000 a month. **Orchid Bay** also has some rentals, with one-bedroom casitas going on www.vrbo.com for around US$100 a night, less for weekly or monthly rentals.

Visiting Corozal

How to Get Here

From Mexico: ADO (in Mexico 0115 5784 4652, www.ado.com.mx) and other Mexican bus lines serve Chetumal, capital of the Mexican state of Quintana Roo and, with a population of more than 300,000, far larger than any city in Belize. Buses run frequently from various towns and cities in the Yucatán, including Playa del Carmen and Mérida. Fares for first class buses — with reserved seats, videos, and bathrooms — are around US$20 at current exchange rates from Playa del Carmen to Chetumal. Chetumal is a little over four hours from Playa del Carmen and six hours from Mérida. The new ADO terminal in Chetumal is on Av. Insurgentes at Calle Palermo. You'll need to get to the old ADO terminal on Av. Insurgentes, from where the Belize buses depart. Buses leave Chetumal for Corozal Town and points south beginning well before daybreak. At the border, which sports a new Belize customs and immigration office, marked by a bridge over the Rio Hondo, you get off the bus to go through customs and immigration and then reboard for the 15-minute ride into Corozal Town. If arriving at the border by means other than bus, a taxi from the border into Corozal Town is around US$10, and a bus from the border is about US$1.50.

Another option for some is the **ADO Express** between Cancún and Belize City and also between Mérida and Belize City. The daily Belize-City-Cancún bus is a comfortable, air-conditioned bus with reserved seats and videos. It costs about US$35 one-way at current exchange rates. The ADO Express Mérida, also known as the hospital run, due to the number of Belizeans who get medical care in Mérida, currently isn't daily but three or four days a week.

Transfer services in Corozal and elsewhere in Belize will also pick you up in Cancun or elsewhere in Mexico and bring you to Corozal. One of the good transfer services is **Belize VIP Transfer Service,** formerly Menzies Tours (www.belizetransfers.com, 501-422-2725). You'll pay around US400 for up to four persons from Cancun to Corozal, US$350 from Playa del Carmen, US$300 from Tulum, and US$45 from Bacalar or US$30-$35 from Chetumal. Other shuttle services also operate.

It's also possible to **rent a car** in Cancún, Playa del Carmen, Chetumal or elsewhere and drive it into Belize (only a few Mexican agencies permit this). You will have to stop at the Belize border and purchase Belize auto insurance.

From points south in Belize: Corozal Town is about 83 miles by road from the international airport in Ladyville and 9 miles from the Mexican border. Figure about two hours by car on the Philip Goldson Highway (formerly Northern Highway) from Belize City. Belize Bus Owners Cooperative (BBOC), Cabrera's, Chell's, Joshua's, Morales, Tillett's, T-Line and Valencia are among bus lines on this route, with frequent service in both directions, starting early in the morning and continuing to the early evening. Fares are about US$6 between Belize City and Corozal Town. Buses on this route use the main bus terminal in Belize City, Novelo's on West Collet Canal; in Corozal Town the bus station is on the main road toward the north end and just a few minutes walk to the main part of town. By regular (local) bus the trip takes about three to four hours. Most buses on this route are retired school buses or other older equipment, and currently there are no express buses.

What to See and Do in Corozal

Ho hum, Corozal Town has few must-see attractions. It's more of a place just to visit, wander around the main plaza or waterfront, have a soft drink or beer and enjoy the Latin-Caribbean ambiance. Outside of Corozal Town, if you have the time for it, you really must drive up the Sarteneja peninsula to experience Belize off-the-beaten track. Also, go for a swim in Four Mile Lagoon near the Mexican border or a take a boat or fishing trip in the beautiful Bay of Chetumal.

Corozal House of Culture. 1st Ave., 501-422-0071, www.nichbelize.org. You'll recognize this place, in a landmark building over 100 years old, by its clock tower and new red roof. In the waterfront park, between 2nd Street South and the bay, the museum has, among other interesting artifacts, hand-blown rum bottles, a traditional Maya thatch hut and displays from the lighthouse that once stood on this site. It also presents rotating art and history displays. After renovation, it reopened in early 2012 and is now operated by the National Institute of Culture and History (NICH). Admission Monday-Friday 8-5, US$5.

Gabriel Hoare Market. This market, which replaced the old one by the bay, is in a two-story concrete building on 6th Avenue near the center of town. The first level has numerous fruit and vegetable stalls, with good seasonal selections of local items such as papaya, mangos, watermelon, citrus, bananas, onions, potatoes, peppers, ginger and beans. Upstairs are several inexpensive restaurants for a quick breakfast or lunch, along with some shops selling clothing and other items. There also are stands beside the main market building. There is also a new **Wholesale Farmer's Market.** Free.

Corozal Town Hall. Stop by on weekdays for a look at the mural by Manuel Villamar Reyes. It depicts the region's history. Nearby, in the center of town, are the ruins of Fort Barley, built to thwart attacks by Maya Indians. Free.

Maya Sites
Cerros

Cerro Maya (sometimes referred to as Cerros) was an important jade and obsidian trading center during the Late Pre-Classic Period, with its heyday being from 400 BC to 100 CE. The site apparently suffered an economic decline and was mostly abandoned in the Early Pre-Classic period after 250 CE, although there were residents there until around 1300 CE.

This site is on 53 acres on a low hill (*cerro* in Spanish means hill) beside the Bay of Chetumal. Cerros was first studied by the amateur archeologist Thomas Gann in the early 1900s. It was surveyed and excavated by David Freidel of Southern Methodist University in the 1970s. More recently a group of archeologists including Debra Walker, Kathryn Reese-Taylor and Beverly Mitchum Chiarulli brought to light several new structures including a ball court and a major monument.

Three main structures have been excavated, along with plazas and ball courts. One structure rises about 65 feet. The site is of special interest because of its location overlooking the Bay of Chetumal. Its waterfront location is reminiscent of the better-known Tulum site in the Yucatán.

A pedestrian and auto ferry across the New River has cut travel time by car to Cerros. Drive to Copper Bank village and turn left, following signs. A faster way is by boat from Corozal Town. Expect to pay around US$20 and up per person for someone with a skiff to take you and your party to Cerros, about 15 minutes away.

Admission: Daily 8-5, US$5.

Santa Rita

The Santa Rita archeological site is thought to be a small remnant of the Maya city of Chetumal, or Chactemal, an important Maya center since it controlled trade routes along the coast and into what is now Mexico and Guatemala. This center was occupied by the Maya from at least 2000 BC to the 16th century CE.

Thomas Gann worked here around the turn of the 20th century. Systematic excavations were by Diane and Arlen Chase from 1979 to 1985.

Only a small area has been excavated, and it is thought that much of the ancient city of Chetumal is now covered by the town of Corozal. One large Post-Classic structure with several chambers is excavated and open to visitors.

Santa Rita is located on a small hill at the northwest edge of Corozal Town, near the Coca-Cola plant. Follow the Santa Rita Road toward the Mexican border. About ½ mile from Corozal, bear to the right at the statue. Then, in a few hundred yards, take the first road to the left and then go about 2/10ths of a mile to the site.

The site is now open to visitors daily 8-5, more or less, and a caretaker is on the grounds. It is being promoted as a wedding venue. Admission US$5.

Corozal Lodging
The price level for lodging in all areas is as follows:
Inexpensive: Under US$75
Moderate: US$75-$150
Expensive: US$151-$300
Very Expensive: Over US$300

Prices are for a double room in high season (usually late November to Easter). Rates, which do not include taxes, service charges or meals (except in some cases breakfast), may be higher during holiday periods, especially Christmas and New Years. If specific prices are mentioned, they are plus 9% hotel tax and in some cases a service charge, usually 10%.

Lodging is listed alphabetically.

Almond Tree Hotel Resort, 425 Bayshore Dr., South End, 501-628-9224, www.almondtreeresort.com. This small inn is a fine upscale choice at fairly moderate rates. Set directly on the bay at the South End of town, Almond Tree has a fresh water pool and bar. There are 10 rooms/suites. Rates range from US$105 to $189 double, plus 9% tax. There is air conditioning in rooms, cable TV, laundry services, bikes and wireless access throughout most of the premises. **Moderate to Expensive.**

George Hardie's Las Vegas Hotel & Casino, Mile 91.5 George Price Hwy., Corozal Free Zone, 501-423-7000, www.lvbelize.com. Located in the Corozal Free Zone area at the Belize-Mexico border, this is the newest and best hotel in the casino area. The main hotel is 106 rooms with a large pool, bar and fitness room. It opened in late 2015. Also here is the smaller, older Las Vegas Gardens Hotel. The hotel is a part of the 54,000 sq. ft. casino, the largest in the region. **Moderate.**

Las Palmas Hotel, 123 5th Ave., Corozal Town, 501-422-0196, www.laspalmashotelbelize.com. This was formerly the budget-level Nestor's Hotel. It has was renovated and rebuilt, moving the whole property somewhat upmarket. The 27 rooms, with A/C, microwave, small fridge and wi-fi, go for about US$60 to $80 a night, double, plus tax. **Inexpensive to Moderate.**

Sea Breeze, 19 1st Ave., 501-422-3051, www.theseabreezehotel.com. The Sea Breeze is a decent budget choice in Corozal. In 2015, the then-owner moved the inn to a new location near the bay about 150 feet from where it had been since 2008. It serves breakfast but no longer has a bar (there's one nearby). The three rooms, two with private baths, are around US$35 plus 9% tax. **Inexpensive.**

Serenity Sands Bed & Breakfast, Mile 3, Consejo Road (P.O. Box 88, Corozal Town), 501-669-2394, www.serenitysands.com. Serenity Sands B&B is serenely hidden away off the Consejo Road north of Corozal Town. On the second floor of a large modern concrete home, there are four tastefully decorated rooms with private balconies, Belizean art and locally made hardwood furniture. Although not directly on the water, Serenity has a private beach on the bay a few hundred feet away. Rates are an excellent value for the high quality you enjoy, from US$90 to $95 in high season, US$80 to $85 off-season, plus tax. There's a 5% discount for payment in cash in U.S. dollars. Breakfasts, mostly organic, are included. Best visited with a rental car. Recommended. **Moderate.**

Tony's Inn, South End, Corozal Town, 501-422-2055; www.tonysinn.com. A longtime favorite of travelers to Corozal, Tony's has 24 motel-like rooms with tile floors, cable TV and A/C. Many of the rooms recently have been renovated and upgraded, and rates for these have gone up. The breezy bayside palapa restaurant is one of the more pleasant places to eat in Corozal. Rates: Upgraded rooms US$125 double January-April, US$115 rest of the year; standard rooms are less. All rates plus 9% tax. **Moderate.**

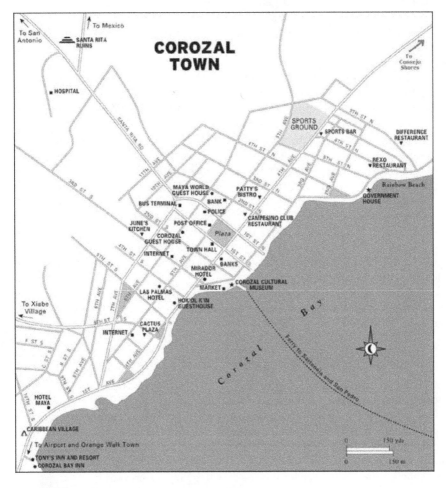

Dining in Corozal Town
The price level for restaurants in all areas is as follows:
Inexpensive: Under US$7

Moderate: US$8-$19
Expensive: US$20-$39
Very Expensive: Over US$40
Prices don't include tips or alcoholic drinks. If not otherwise stated, the price range is for one person for dinner.

Restaurants here are listed alphabetically.

Blue Iguana, Consejo area, 501-630-5595. Blue Iguana is an expat hangout between Corozal Town and Consejo, in a large screened palapa on Corozal Bay. It's a little hard to find, so ask for directions. There's usually a breeze off the water to keep things cool. Steve, the owner, is an interesting guy who knows just about everybody, at least in the expat community, in Corozal Town and Consejo. The grilled fish is good, and the rum and tonics and Belikin are cold. There's a regular poker game here, a darts night and a movie night. **Moderate.**

Corozo Blue, South End, Corozal Town, 501-422-0090. In a beautifully redone stone building on the bay, this is a good spot for drinks and wood-fired pizza. **Moderate.**

June's Kitchen, Third St. South/College Ave., Corozal Town, 501-422-2559. Miss June stands at her stove while her husband bikes through Corozal Town to deliver take-out from this popular Belizean eatery. With three tables on the family's porch and folks going in and out, you'll feel cozy and welcomed. Lunch is delicious, and the menu can (and will) be spoken in a few words: likely stew chicken, stew beef, or stew pork, plus a daily special. Breakfast is the best in town, and a full order including pepper sausage and Miss June's warm bread is US$5. Open for breakfast and lunch daily except Monday. **Inexpensive to Moderate.**

Patty's Bistro. 2nd St. North, Corozal Town, 501-402-0174. You can eat your fill of fried chicken, pork chops, stew chicken, conch soup and other local dishes for very modest prices. **Inexpensive to Moderate.**

Venky's. 5th Ave., across from the Immigration office, Corozal Town, 501-402-0536. For takeout curries and other Indian food at modest prices, Venky's is the place. **Inexpensive to Moderate.**

Other favorites in Corozal include **Scotty's Crocodile Cove** and **RD's Diner** in Corozal Town. Also, check out the **Buccaneer Palapa** and **Smuggler's Den** in the Consejo area.

Rural Corozal District
COPPER BANK/CERROS AREA
Getting Here from Corozal Town: You can drive from Corozal Town, crossing the New River on the hand-pulled ferry. To get to the ferry from Corozal, take the Northern Highway south toward Orange Walk Town and watch for ferry sign. Turn left and follow this unpaved road for 2½ miles to the ferry landing. At a T-intersection, turn left for Copper Bank. The trip to Copper Bank takes about a half hour, but longer after heavy rains, as the dirt road can become very bad. As you enter Copper Bank, watch for signs directing you to Cerros Maya.

You can also hire a boat in Corozal to take you across the bay. Rates vary but can be as low as US$20 one-way.

Where to Stay

Cerros Beach Resort, near Cerros Maya site on north side of Cerros peninsula, 501-623-9763, www.cerrosbeachresort.com. Directions: Entering Copper Bank village, watch for signs on the left to Cerros Beach Resort, then follow signs on a dirt track. This is a laid-back, off-the-grid option for good food and simple lodging on Corozal Bay, near the Cerros ruins. For overnight stays, four small solar-powered cabañas are far from fancy, but the price is right, and your hosts are friendly. Cerros Beach Resorts offers complimentary kayaks, bikes, snorkeling gear, fishing poles and wi-fi. There's TV in the lounge. **Inexpensive.**

ORCHID BAY
Where to Stay

Crimson Orchid Inn, 59 Pescadores Park, Orchid Bay, Chunox, 501-669-5076; www.thecrimsonorchidinn.com. Opened in late 2012, the Crimson Orchid Inn is located in the heart of the Orchid Bay development. Those checking out Orchid Bay for a lot or home stay here while visiting the property, but it's also open to the public. Stephen and Laurene Honeybill, who were in the theatre and entertainment in Britain, are the innkeepers. The B&B-style inn has nine rooms, Casitas at Orchid Bay also are offered for overnight guests. Crimson Orchid Inn guests can eat at the restaurant at Orchid Bay, Tradewinds *(see below)*. **Moderate to Expensive.**

Dining at Orchid Bay

Tradewinds Restaurant, Orchid Bay, 501-650-1925. Although most of the diners here are part of the "captive audience" of residents, visitors and would-be buyers at Orchid Bay, the food is pretty good, and the beer is cold. The menu is a combination of bar food, seafood and Belizean-American dishes. The clientele seems friendly and happy to be here. **Moderate to Expensive.**

SARTENEJA
This small Mestizo and Creole community enjoys a waterside setting that makes it one of the most relaxed and appealing villages in all of Belize. It's one of the few places where you can see the sunset over the water. Lobster fishing and pineapple farming are the town's two main industries, although tourism is creeping in, and Sarteneja is also known for building wooden boats. Most residents speak Spanish as a first language, but many also speak English. Real estate investors are beginning to discover Sarteneja.

How to Get There: Driving to Sarteneja from Corozal Town takes about 1½ hours via the New River ferry and a second ferry across the mouth of Laguna Seca. The road is unpaved and can be very muddy after heavy rains. On the way here you'll pass several developments, including Orchid Bay. You also can drive to Sarteneja from Orange Walk Town, a trip of about 40 miles and 1½ hours. There are several buses a day, except Sunday, from Belize City via Orange Walk Town.

The daily water taxi, Thunderbolt, between Corozal Town and San Pedro, will drop you at Sarteneja on request.

Where to Stay

Backpackers Paradise Hostel, Bandera Rd, Sarteneja, 501-423-2016; https://cabanasbelize.wordpress.com. Rates for this hostel are US$13 double for a small cabaña with share outside bathrooms or US$6 person for camping. A "honeymoon cabaña" with private bath is US$40 double. The cabañas are barely large enough for a double bed, lacking chairs, closet and frills. A common kitchen is available for those who want to cook their own meals. You can pick your own mangos and other fruit free. Free wi-fi, too. **Inexpensive.**

Fernando's Seaside Guesthouse, 62 N. Front St., Sarteneja, 501-423-2085, www.fernandosseaside.com. This was one of Sarteneja's first lodging spots, and it still enjoys a great location, on Front Street across a quiet dirt street from the water. Rooms are clean and have A/C and TV, but only the two at the front have views of the water. Rates around US$50 double, plus tax. **Inexpensive.**

The **Sarteneja Homestay Program**, 501-634-8032, email sartenejahomestay@gmail.com, can provide accommodations in local homes. **Inexpensive.**

Our long-time favorite, **Candelie's Seaside Cabañas**. N. Front St., Sarteneja, on the seafront at the west end of the village, 501-423-2005, as of this writing doesn't seem to be open, but perhaps it will reopen. Candelie's has two charming cottages by the sea -- Wood Stork and Brown Pelican. When open, they rented for around US$60 double. **Inexpensive.**

Where to Eat in Sarteneja

Liz's Fast Food, Av. Primativo Aragon, 501-665-5998. Liz's is a snack shack two blocks back from the water, in the center of town near the old Catholic church. It's super cheap, with three small tacos for BZ$1 or two salbutes for BZ$1 – very tasty! Usually open for breakfast, lunch and dinner daily. **Inexpensive.**

Crabby E's, N. Front St., Sarteneja, 501-668-1531. Formerly Richie's, this spot across a quiet dirt street from the bay has been around for a good while, serving fried seafood, pizza (US$10) and other dishes. Good drinks. Good breakfasts. **Inexpensive to Moderate.**

Martineja, N. Front St., 501 634-1021. Sarteneja's newest restaurant brings a touch of sophistication to Northern Belize. Very attractive place, with some of the best food in the region. Good pizzas (from US$13 for a large), fried chicken with waffles and maple syrup, pulled pork sandwiches and more. **Moderate.**

Tropical bougainvillea flourishes in Belize

Orange Walk District

BUG OUT RATINGS

Ratings are on an A to F scale, just like your old high school report card. A is the top grade; F is failing. Grades are relative compared to other areas in Belize.

Popularity with Expats	D
Safety	B-
Overall Cost of Living	B
Real Estate Bargains	B
Investment Potential	C-
Leisure Activities	C+
Restaurants	C-
Cultural Activities	D
Infrastructure	C+
Business Potential	C
Medical Care	C+
Shopping	C
Farming & Ranching	B+
Safety in Nuclear War	B
Sustainable Living	B+
Overall Bug Out Rating	**C+**

ADVANTAGES OF ORANGE WALK: • Low land prices in rural areas • Offers some of the most natural areas of Belize, with excellent birding and wildlife spotting • Proximity to Mennonite centers of Shipyard and Blue Creek • Good agricultural area

In what is now Orange Walk District, the early greatness of the Maya empire was on display at Lamanai, La Milpa and elsewhere. During the centuries before the time of Christ, the Maya built temples that were higher than any modern building in Belize, and one at Lamanai still stands about 100 feet above the jungle floor. Many Maya sites in Orange Walk were occupied up to colonial times. For a while the Maya were even able to resist the Spanish *conquistadores*, in the 17th century driving the Spanish out of the area around Lamanai and burning Catholic churches. Mestizos fleeing the Maya rebellions in the Yucatán settled modern Orange Walk around 1849, and Corozal about the same time.

Mahogany logging in the late 18th and early 19th centuries was the first major industry of the region, with some 5,000 giant mahogany trees harvested every year. A big British-based company, Belize Estate and Produce Company, once owned one-fifth of the land in Belize and was a major force in British Honduras' economy and politics until the mid-20th century. When the mahogany industry died down due to over logging, sugar cane and citrus became staple crops. But boom and bust continued, and with the global oversupply of sugar, small Orange Walk farmers turned to marijuana cultivation. The U.S. government, with its take-no-prisoners approach to drug control, forced Belizean authorities to shut down airstrips, spray chemicals on fields and destroy this cash crop. Today, subsistence agriculture and the remnants of sugar cane and citrus farming occupy the time of rural residents. Rum is distilled near Orange Walk Town, logging still is going on and Mennonites farm productively in the Shipyard (home to conservative Mennonites), Little Belize and Blue Creek (progressive) areas.

The road west from Orange Walk Town, past Cuello distillery, Yo Creek, and then back south to August Pine Ridge village and San Felipe village leads through agricultural areas to the 240,000-acre Programme for Belize Rio Bravo Conservation area and the 250,000-acre private estate of the late Sir Barry Bowen. Or, if you go southeast from San Felipe, you end up at Lamanai near Indian Church village. Two world-class jungle lodges, Chan Chich at Gallon Jug, and Lamanai Outpost Lodge on the New River Lagoon, await you in this part of Orange Walk District. Another route is via Shipyard, on an unpaved road just south of Orange Walk Town.

Orange Walk Practicalities

Banks: ScotiaBank, Heritage Bank, Atlantic Bank and Belize Bank all have branches in Orange Walk Town.

Groceries and Other Stores: M & A Supermarket and P & P Supermarket, both fairly small, are among your choices. The main drag, Queen Victoria aka Belize-Corozal Road, has a large variety of shops and stores. There's a public market in the middle of town.

Medical: Orange Walk Town has the Northern Regional hospital, though it is not one of the more modern hospitals in Belize. Chetumal, Mexico, a little over an hour away, offers low-cost and often high-quality dental and medical care. About the same distance to the south is Belize City, with its private and public hospitals and many physician and dental offices. Mérida, Mexico, also is a popular place for Belizeans and expats to get expert medical care at modest costs. In fact, the ADO Express bus from Belize City to Mérida is often called the "hospital run."

Restaurants and Hotels: Among the good restaurants in Orange Walk Town are Nahil Mayab and Maracas Bar & Grill. Among the good lodging in and near town are Hotel de la Fuente and El Gran Mestizo Riverside Cabins. In remote areas are two outstanding lodges, Chan Chich Lodge and Lamanai Outpost Lodge, plus La Milpa Field Station.

Infrastructure: Orange Walk Town and some larger villages have municipal water and sewerage systems. More remote areas have to rely on wells and cisterns for water, septic systems for sewerage and satellite for internet.

Real Estate

The real estate market in Orange Walk District is not very active. Undeveloped land in large tracts starts at under US$500 to $1,000 an acre and goes up to around US$2,500 an acre for well-sited medium-sized tracts with good road and utility access.

Property Listings

Here are properties available in 2018 in Orange Walk District. Prices shown are asking prices.

• Small hotel and restaurant on about 2 ½ acres in Carmelita village, with owner's house, swimming pool and more, US$134,000

• 110' x 160' lot near Honey Camp Lagoon, US$24,500

• 56 acres on New River Lagoon, about 2 miles from Lamanai Maya site, 700 feet lagoon frontage, fruit and cacao trees already planted, US$165,000

• One-bedroom two-level concrete house on almost 2 acres directly on New River, upper level has 600 sq. ft. studio apartment with kitchenette, full bath and A/C, lower level is utility area, ecotourism potential, US$105,000

• 134-acre private island in New River, with a total of 2 ½ miles of river frontage, for private estate or ecotourism, US$82,000

• 15,000 acres near Blue Creek Mennonite community, about two-thirds of acreage is in timber, US$1,000 an acre

• Two-bedroom fixer upper in Orange Walk Town, US$40,000

Real Estate Agents

Real estate companies in Belize City and elsewhere in Belize handle property in Orange Walk.

Visiting Orange Walk

Your first introduction to Orange Walk District likely will be the sugar cane fields — and concomitant hulking sugar cane trucks — near Orange Walk Town on the Philip Goldson Highway. Orange Walk Town itself is a somewhat scruffy, bustling place with more of a Mexican than Belizean ambiance, having not a great deal of interest for most visitors. There's a formal plaza, and the town hall is called the Palacio Municipal. The businesses and houses along the main drag — Queen Victoria Avenue or the Belize-Corozal Road — have barred windows, and a few of the hotels and bars are in fact brothels.

The real Orange Walk is the big, wide and lightly populated area to the west of Orange Walk Town, up against the Guatemala border. Here you'll find large tracts of public and private land, teeming with deer, oscellated turkey, toucans and all manner of other wildlife. A handful of remote jungle lodges offers you the chance to see crocodiles, howler monkeys and even the illusive jaguar. Maya sites, discovered and undiscovered, are everywhere, including one of the most impressive and beautifully situated ones in the region, Lamanai.

Mennonites are a potent agricultural and economic force in Orange Walk, especially in the Shipyard and Blue Creek areas. Farmland would be the appeal for expats in this part of Belize.

Getting There: By car via the Goldson Highway, Orange Walk Town is about 55 miles north of Belize City and 35 miles south of Corozal Town. From Belize City or Corozal Town to Orange Walk Town, several bus lines offer frequent bus service, every hour or so. There is charter air service to Orange Walk Town on Tropic Air.

To Lamanai: By road from Orange Walk Town, take the all-weather road west to Yo Creek, then southwest to August Pine Ridge and San Felipe, bearing left (southeast) at San Felipe to Indian Church Village near the Lamanai ruins, a total distance of about 36 miles from Orange Walk. Alternatively, you can go from near Orange Walk Town through the village of Guinea Grass to Shipyard. Figure about 3 hours by car from Belize City. There's limited non-daily bus service to Indian Church from Orange Walk. A more scenic option is a boat trip up the New River to the New River Lagoon, about 1 1/2 hours and around US$45 per person. If you are staying at Lamanai Outpost, the hotel will arrange your transportation. If not, boat trips can be arranged at the New River bridge or in Orange Walk Town.

To Gallon Jug/Chan Chich: You follow the same route as to Lamanai, but at San Felipe you turn right and go west to Blue Creek Village, a Mennonite settlement. The Mennonites have paved part of the road here. From Blue Creek, it's about 35 miles to Gallon Jug. Figure about 4 hours by car from Belize City. Charter flights are available from Belize City to Gallon Jug's modern little airstrip.

What to See and Do in Orange Walk

In Orange Walk Town, the **Banquitas House of Culture** (Main Street, 501-322-0517, www.nichbelize.org) has displays on the Mestizo history of Orange Walk area, the sugar industry and archeology. Open 9-5 Monday-Friday, free.

Created with the help of British naturalist Gerald Durrell, **the Río Bravo Conservation & Management Area** covers 260,000 acres in rural Orange Walk District west of Orange Walk Town. The three-hour drive from Orange Walk Town takes you through wild lands where you may encounter a troupe of spider monkeys, wildcats, flocks of oscellated turkeys, a dense shower of butterflies—almost anything but a lot of other vehicles. Managed by Belize City–based **Programme for Belize** (www.pfbelize.org), a not-for-profit organization whose mission is the wise use and conservation of Belize's natural resources, the Río Bravo Conservation Area contains some 400 species of birds, 70 species of mammals, and 200 types of trees. About one-half of Río Bravo is managed as a nature reserve, and the rest is managed to generate income, from forestry and other activities, including tourism.

Maya Sites

Within the Rio Bravo reserve's borders are more than 60 Mayan sites, many still unexplored. The most important is **La Milpa**. At its height between CE 400 and 830, La Milpa was home to almost 50,000 people. The suburbs of this city spread out some three miles from the city center, and the entire city encompassed some 30 square miles in area. So far, archaeologists have discovered at least 20 large courtyards and 19 stelae.

Visiting Río Bravo, like most other areas of rural northwestern Orange Walk, is best done in a four-wheel-drive vehicle. You must make arrangements to visit in advance with Programme for Belize, as the entire Río Bravo conservation area is managed by this private, nonprofit organization, and the main road through its lands is gated.

You also need advance reservations to stay at La Milpa Field Station *(see below)*. Staying overnight or longer at this field station is the best way to see Río Bravo, but you can visit it briefly on a day trip. Another field station at Hill Bank, primarily serves as a research base for sustainable forest management but visitors with an interest in forest research can be accommodated in two cabañas and a dorm that sleeps six. Contact Programme for Belize for information.

Guides and information are available at La Milpa Field Station. Chan Chich Lodge, Lamanai Outpost Lodge, and other hotels also can arrange visits with guides to La Milpa and the Río Bravo Conservation & Management Area.

La Milpa Field Station, Programme for Belize, 1 Eyre St., Belize City, 501-227-5616; www.pfbelize.org. About 3 miles from La Milpa Maya site, this field station is a combination of summer camp and lodge. Stay in rustic thatch cabañas with private bath or in a dorm. Since you're in a remote area, you'll take all your meals, generally simple Belizean-style dishes such as rice and beans with stew chicken or pork, at the field station. Hiking trails are maintained around the lodge, and guides are available to take you to La Milpa and other Mayan sites. In spring and summer you can visit archaeological teams working at La Milpa. Meals are included. **Moderate.**

Blue Creek

The Blue Creek Mennonite settlement gives you a fascinating glimpse into one aspect of Mennonite culture in Belize. Progressives dominate here, so you will see vehicles and diesel tractors. The village manages its owns affairs, including paving streets. A gas station (closed Sunday) is on the hill just past the village, near Hillside Bed & Breakfast. If you're driving, definitely fuel up here. (Don't confuse the Blue Creek in Orange Walk District with the Blue Creek in Toledo.)

At Blue Creek, you can legally cross into Mexico. Belize customs and immigration is in the police station. There is no road access to Mexico, but you can take a small boat (BZ$1) across the Rio Hondo.

Hillside Bed & Breakfast, P.O. Box 2, Blue Creek Village, 501-323-0155. Mennonites John and Judy Klassen opened this small B&B at the edge of Blue Creek settlement. It has five motel-like rooms on a hill overlooking Blue Creek village, with two larger thatch cabañas nearby, down steep wood stairs. Kitchen facilities available, and breakfast is included in the rates. **Inexpensive.**

Lamanai

With its stunning setting on the New River Lagoon and many excavated ruins, Lamanai is the top Maya site to see in Orange Walk District. Hundreds of structures have been identified in a 2-square-mile area by archeologist David Prendergast of the Royal Ontario Museum and others. Lamanai is believed to have been continuously occupied from around 1,500 BCE to the 19th century CE, longer than any other Maya site in the region. There are four main temples to see, a residential area and a reproduction of a Lord Smoking Shell stela. The High Temple, at 100 feet, is the tallest known Pre-Classic temple (other, later Maya structures in Belize are higher) in the Maya world. Admission: Daily 8 to 5, US$10.

Due to day trips from cruise ships, Lamanai can get quite busy. There's a nice visitor center and local people sell souvenirs and snacks. Most tour operators in Belize City, Ambergris Caye, Caye Caulker, Orange Walk Town and even Corozal Town can arrange trips day trips to Lamanai, or you can take a boat up the New River from Orange Walk Town (around US$45 round-trip.)

Orange Walk District Lodging
The price level for lodging in all areas is as follows:
Inexpensive: Under US$75
Moderate: US$75-$150
Expensive: US$151-$300
Very Expensive: Over US$300
Prices are for a double room in high season (usually late November to Easter). Rates, which do not include taxes, service charges or meals (except in some cases breakfast), may be higher during holiday periods, especially Christmas and New Years. If specific prices are mentioned, they are plus 9% hotel tax and in some cases a service charge, usually 10%.

Lodging is listed alphabetically within each area.

Chan Chich Lodge, Gallon Jug, 501-223-4419 or 877-279-5726 in U.S./Canada; www.chanchich.com. Very simply, this is one of the classic jungle lodges of the world. It was developed by the late Sir Barry Bowen, a fifth-generation Belizean whose family has the Coca-Cola bottling franchise in Belize and brews Belikin beer, among many other endeavors. The lodge literally is built in the middle of a Maya site – the mounds around the lodge are unexcavated Maya buildings and temples. Chan Chich, in a setting of incredible beauty, is in a 30,000-acre private nature reserve, which adjoins the half million wild acres of Programme for Belize lands and other reserves. Nearby is the large working Gallon Jug farm, also operated by the Bowen family. The Bowen management is dedicated to sustainability.

The trip here by car from Orange Walk Town is an incredible experience. If you don't have a rental car, the lodge offers road transfers from the international airport near Belize City for around US$300 for two people, US$50 each for additional persons.

The drive takes you through deep bush, including the Programme for Belize lands next door, and around every curve you might encounter anything but another vehicle — deer, a quash, a snake sliding across the road, one of Belize's cats, a flock of oscellated turkeys, a dense shower of butterflies. Closer to the lodge, which is on a quarter million acres of private land, you'll spy the neatly fenced fields of the 2,500-acre Gallon Jug farm, which raises cattle, corn, soybeans, cacao and coffee. Gallon Jug is the only place in Belize that produces coffee in any commercial amount. The lodge, across a suspension bridge at the end of a short paved road, enjoys an astounding setting. It was built literally on top of a Maya plaza. Around the lodge are tall, unexcavated mounds. If you want to get here more quickly, you can come by charter plane. The lodge will assist you in arranging the charter.

Chan Chich has 12 standard and superior thatch-roof cabañas, comfortable rather than luxurious, 24-hour electricity (but not air-conditioning), bath with hot and cold water shower, and a wrap-around verandah. There also is a two-bedroom villa with A/C. Meals are served in a large thatch cabaña, which also houses a gift shop, and the bar is next door — guests congregate there for a social hour before dinner. (About 60% of the food served here is grown or raised on Gallon Jug farm, including its 3,000-acre organic farm.) A lovely swimming pool, located at the edge of the jungle, is screened to keep out bugs. Wi-fi is available only around the main lodge building, not in the cabañas.

Around the lodge grounds is a series of cut and raked trails, ideal for wildlife spotting and birding. You can enjoy the jungle setting without having to wrestle snakes and briars. Will you see a jaguar? There's a better chance here than at most other places in Belize. The lodge has been averaging about one to two jaguar sighting a week.

Even if you don't see the elusive big cat, you'll definitely see plenty of other wildlife including howler monkeys, whether you walk the trails on your own or go on one of the nature tours offered by the lodge. Guides at Chan Chich are very knowledgeable. Birding is terrific here, with more than 350 species identified; often 40% or more of guests are birders. Canoeing, horseback riding, birdwatching and nature tours, and trips to Maya sites are available.

With meals and activities, you'll pay around US$500 double per night, or more, but it's worth it. **Very Expensive.**

Lamanai Outpost Lodge. Indian Church Village, 501-235-2441 or 954-636-1107 in the U.S., www.lamanai.com. Lamanai Outpost is another extraordinary jungle lodge. One of the reasons it's so special is the setting. Built by the late Colin Howells, a pioneer in hospitality circles in Belize, Lamanai Outpost perches on a low hillside with a view of the beautiful New River Lagoon. The lodge has 20 rooms in thatch cabañas set among hillside gardens. Lamanai Outpost Lodge is closely involved with archeological and nature study programs. Kids love Lamanai, as there always seem to be monkeys, parrots and other creatures around. A dock extends 130 feet into the lagoon and is good place for stargazing and swimming — just keep an eye out for Ol' Mister Croc. Birding is superb in this area, with at least 375 species identified nearby. The Lamanai ruins and archeological reserve are within walking distance. Indian Church village is also within walking distance, and near the village are the ruins of two Spanish churches. Package rates including lodging, meals, two tours and transfers from the international airport are not cheap. **Very Expensive.**

Orange Walk Town Lodging

Few tourists linger long in Orange Walk Town, and most hotels cater to visiting Belizeans and Mexicans. However, the number of good quality lodging is increasing here.

El Gran Mestizo Riverside Cabins, Naranhal St., Orange Walk Town, 501-322-2290, www.elgranmestizo.com. Associated with Hotel de la Fuente, the relatively new El Gran Mestizo is now a top lodging choice in Orange Walk Town. It has pleasant cabins with handcrafted furniture, air-conditioning, cable TV and wi-fi. El Gran Mestizo is on the New River, conveniently located but a bit away from the bustle of the town center. Premium cabins on the river (about US$100 plus tax) are worth the extra money over the standard ones. **Moderate.**

Hotel de la Fuente. 14 Main St., Orange Walk Town, 501-322-2290, www.hoteldelafuente.com. Orlando de la Fuente and his wife run this affordable, clean and centrally located in Orange Walk Town. The low rates (around US$40 to $85 plus tax) put it among the best values in Northern Belize. All 23 rooms and suites have air conditioning and wi-fi, and suites have kitchenettes. **Inexpensive to Moderate.**

Lamanai Landings, Philip Goldson Hwy. at Tower Hill, Orange Walk, 501-670-7846, www.lamanailandings.com. White-tiled and spare, the rooms here could be any place, but the New River scene, at Tower Hill a little south of town, from your private balcony places you in the Belize of jungle and hummingbird. Groups are well accommodated. In a thatch pavilion, Shuga City serves tasty ceviche and other standards, plus flashier dishes like habanero-glazed chicken. At night shine your flashlight on the river to catch the red eyes of crocodiles. Discounted rates are usually available. Moderate.

St. Christopher's, 10 Main St., Orange Walk Town, 501-322-2420. This well-established in-town hotel on the New River has comfortable rooms at modest rats. Doubles have A/C and wi-fi. Inexpensive

Dining in Orange Walk Town
The price level for restaurants in all areas is as follows:
Inexpensive: Under US$7
Moderate: US$8-$19
Expensive: US$20-$39
Very Expensive: Over US$40
Prices don't include tips or alcoholic drinks. If not otherwise stated, the price range is for one person for dinner.

Restaurants here are listed alphabetically.

Cocina Sabor, Belize-Corozal Rd., Orange Walk Town, 501-322-3482. Cacti populate this restaurant's patio, as do locals and a smattering of tourists who know good food. Flavors such as coconut rum salsa and ginger-citrus glaze give Belizean classics an energetic twist of flavor (the restaurant earns its name). Come on Thursday for popular Dollah Wing Day or any time, except Tuesday when it's closed, for great frozen mojitos and a very good meal. Open for lunch and dinner. **Moderate.**

Maracas Bar & Grill, Naranhal St., Orange Walk Town, 501-600-9143. Located beside the New River at El Gran Mestizo Riverside Cabins, Maracas is one of the top spots to eat in Northern Belize. Try the shrimp, conch or lobster ceviche, fajitas, grilled fish or chaya empanadas. Open for lunch and dinner Wednesday-Sunday. **Moderate.**

Nahil Mayab, Santa Ana and Guadalupe Sts., Orange Walk Town, 501-322-0831, www.nahilmayab.com. Lovely and not overdone Maya-themed decor, good service and the best ceviche we've had in years, only a few U.S. dollars for a serving of shrimp and conch ceviche, beautifully presented and big enough for two. There's air-conditioned dining inside and a lovely outdoor patio. Most entrees are around US$10 to $12. Closed Sunday. **Moderate.**

Tan's Pizza, 47 Castillo Alley, Orange Walk Town, 501-322-2669. Tan's is all about pizza, and it's really, really good. (Owners Tan and Randy also serve lasagna, burgers and wings.) The seating is open air under a big thatch palapa, where you can also enjoy rum and cold beer. Open Wednesday-Sunday, takeout available daily. **Inexpensive to Moderate.**

The small stalls and restaurants in **Central Park** (aka Fort Cairns) serve garnaches, tacos, empanadas, burgers, waffles and other breakfast, lunch and snack dishes for amazingly low prices. Open daily until around dark (**Inexpensive**). An excellent bakery in central Orange Walk Town is **Panificadora la Popular (Inexpensive).**

Western Belize

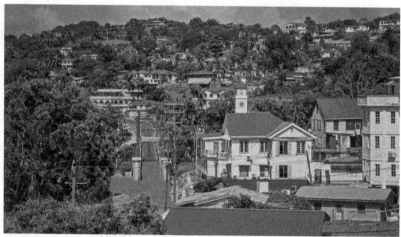

Hillside view of San Ignacio Town   Photo:Shutterstock

BUG OUT RATINGS

Ratings are on an A to F scale, just like your old high school report card. A is the top grade; F is failing. Grades are relative compared to other areas in Belize.

Popularity with Expats	B+
Safety	B-
Overall Cost of Living	B
Real Estate Bargains	B
Leisure Activities	B+
Restaurants	B
Cultural Activities	C+
Infrastructure	B
Medical Care	B
Shopping	B-
Farming & Ranching	A
Safety in Nuclear War	A-
Sustainable Living	B+
Bug Out Rating	**B+**

ADVANTAGES OF CAYO: • Relatively low cost for rural land and for houses in San Ignacio and Belmopan • Offers some of Belize's most beautiful inland scenery • Access to outdoor activities on beautiful rivers and mountains • Friendly mix of Mestizo and Maya residents • Agricultural area for citrus, cattle ranching and other • Good place to escape from hurricanes and other catastrophes

To exaggerate just a bit, Cayo is the "Wild West" of Belize. For would-be expats, it's an area where you can buy a small spread (or a large one) to raise citrus or Brahma cattle. For tourists, it is the turf in the traditional "surf 'n turf" visit to Belize — a few days on the cayes, typically Ambergris Caye or Caye Caulker, or perhaps on the beaches of the Southern Coast around Hopkins or Placencia, combined with some time on the mainland exploring ruins, rivers and rainforests.'

Cayo District has an area of more than 2,000 square miles, beginning near Belmopan and extending west and southwest to the Pine Ridge and into the Chiquibul wilderness and Maya Mountains. Belmopan City, Belize's capital, about 48 miles west of Belize City, has a reputation as a Nowheresville. Truth to say, the capital is not exactly a jumping place, but nearby is the Hummingbird Highway, the most scenic road in Belize. Also in the area are several top-notch jungle lodges. Belmopan is also in a growth spurt, with the population reaching around 20,000 and a lot of new development going on. San Ignacio and its sister town Santa Elena, total population also around 20,000, have an unassuming small town atmosphere.

Nothing in the twin towns of San Ignacio and Santa Elena will knock your boots off. There are few big cultural sights or museums, though there is an attractive Welcome Center with historical artifacts in downtown San Ignacio, and several important Maya sites are nearby. The shopping and other urban activities are somewhat limited. But San Ignacio, often just called Cayo or El Cayo, is a pleasant little burg. Locals are friendly, easy-going folk, mostly Mestizos with the usual Belizean mix of others, from Maya to Creoles to Chinese and Americans. Here you can buy groceries, check your email, do your banking and get a good cheap meal.

Progressive Mennonites have a large farming and commercial presence in the Spanish Lookout area northeast of San Ignacio. Some of the largest stores in Belize are in Spanish Lookout, with some of the lowest prices. There also are conservative Mennonites near San Ignacio/Santa Elena. Mostly to the southwest of San Ignacio are the green rolling hills of lodge country. Some of Belize's best jungle lodges are here.

Much of the land here is in cattle farms and citrus orchards. As you go west, you begin to see the influences of Guatemala. Maya women wash clothes in the river, and Benque Viejo del Carmen (population 7,000) strikes many as more Latin American and less Caribbean than most Belizean towns. Cross the border to Melchor de Mencos, Guatemala, and you're really in another world, one of more poverty, crime and where English is rarely spoken. However, prices for nearly everything are lower in Guatemala than in Belize.

In 2005, an oil drilling company, Belize Natural Energy, then run by two Irishwomen and three geologists, found oil near Spanish Lookout. The wells there currently are pumping light sweet crude at the rate of several thousand barrels a day. How long the oil will last, however, is another matter.

Cayo District Practicalities
Welcome Center: Cayo Welcome Center is in downtown San Ignacio, near Burns Avenue. In addition to tourism information and some interesting historical

and cultural displays, the complex has dining, shopping and a nice pay parking lot.

Banks: Heritage Bank, ScotiaBank, Belize Bank and Atlantic Bank have branches in San Ignacio. Heritage Bank, Atlantic Bank and Belize Bank also have offices in Belmopan, along with the home office of the new National Bank of Belize. Currently, only Heritage Bank has an office in Benque Viejo del Carmen.

Groceries: The two largest and generally cheapest grocery stores in the San Ignacio area are Mega Food in Santa Elena and Costless, near Cahal Pech on Benque Viejo Road. Both have the same owners. Celina's Superstore on Burns Avenue is a small friendly place to shop for groceries and other items. The San Ignacio market near downtown across from the football field has fruit, vegetables and some clothes and household items. Saturday morning is the best time to visit, but some stands are open daily. There also are fruit and vegetable stands downtown near the Welcome Center.

Restaurants: San Ignacio has many good small dining spots, including Guava Limb Café, Ko-Ox Han-Nah (formerly Hannah's), Sanny's, Pop's, The Crave, Erva's, Mr. Greedy's Pizzeria, Hode's, Cenaida's, Serendib and others. Benny's Kitchen in San José Succotz is a local favorite. Belmopan has several good places to eat, including Corkers, which is the best of the bunch, Bull Frog Inn and Caladium.

Medical: A private hospital, La Loma Luz, is in Santa Elena. Among public facilities, there is a district hospital in San Ignacio in a newish facility off the road to Bullet Tree and a regional hospital in Belmopan. Mopan Clinic is in Benque Viejo.

Infrastructure: Belmopan, San Ignacio/Santa Elena and Benque Viejo have municipal water and sewerage systems. More remote areas of Cayo are off the electrical grid and have to depend on cisterns and wells for water and on satellite internet. A new bridge in Santa Elena across the river should reduce the number of bridge closings due to floods down the Macal and Mopan.

Real Estate

Cayo covers a fairly large area, with a lot of agricultural land along with wild bush. It includes the capital, Belmopan, and the twin towns of San Ignacio/Santa Elena, plus Spanish Lookout and Benque Viejo. Thus property values vary widely. Land in tracts of under 50 to 100 acres along the beautiful Hummingbird Highway is selling in the range of US$1,500 to $4,000 an acre. These tracts usually have some road frontage and electricity. Large tracts in Cayo go for as little as US$500 to $1,000 an acre, but some opportunistic owners are asking blue sky numbers such as US$10,000 an acre or more. The same blue-sky prices are being asked for some homes, especially those offered by real estate agents. Belizean-style homes start at around US$30,000, or even less, but you can pay up to half a million or more for a large U.S.-style home on an estate tract.

Property Listings

Here are a few of the properties available in 2018, offered by individuals and real estate firms. Prices shown are in U.S. dollars and are asking prices.

• Four-bedroom, two-bath house in San Ignacio Town, near shops and stores, on 75' x 100' lot, tile floors, burglar bars, US$87,500

• Three-bedroom, two-bath 2,000 sq. ft. concrete home in Belmopan City, US$115,000

• 107 acres near Negroman area west of San Ignacio, 500 ft. river frontage, currently used as cattle and goat ranch, US$107,000

• 51 acres near Spanish Lookout, with small house, 5 acres planned in fruit trees, US$55,700

• 10-acre farm near Camalote village already producing truck crops including peppers, lettuce and okra, with small wooden solar-powered house and a 2,000 sq. ft. steel warehouse or work building, municipal water, US$145,000

• Corner lot in Cristo Rey village, ready to build on, US$11,000

• Two-bedroom, two-bath air-conditioned 1,270 sq. ft. concrete house in Georgeville on fenced 1-acre lot, with saltwater swimming pool, 18,000 gallon water tank, sold completely furnished, US$195,900

• 80 acres of mostly cleared, fully fenced fertile land, suitable for farm or ranch, about 5 miles from Spanish Lookout in Billy White area, access by gravel road (reportedly soon to be paved), power nearby, US$165,000

• 150 acres of jungle land in Yalbac area about 8 miles from Spanish Lookout, 400 ft. frontage on gravel road, strong creek as water source, 2 acres cleared and planted in fruit and citrus trees, US$180,000

• 5.3 acres in the Mountain Pine Ridge, with bold stream, truly a private hideaway in the Maya Mountains, US$45,000

• 9-hole "jungle golf course" near Belmopan, the only completed public course on the mainland, total of 30 acres, four new 800 sq. ft. air-conditioned deluxe, cottages, restaurant and club house, and other buildings on Roaring River, US1,600,000

Local Real Estate Agents

Ceiba Realty (Jonathan Lohr), 161 George Price Hwy., Santa Elena, 501-824-4050; www.ceibarealestatebelize.com

Keller Williams Rainforest Realty (Macarena Rose), 22 Benque Viejo Rd., San Ignacio, 501-804-0195, www.rainforestrealty.com

Tropic Real Estate (Howard Oldham), P.O. Box 453, Belmopan City, 501-824-3675; www.realestatebelize.com.

Visiting Cayo District
How to Get There
San Ignacio is about 67 miles, or about 1 3/4 to 2 hours by car, west of Belize City, and the Guatemala border is another 9 miles west. Belmopan City is about 45 miles or about an hour west of Belize City.

The George Price Highway (formerly Western Highway) is a paved two-lane road from Belize City to Belmopan and then on to San Ignacio. It continues (as the Benque Highway) to Benque Viejo Town and the Guatemala border. After rain parts of the road can be extremely slick, and in most places there are no shoulders, so accidents are common. As of 2018, there are plans to resurface and improve the entire highway.

Several bus lines run from Belize City to Belmopan and San Ignacio, with frequent, inexpensive service (US$4 to $5) from Belize City. The buses run from the main terminal (the old Novelo's terminal) in Belize City. If coming from the international airport, you'll have to take a taxi into town (US$25 for two people, US$5 extra for each additional person) or lug your bags by foot or take a taxi, if available, about 2 miles to the Philip Goldson Highway, where you can catch a bus into Belize City (US$1) and connect with a San Ignacio bus at Novelo's.

In addition, several operators have shuttle vans running from the airports and water taxi places in Belize City to San Ignacio. Fare is about US$40 to $75 per person one-way. You need to book ahead. Here are some of the shuttle services. William's Shuttle, run by a longtime local expat in Cayo, is probably the most recommended. Rates to Belmopan are usually lower.

William's Shuttle Belize (www.williamsshuttlebelize.com)
Discounted Belize Shuttles and Tours
(www.discountedbelizeshuttlesandtours.com)
Belize Shuttles and Transfers (www.belizeshuttlesandtransfers.com)
Belize Transportation Services
(www.belizeshuttleservices.sanignaciotown.com)
Mayan Heart World (www.mayanheartworld.net)
PACZ Tours (www.pacztours.net)

Most hotels and lodges around San Ignacio and in the Mountain Pine Ridge also will provide transport for US$120 to $200 for up to four persons.

Guatemalan transportation services **Linea Dorado** and **Fuente del Norte** run daily from the Belize City Marine Terminal near the Swing Bridge to Flores, Guatemala, near Tikal, for around US$25. These buses are not supposed to pick up or drop off passengers in Belize (except in Belize City), but usually you can get off at the Belize-Guatemala border, or even in San Ignacio.

Finally, some taxis at the international airport will drive you to San Ignacio. Bargain, but expect to pay around US$125 for up to four people.

Flights to Belmopan and San Ignacio: Tropic Air (www.tropicair.com) has four daily flights from the international airport near Belize City to Belmopan and to Maya Flats between San Ignacio and Benque Viejo. Cost one-way to Belmopan is US$98 and to San Ignacio/Benque US$137.

Getting Around the Mountain Pine Ridge: To explore the Mountain Pine Ridge on your own, you must have a car, or go on a tour, as there is no bus service. Two roads lead to the Mountain Pine Ridge reserve. The first, the Pine Ridge Road (also known as the Chiquibul Road) turns off the George Price Highway at Georgeville, at about Mile 63. This road, unpaved and very rough in places, depending on when it has rained and when it was last scraped, runs past the Barton Creek area, large farms and the Slate Creek preserve, leading to the entrance of the Mountain Pine Ridge reserve. It's about 10 miles from Georgeville to the reserve gate, where you must stop and register with the guard, who will take your name, vehicle information and destination, but there is no entrance fee.

The other route to the Pine Ridge is the Cristo Rey Road, which turns off the George Price Highway at about Mile 68½, at Santa Elena just before you enter San Ignacio. The mostly unpaved road runs through Cristo Rey and San Antonio villages. It is about 12½ miles by this route to the junction with the Pine Ridge Road, and then another 1½ miles to the reserve gate, the same gate you would reach from Georgeville.

Note: Loans were arranged in late 2017 to fund the improvement and paving of the entire Caracol Road. Completion date is not definite.

From the Pine Ridge gate, you continue on an unpaved road. At some points the roadbed is sandy, and at others red clay. If you are going to Hidden Valley Inn or Hidden Valley Falls, about 4 miles into the reserve you turn left (watch for a sign) and go a few miles to the lodge or falls. If, instead of turning, you go on, you'll soon see the Pine Ridge Lodge, on the right, a little more than 4 miles past the entrance gate. About 1/2 mile farther, there's a turn to the right to Blancaneaux Lodge; Five Sisters Lodge is a little farther on the same spur road. If you continue on the "main road" rather than turning on the spur road to Blancaneaux and Gaia Lodge, you will pass near the Rio On, a popular swimming area, and the Rio Frio cave. At about 14 miles into the reserve, you'll reach Douglas De Silva (formerly called Augustine), a tiny collection of small white frame houses with tin roofs. Turn left here and you'll be on your way to Caracol. Ten miles from Douglas De Silva, you cross the Macal River and are in the Chiquibul wilderness. Caracol is about 50 miles from the reserve entrance gate.

Note that due to occasional bandit attacks in the Mountain Pine Ridge, you are asked not to go on your own to Caracol. You are supposed to go in a convoy guarded by Belize Defence Forces troops. Check locally to see if this plan is still in effect and for time and place to meet up with the convoy. You can drive alone to the four lodges in the Pine Ridge, but not all the way to Caracol (although some do.)

Keep in mind that most of the roads in this region are logging roads. After heavy rains, the clay sections in particular can become extremely slick and difficult to negotiate, even with a four-wheel drive vehicle. If you do not have your own vehicle, you can take a taxi from San Ignacio to the lodges in the Pine Ridge (perhaps US$75-$100 for up to four or five people). A Mesh bus makes trips daily except Sunday from San Ignacio to Cristo Rey and San Antonio villages (about US$1.50, ask locally for schedule). It gets within about 1½ miles of the Mountain Pine Ridge entrance gate. The lodges in the Pine Ridge also provide transfers from Belize City to the Pine Ridge (about US $150 to $200 per party, one-way). Hotel packages usually include transfers from Belize City. You also take a charter flight to Blancaneaux's airstrip.

What to See and Do in Cayo

This part of Western Belize offers some of the best caving in Central America. **Actun Tunichil Muknal** near Teakettle village is a must-see. A full-day guided tour from San Ignacio is around US$100-$125, including transport, a guide –you cannot go into this cave without a licensed, trained guide, and lunch. Many other caves are in the region, including **Barton Creek Cave** off the

Chiquibul Road – it is best viewed by canoe. **Che Chem Ha** cave is on private property about 25 minutes from San Ignacio, and **Flour Camp Cave** is another popular cave. **Rio Frio** is an open cave in the Mountain Pine Ridge. **St. Herman's Cave** is off the Hummingbird Highway near the inland Blue Hole.

There also excellent hiking, mountain biking, birding, cave tubing, canoeing and horseback riding. There are important Maya sites, including **Caracol, Cahal Pech, El Pilar** and **Xunantunich**.

The **Belize Botanic Gardens** (www.belizebotanic.org, open daily, admission US$15 for self-guided tour and US$30 for guided tour) at duPlooy's Lodge are the largest gardens in Belize, and well worth visiting. **Green Hills Butterfly Farm** (Mile 8, Chiquibul Rd., 501-834-4017, www.greenhills.net, open daily, admission US$10) is the most interesting butterfly operation in Belize. There is also a small butterfly center at Chaa Creek Lodge.

There are government-sponsored **Houses of Culture** in San Ignacio/Santa Elena (7 King St., San Ignacio, 501-824-0783) and Benque Viejo (64 Joseph Street, 501-823-2697, both www.nichbelize.org).

For zipline enthusiasts, **Calico Jack's zipline** is at Seven Mile/Progresso off the Chiquibul Road toward the Mountain Pine Ridge, and **Jaguar Paw zipline** is at Cave's Branch near Belmopan.

There's even a small golf course, the nine-hold **Roaring River Golf Course** near Belmopan off Mile 50½ of the George Price Highway. You can play all day for US$25. Rental clubs available. Watch out for the crocs in the water traps. Roaring River Golf Course also has five nice cabins to rent (Expensive), with a Jacuzzi-style pool, and a restaurant, The Meating Place, open to the public with advance reservations. Guest staying here can play golf free.

Also near Belmopan – actually in Belize District, not Cayo – but an easy stop when traveling between San Ignacio/Belmopan and Belize City- is the wonderful **Belize Zoo** (Mile 29, George Price Hwy., 501-822-8000, www.belizezoo.org). It's fairly small, on 29 acres, but it has 125 of Belize's native mammals and many of its birds and reptiles, all in natural settings. Absolutely worth seeing anytime you're in Belize. Open daily 8:30 to 5, admission US$15 adults, US$3 children.

Near Belmopan, too, is the **Hummingbird Highway.** This is Belize's most scenic road. You'll take this road when going to Dangriga, Hopkins, Placencia or Punta Gorda. Along the way, don't miss stopping and taking a swim in the inland Blue Hole (**St. Herman's Blue Hole National Park,** open daily 8 to 4:30, admission US$4.) While you're there, also visit St. Herman's Cave. A little farther south is **Five Blues Lake National Park** (Mile 32, Hummingbird Hwy., admission US$5), where there are small Maya sites as well as a lake. The lake mysteriously drained to almost nothing in 2006, but strangely filled back up in 2010.

In Belmopan City, of course, are many Belize government buildings as well as a number of embassies, including the US$50 million U.S. Embassy complex.

About a half an hour southeast from San Ignacio is the **Mountain Pine Ridge** reserve, which covers more than 100,000 acres. Visitors here are surprised by what they find. Instead of low-lying, bug-infested tropical vistas, they find hills and low mountains with few mosquitoes and temperatures that can dip into the 40s and 50s F. in winter. Instead of lush Tarzan-style jungle, in some parts of the region they find pinewoods, sparse grass and red clay mindful of the Southern Appalachians. Many of the Mountain Pines (also known as Honduras Pines) in this area have been killed by the Southern Pine Beetle, but the pines are coming back.

Except for a small settlement at Augustine/Douglas de Silva, groups of workers living at the area's handful of lodges and some remote squatter settlements occupied by illegal immigrants from Guatemala, few people live in the Mountain Pine Ridge. Much of the land is government property, and some is owned, mostly in large tracts, by foreign interests or wealthy Belizeans. The roads in the region are former logging roads, most hardly better than dirt tracks. Controlled logging continues, and the area is also the site of occasional Belize Defence Force or U.S. Army training exercises. In the dry season, usually March to late May or early June, the area sees higher temperatures (though still cooler than in most of the rest of inland Belize), and forest fires are a threat.

Also in this area is **Noj Koxx Meen Elijio Panti National Park** (www.epnp.org), a 13,000-acre park named after the fame Guatemalan natural healer who died at age 103 in 1997. There is as yet little good access or development of this park for visitors.

Beyond the Mountain Pine Ridge is **Chiquibul,** a great wilderness area and forest reserve. It is home to Caracol, the largest and most important Maya site in Belize. Once into the Chiquibul, the vegetation turns to broadleaf rainforest, more like the jungle you've seen in the movies. It is beautiful country, with isolated waterfalls where you can slip in for a skinny dip, incredible cave systems, unpolluted streams and blue skies.

San Ignacio has many tour operators that can take to Maya sites and other attractions in Cayo. These include PACZ Tours, Yute Expeditions, River Rat, Belizean Sun Tours, Paradise Expeditions and others. You'll typically pay about US$80 to $90 per person for a tour, including lunch.

It's not really a visitor destination, but especially if you're thinking seriously of living in Belize, you must visit **Spanish Lookout.** This is a progressive Mennonite community just north of San Ignacio. It's the farming center of Belize, producing most of the country's chickens, eggs, cheese and truck crops. It's also where you can look at and buy Mennonite prefab houses. There are a number of large (for Belize) stores such as Westrac auto parts, Reimer's Feeds and Farmer's Trading Centre, places where you can buy hardware, building supplies, auto parts, tires and other necessities at good prices. There are gas stations, a couple of restaurants but no hotels. It's also worth seeing what hard work and self-sufficiency can do.

An offbeat attraction west of San Ignacio is **Poustinia Land Art Park** (www.poustinialandart.org), a former 100-acre cattle ranch that is now home to a collection of about three dozen outdoor sculptures and installations. Poustinia was established by an architect in Belmopan. Admission requires an appointment and costs US$10. Call the Benque House of Culture at 501-823-2697 for information on how to visit.

Maya Sites
Caracol (www.caracol.org), Spanish for "snail," perhaps named for the many snail shells found on the site, is located on the Vaca Plateau in the Chiquibul Forest

Preserve at about 1,600 feet elevation. It was one of the most important Maya political and population centers of the Classic Period. At its height it covered more than 75 square miles in area and had a population of nearly 200,000, more than twice the population of present-day metropolitan Belize City, and some 36,000 structures. It rivaled Tikal in size and power, and in the middle of the 6th century CE it fought wars with that mighty city-state. At one point Caracol's rulers conquered Tikal, at least for a time.

Archeologists Diane and Arlen Chase of the University of Central Florida have been working at Caracol for many years, along with other archeologists. Still, only a small percentage of the buildings have been excavated. **Caana** is the centerpiece. At 136 feet, this temple is still the tallest human-built structure in all of Belize. You can climb Caana and view much of Caracol, which has been partly cleared of vegetation and undergrowth.

Tour operators in San Ignacio and at various lodges in Cayo will take you to Caracol for around US$100 to $125 per person including transport, lunch, guide and admission fee. You can drive yourself, but at most times, due to the ongoing risk of bandits in the area from Guatemala, drivers go in convoys accompanied by Belize Defence Force soldiers. Check locally for the time when you meet up with the BDF at Douglas de Silva. It is about a 50-mile, two to three-hour drive, depending on road conditions, from San Ignacio. Roads to Caracol are being improved, but in the rainy season especially it can be slow going. Gas up before you go as there are no gas stations along the way. Caracol has a good visitor center, and the site is open daily from around 8 to 5. Admission US$15. If not with a group, you can hire a guide at the site.

Xunantunich ("Stone Woman" from the Yucatec and Mopan Maya languages and pronounced shoo-NAN-ta-nitch) is 8 miles west of San Ignacio, just off the Benque Road/George Price Highway. It is on a hill overlooking the Mopan River. It was settled around 400 BC and abandoned around 1000 CE. At its height, some as many as 10,000 people lived here. While it's not a huge site, it's popular because it's easy to get to from San Ignacio by bus (BZ$1.50), taxi (around US$10) or car. You cross the river on a hand-pulled pedestrian and car ferry, free but it's nice to tip the hard-working operator, and then go up a hill to the informative new visitor center. El Castillo is the most prominent building at Xunantunich and is only one foot shorter than Caana at Lamanai. From the top, there are amazing views into Guatemala. Open daily during daylight hours. Admission US$10. Licensed guides (not necessary but can add to the value of your visit) charge around US$20 for a small group. If you choose to go on a tour from San Ignacio, you'll pay US$45 to $50 per person, including transportation from downtown San Ignacio, guide, entrance fee and a snack.

El Pilar, about 7 miles north from Bullet Tree Falls on the Guatemala border, provides a quiet experience for the few visitors. It is also an excellent birding site. There are two groupings of temple mounds, ball courts and courtyards. The excavations here so far are minor, and the site is overgrown with vegetation. Before going, visit Be Pukte Cultural Center in Bullet Tree Falls. Admission is US$10. If you're not driving, you can probably get a taxi for around US$25 to $30. Only a few tour companies visit El Pilar.

Cahal Pech, ("Place of the Ticks" although you probably won't be bothered by any) located on a high hill just west of San Ignacio, near the Cahal Pech Village hotel. Cahal Pech was re-discovered in the 1950s, but archeological work didn't begin in earnest until 1988, when a team from San Diego State, along with Belizean archeology expert Dr. Jaime Awe, found almost three dozen structures on a three-acre site. Excavation is on going. This isn't nearly as impressive as Caracol or Xunantunich, but it's easy to get to and has an informative visitor center (501-824-4236.) Cahal Pech is open 8 to 5 daily. Admission is US$5. Until you're in good shape, we recommend you drive or take a taxi up the steep hill to Cahal Pech.

Belmopan City Lodging
The price level for lodging in all areas is as follows:
Inexpensive: Under US$75
Moderate: US$75-$150
Expensive: US$151-$300
Very Expensive: Over US$300
Prices are for a double room in high season (usually late November to Easter). Rates, which do not include taxes, service charges or meals (except in some cases breakfast), may be higher during holiday periods, especially Christmas and New Years. If specific prices are mentioned, they are plus 9% hotel tax and in some cases a service charge, usually 10%.

The lodging choices in Belmopan proper are small motels and hotels, geared more toward the needs of government bureaucrats and others on government business than of tourists. Jungle lodges and other more interesting lodging choices are located outside of Belmopan along the George Price and Hummingbird highways.

Bull Frog Inn, 25 Half Moon Ave., Belmopan City, 501-822-2111; www.bullfroginn.com. This will remind you of a small mom 'n pop motel in the U.S. or Canada. The 25 rooms have air-conditioning, cable TV and wi-fi and are clean and comfortable enough, though your bed may not be quite as new as you'd like. Rates are geared to business people and government officials who make up 70% of the guests here. There's a restaurant with open-air and indoor seating. **Moderate.**

El Rey Hotel. 23 Moho St., Belmopan City, 501-822-3438, www.elreyhotel.com. A budget spot in Belmopan for more than two decades, a change in management in 2012 upgraded it some with A/C, cable TV and wi-fi. Rates here start at around US$35 double for the economy rooms. The standard rooms go for US$65. All rates plus tax. There's also one more expensive suite. **Inexpensive.**

Hibiscus Hotel, Hibiscus Plaza, Melhado Parade, Belmopan City, 501-633-5323; www.hibiscusbelize.com. This six-room hotel is one of Belmopan's better values, and it's next door to a good restaurant, Corker's (under the same family ownership). Rooms have king or twin beds, A/C, cable TV, wi-fi and mini-fridges. Room rates are US$60 double plus tax. Choose this for central location and honest value. **Inexpensive.**

KenMar's Bed & Breakfast, 22-24 Halfmoon Ave., Belmopan City, 501-822-0118; www.kenmar.bz. This attractive guesthouse, located near the Bull Frog

Inn, has 10 spotless, air-conditioned rooms, with mini-fridges and cable TV. Get one of the larger rooms if possible. Cooked-to-order breakfast included in rates. **Moderate.**

Inn at Twin Palms, Mile 54, Hummingbird Hwy., Belmopan City, 501-822-0231. A few years ago, this inn was named one of the best of its kind in the world by a major social media site. It has since expanded to 16 rooms, with gardens, gym and a nice swimming pool. A continental breakfast with lots of fruit is included in the rates. **Moderate.**

Yim Saan Hotel & Restaurant, 4253 Hummingbird Hw., Belmopan City; 501-822-1356; www.yimsaan-hotel.com. This Chinese-owned property is among the nicer lodgings in Belmopan. The 25 5ooms are modern and clean, with A/C, wi-fi and cable TV, and 15 of them have been upgraded. There's a Chinese restaurant on the first floor. **Inexpensive to Moderate.**

Belmopan Area Lodges

Pook's Hill, off Mile 52½, George Price Hwy., Teakettle Village (P.O. Box 14, Belmopan City); 501-832-2017; www.pookshillbelize.com. *Directions: Turn south off the Western Hwy. at Mile 52 1/2 at Teakettle village. Go about 4 miles on a dirt road, then turn right and go another 1½ miles to the lodge (the route is well-signed.)* How about a remote lodge in deep jungle, next to a river, near Actun Tunichil Muknal and on the site of a Maya plaza, run by an engaging international staff where meals and drinks are by lantern-light and you're isolated from the cares of civilization? That pretty much describes Pook's Hill, a collection of thatched, Maya-style cabañas on 300 acres next to Tapir Mountain Reserve and the Roaring River. Hiking, tubing and river swimming in the Roaring River and excellent birding are available. You can take an Actun Tunichil Muknal tour from the lodge – it's a 45-minute hike away. Meals, served buffet-style by with a common table sure to get everyone talking, are tasty and filling. Pook's Hill, by the way, is named after Rudyard Kipling's Puck of Pook's Hill. **Expensive.**

Belize Jungle Dome, off Mile 47, George Price Hwy., Belmopan City, 501-628-8550, www.belizejungledome.com. *Directions: From George Price Highway, turn north at Mile 49 and cross bridge over Belize River. Follow gravel road 3 miles until you see Banana Bank sign. Turn right and follow dirt road 2 miles.* Owned by a former English professional soccer player and a former MTV Europe VJ, the suites and rooms at this inn have tile floors, lots of windows, air-conditioning and an uncluttered look. There's a full complement of tours available. For large groups, a three-bedroom house is available. **Moderate.**

Banana Bank Lodge & Belize Horseback Adventures, off Mile 49, George Price Hwy. (P.O. Box 48, Belmopan City), 501-832-2020, www.bananabank.com. *Directions: From George Price Highway, turn north at Mile 49 and cross bridge over Belize River. Follow gravel road 3 miles until you see Banana Bank sign. Turn right and follow dirt road 2 miles.*

You're guaranteed to see a jaguar at this lodge. A spotted jaguar called Tika lived here for 26 years and after her death was replaced by Tika 2. The Belize government has granted permission for the lodge to have the jaguar. (Note that some wildlife rescue organizations and other groups in Belize strongly oppose the practice of keeping wild animals and birds in captivity, even with government permission.)

Banana Bank is especially good for those who like to ride, as the lodge keeps about 100 horses. John Carr, who in his youth was a real Montana cowboy and rodeo star, in 1973 with a partner bought Banana Bank, then a 4,000-acre ranch with 1,500 head of cattle. Carr and his wife, Carolyn, have lived on the ranch since 1977, one of a small group of pioneering American expats who adopted Belize as their home. Carolyn is a noted artist. Her paintings of wild creatures and Belize City street scenes have been widely exhibited, and her work has appeared on the cover the Belize telephone book twice, most recently in 2009. She has a studio at the lodge.

The lodge offers a variety of accommodations: three budget rooms, six standard rooms with air-conditioning, five thatch cabañas (one with A/C), and three suites with air-conditioning. Packages, including equestrian packages, are available. Banana Bank is a family-oriented spot. The Carrs' daughter Leisa helps run the lodge. The food is filling and tasty, served family-style at moderate prices. There is something of a Christian atmosphere here, with prayers sometimes offered at meals. There's a nice swimming pool, with a bar and dining area. **Moderate to Expensive.**

Dream Valley Belize, Young Gyal Rd., Teakettle Village, 501-665-1000, www.dreamvalleybelize.com. Set at the jungle's edge on 60 acres on the Belize River, Dream Valley is a Belizean-owned lodge. There's a selection of rooms and cabañas, all with A/C, TV and wi-fi. **Expensive.**

Ian Andersons's Caves Branch Adventure Co. & Jungle Lodge. Hummingbird Highway (P.O. Box 356), Belmopan City), 501-610-3451 or toll-free 866-357-2698 from U.S./Canada, www.cavesbranch.com. *Directions: About 14 miles from Belmopan at Mile 41½ of the Hummingbird Highway (mile markers on the Hummingbird from Belmopan run backwards, starting at Mile 55 at the George Price Highway), turn left and follow a dirt road less than a mile to the lodge grounds.*

Set in a large chunk of private land on the Caves Branch river, this is one of Belize's premier jungle lodges for travelers who like to do things outdoors. Ian Anderson, a Canadian, and his teams run strenuous caving, hiking and river trips, and they do a top-flight job. They call them adventure trips, not sightseeing. In short, this is not a place for couch potatoes. More than a dozen adventure tours are offered, open to non-guests as well as guests. Each Caves Branch guide has been trained in first aid and in cave and wilderness rescue.

For years, the lodge has been going more upscale, with a new swimming pool, botanical garden and tony treehouse suites. The treehouses are operated by Viva, which also runs Sleeping Giant Rainforest Lodge nearby as well as Jaguar Reef and Almond Beach in Hopkins and other properties. Note that in the late spring dry season the river that runs by the lodge may be completely dry. **Expensive to Very Expensive.**

Rock Farm Guest House, Roaring River Rd. (P. O. Box 259), Belmopan, 501-610-0400, www.rockfarmbelize.com. Directions: *From Mile 49 George Price Highway about 3 miles west of Belmopan turn south (left if you're coming from Belize City) at the big Westar service station. Go about 1.2 miles on the unpaved* *road and watch for Rock Farm and Belize Bird Rescue signs on left. Open gate and drive to guest house.* You'll like the conviviality and hospitality of the British hosts and the homey comforts at Rock Farm, on a 50-acre property a few miles from Belmopan City. Jerry Larder grew up in Fiji and has been in more than 160 countries, mostly as an oil and gas consultant. Wife Nikki Buxton heads up the bird rescue program. Three air-conditioned guestrooms with wi-fi are on the second level of the large and well-designed home of the owners. There also are one-bedroom, one-bath cabañas and a two-bedroom, two-bath cottage (none air-conditioned) for short- or long-term rental. Rates range from around US$90 to $110 double for rooms and US45 to $120 for the cabañas and cottage. Home cooked meals are extra but are reasonably priced. The inn is licensed to sell beer and wine, and you can bring your own bottle. As a guest, you can get a tour of the Belize Bird Rescue operation. Typically, around 200 parrots are cared for here, along with some raptors, owls and other birds. Birds that can be rehabilitated are released to the wild, while others, too ill or maltreated, have to be cared for indefinitely. The rescue operation is a labor of love for the owners, one that they have mostly paid for out of their own pockets. Revenue from the Rock Farm Guest House goes toward supporting this worthy cause. You must see the famous "water wheel" that Jerry designed and built to pump water from Roaring River -- it's amazing! **Inexpensive to Moderate.**

Sleeping Giant Rainforest Lodge, Mile 36, Hummingbird Hwy., 888-822-2448, www.vivabelize.com. Part of the Viva Belize group that includes Jaguar Reef and Almond Beach in Hopkins, plus the treehouses at Ian Anderson's Caves Branch, Sleeping Giant is one of the newer jungle lodges in Cayo. It's set on a hillside at the edge of the Sibun Forest Reserve on the Sibun River, which is swimmable, but there is also a swimming pool and hot tub. The accommodations include garden view, river view, Spanish casita and new mountain view units. Most an attractive combination of stone, stucco, tile and thatch, with ceiling skylights. They're air-conditioned and nicely furnished but don't have TV. Dining at Sleeping Giant is from a la carte menus at the highly rated **Grove House** restaurant. Dinner entrees are mostly in the US$24 to $32 range. The well-run lodge offers a variety of tours and trips, including ziplining, horseback riding, cave tubing, river kayaking and visits to Maya sites and caves. **Expensive to Very Expensive.**

Dining in Belmopan

The price level for restaurants in all areas is as follows:
Inexpensive: Under US$7
Moderate: US$8-$19
Expensive: US$20-$39
Very Expensive: Over US$40
Prices don't include tips or alcoholic drinks. If not otherwise stated, the price range is for one person for dinner.

Restaurants here are listed alphabetically.
Caladium. Near Market Square, Belmopan City, 501-822-2754. Caladium is an old-school Belizean-owned restaurant serves good breakfasts and Belizean

224

favorites such as stew chicken, plus burgers and even steaks. Air-conditioned, and it has a bar. Often busy. Open daily for breakfast, lunch and dinner. Closed Sunday. **Inexpensive to Moderate.**

Cheers, Mile 31¼ , George Price Hwy. near Belize Zoo, 501-822-8014. This open-air roadside restaurant (it also has some cabañas for overnight) is not in Belmopan City or even in Cayo District but is on the way, not far from the Belize Zoo. It's a good stopping point for a Belikin and a beefburger or some Belizean food. Friendly staff and cool atmosphere. **Inexpensive to Moderate.**

Corker's Restaurant and Wine Bar, Hibiscus Plaza, corner of Constitution and Melhado Parade, Belmopan City, 501-822-0400. This is one of our favorite places to stop for a meal and a drink in Belmopan. It's on the second floor of Hibiscus Plaza and next door to the Hibiscus Hotel (owned by members of the same family.) The menu has a huge number of choices, from around a dozen kinds of salads and more than 15 varieties of beef and chicken burgers to fish and chips to ribs and steaks and several Italian pasta dishes. The combo platters, while not cheap, are huge. Drinks are good pours and not overpriced. Open for lunch and dinner. Closed Sunday. **Moderate to Very Expensive.**

Everest Indian Restaurant, Belmopan City, 501-600-8850. Located behind the fire station, near the market and bus station, in a small, unprepossessing shack, the Everest serves wonderful Indian and Nepalese food. Owner Raj is friendly and works hard to please. Try the vegetarian platter, but there are chicken and other non-veg dishes as well. It's all well prepared and delicious, not to mention being a good value. **Inexpensive to Moderate.**

Farm House Deli, Rio Grande Ave., Belmopan City, 501-822-3354. Small deli with big sandwiches. Authentic deli sandwiches like Reubens, pastrami and corn beef on rye, plus burgers, pork barbecue and a great smoked fish chowder. Closed Monday. **Moderate.**

San Ignacio/Santa Elena Area Lodging

The price level for lodging in all areas is as follows:
Inexpensive: Under US$75
Moderate: US$75-$150
Expensive: US$151-$300
Very Expensive: Over US$300

Prices are for a double room in high season (usually late November to Easter). Rates, which do not include taxes, service charges or meals (except in some cases breakfast), may be higher during holiday periods, especially Christmas and New Years. If specific prices are mentioned, they are plus 9% hotel tax and in some cases a service charge, usually 10%.

These hotels and guesthouses are listed alphabetically.

Aguada Hotel & Restaurant, Aguada St., Santa Elena, 501-804-3609; www.aguadabelize.com. Just north of the George Price Highway near La Loma Luz hospital, this motel is a real find. You can stay here in a clean, modern room or small suite with air-conditioning for around US$50 to $80 double year-round, plus 18% room tax and service. The 18 rooms — some were added on the second floor and in a new building in the back — are not overly large. There's even a swimming pool. The café is a friendly, casual place serving Belizean and American dishes at moderate prices. **Inexpensive to Moderate.**

Amber Sunset Jungle Lodge, Mile 59, George Price Hwy., Unitedville, Cayo, 501-824-3141, www.ambersunsetbelize.com. This Belizean-owned small lodge is perched on a 28-acre hillside not far off the Price Highway, about midway between San Ignacio and Belmopan. Lodging is in five thatch cabañas, up a long series of steps (so this is not for the physically challenged). There's a small pool with bar and an open-air restaurant, The Jungle Pot, with scenic views. Not deluxe, but it offers a pleasant family-run experience. **Expensive.**

Cahal Pech Village Resort. Cahal Pech Rd., 1 mile west of town off George Price Hwy., San Ignacio, 501-824-3740; www.cahalpech.com. This resort is set on a high, steep hill at the western edge of San Ignacio, near the Cahal Pech Maya site. It is very popular and often full, due to the relatively moderate rates and scenic views over the valley. Ever expanding, the property now has more than 50 rooms, suites and cabañas. More recent additions are new hillside cottages and a two-level swimming pool, guarded by a giant statue of a pteryldactl. **Moderate.**

Casa Blanca Guest House. 10 Burns Ave., San Ignacio, 501-824-2080; www.casablancaguesthouse.com. While it's near the center of busy San Ignacio, this small guesthouse, winner of the Belize Tourism Board's "best small hotel award" a few years ago, is a great choice if you want to save money but be comfortable. The eight rooms, with white walls trimmed in mahogany and locally made wood furniture, are a step above typical budget lodging. All rooms have TV and more-expensive ones have air-conditioning. You can prepare snacks or meals in the shared kitchen. Casa Blanca is often fully booked. **Inexpensive.**

Hi-Et Guest House. West St., San Ignacio, 501-824-2828. This 10-room guesthouse may be your best option in the cheapie segment. There's a common room with fridge and free wi-fi. No air-conditioning. Cash only. **Inexpensive.**

Ka'ana Boutique Resort and Spa, Mile 69¼, George Price Hwy. San Ignacio, 501-824-3350, 305-735-2553 in U.S., www.kaanabelize.com. Ka'ana is your most upscale non-jungle lodge option in or near San Ignacio. It has a wine cellar, bar, spacious suites outfitted with extras like iPod docks and espresso machines and flat-screen TVs, plus one- and two-bedroom villas with private plunge pools. The main infinity swimming pool with waterfall uses a saltwater filtration system. **La Ceiba** restaurant, while attractive and serving vegetables from the resort's organic garden, is expensive. **Very Expensive.**

Rumors Resort, Mile 68, George Price Hwy., San Ignacio, 501-824-2795, www.rumorsresort.com. About 3 miles west of downtown San Ignacio, Rumors sits on a low hill. The Belizean-owned property has a nice pool, a restaurant and affordable prices.

San Ignacio Resort Hotel, 18 Buena Vista St., San Ignacio, 501-824-2125 or 855-488-2624 in U.S. and Canada, www.sanignaciobelize.com. The 26-room San Ignacio Resort Hotel is the closest thing to an international-style hotel in San Ignacio Town. But, in Belize, that can mean anything, and in this case it means a green iguana project out back, with 14 acres of bush. The location is convenient, on a low hill on the west side of town. The redone rooms are comfortable, the pool relaxing, the **Running W Steakhouse & Restaurant** satisfying, the Lobby Bar a good place to grab a cool one and the management and staff accommodating. A branch of the **Princess Casino,** with about 170 video slot machines and five live tables, adjoins the hotel. **Expensive.**

Western Guest House. 54 Burns Ave., 501-669-7230, San Ignacio. Located above a hardware store, this inexpensive guesthouse has eight large, clean rooms with private baths and wi-fi. There's a common kitchen. **Inexpensive.**

Other budget options include **Tropicool Hotel** (30A Burns Ave.), **J & R's Guest House** (26 Far West St.) and **Venus** (29 Burns Ave.)

Benque Viejo/Succotz Area Lodging and Dining

Trek Stop, Mile 71½ George Price Hwy. (Benque Rd.), 501-660-7895, www.thetrekstop.com. This collection of little wood cottages near the Xunantunich ruins and Succotz village, across the highway from the river, is a good budget choice, although cabin prices have gone up some recently. Camping available. There's a little restaurant on site and a small butterfly exhibit (US$5), plus a disc golf course. **Inexpensive.**

Benny's Kitchen, 139 Belize St., San José Succotz Village, across Benque Road from ferry to Xunantunich, 501-823-2541. This little open-air restaurant near Xunantunich is a local find. Lots of local Maya, Creole and Mestizo dishes, including *pibil* (Mayan pork), *chilimole* (chicken with mole sauce) and *escabeche* (onion soup with chicken) and of course stew chicken with rice and beans. Low prices and large portions. Open daily for breakfast, lunch and dinner. **Inexpensive to Moderate.**

Jungle Lodges on the Macal River

Most of Cayo's jungle lodges are on either the Macal or Mopan rivers. In general, the lodges on the Macal are more upmarket. With some exceptions don't expect to be in a "movie jungle" or rainforest. Most lodges share their locations with cattle ranches or citrus farms and second-growth bush, though the jungle is seldom far away. Lodges are listed alphabetically.

Black Rock Lodge, off Chial Road, 501-834-4038; www.blackrocklodge.com. *Directions: From San Ignacio, go 4 3/4 miles west on Benque Road (George Price Highway) and turn left on Chial Road. Look for signs to Chaa Creek, duPlooy's and Black Rock lodges. Follow unpaved road, past Maya Flats airstrip, to a dirt track turning right – watch for sign to Black Rock Lodge. Follow to its end at Black Rock.* Black Rock enjoys a stunning location overlooking the Macal River. It's also one of the most isolated lodges in the area, at the end of a long, mostly dirt road that winds for miles through citrus groves, teak plantations and farms off the graveled Chial Road. There are 14 cottages, including the premium river view suites with marble floors and decks. All are a good value. Even if you have a car, you're unlikely to go anywhere else for meals, due to the distance involved. The lodge offers a wide selection of trips and tours. **Moderate.**

Chaa Creek, Chaa Creek Rd., off Chial Rd. (P.O. Box 53, San Ignacio), 501-824-2037 or 877-709-8706, www.chaacreek.com. *Directions: From San Ignacio, go 4 3/4 miles west on Benque Road. (George Price Highway) and turn left on Chial Road (look for signs to Chaa Creek, duPlooy's and Black Rock lodges). Follow signs on this unpaved road, past Maya Flats airstrip, 3 1/2 miles to Chaa Creek.* Mick and Lucy Fleming started Chaa Creek in 1980 when tourists were almost unknown in Cayo. Over the years, they've expanded, improved and fine-tuned their operation until it has become one of the best run, most-professional operations in all of Central America. Everything works here: The grounds, comprising a total of about 400 acres on the Macal River, are beautifully planted and maintained. A gorgeous swimming pool was added in 2009. The 23 large rooms and suites (not including new villas) are mostly in thatch cottages, and all have high-quality furnishings set off with Guatemalan wall hangings and bedspreads, the perfect marriage of comfort and exoticism. The honeymoon new air-conditioned Ix Chel Villas and the Treetop Suites, Garden Suites, Orchid Villa, Spa Villa, Macal Cottage and Sky Room offer more privacy and extra room. Staffers are friendly, not fawning, and move quickly to solve any problem. There's electricity, plenty of hot water and cold beer, and, if you like, Chaa Creek will sell you a good cigar to enjoy after a great dinner with your cognac. There's a fully equipped, modern spa, arguably the best in Belize, offering everything from aromatherapy to seaweed wraps, and a conference and meeting center. You won't run out of things to do here, either. You can visit the Chaa Creek Natural History Centre and Blue Morpho Butterfly Breeding Centre, tour the Rainforest Medicine Trail, visit a Maya-style cacao plantation and other farming projects, go horseback riding or canoeing, or take one of the many top-notch but pricey tours offered by Chaa Creek Expeditions. Chaa Creek helped reintroduce howler monkeys to the Macal River Valley. Birding is excellent, with some 250 species spotted on the grounds. Chaa Creek has won a number of environmental and other awards. For all this, you pay a premium price, around US$500 to $900 including tax and service charge. For those who want the Chaa Creek experience at a Walmart price (around US$130 double including breakfast and dinner, plus hotel tax and service), the **Macal River Camp** (Moderate with most meals), has 10 small "cabinettes" on raised platforms and very good Belizean-style meals. Both the lodge and river camp are highly recommended. **Very Expensive.**

Crystal Paradise, Crysto Rey Village (P.O. Box 126, San Ignacio, Cayo), 501-824-2772. Operated by the local Tut family (pronounced Toot), many of the numerous clan pitch in and help at the lodge, which is located near the village of Cristo Rey on the Macal River. The lodge has 17 rooms and units with private bath with hot and cold water, ceiling fan and 24-hour electricity. The Tuts offer horseback riding, have mountain bikes to rent and offer a variety of tours. **Moderate.**

duPlooy's Lodge, 10 miles from San Ignacio, Cayo, 501-824-3101 or 512-243-5285 in the U.S., www.duplooys.com. *Directions: From San Ignacio, go 4 3/4 miles west on Benque Road (George Price Highway) and turn left on Chial Road (look for signs to Chaa Creek, duPlooy's and Black Rock lodges). Follow signs on this unpaved road past Maya Flats airstrip about 4 miles to duPlooy's.* Since it opened in the late 1980s, duPlooy's has been seen by some to play second fiddle to its Macal River neighbor, Chaa Creek. But that's unfair, because duPlooy's has its own style — a little more casual, a little more oriented to birders and tree-huggers and nature lovers. On part of the lodge's grounds about 10 miles from San Ignacio, Judy and the late Ken duPlooy created something very special: the 45-acre **Belize Botanic Gardens** (www.belizebotanic.org), with plantings of some 2,500 trees from all over Belize and Central America. For most guests, the focus of the lodge is the remarkable deck, which rambles 200 feet off from the bar. From vantage points on the long walkway beside the Macal River, you're sure to see a variety of birds, iguanas and other wildlife. Bring your camera and binoculars. About 300 species of birds have been identified within 5 miles of the lodge. In accommodations, duPlooy's offers something for anyone, with bungalows, suites, rooms and a large house. duPlooy's does not serve beef in its restaurant, but it does serve good pork, chicken and seafood, along with vegetarian dishes. The lodge also has selection of tours to Cayo and Petén sites. duPlooy's has sold some of its lodge units as residences. **Expensive to Very Expensive.**

Mystic River Resort, Mile 6, Cristo Rey Rd., Negroman Village, 501-672-4100, U.S. number 336-510-0675, www.mysticriverresort.com. This upscale lodge sits on a bank above the Macal River. It has deluxe suites and cottages, some with fireplaces and plunge pools (but not air-conditioning or TVs), an open-air restaurant, La Ranita, overlooking the river and serving Belizean, Thai and other cuisines. There is a small onsite spa and yoga. **Very Expensive.**

Table Rock Lodge, Cristo Rey Rd., Cristo Rey Village, 501-672-4040; www.tablerockbelize.com. This small ecolodge, owned by an American couple, has already made a big name for itself, rating high on social media sites and winning awards from the Belize Tourism Board. The lodge has only a handful of thatch cottages, all with tile floors and four-poster beds, plus one house. It is part of a small working farm, perched just above the Macal River. You can explore winding pathways and cut trails down to the river, or visit with the donkeys. Meals here are excellent. Riverside camping also is available for including tent, set up and break down and firewood. Highly recommended. **Inexpensive (camping) to Expensive.**

The Actun Tunichil Muknal Maya site in a cave in Cayo is one of the top attractions in Central America

Lodges on the Mopan River

Vanilla Hills Lodge, Guana Belly Dr., off Bullet Tree Falls Rd., 501-634-0011, www.vanilla-hills.com. This little lodge on 30 acres between San Ignacio and Bullet Tree Falls, about five minutes from San Ignacio, has become popular because of its affordable rates and comfortable accommodations in three cabins and one two-bedroom villa. Food is freshly prepared from local markets and the lodge's own greenhouse and chickens. Recommended. **Moderate to Expensive.**

Clarissa Falls Resort, Mile 70, George Price Hwy./Benque Rd., 501-833-3116, www.clarissafalls.com. Friendly owner Chena Galvez has spent her life on a cattle ranch here, 5½ miles west of San Ignacio, on a rolling 800-acre expanse of grassy, hilly pasture and bush. The family has built pleasant though very simple thatch cabañas. A large family cabaña is perhaps overpriced. Inexpensive camping also is available. You can swim or tube on the river, go horseback riding or take one of the tours that the lodge can arrange. The little restaurant serves tasty Creole and Mestizo dishes at modest prices. **Inexpensive (camping) to Expensive.**

Mahogany Hall Boutique Resort, Paslow Falls Rd., Bullet Tree Falls, 501-664-7747, U.S. number 228-331-0234, www.mahoganyhallbelize.com. In a large house that looks like an old mansion but that was built relatively recently, Mahogany Hall sits close to the Mopan River in Bullet Tree village, about 3 miles from San Ignacio. Rooms are pleasant but most are fairly small, with A/C that's nice and cold. There's a beautiful swimming pool, a bar and restaurant. **Expensive.**

Parrot Nest Lodge, Bullet Tree Falls, 501-660-6336, www.parrot-nest.com. Set on shady grounds on the Mopan River 3 miles or a US$2.50 *colectivo* ride from San Ignacio, Parrot Nest has nine cabins with thatch roofs, including tree houses. Good breakfasts and affordable dinners are served in its open-air restaurant. **Inexpensive to Moderate.**

Mountain Pine Ridge Lodging

Blancaneaux Lodge, Mountain Pine Ridge, 501-824-4912 or 877-611-9774 in the U.S. and Canada; www.thefamilycoppolaresorts.com/w/blancaneaux-lodge. *Directions: From San Ignacio, go 12½ miles via the Christo Rey Road to the entrance to the Mountain Pine Ridge reserve or go by way of the Pine Ridge/Chiquibul Road from Georgeville, then 4½ miles (watch for sign) and turn on dirt road. Go approximately 1/2 mile to the lodge. You also can fly here via a charter plane or helicopter, as the lodge has an airstrip.* Francis Ford Coppola ought to win another Oscar for his incredible lodge, to add to the collection he won for the *Godfather* movies and other parts of his oeuvre. Coppola has said Belize reminds him of the verdant jungles of the Philippines, where he filmed *Apocalypse Now,* the movie that best caught the crazed atmosphere of the Vietnam War. In 1981, he bought an abandoned lodge, spent a fortune on fixing it up and reopened it in 1993. Mexican architect Manolo Mestre created the jungle chic look, and Francis and Eleanor Coppola themselves chose the Mexican and Guatemalan furnishings for the villas and cabañas.

The result is simply one of the most extraordinary lodges in the world. Blancaneaux looks better and better each time we visit, even considering the loss of a number of pine trees due to Southern Pine Beetle blight. The grounds are beautifully maintained, with native flowers accenting pathways, grass areas are manicured. Note that getting about Blancaneaux's hilly grounds requires climbing many steps up and down.

The lodge has a total of 20 units. The regular cabañas are less of a burden on your credit card than the luxury cabañas with plunge pool, the two-bedroom villa, Coppola's personal villa and the Enchanted Cottage on a hill away from the main lodge grounds. The lodge has 24-hour electricity provided by a hydroelectric plant. Staffers can enjoy satellite TV in their rooms, but nothing so pedestrian is available in the guest lodging. The dining room in the main lodge building is comfortably upscale. The Italian and other dishes in the restaurant are excellent, if a little pricey, and gradually a wider variety of choices has been added, a boon to those staying for more than a few days. You can even get real espresso and pizza from a wood-burning pizza oven. Most of the fruits and vegetables served are grown in the lodge's organic gardens. Wines from the Niebaum-Coppola Estate Winery in Napa Valley are available. A second restaurant serving Guatemalan food is at the far end of the pool.

When you're in the bar, just off the lobby, note the slate bar top carved by the Garcia sisters of San Antonio village, and the ceiling fan, which was used in *Apocalypse Now.* In the winter, the fireplace in the bar adds a cozy touch when nights drop into the low 50s. The hotel and restaurant service is excellent. Many tours are available. Coppola also operates the Turtle Inn in Placencia and La Lancha near Tikal in Guatemala. **Very Expensive.**

Hidden Valley Inn, 4 Cooma Cairn Rd., Mountain Pine Ridge. 501-822-3320 or 844-859-2227 in U.S., www.hiddenvalleyinn.com. *Directions: From San Ignacio, go 12½ miles on Cristo Rey Road to the entrance to the Mountain Pine Ridge reserve, (or go by way of the Pine Ridge/Chiquibul Road from Georgeville), then 4 miles (watch for sign to Hidden Valley Falls and Inn) and turn left on dirt Cooma Cairn Road to the lodge. You can also fly to Hidden Valley on a charter flight or by helicopter.* With its 7,200 acres of surrounding property, private waterfalls and great birding, Hidden Valley Inn, owned by the Roe family in Belize City, is one of the best lodges in Belize. The 12 private cottages, each with a bedroom living room and tiled bath, are not your traditional thatch but marl daub with zinc roofs. They've been spruced up, and two cottages are deluxe units. All have salt tile floors and comfortable furnishings, and the fireplaces come in handy in the winter.

There's a beautiful swimming pool and a hot tub, in a grand setting by the side of the main lodge building. The lodge also has a spa. Delicious meals are served in the comfortable lodge dining room. It's wonderful to wake up early in the invigorating air of the Pine Ridge and walk some of the trails around the lodge. There are some 90 miles of trails, several leading to waterfalls that are open only to Hidden Valley guests. Honeymooners or even old married folks can reserve Butterfly Falls or other falls for your own private day at a waterfall, complete with champagne. You can also walk through a small coffee finca — the lodge grows and roasts its own coffee. Yes, many of the pines in this area have succumbed to the beetle infestation, but they are quickly regenerating. Many already 20+ feet tall. The birding is actually better than ever here, as it's now much easier to spot the little feathered friends. A sizable percentage of Hidden Valley Inn guests are birders, who want to add to their life lists rare birds such as the Orange-breasted Falcon, King Vulture and Keel-billed Motmot. **Very Expensive.**

Gaia Riverlodge, Mountain Pine Ridge (P.O. Box 173, San Ignacio, Cayo), 501-834-4005, www.gaiariverlodge.com. Gaia Riverlodge is owned by the same folks who operate Matachica on North Ambergris. It has upgraded mountain and garden thatch cabañas and waterfall view cabañas and rooms situated above Five Sisters Falls not far from Blancaneaux Lodge. There's a riverside villa, too. It's 360 steps down – and up – if you go to the falls, but there is a tram. Gaia Riverlodge has been honored by the BTB as one of the top hotels in Belize. **Expensive to Very Expensive.**

Dining in San Ignacio
The price level for restaurants in all areas is as follows:
Inexpensive: Under US$7
Moderate: US$8-$19
Expensive: US$20-$39
Very Expensive: Over US$40
Prices don't include tips or alcoholic drinks. If not otherwise stated, the price range is for one person for dinner.

Restaurants here are listed alphabetically.

If you're staying at a jungle lodge, you'll probably take most of your meals there. Chaa Creek, Blancaneaux, Hidden Valley Inn, duPlooy's, Caves Branch, Table Rock and other lodges have excellent, if fairly pricey, meals. San Ignacio is the center for dining in Cayo, with a host of small, generally inexpensive restaurants.

Cenaida's, off 10 Bullet Tree Rd. on West St., San Ignacio, 501-631-2526. One of the best values in simple but well-prepared Belizean and Caribbean food. The coconut chicken is excellent, and the stew meats with beans and rice are classics. It has a loyal local clientele. **Inexpensive to Moderate.**

Crave House of Flavors, 24 West St., San Ignacio, 501-602-0737. At this very tiny spot, with just a few seats inside and outside, Chef Alejandro serves up some of the best food in Cayo. Reservations are a must. Try the steaks, Italian dishes, lamb chops and lamb ribs, pork chops or whatever the special may be. Wine only. **Moderate to Expensive.**

Erva's, 4 Far West St,, San Ignacio, 501-824-2821. A favorite for simple Belizean Mestizo food, rum punch and also pizzas. **Inexpensive to Moderate.**

Guava Limb Café, 75 Burns Ave., San Ignacio, 501-824-4837. Opened by Chaa Creek Lodge, Guava Limb is now widely considered the best restaurant in San Ignacio. Its menu changes frequently, with a variety of creatively presented international dishes from seafood stew to pepper rubbed steak to beer-battered fish with cassava Lyonnaise. Shrimp wontons are a hit, as are the pasta dishes. Desserts (cheesecake flavors from papaya to Oreo) come tall and artful. Excellent breakfasts, and it's a good place to drink, too. Great service and a charming atmosphere. Open for breakfast, lunch and dinner Monday to Saturday and brunch/lunch and dinner on Sunday. **Expensive.**

Hode's Place Bar & Grill, Savannah Rd., San Ignacio, across from soccer stadium, 501-804-2522. With a large shaded patio and swings and slides for the kids at the back, plus an ice cream stand, Hode's has good food in large portions and at modest prices. It has long been popular for its traditional menu, cold beers, karaoke and billiards. Outdoor seating at the edge of an orange grove. **Inexpensive to Moderate.**

Ko-Ox Han-Nah, 5 Burns Ave., 501-824-3014. Formerly Hannah's (the new name in the Maya language means "Let's go eat"), this is probably San Ignacio's most popular restaurant, and deservedly so. It's not fancy—you eat on simple tables in a room opening on busy Burns Avenue—but the food is moderately priced and well prepared. In addition to beans-and-rice dishes, Hannah's serves salads, sandwiches and East Indian curries. Open for breakfast, lunch and dinner daily. **Moderate.**

Pop's, West St., San Ignacio. This is where to go for some of best breakfasts in Cayo. Try the chaya scrambled eggs, fry jacks and freshly squeezed juice. Open daily for breakfast from 6:30 a.m. until 1 p.m. **Inexpensive to Moderate.**

Sanny's Grill, East 23rd Street, San Ignacio, 501-824-2988. Heading west of San Ignacio, look for sign on the Benque Road just beyond UNO station. On a good night, this is one of the best restaurants in Cayo. Sanny's restaurant transforms Belizean basics, like chicken or pork chops, beyond standard fare. Eat in the casual dining room or out on the covered deck. Open for dinner only. **Moderate to Expensive.**

Serendib, 27 Burns Ave., San Ignacio, 501-824-2302. This was Belize's only Sri Lankan restaurant, but it has changed owners. You can still get a curries, plus burgers and such. On busy Burns Avenue, with access from the Cayo Welcome Center. Indoor and outdoor seating. Closed Sunday. **Moderate.**

For ice cream, **The Ice Cream Shoppe** (24 West St., San Ignacio) is tops. The best bakery in the area is **The French Bakery** (Savannah Rd.).

Sign for Chef Rob's restaurant in Hopkins

Dangriga/Hopkins and Stann Creek District

BUG OUT RATING

Ratings are on an A to F scale, just like your old high school report card. A is the top grade; F is failing. Grades are relative compared to other areas in Belize.

Popularity with Expats	B-
Safety	B-
Overall Cost of Living	B
Real Estate Bargains	C+
Farming	B
Investment Potential	B-
Leisure Activities	B
Restaurants	C+
Cultural Activities	C
Infrastructure	B
Business Potential	B
Medical Care	C+
Shopping	C+
Farming & Ranching	B-
Safety in Nuclear War	B-

Sustainable Living	B-
Overall Bug Out Rating	**B-**

ADVANTAGES OF HOPKINS/DANGRIGA AREA: • Lower prices for beachfront property than on Ambergris Caye or Placencia • Friendly, interesting Garifuna culture • Provides excellent opportunities for water sports – boating, fishing, diving • Proximity to Cockscomb Basin Wildlife Sanctuary and other natural areas

This part of Stann Creek District is Belize at its most exotic, with Garifuna settlements that may remind you more of a coastal village in Senegal than Central America. Rural Maya villages look much as they did hundreds of years ago. A few miles inland are a wild jaguar preserve and the highest mountains in Belize. The Cockscomb Basin Preserve west of Hopkins is real rainforest jungle, and the tallest peaks in Belize, Doyle's Delight at 3,688 feet and Victoria Peak at 3,675 feet, are in the Maya Mountains.

Unlike most of the rest of Belize's mainland coast, the Hopkins area has real beaches. The beaches here are similar to those in Placencia *(see below)* —ribbons of khaki-colored sand, with a good deal of seagrass in the water off the beach. Swimming is possible, especially in areas where the seagrass has been removed, as at the end of a dock. The snorkeling off the shore usually is not very good, although you can see some fish and possibly even a manatee.

The barrier reef is about 12 to 15 miles offshore from Hopkins and Dangriga, so it takes a while to get out to the reef for diving.

The Garifuna (usually pronounced Gah-RIF-u-nah) people who settled in this area have a fascinating history. Before the time of Columbus, Indians from the South American mainland came by boat to the island of St. Vincent in the southeast Caribbean. They conquered, and then intermarried with, Arawak Indians, adopting much of the Indian language. They went by the name Kwaib, from which the names Carib and Garifuna, meaning cassava-eaters, probably evolved.

Then, in the 17th century, slaves from Nigeria were shipwrecked off the island of St. Vincent. They too mixed with the Caribs or Garifuna. For years, Britain tried to subdue these free people of color, but the Garifuna, with the support of the French, fought back until the late 1700s, when the French and Garifuna finally surrendered to the British. In 1797, several thousand surviving Garifuna were taken by ship to Roatán in Honduras. Over the 150 years or so, many Garifuna moved from Roatán up the coast of Central America to Belize, where they worked in logging. The largest migration to Belize took place in 1823, and today that is commemorated nationally on November 19 as Garifuna Settlement Day.

Many settled in Stann Creek Town, what is now Dangriga. Hopkins, Seine Bight and, in Toledo, Punta Gorda Town and Barranco village also have sizable Garifuna populations. Initially, Dangriga was called Black Carib Town and then Stann Creek. The Garifuna in Belize are working hard to continue their language and culture. They have a complex system of religious beliefs, combining African and South American elements as well as Catholicism. Dugu or

"Feasting of the Dead" is one of the ancestral rites practiced by Garifuna. There is a good small museum near Dangriga, Gulisi Garifuna Museum, with displays on the Garifuna people, their culture and their art.

Dangriga Town itself is not very popular for expats, but the rural areas around Dangriga offer sustainable living options, and the Hopkins/Sittee Point area south of Dangriga is attracting a lot of attention, especially among those wanting a home on or near the sea or river. An American developer based in Texas, British-American Cattle Company, subdivided a large tract near Hopkins and before retiring sold a sizeable number of lots. Not too many homes have yet been built in this area, but more building is likely to take place over the next few years. Several upscale seafront condo developments, including Belizean Dreams and Hopkins Bay, have opened, with units sold to investors who let a management company rent out the units on a nightly or weekly basis.

Hopkins is a delightfully friendly and still mostly unspoiled village, though it is changing fast. In Hopkins and nearby are several excellent beach resorts, notably Hamanasi, along with many smaller, less expensive lodging options. You'll find some good spots for dining as well. The Sittee River and the Caribbean waters offer some of Belize's best fishing. The barrier reef isn't close to shore here, but once you get to the reef there's good diving. There's also good diving in the Southwater Marine Reserve. Inland you're only a few miles from the world's first jaguar preserve, Cockscomb. Also within a short drive are Maya ruins and waterfalls at Mayflower, along with a revitalized jungle lodge, Mama Noots, with the country's longest zipline.

In Dangriga you'll find some shopping and a regional hospital for medical care. The access road from the excellent Southern Highway to Hopkins has been rebuilt and surfaced. If there's a rub to this paradise, it's the sand fleas, which can be fierce in this area.

Dangriga/Hopkins Practicalities

Dangriga is the hub of this area, and for medical care, shopping and other services this is where you will need to go. Hopkins has only a few small shops.

Banks: Belize Bank, Heritage Bank and ScotiaBank have branches in or near Dangriga. There are no banks in Hopkins, although there is a Belize Bank ATM.

Groceries: There are several sizeable groceries in Dangriga. Try the one near Pen Cayetano's home and studio. Hopkins has several small groceries.

Restaurants: The restaurant at Pelican Beach Resort is the best Dangriga has to offer. Hopkins has several small restaurants owned and operated by local ladies, including Innie's that serve good local food and low prices. Chef Rob's, now at Parrot Cove Resort, is one of the top restaurants in Southern Belize. The restaurant at Beaches and Dreams is very good, and there are a number of other good restaurants around Hopkins.

Medical: The Southern Regional Hospital (501-522-2078) at Mile 1.5 of the Stann Creek Valley Road opened in 1999. Dangriga is a regional medical center for Southern Belize.

Infrastructure: Dangriga and Hopkins have municipal water and in most areas sewerage systems. These areas as well as most villages are on the electrical grid. Cable TV, DSL and cellular internet are available. More remote areas are not on the grid and must depend on their own resources for water, sewerage and satellite internet. Some Maya villages have homes with no running water.

The main drag in Dangriga   Photo by Matyas Rehak/Shutterstock

Real Estate

Prices have gone up considerably in recent years in the Hopkins/Sittee area, due to resort development in and around Hopkins. Beachfront lots generally go for US$150,000+ though occasionally one is available for less. Larger lots of more than half an acre with both Caribbean and canal or lagoon access are around US$150,000-$250,000. Seaview lots are much less, starting around US$35,000, and lots on the Sittee River can be had for US$40,000. These lots have utilities (electricity, telephones, public water and cable TV) and road access. Small recently built homes in this area, near but not on the water, are going for US$125,000 to $400,000+, occasionally with some owner financing available. New or resale beachside luxury condos are US$300,000 to $600,000.

Prices for tracts of land along the Southern Highway between Dangriga and a little south of the road to Placencia are still affordable. Some larger tracts of 100 acres or more, with access to municipal power and with creek or river frontage, start at around US$1,000 an acre.

Properties in Dangriga/Hopkins

These are offerings by individuals and real estate agencies in 2018. Prices shown are asking prices.

• 5 acres on Stann Creek River near less than 2 miles from Dangriga, US$55,000

• Large lot in Sittee River Subdivision, about 2.2 acres near Sittee River, with reserved access to river, US$50,000

• 1,400 sq. ft., two-story concrete house with Sittee River views, separate garage, on 1/3 acre lot about 3 miles from Hopkins, US$199,000

• 113 acres near Silk Grass village with 1,400+ feet frontage on the Southern Highway, US$139,000

• 47 acres in two parcels just off Southern Highway, short drive to Hopkins, fully planted in oranges, with year-round creek bordering back of tracts, US$71,000

• 58 acres with frontage on Southern Highway at Mile 3.5, creek frontage in back, cleared land with municipal power, US$50 pays the annual property tax, US$87,000

Real Estate Developments

Here are selected real estate developments in the Dangriga-Hopkins area. Most market primarily to foreign buyers. As always in Belize, it's buyer beware. For example, a large "development" was divided on paper into more than 1,000 lots. Located near Mullins River and called "Dreamscapes," (several different versions of the name were used) the "developer," allegedly a disbarred Florida attorney who had served time in prison on a federal felony racketeering charge, reportedly sold lots to buyers, some of whom had never seen the property, for some US$20,000 to $30,000 each. In 2015, a group of investors, who sued in a Florida court, claimed that some 300 lots had been sold, but that none of the money had been escrowed, and that besides the grading of a few roads nothing had been done to the property to prepare it for home building.

Hopkins Bay, 412-860-1418; www.hopkinsbayrealestate.com Developers of the successful Belizean Dreams condos near Jaguar Reef Resort originally put together the Hopkins Bay project at the north end of Hopkins village. Now, a "Canadian-American-South African consortium" is offering lots and villas on a 48-acre tract. A number of condo units, which range in price up to around US$750,000, are offered for sale. A master plan calls for a casino, marina, hotels and golf course, but those are years in the future if they materialize at all.

Sanctuary Belize, Dangriga, 1401 Dove St. #610, Newport Beach, CA 92660, 949-757-0949 or 830-443-4595; www.sanctuarybelize.com. Sanctuary Belize, a large and controversial development formerly called Sanctuary Bay, on a 14,000-acre tract of land, of which about 9,000 to 11,000 acres (various numbers have been put forth over the years) is a protected reserve. The property is located between the Placencia peninsula and Hopkins, bordering the Sapodilla Lagoon and the Sittee River. Sanctuary Belize has something of a checkered history. Two Americans initially involved in Sanctuary served prison terms in the U.S. Andris Pukke, founder of a U.S. credit counseling company accused of cheating 300,000 debtors out of millions of dollars and reportedly the original owner/developer of Sanctuary Bay, and Peter Baker, a long-time Pukke friend and associate who was also a principal in Sanctuary Bay, were jailed by a U.S. District Court judge in Maryland. Pukke was held in contempt of court for failing to turn over assets to a fund set up, in a U.S. Federal Trade Commission agreement, to repay the debtors. Peter Baker, the son of Joan Medhurst, whose firm in the 1990s had the international public relations contract for the Belize Tourism Board, was jailed because the judge concluded Baker and Pukke colluded to shield assets both in Belize and in

California. New management at Sanctuary Belize was installed, but it is now alleged that Pukke is back in the saddle. At this time, we cannot recommend buying in Sanctuary Belize.

Real Estate Agents

Belize Property Agents, Mile 6, Hummingbird Hwy., Dangriga, 501-670-1412, www.belizepropertyagent.com

Caribbean Property Consultants, P.O. Box 149, Dangriga, 501-672-9000, www.belizeproperty.com.

Local buses serve parts of the Southern Zone

VISTING DANGRIGA/HOPKINS

Getting There

Dangriga is connected with the north by the Hummingbird Highway and by the Coastal Highway, which is also known as the Manatee Highway. Running south from Dangriga to Punta Gorda, a distance of about 100 miles, is the Southern Highway. Once this was widely considered the worst "main" road in Belize, with cars and big trucks raising thick clouds of dust in dry weather and bogging down in the mud in wet.

Things have improved a lot. The Southern Highway is now completely paved and one of the best roads in the country. **James Bus Line** (www.jamesbusline.com) buses connect Dangriga with Belize City (US$8). Dangriga has an airstrip, with regular service on **Maya Island Air** (www.mayaislandair.com) and **Tropic Air** (www.tropicair.com) from Belize City. One-way fares from the international airport are around US$100, and from municipal about US$70. There also are shuttle services from Belize City, San Ignacio and elsewhere that will take you in a van to Dangriga or Hopkins.

The road into Dangriga Town from Belmopan is completely paved. The access road to Hopkins from the Southern Highway also is now paved, and that to Sittee River is paved as well (though the paving ends around Sittee village before you get to Hopkins).

You'll probably get wet, you'll probably get eaten up by mosquitoes, but you'll get to experience the "real jungle" at **Cockscomb Basin Wildlife Sanctuary**. This preserve covers nearly 150 square miles of broadleaf rainforest. Much of it has been selectively logged for mahogany and other valuable trees, and some of it was affected by hurricanes, but to the novice bushwalker the rainforest canopy, up to 130 feet high, and the exotic plants and trees are nothing at all like back home. Parts of the preserve get up to 180 inches of rain a year, and the preserve includes the two highest peaks in Belize, Doyle's Delight at 3,688 feet and Victoria Peak at 3,675 feet.

Cockscomb has the most extensive trail network of any park in Belize. Trails at the preserve vary from short self-guided hikes near the visitor center to a 17-mile multi-day trek to Victoria Peak, only for the physically fit and best done with a local guide during the dry season. While it's unlikely that you will see one of the 200 or so jaguars in the preserve, you may well see tracks or scat, as the jaguars do frequent the trails and entrance road at night. If you hike long enough, however, you will run into quite a few other wild creatures. The preserve is home to some 300 species of birds, along with all five types of Belize's wild cats, black howler monkeys, peccaries and snakes of all types and biting abilities. The best time to see wildlife is at the start of the rainy season, usually mid-June to early August, although with luck you will see wild creatures anytime you are in the preserve. Animals are most active on cooler, cloudy days.

Mayflower Bocawina is a smaller park, but perhaps more interesting to the casual visitor than Cockscomb, as it has several beautiful waterfalls and some Maya sites.

Dangriga, with a population of around 9,000, is the largest town in Belize south of Belize City. Until the 1980s it was known as Stann Creek, when it was renamed Dangriga, meaning "sweet waters" in the Garifuna language. Dangriga, like Orange Walk Town, is not much of a visitor destination, though it is a useful jumping off spot for some of the central and southern cayes. Physically, it slightly resembles the older sections of Belize City, although it is much smaller.

What to See and Do in Dangriga and Hopkins

Few visitors stay for long in Dangriga. In many ways that's a shame, because Dangriga is home to a unique culture, the Garifuna. It is also home to a number of nationally and internationally known painters and drum makers. The town, scruffy at first look, is actually quite photogenic.

One interesting attraction in Dangriga is the **Gulisi Garifuna Museum** (George Price Drive, 501-669-0539, open 10 to 5 Monday-Friday and 8 to noon Saturday, admission US$5). It has excellent displays on Garifuna culture, art and history.

Another must-see near Dangriga is the **Marie Sharp's Factory** (Melinda Road, off Stann Creek Valley Road, 501-532-2087, www.mariesharps-bz.com.) It's open 9-4 Monday-Friday. You can usually take a brief free tour, or at least a look, at the small factory that produces the famous hot sauce and other condiments. You can also buy all the Marie Sharp's products at a shop there. Marie Sharp herself is often there. There is another Marie Sharp's store in Dangriga (near Stann Creek Bridge, 501-522-2370, open 8-5 Monday-Friday.

Dangriga is also something of an art center, with **Pen Cayetano's Studio Gallery** (3 Aranda Crescent, Dangriga, 501-628-6807, www.cayetano.de). Pen Cayetano painted an impressive mural for the Dangriga Town Hall in 2012. He now spends much of his time in Germany.) **Austin Rodriguez's drum workshop** is in Dangriga, too.

The biggest event of the year here is **Garifuna Settlement Day,** celebrated on November 19 and the days around that date. There's a reenactment of the Garingu landing in British Honduras, along with drumming concerts, dancing, music concerts, art exhibits and more.

Dangriga is also a **jumping off point** for many offshore cayes, including Southwater Caye, Tobacco Caye, Cocoplum Caye and Thatch Caye, all with accommodations or resorts. It's also a good place for departures to the wonders and the several resorts on Glover's Reef Atoll.

A little farther south, the **village of Hopkins** offers Garifuna culture is an easier-to-absorb form, and of course the beaches, restaurants, dive resorts and small guesthouses are draws here. Hopkins bills itself as being midway between the reef and the rainforest. You can go diving one day, and the next tour the jungles of **Cockscomb Basin Wildlife Sanctuary** and **Mayflower Bocawina National Park.**

Cockscomb, often called the Jaguar Preserve, consists of more than 150 square miles of pure nature. As many as 200 jaguars are believed to be in and around the sanctuary. There also are other cats including margay, ocelot, puma and jaguarondi, along with tapirs, howler monkeys, deer, crocodiles and many species of birds. Take the entrance road to Cockscomb at Maya Centre, where a women's co-operative sells Maya and other local crafts. There's also a small private museum here, Maya Centre Maya Museum (admission US$7.50). Sanctuary admission is US$5. If you don't have your own transport, you can hire a taxi at Maya Centre for around US$15. Near the visitor center at the sanctuary is a campground (US$10 per person per night) and rustic cabins from around US$20 to $55. Reservations can be made through the **Belize Audubon Society** (www.belizeaudubon.org.) Bring your own food and water.

Mayflower Bocawina National Park (admission US$5) comprises about 7,000 acres. In the park are five waterfalls and a small Maya site. Getting to the waterfalls requires a fairly strenuous hike. Also in the park is a jungle lodge, **Bocawina Rainforest Resort,** (501-670-8019, www.mamanootsbocawina.com, **Expensive**) formerly Mama Noots Eco-Lodge. Bocawina Rainforest Resort has a variety of accommodations. There's also a restaurant and bar at the resort and what is billed as the longest zipline in Belize.

Dangriga Lodging
The price level for lodging in all areas is as follows:
Inexpensive: Under US$75
Moderate: US$75-$150
Expensive: US$151-$300
Very Expensive: Over US$300
Prices are for a double room in high season (usually late November to Easter). Rates, which do not include taxes, service charges or meals (except in some cases breakfast), may be higher during holiday periods, especially Christmas and New Years. If specific prices are mentioned, they are plus 9% hotel tax and in some cases a service charge, usually 10%.

Pelican Beach Resort. Scotchman Town, on the sea near the airstrip, 501-522-2044, www.pelicanbeachbelize.com. The rambling white wood-frame main building at Pelican Beach, reportedly once a dance hall, always reminds us of boarding houses of our youth in Florida; others say it reminds them of old hotels on the coast of Maine. Inside, though, it's vintage Belize, with simple wood paneling and furniture that wasn't selected by any interior designer. There are about a dozen rooms in the main building and others in a separate structure. All rooms have fans, and some have air conditioning. In any event, this is the best hotel in Dangriga. It's on the water at the north edge of town, and there's a beach area and a breeze-swept pier. Some people swim here, but it's not exactly Cane Garden Beach in the British Virgin Islands. **Coconuts Grill & Bar** is quite good, if a bit expensive for dinner. **Moderate to Expensive.**

Chaleanor Hotel, 35 Magoon St., 501-522-2587. This is a decent budget/low moderate choice in Dangriga. It's well run and a good value. The 18 rooms in this tall, three-story hotel are larger than at many budget hotels, and all have private baths. Some rooms with TV and air-conditioning. Great views from the rooftop. **Inexpensive to Moderate.**

Another budget spot nearby is the recently upgraded, 16-room **Pal's Guesthouse** (868 Magoon Street, 501-660-1282). **Inexpensive.**

Dining in Dangriga
Your best option in Dangriga is the **Coconuts Grill** restaurant (**Expensive**) at **Pelican Beach Hotel.** It has a nice setting with a sea view. For something more local, try the **Riverside Café (Inexpensive)**, a good choice for breakfast, or **King's Burger (Inexpensive)**, which does have good beefburgers along with standard Belizean dishes such as stew chicken.

Hopkins Lodging
A seaside Garifuna village of about 1,400 people living in unpretentious frame houses, Hopkins was first settled in1942 after a hurricane devastated New Town, a Garifuna community just north of present-day Hopkins. The village gets its name from Frederick Charles Hopkins, a Catholic bishop of the early part of the 20th century. Hopkins was itself leveled by Hurricane Hattie in 1961. The village only got electricity and telephones in the mid-1990s. If "poor but proud" fits anywhere, it fits here. Villagers have gotten by on subsistence fishing and farming, and some are now earning cash money from tourism. You'll find most folks friendly. Many

are eager to share their thoughts with visitors, and it's safe to walk around the village most anytime. The beach is nice, though many coco palms have died. Just south of Hopkins is the Sittee Point and False Sittee Point area, where hotel and real estate development are taking off. Many lots have been sold to expats looking for their little piece of the Caribbean, though only a few homes have so far been built.

You may have heard about the ferocious sand flies in this area, and, yes, they can be pretty bad. At other times, they're hardly to be noticed. Sorry, but we're not able to predict exactly when they are at their worst. The hotels here do their best to control the little devils, without resorting to hydrogen bombs, but at times the sandflies can be a pain in the neck, and also the foot, leg and everywhere else. An oily lotion such as baby oil or Avon Skin-So-Soft and a bug spray with DEET may help.

The price level for lodging is as follows:
Inexpensive: Under US$75
Moderate: US$75-$150
Expensive: US$151-$300
Very Expensive: Over US$300
Prices are for a double room in high season (usually late November to Easter). Rates, which do not include taxes, service charges or meals (except in some cases breakfast), may be higher during holiday periods, especially Christmas and New Years. If specific prices are mentioned, they are plus 9% hotel tax and in some cases a service charge, usually 10%.

Lodging places are listed alphabetically.
Hamanasi, Sittee Point, (P. O. Box 265, Dangriga), 844-235-4930 in U.S, 877-552-3483 in U.S. and Belize, www.hamanasi.com. Opened in 2000, Hamanasi quickly became one of the top beach and dive resorts in Belize. It has been named "Hotel of the Year" by the Belize Tourism Board and gets high ratings on social media sites. On about 22 acres with 400 feet of beach frontage, the resort is just south of Hopkins village. The restaurant and lobby are attractive, graced with local art, the grounds well kept and the pool, with a "zero effect," one of the nicer ones in Belize. There are several types of accommodations including rooms and suites in beachfront buildings and deluxe and regular "tree houses" (actually just units raised on stilts and set in the trees in the back). All the accommodations are air-conditioned and attractive, though we like the beachfront suites best. None of the units have TV or phones. Hamanasi's dive operation provides full diving services. Hamanasi has several dive boats, including big 45- and 43-footers. The resort also offers inland trips. Room rates are way up there, over US$400 double in high season. Continental breakfast is included in room rates. The hotel's restaurant is very good, if very expensive. There are usually minimum-stay requirements of three to five days, depending on the season. **Very Expensive.**

Jaguar Reef Lodge & Spa. Sittee Point, 501-523-7365, or 888-822-2448 in the U.S. and Canada, www.vivabelize.com. Jaguar Reef is jointly operated with Almond Beach Resort and two luxury suites buildings next door. These Hopkins properties are part of the Viva Belize group that also includes Sleeping Giant Lodge on the Hummingbird Highway and the treehouses at Ian Anderson's Caves

Branch Lodge. The attractive main building at Jaguar Reef houses a glassed-in beachfront restaurant that serves all the guests at the complex, bar, gift shop and front desk. There's a large variety of accommodations, from thatch duplex cabañas to luxury rooms and suites, all air-conditioned. The beach here is nice. Jaguar Reef runs a variety of tours, both on land and sea. Packages and specials are available. **Expensive to Very Expensive.**

Belizean Dreams, Hopkins, 501-523-7272 or 800-456-7150; www.belizeandreams.com. This condo colony just north of Jaguar Reef is among the most upscale accommodation choices on the Southern Coast. All villas have the same floor plans and furnishings, but some are directly on the beach, and the others have sea views. The units can be reserved as a complete three-bedroom villa, or choose a single bedroom or two-bedroom suite. The bedrooms have vaulted ceilings with exposed beams and four-poster king beds. **Very Expensive.**

Beaches and Dreams Seafront Inn, Sittee Point, 501-523-7259; www.beachesanddreams.com. This beachfront inn has two octagonal cottages, each with two units with vaulted ceilings and rattan furniture. The main building has been redone, adding six beachfront rooms plus a "treehouse" (not really) that sleeps up to five. The Barracuda Restaurant is one of the better eateries on the southern coast, and the Sea Bar offers drinks with a seaview. **Moderate.**

Jungle Jeanie by the Sea, Hopkins, 501-533-7047, www.junglejeanie.com. These cabañas are on a nicely shaded stretch of beach a little south of Hopkins village. Founders "Jungle Jeanie" Barkman and husband, John (who died in 2014), Canadians who lived in Belize for years, made this into one of the nicest little moderate range beach resorts in southern Belize. Cabañas, without A/C but with wi-fi, are on or near the beach. Yoga is available. **Inexpensive to Moderate.**

Hopkins Inn, Hopkins, 501-665-0411, www.hopkinsinn.com. In the heart of the village, Hopkins Inn has attractive cottages on the beach, with full bath, fridge, fan and private verandah with sea views. New owners, Will and Leslie, an enthusiastic young couple, have taken over, doing some upgrades and improvements. The affordable rates include continental breakfast. **Moderate.**

Tipple Tree Beya Inn, Hopkins, 501-533-7006; www.tippletree.com. If you're looking for an affordable simple little place on the beach in the village, this is a great choice. The hotel is popular, so reserve in advance. Beachside room, apartment and cabins, some with A/C, range from US$45 to $103 double, plus tax. There's also a two-bedroom apartment with A/C sleeping up to four persons for US$175. All rates plus 9% tax. German spoken. Rooms, cabin and apartments **Inexpensive to Moderate,** two-bedroom apartment. **Expensive.**

Dining in Hopkins
The price level for restaurants in all areas is as follows:
Inexpensive: Under US$7
Moderate: US$8-$19
Expensive: US$20-$39
Very Expensive: Over US$40
Prices don't include tips or alcoholic drinks. If not otherwise stated, the price range is for one person for dinner.

Restaurants here are listed alphabetically.

The larger resorts, including **Hamanasi** and **Jaguar Reef,** have attractive if expensive dining rooms, but you don't need to limit yourself just to hotel dining. There are several excellent chefs and cooks in Hopkins, and a number of new eateries have opened in the past several years.

Barracuda Bar and Grill, Sittee Point, 501-523-7259. A part of Beaches and Dreams inn, this waterfront restaurant has a long-time reputation for tasty seafood and interesting takes on Belizean dishes, along with good pizza. **Moderate to Expensive.**

Chef Rob's Gourmet Café, Parrot's Cove Lodge, Sittee River Rd., south of Hopkins village at Sittee Point, 501-523-7275. For upscale dining, Chef Rob Pronk's al fresco spot with a close-up view of the beach is the number one restaurant in Hopkins and one of the best in Southern Belize. Chef Rob also does Love on the Rocks, his cook-your-own concept where you grill your seafood or meat on 700-degree lava slabs. Open for dinner daily. **Expensive.**

Driftwood Beach Bar and Pizza Shack, Beachfront at north end of village, 501-667-4872. Popular seaside place at the north end for drinks and wood-fired pizza. Wings, conch fritters and other dishes, too. Open for lunch and dinner. Live music and drumming some nights. Closed Wednesday. **Moderate.**

Ella's Cool Spot, Main St,, Hopkins. With upholstered chairs in the sand and Christmas lights blinking, Ella's joint seems to have assembled itself casually beside Hopkins' main road. It's a great find. Her lunch and dinner menus, both in good favor with the locals, change daily. If you crave spice, go for the jerk chicken. **Moderate.**

Gecko's, 101 North Rd., Hopkins, 501-629-5411. Laidback spot for a really good meal. Check the blackboard for what's cooking -- dishes like jerk chicken, a huge pork chop and fish tacos. Open for lunch and dinner. Very popular and often packed. Closed Sunday and sometimes Tuesday. **Moderate to Expensive.**

Innie's, Main St., Hopkins, 501-503-7333. Not as cheap as it used to be, but it still serves authentic local Garifuna dishes, such as *hudut* (fish in a coconut broth with plantains) and seafood at moderate prices. Open daily for breakfast, lunch and dinner. **Moderate.**

Loggerheads Pub & Grill, Sittee Village Rd., south of Hopkins, 501-667-4872. This second-story bar and grill is the best place in the area for a beefburger or seafood sandwich and a cold beer. **Moderate.**

Lucky Lobster Bar & Grill. Lot 6, Sittee River Rd., Hopkins, 501-676-7777. You've been here before, or you may think you have. See the koozies and tee-shirts ("I Got Lucky at Lucky Lobsters") for sale? You didn't stumble back into the States, but this open-air bar with TVs, nice restrooms and efficient service has all the trappings. If craving fried-not-greasy food, get the Chicklets (chicken tenders), skillfully battered in buttermilk and cornmeal, or the Lucky Clucker Lollipops (chicken skewers). Chew the fat with friendly staff, and, later in the evening, with travelers who make this a night scene. Closed Monday-Tuesday. **Moderate.**

Thongs Café, Main St., Hopkins, 501-662-0110. This café is popular for morning coffee and breakfast (everyone loves the special French Toast) as well as for light lunches (sandwiches, salad). **Inexpensive to Moderate.**

Fruit and vegetable sellers in PG

Punta Gorda and Toledo District

BUG OUT RATINGS

Ratings are on an A to F scale, just like your old high school report card. A is the top grade; F is failing. Grades are relative compared to other areas in Belize.

Popularity with Expats	C-
Safety	B+
Overall Cost of Living	B
Real Estate Values	B+
Investment Potential	C+
Leisure Activities	C+
Restaurants	C-
Cultural Activities	C-
Infrastructure	C+
Business Potential	C
Medical Care	C
Shopping	C-
Farming & Ranching	A
Safety in Nuclear War	A-

Sustainable Living   A
Overall Bug Out Rating   **B+**

ADVANTAGES TO PUNTA GORDA AREA: • Lush, beautiful tropical scenery • Excellent fishing • Diverse mix of Maya, Garifuna and other cultures • Moderate land prices • Proximity to Rio Dulce area of Guatemala • Increasing interest in area for tourism due to completion of Southern Highway and construction of new road to Guatemala with border crossing

You've probably heard stories about Punta Gorda being the end of the earth and all that. You may be surprised, then, at how inviting a town it is. With about 5,500 people, it has a mix of Mopan and Ket'chi Maya, Garifuna and a dollop of Creoles, Lebanese and Chinese, plus a few American expats, missionaries and dreamers.

PG, as it's known in Belize, is colorful and friendly. There's usually a breeze blowing from the Bay of Honduras. On Wednesdays and Saturdays, the downtown market draws Maya from surrounding villages. PG's waterside setting is, like that of Corozal Town, truly pleasant, even beautiful.

Business activity in the town is not exactly hot and hopping. With a few exceptions, hotels in and around PG have low occupancies most of the year, though several new ones have opened -- hope springs eternal. The overall annual hotel occupancy rate is under 30%. As yet, only a few tourists make it all the way down the Southern Highway from Belize City or Placencia. Some backpackers do pass through on their way to cheaper towns in Guatemala and Honduras. With the completion of the paving of the Southern Highway, and the opening of a new paved road, with a planned border crossing to Guatemala, conventional wisdom is that PG will soon explode with new hotels, real estate developments and other businesses. We're not so sure that will happen to any great extent, but certainly things are getting a bit busier.

Outside of PG, the land in Toledo District is lush, wild and wet, fed by 160 inches or more of rain each year — the only "dry" months are February through May. Emerald green valleys lay between low peaks of the Maya Mountains. Rice grows in flooded fields, and giant bromeliads line the roads. There are no beaches to speak of around PG, but the rocky shorelines are cooled by near constant breezes from the Bay of Honduras. Offshore are isolated cayes and the straggling end of the barrier reef.

The Maya have lived in this part of Belize for millennia. Among the Maya ruins here are Lubaantun ("Place of the Fallen Stones") Lubaantun was occupied only from around 700 to 900 CE. The famous, or infamous, "crystal skull" was supposedly discovered here in 1926 by F.A. Mitchell-Hedges, on assignment from the British Museum, though most experts believe the skull is a hoax. Nim Li Punit ("Big Hat") was occupied about the same time as Lubaantun, in the Late Classic period. At its height, several thousand people may have lived there. Among other notable Maya sites in the area is Uxbenka (pronounced Ush-ben-ka and meaning "Ancient Place").

The Maya were joined in the early 19th century by Garifuna from the Bay

Islands of Honduras and, after the American Civil War, by a group of former Confederate soldiers and their families who attempted to settle here, with relatively little success. In modern times, Punta Gorda has held an attraction for missionary groups, mostly fundamentalists from the U.S.

Who knows? You may find PG is precisely your kind of place, too.

Punta Gorda Practicalities

Banks: Belize Bank and ScotiaBank have branches and ATMs in PG.

Groceries: All of the groceries in Punta Gorda are small. Try Mel's Mart or one of the several Supaul Stores (usually referred to by color, "green Supaul's," "white Supaul's," etc. The old PG market, where vendors sell fruit, vegetables and other items, has been renovated.

Restaurants: Asha's Culture Kitchen, Walucca's, Mangrove Inn, The Snack Shack, Gomier's and Grace's.

Medical: Punta Gorda Hospital (south end of Main Street) can provide basic emergency care; you may want to upgrade to the Southern Regional Hospital in Dangriga or to hospitals in Belize City.

Infrastructure: Punta Gorda has power, municipal water and sewerage system. Cable TV, DSL and cellular internet are available in PG. Many remote areas of Toledo District are not on the grid, and residents must depend on their own resources for water, sewerage and satellite internet. Some Maya villages have homes with no running water and no power.

Real Estate

Toledo does not have a very active real estate market, and sometimes it is difficult to establish market value. Accessible land in smaller tracts (under 50 acres) often goes for US$1,000 to $2,000 an acre. Large parcels with river frontage might go for US$500 to $1,000 an acre. Building lots in or near Punta Gorda not on the bay are inexpensive, usually no more than a few thousand dollars, but waterfront lots are more expensive. Smaller concrete houses on the bay in PG have sold for under US$75,000.

Properties Offered in Toledo

Here are a few properties offered by individuals and real estate companies in 2018. Prices shown are asking prices in U.S. dollars.

• Three-bedroom, one-bath fixer-upper in PG, concrete construction, not on the bay but if you added a palapa on the roof you could see the water, US$54,500

• 44-acre parcel near Big Falls village, with 400 ft. frontage on Southern Highway, fertile soil, all utilities nearby, good spot for lodge, great building site with long-distance views over Toledo and the Bay of Honduras, US$149,900

• Small concrete house in Cattle Landing adjoining PG just yards from the Bay of Honduras – could be commercial or residential, all utilities available, US$100,000

• Four-bedroom, two-bath house on 29+ acres near village of Barranco, US$75 annual property tax, motivated seller open to offers, US$124,500

• 200-acre farm at Manfredi village off new San Antonio Hwy., high ground

for building, with 80 acres low land cleared and formerly used for rice farming, power to property, water from well, US$149,000 (US$745 an acre)
• 2½-acre beachfront lot near Punta Negra and Monkey River, 175 ft. of golden, pristine beach on the sea, US$200,000

Real Estate Agents
Real estate companies in Belize City and elsewhere also have some listings for Toledo. PG tourism operators and entrepreneurs sometimes hustle real estate on the side.
CPC Real Estate Solutions Ltd., #168 Beach Front, Hopeville, Punta Gorda, Toledo, 501-667-3254. www.belizeproperty.com.

Rio Grande in Toledo District

VISITING TOLEDO DISTRICT

Getting There
Via the Southern Highway, Punta Gorda is about 100 miles by car from the junction with the Hummingbird/Stann Creek Valley Highway near Dangriga. Since the Southern Highway is now fully paved, if you push it a little you can make the trip in about two hours. Add up to three hours if leaving from Belize City, and two hours from San Ignacio, depending on your route and driving habits.
By bus from Belize City -- **James Line** (www.jamesbuslines.com) is your best choice -- figure about six hours minimum. Besides regular buses, James has two daily express buses that are a little faster. Fare from the Novelo's bus station in

Belize City to PG is around US$8.

Both **Tropic Air** (www.tropicair.com) and **Maya Island Air** (www.mayaislandair.com) each have about four or five flights a day from Belize City to PG. From the international airport to Punta Gorda, the fare is around US$187 one-way and from municipal, US$163.

One of these days soon, thanks to the new San Antonio Road a new border crossing with Guatemala will open, connecting Belize's Far South with the Pan American Highway. That is expected change the dynamics in Toledo, not just in tourism but also in other areas such as retailing and agriculture.

Moving on from PG, there is regularly scheduled pedestrian water taxi service between PG and Puerto Barrios, Guatemala. Currently, there are four boats daily to Puerto Barrios – Requena's, Tek-Dat, Pichilingo and Sharkboy. The trip takes about an hour and the one-way fare is US$20 to $25. There's one boat daily to Livingston, Guatemala, Memos. Fare depends on the number of people going.

What to Do and See in PG and Toledo

The Deep South of Belize offers a lot to do on land and sea. It's too bad that so few visitors make it here. Unfortunately, prices for tours tend to be high, due to lack of volume and the distances involved.

Punta Gorda Town has an attractive waterfront location. However, there are no real beaches in or near PG. The town, with its mix of Garifuna, Creole, Maya, Guatemalans and quite a few expat Americans, is generally safe. There's not much to see or do in town, except for a few small shops along Front Street and elsewhere in town. At Central Park is a large clock tower and a market with lots of shops selling used clothing and other miscellaneous junque. **Fajina Women's Group Craft Center** (Front Street near the pier) is a small co-op selling Maya crafts.

Cacao growing is big business (but with a lot of small cacao farmers) in Toledo. The Toledo Cacao Growers Association (www.tcgabelize.com) has some 600 members. Most grow their cacao organically and bring it to a central facility for processing. A small chocolate factory (**Cotton Tree Chocolate Shop**, 2 Front Street, 501-621-8772, www.cottontreechocolate.com) is in PG. Other chocolate making operations include the **Ixcacaco May Belizean Chocolate** (San Felipe village, 501-742-4050, www.ixcacaomayabelizechocolate.com).

Near Mafredi village is the **Maya House of Cacao** (San Antonio Road, 501-722-2992), which opened in late 2015. It has exhibits on cacao, chocolate making and a gift shop.

The **Chocolate Festival** (www.chocolatefestivalofbelize.com), usually held the third week in May) is a growing annual event held downtown and in other venues in Toledo.

PG has a couple of Garifuna drumming schools, including Ray Mcdonald's **Warasa Drum School** (501-632-7701, www.warasadrumschool.com) and **Maroon Creole Drum School** (501-632-7841) run by noted drummer and drum-maker Emmeth Young. Mr. Young's drums are sold in PG.

In rural Toledo, you'll see true rainforests, lush and green, Maya villages that are little changed from 1,000 years ago and several interesting Maya sites, including Lubaantun and Nim Li Punit. You can also hike in the national parks and forest reserves and go caving.

While you're here you must visit the rural areas where there are a number of Mayan villages, both Mopan and Ket'chi. **San Pedro Columbia** and **San Antonio,** a Ket'chi village, are two of the largest.

San Pedro Columbia is home to **Eladio Pop's Agouti Cacao Farm Tour** (501-624-0166, https://agouticacaofarm.wordpress.com). Mr. Pop will take you on a tour of his 30-acre cacao farm and demonstrate how the ancient Maya made chocolate. Camping is also available here.

Other interesting villages are **Blue Creek** (Ket'chi and Mopan), home to **Blue Creek Cave.** You'll need a guide to explore the cave, although you can swim a few hundred feet into the cave on your own. The **Tumul K'in Center of Learning** (501-608-1070, www.tumukinbelize.org), dedicated to preserving Maya heritage and practices, is also in Blue Creek. **International Zoological Expeditions** (IZE, 501-532-2404, www.izebelize.com), which runs educational and research programs in several parts of Belize, has a small lodge and research station at Blue Creek with a couple of treehouse cabins and a dorm. Rates for lodging, meals and a couple of tours are around US$115 per person per night.

Maya House of Cacao (Mile 18, San Antonio Rd., 501-722-2992, www.mayahouseofcacao.com) is a 2,000 sq. ft. chocolate museum and learning center, run by the Toledo Cacao Growers Association. Is is open daily 10-3.

At **Santa Cruz** village is **Río Blanco National Park,** a small (105-acre) park with a waterfall, small lake and a cave. Near **San Miguel village** is **Tiger Cave.**

Near **Big Falls** village is the **Living Maya Experience** (501-627-7408), which provides visitors with an immersion experience in Ket'chi Maya culture, including farming, making tortillas and basket weaving with a Maya family in Big Falls.

Not associated with the Living Maya Experience but in the same area is a zip line, **Big Falls Extreme Adventures** (Southern Hwy. south of Big Falls village, 501-634-6979). Doing the zip line costs around US$40 per person. Tubing on the river is also available.

Near **Golden Stream** village about 30 miles north of PG is the **Belize Spice Farm & Botanical Gardens** (501-732-4014, www.belizespicefarm.com). This farm, owned by an American couple of East Indian descent, is one of the largest vanilla and black pepper farms in Belize. Tours are in a trailer behind a tractor. They cost a surprisingly high US$20 per person.

Ya'axché Ranger Program (www.yaaxche.org) allows you to experience time with a ranger in the rainforest. The program starts at Golden Stream Field Center. A half-day hiking tour is US$62 per person.

Payne's Creek National Park, north of PG, covers more than 37,000 acres of mixed saltwater, freshwater and savannah land habitat. It has manatees, yellow-headed parrots, howler monkeys and all five species of Belize's wild cats including jaguars. It is administered by the Belize Forestry Service and the Toledo Institute for Development and Environment (TIDE).

Barranco is a Garifuna fishing village of about 600 people near the Sarstoon-Temash National Park. It was the home of Andy Palacio and a number of other well-known musicians and artists. There is a dügü, a Garifuna temple, here, along with the **Barranco House of Culture.** A TIDE tour of Barranco is around US$100 for two people.

Maya Sites

Nim Li Punit, near Indian Creek village off Mile 75 of the Southern Highway, 501-665-5126, open 8 to 5 daily, admission US$5, is a late Classic period site noted for its stelae. More than 25 large stelae have been found at the site. Some of the stelae and other artifacts are on display at the informative visitor center. Nim Li Punit is on a hilltop with good views of the surrounding rainforest. Maya women and children from Indian Creek set up tables near the exit area, selling their Maya crafts.

Lubaantun, near San Pedro Columbia village off the San Antonio Road, is a late Classic period site. There is a visitor center. Lubaantun was at its peak from around 730 to 900 CE. The site has 18 plazas. From the tallest structure in the plaza, about 50 feet high, you can see the sea. Lubaantun was first rediscovered in 1875 and has been excavated by a number of different archeologists, including F.A. Mitchell-Hedges, Thomas Gann and Norman Hammond. The so-called "Crystal Skull" allegedly was discovered here in 1924 by Anna Mitchell-Hedges, the daughter of F.A. Mitchell-Hedges. In fact, F.A. likely bought the skull at an auction in London in 1943. Tests suggest the skull is of modern origin. The site is open daily from 8 to 5. Admission is US$5.

Pusilhá and **Uxbenka** are two other Maya sites in Toledo. Neither is much excavated Both are difficult to visit except on a tour (around US$100 for two people).

Maya Villages and Offshore Cayes

Getting to the Maya villages areas is easiest done with your own transportation, but you can also go on a tour or take a bus. A bunch of local buses leave from the clock tower area to go to various Maya villages and to Barranco in Toledo. Usually there is just one or two buses a day to each village. Ask locally for current schedules, or look in the local tourist newspaper, *The Toledo Howler.*

Off the coast of Toledo are some of Belize's most pristine cayes and excellent diving, snorkeling and fishing.

Closest to PG are the **Snakes Cayes** in the **Port Honduras Marine Reserve.** These cayes offer good snorkeling, diving and swimming about a 30-minute boat ride from town. There are **East, South, West and Middle Snake** cayes. The best beach is on West Snake Caye. South Snake Caye has abundant sea life on view for snorkelers and divers. East Snake Caye has a lighthouse. Middle Snake Caye is for researchers only, off limits to regular visitors. There is a US$5 per person per day reserve fee for visiting Port Honduras Reserve.

Farther out are the **Sapodilla Cayes** in the **Sapodilla Cayes Marine Reserve.** It's about a 90-minute boat ride from PG, and when the weather is bad it's a rough ride. Hunting Caye and Lime Caye both have good swimming and snorkeling, and you can overnight at either one. On **Lime Caye** is Garbutt's Fishing Lodge (501-73209979, www.garbuttsfishinglodge.com) offers several packages for US$350 to $700 per person including transportation, lodging, meals, snorkeling, fishing and park fees. (This marine reserve has a US$10 per person per day reserve fee.) **Hunting Caye** is the site of one of the University of Belize's small satellite campuses, and it sometimes rents out its basic rooms for visitors (around US$40 per person). The Belize Coast Guard is also stationed here. Camping on the island is US$5 per person.

Reef Conservation International (501-702-0229 in Placencia , www.reefci.com) has a combination research operation and dive lodge on Tom Owens Caye in the Sapodilla Cayes Marine Reserve. Rates for divers are around US$1,350 per week per person.

Tours and Information

There are about a dozen registered and licensed tour operators in Toledo, including the ones below. They can arrange land and marine tours. The larger lodging properties also run tours. Full-day land tours range from about US$100 to $150 per person. These tours include guide, transportation from PG and lunch. Full-day snorkel and swimming tours to the Snake Cayes cost around US$250 for two persons on a private tour. If you can join a group, the rate may be lower.

Garbutt's Marine, Joe Taylor Creek, Punta Gorda, 501-722-0070, www.garbuttsfishinglodge.com.

PG Tours, 501-629-4266, Punta Gorda, www.pgtours.com.

TIDE Tours, 501-722-2129, www.tidebelize.org.

Toledo Cave & Adventure, 501-604-2124, www.tcatours.com.

For more information on tours and about the Toledo area in general, visit the Belize Tourism Industry Association (BTIA) office on Main Street, Punta Gorda, 501-722-2531.

Punta Gorda Lodging

The price level for lodging in all areas is as follows:

Inexpensive: Under US$75

Moderate: US$75-$150

Expensive: US$151-$300

Very Expensive: Over US$300

Prices are for a double room in high season (usually late November to Easter). Rates, which do not include taxes, service charges or meals (except in some cases breakfast), may be higher during holiday periods, especially Christmas and New Years. If specific prices are mentioned, they are plus 9% hotel tax and in some cases a service charge, usually 10%.

Lodging places are listed alphabetically.

Blue Belize Guest House, 139 Front St., Punta Gorda, 501-722-2678; www.bluebelize.com. This pleasant, well-located guesthouse is owned by marine biologist Rachel Graham, though it is now managed by a local Belizean couple. You can do your own thing in one of the six attractive self-catering flats or suites, with kitchenettes, large bedrooms and verandas with hammocks. The guesthouse is set on a bluff overlooking the water, within a short stroll of everything in town. A continental breakfast is included. Bikes are complimentary. **Moderate to Expensive.**

Copal Tree Lodge, Wilson Rd., 5 miles north of PG, 501-722-0050 or 844-238-0216 in the U.S. and Canada, www.copaltreelodge.com. Formerly the fishing lodge known as El Pescador PG, and then Machaca Hill Lodge, and then Belcampo

Lodge, the property in early 2018 was relaunched once again, this time as Copal Tree Lodge. A member of National Geographic Unique Lodges of the World, the lodge has added a rum distillery to its complement of facilities and activities, including cacao classes, organic gardens and inland and sea tours. The lodge is beautifully situated on a steep hill, on 470 acres above the Rio Grande. A small tram takes guests down to the boats docked on the river at the base of the hill. Up top, on a clear day, you have views of the Gulf of Honduras, with Guatemala and Honduras in the distance. Troops of howler monkeys come by frequently. After a day exploring the Toledo rain forest, dive into the pool, then dine on in the second-floor restaurant, with vegetables from the lodge's organic garden. The 16 renovated cottage suites have vaulted ceilings, tile floors and air-conditioning, and there's also a three-bedroom villa. Rates have always been very high here, probably one reason that it has changed personalities every few years. **Very Expensive.**

Coral House Inn, 151 Main St. (P.O. Box 43, Punta Gorda), 501-722-2878; www.coralhouseinn.net. Americans Rick and Darla Mallory bought and renovated a 1938 colonial-era house and turned it into one of the coolest guesthouses in Belize. You'll recognize it by the coral color and the vintage red and white VW van parked in front. There's a small swimming pool and use of bikes is complimentary. Nearby are Confederate graves in a cemetery, a legacy of the Confederate immigration to Toledo after the U.S. Civil War. The five guest rooms and suite have tile floors, good beds, cable TV, air-conditioning and free wi-fi. A continental breakfast is included, and there's a newly upgraded outdoor bar and swimming pool. Nearby os rental house with apartments managed by the Coral House Inn owners. Highly recommended. **Moderate for inn, Expensive for rental apartments.**

Cotton Tree Lodge, San Felipe Village (P. O. Box 104, Punta Gorda), 501-670-0557 or U.S. number 212-529-8622, www.cottontreelodge.com. Named after the silk cotton tree, aka kapok or ceiba, an example of which stands on the grounds, Cotton Tree Lodge sits on 100 acres beside the Moho River about 15 miles from Punta Gorda. Cotton Tree accommodations include rooms, one- and two-bedroom cabañas and even a river cabaña anchored in the middle of the Moho River. The lodge has raised wooden walkways; in the summer rainy season the Moho sometimes floods, and at times the lodge grounds become a shallow pond. Filling meals are served in a huge thatch palapa. Meals-included and all-inclusive rates are available, along with room-only rates. **Expensive (rooms only), Very Expensive with meals or as all-inclusive.**

Hickatee Cottages Lodge, Mile 1.5, Ex-Servicemen Rd., Punta Gorda, 501-662-4475, www.hickatee.com. This charming and down-to-earth lodge on 20 acres just south of Punta Gorda was created by a British couple, Ian and Kate Morton. It opened in late 2005 and soon became one of the best little inns in Belize. In 2016, it changed hands and is now run by another couple who seem to be continuing the sustainable, eco-conscious and locavore policies of the founders. The Caribbean-style cottages, with zinc roofs and private porches, are nestled in lush foliage. There's a small but well-stocked bar with free wi-fi. Continental breakfasts are included. On certain days, the lodge offers guests free visits to Fallen Stones Butterfly Farm, and usually there's Garifuna drumming one night a week. A hickatee, by the way, is a river turtle, *Dermatemys mawii.* Recommended. **Moderate.**

The Farm Inn, San Antonio-Santa Cruz Rd., Toledo, 501-732-4781; www.thefarminnbelize.com. The Farm Inn is a small lodge on 52 acres just off the newly paved San Antonio-Santa Cruz Road. The managers, Kevin and Renee, are from South Africa. The Farm Inn has three rooms in a two-story building near a small creek, plus two other rooms closer to the lodge office. All rooms have private baths and fans, no air-conditioning (power at the lodge is solar, except for a generator). There's a pool. The restaurant serves excellent food, with many items from the lodge's own garden. Guinea fowl and other creatures scamper around the cacao trees. **Moderate to Expensive.**

Lodge at Big Falls, Big Falls Village (P.O. Box 103, Punta Gorda), 501-732-4444; www.thelodgeatbigfalls. This lodge, on about 30 acres on the banks of the Rio Grande River near the village of Big Falls, is an attractive option for birders, nature lovers and outdoor lovers. The accommodations are what most visitors are looking for in a lodge —there are thatch cabañas, but nice ones, with tile floors and private baths. In addition, the lodge has three newer cabins with air-conditioning. There's a swimming pool, but you can also swim in the Rio Grande. The main lodge building has a restaurant and library. **Expensive.**

Sirmoor Hill Farm Bed and Breakfast, Mile 3, New Rd., Punta Gorda, 501-722-0052, www.sirmoorhillfarm.com. In a century-old colonial house, beautifully set on a low hill on a 775-acre farm and ranch, Sirmoor Hill Farm B&B is one of the most appealing places in Southern Belize. The owners will make you feel welcome. There are just two rooms, a one-bedroom and a two-bedroom suite. **Moderate to Expensive.**

Tate's Guest House, 34 José Maria Nuñez St., Punta Gorda, 501-722-0147. Run by William Tate, a long-time post office worker in PG, and his family, this guesthouse on a quiet residential street is a good value. The rooms are clean, and the atmosphere friendly. There's a small common kitchen with refrigerator and microwave for guest use. **Inexpensive.**

Homestays and Guesthouse Program

For a more complete immersion in Maya life, consider a **homestay** or **guesthouse stay** in a Maya village. Several different programs are available in Toledo.

One is the **Toledo Ecotourism Association** (TEA) program (501-633-9954, www.teabelize.org. TEA offers stays in guesthouses (not individual homes) in five villages: Laguna, San Antonio, Santa Elena, San Jose and San Miguel starting at US$28 per person. A one-day, one-night program including guesthouse stay, three meals and various activities is US$100 per person. TEA also offers farm, village, cave, chocolate making and other day tours, most from about US$10 to $30 per person.

Another is the **Aguacate Belize Homestay Program** (501-633-9954, www.aguacatebelize.com). Stays in a Maya home in Aguacate village, a Ket'chi community, are around US$8 per person per night, with meals US$3.50 per meal, plus a one-time US$5 registration fee. Keep in mind you will stay in a Maya thatch home with dirt floor that will not have electricity or running water. You'll sleep in a hammock, bathe in a creek and eat simple meals of tortillas, beans and eggs that the family eats.

Dining in Toledo
The price level for restaurants is as follows:
Inexpensive: Under US$7
Moderate: US$8-$19
Expensive: US$20-$39
Very Expensive: Over US$40
Prices don't include tips or alcoholic drinks. If not otherwise stated, the price range is for one person for dinner.

In addition to the restaurants listed below, Copal Tree Lodge has a restaurant, **(Expensive to Very Expensive)** open to the public by reservation. **The Farm Inn** restaurant, **(Moderate)** serves an unusual combination of Belizean and African dishes. The South African dishes are cooked in a three-legged cast iron pot.

Restaurants here are listed alphabetically.

Asha's Culture Kitchen. 80 Front St., Punta Gorda, 501-632-8025. This is one of our first stops for dinner in PG. For one thing, the setting is great: Asha's is in a wooden building over the water, with a windy deck with views of the sea. For another, its serves tasty seafood and other Creole dishes in large portions at modest prices. Open for dinner daily except Tuesday. **Inexpensive to Moderate.**

Coleman's Café. Big Falls village, near the rice mill, 501-720-2017. This restaurant in Big Falls village serves simple but tasty Belizean dishes such as stew chicken with beans and rice. Sit at tables with under a covered patio, open to the breezes, and enjoy real Belizean hospitality. **Inexpensive to Moderate.**

Gomier's Restaurant and Soy Centre. 5 Alejandro Vernon St., Punta Gorda, 501-722-2929. This restaurant opens only if the St. Lucia-born owner, Ignatius "Gomier" Longville, feels like cooking. If open Gomier's does excellent vegetarian meals, from organic ingredients mostly grown by the owner. Closed Sunday and some other days. **Inexpensive to Moderate.**

Grace's. Main St., Punta Gorda, 501-702-2414. This long-established local place is especially good for breakfast. Open for breakfast, lunch and dinner daily. **Inexpensive to Moderate.**

Mangrove Inn at Casa Bonita, Front St. in Cattle Landing area, Punta Gorda, 501-722-2270. The cook and co-owner of this little restaurant, Iconie Williams, formerly operated one of PG's best eateries, also called Mangrove Inn, and she reopened it here in the B&B in her home. Iconie cooks different dishes every evening, but you'll usually have a choice of seafood (snapper, snook, or shrimp) or hearty fare like roasted chicken. Open daily for dinner only. **Inexpensive to Moderate.**

A Piece of Chicken, 1050 Pelican St., Punta Gorda, 501-665-2695. This fairly new spot is making a name for itself for its chicken burgers and other chicken dishes, such as chicken with chili and fries. It also has veggie burgers and other items. **Inexpensive to Moderate.**

Snack Shack, Main St., Punta Gorda, at Belize Telemedia Ltd. parking lot,

501-702-0020. This is PG's version of fast food – build-your-own burritos, freshly made flavored tortillas, pancakes, fruit smoothies and such. Try the papaya shake. Open Monday-Saturday for breakfast and lunch. **Inexpensive.**

Walucca's, 1 Mile, Hopeville, Punta Gorda, 501-702-2129. Across the street from the bay near the entrance to Punta Gorda proper, Walucca's has some of the best food in the area, a great location with views of the water and the cooling feel of sea breezes, and on top of that a portion of profits goes to support the conservation efforts of Toledo Institute for Development and Environment (TIDE). Depending on what's on the menu when you're there, try the grilled snook fillets, the whole fried snapper or pork chops. It's all good, and the beer and drinks are cold and well priced. **Moderate.**

Clock tower in downtown PG

Coffee and art on Front Street, Caye Caulker

Caye Caulker

Note: Being a small island, with tourism as its main industry, Caye Caulker is probably not what you're looking for as an escape spot. However, we're including it here for those who may want island living, and, besides, it a great place to take a vacation from the Belize mainland.

BUG OUT RATINGS
Ratings are on an A to F scale, just like your old high school report card. A is the top grade; F is failing. The ratings are relative to other places in Belize.

Popularity with Expats	C+
Safety	B
Overall Cost of Living	B
Real Estate Bargains	B
Investment Potential	B+
Leisure Activities	C
Restaurants	B
Cultural Activities	D
Infrastructure	C
Business Potential	C+
Medical Care	D+
Shopping	D
Farming & Ranching	F

Safety in Nuclear War   D
Overall Bug Out Rating   **C-**

ADVANTAGES OF CAYE CAULKER: • Small, laid-back island atmosphere • Provides excellent opportunities for water activities – boating, fishing, diving • Less expensive than San Pedro • No need for a car

Caye Caulker is Ambergris Caye's "little sister" island – smaller, less developed and a cheaper date. Caulker, whose name derives from the Spanish word for coco plum, *hicaco,* has the kind of laidback, sandy-street, tropical-color, low-key Caribbean charm that travelers pay thousands to experience, but here they can have it for peanuts. Well, almost. Less than 10 miles and about 30 minutes by boat from San Pedro or 45 minutes from Belize City, Caye Caulker is definitely worth a visit, and perhaps you'll like it well enough to stay.

A majority of local residents are Mestizos who originally came to the island from Mexico, and who until recently made their living by fishing, but the island also has Creoles, some of whom consider themselves Rastafarians, gringos and others.

While it is quickly going upmarket, Caye Caulker remains to some extent a budget island. In the 1960s and 1970s, the island was on the "back-packer trail," a cheap place for longhaired visitors to relax and smoke a little weed or sip a beer. Today, a very expensive hotel on Caulker goes for around US$250 a night, and most of the hotels charge under US$100 double, with some as low as US$15. Many of the older buildings on the island are wooden clapboard, often painted in tropical colors, but more recently constructed houses and hotels are of reinforced concrete. Only a few hotels on the island have swimming pools.

In the past several years, a flood of new restaurants has opened on Caulker, and you now have a much broader selection of types and quality of restaurants.

Beaches? Caulker has much less beachfront than Hopkins, Placencia or Ambergris Caye. Beach reclamation projects did widen and improve the beach along the east side of the village (though storms have taken away and then given back sand). Swimming in the shallow water close to shore is mainly from piers and at "the Split," which is very popular for sunning and swimming, and there's are good bars with cold beer close by.

In the past, the pipe water on Caulker was not very good. It often had a sulfur smell and came from shallow wells, some which were close to septic systems. However, a reverse osmosis water plant is now operating on the island, but not all homes and businesses are on it.

Caye Caulker, like most other coastal areas and cayes, also has sandflies. Especially on calm days, they can be a nuisance.

Caye Caulker Practicalities
Banks: Caye Caulker has only one bank, Atlantic Bank. It has an ATM that accepts international debit cards.

Groceries: Chan's Mini-Mart on Middle Street near the Caye Caulker Plaza Hotel is the most-frequented grocery, although there are other places to buy beer, booze, snacks and other basics on Front Street and elsewhere. Near Chan's are some fruit and vegetable vendors.

Other Stores: Caye Caulker doesn't have much shopping, beyond some gift shops on Front Street, a couple of art galleries and a few other shops. Most residents go to Belize City for their big shopping trips.

Medical: Caye Caulker doesn't have a hospital, but there is a small medical clinic (Front Street at the south end, 501-226-0190. For a real emergency, fly or take a water taxi to Belize City. Your hotel will assist in getting you to Belize City the fastest way.

Infrastructure: Caye Caulker now has a reverse osmosis municipal water system in the village. Sewerage is still an issue. DSL and cellular internet are available. North of the Split most residents must rely on their own resources for power, water and sewerage, though there is now power to North Island areas close to the Split.

Real Estate on Caye Caulker

Most of the development on Caulker is concentrated in the one small village, although North Caye, across the Split, and the area of the far south of the main island, are getting more development. Many families have long ties with the island and aren't interested in selling. Thus, the number of available properties is small. When properties do come on the market, the owners sometimes have an inflated idea of their value. One small budget hotel was offered for years for US$3,500,000, not much less than the total annual gross tourism revenue of the entire island!

Indeed, small is the key word to keep in mind when looking for property on Caye Caulker. Most lots are small, around one-tenth of an acre or smaller. Typical houses for sale have less than 1,000 sq. ft. of indoor space, not including decks, porches or rooftop verandas.

Properties on Caye Caulker

Here are some of the properties for sale on Caye Caulker in 2018. Prices shown are asking prices in U.S. dollars.

• Small renovated wooden beach house with 50 ft. of Caribbean beach frontage, 100 ft. deep, about ¼ mile north of the Split, power and municipal water to the house, plus well for irrigation, US179,000.

• Custom-built concrete home of almost 1,200 sq. ft., beautifully designed and constructed to last, plus 430 sq. ft. apartment and small caretaker's unit, tile floors, beautiful cabinets, in center of village, municipal power and water, plus catchment vat, US$449,000

• Three-bedroom, one-bath wooden house on stilts in Bahia Puesta del Sol area south of the village near the back side of the island, needs some work but is on a solid foundation, US$125,000

• Lots on North Caye (north of the Split), some with sea or lagoon frontage and some back from the water but with water views, most about 60 x 90 feet, access by boat, no utilities, US$25,000 to $220,000, owner financing available with 20% down.

• 60' x 90' lot on south end of the island, near nature reserve and two lots back from the back side, buyer will have to use solar and a well or catchment,

US$49,000

• Three-bedroom, two-bath concrete house off Front Street in village, but with privacy, built solidly in 1970s, currently used for vacation rental, nice garden area, US$319,000

• Four-unit hotel in two buildings, with two studio apartments, a three-bedroom two-bath unit and a one-bedroom wooden house, all units with kitchens, top-rated on social media, high occupancy with substantial vacation rental income, or live in one and rent the others, US$839,000

Real Estate Agents on Caye Caulker

Caye Living Properties, Middle St. near Atlantic Bank, 501-226-0375, www.cayecaulkerproperties.com

RE/MAX Island Real Estate (Anita Durham), Caye Caulker, 501-225-0404, http://anitadurham.point2agent.com

VISITING CAYE CAULKER

Getting to Caulker

Normally, you can fly to Caulker's little airstrip on **Tropic Air** (www.tropicair.com) or **Maya Island Air** (www.mayaregional.com) from Belize City. However, in September 2017, both Tropic and Maya Island temporarily suspended flights to and from Caye Caulker due to the condition of the Caulker runway.

In any case, most visitors to Caulker come by boat. Two water taxi companies, with fast boats that hold up to 110 passengers, connect Belize City with Caye Caulker.

From Belize City it's a 45-minute ride to Caulker. **Ocean Ferry** (501-223-0033, www.oceanferrybelize.com) boats leave from the Marine Terminal in Belize City at 10 North Front Street near the Swing Bridge. **San Pedro Belize Express** (501-223-2225, www.belizewatertaxi.com) boats leave from the Brown Sugar dock at 111 North Front Street near the Tourism Village. Ocean Ferry has five or six departures daily to and from Caulker. The rates are from US$12 one-way and US$22 round-trip between Belize City and Caye Caulker. San Pedro Belize Express, which has around eight or nine departures to Caulker, charges US$18 one-way and US$28 round-trip between Belize City and Caye Caulker.

The water taxi business in Belize is in flux; schedules, rates and companies are subject to change.

GETTING ORIENTED

The water taxis boats mostly come in at piers on the front side of the island. If you come ashore at the main public pier, the pink and green Trends Beachfront hotel is on your right, and the mustard-colored Seaside Cabañas is on your left.

Walk a few sandy feet and you'll come to Front Street. Go right, or north, and in 15 minutes or so you'll pass several good hotels, some restaurants, shops and tour operators, plus a few touts, and end up at "the Split," the main place to swim on the island. Go left or south and you'll find some of the island's better beachfront properties. Many of the island's restaurants, shops and hotels are on Front Street or on the beachfront. Go straight west, and you're in the heart of the village.

In general, hotels to the south are quieter than those north toward the Split. However, if you're staying south, it's a bit more of a walk to restaurants and most bars. For those who really want to get away from things, try the North Island, the area north of the Split. However, this part of the island is only accessible by water. There is power and municipal water to part of the North, but other parts are off-the-grid. A new bar and restaurant, KOKO King, has recently opened on the North just across the Split. There's a small ferry to take you back and forth to North Island.

What to Do and See on Caye Caulker

Caye Caulker isn't so much about seeing and doing as being. This is a little island to kick back, relax and just enjoy life.

From Caulker, you can do visit most of the same attractions as from Ambergris Caye, such as **Hol Chan Marine Reserve** and other dive and snorkel sites. The **Caye Caulker Marine Reserve** is Caulker's own mini-Hol Chan snorkeling area, just 10 minutes from Caulker.

In addition, you may also want to visit **Swallow Caye Wildlife Sanctuary** (www.swallowcayemanatees.org), 9,000 acres of protected sea and mangrove habitat for manatees and other wildlife. Swallow Caye trips are around US$85.

There is no shortage of tour operators and snorkel and dive shops to take you out. There are at least three dive shops on the island and perhaps a dozen snorkel and tour operators, most of which have locations on the beachfront along Front Street.

Frenchie's Diving Services (beachfront pier, toward the Split, 501-226-0234, www.frenchiesdivingbelize.com) is the island's oldest dive shop under continuous ownership. It has four dive boats.

Belize Diving Services (Chapoose St., near soccer field, 501-226-0143, www.belizedivingservices.com) is a well-respected dive operation, founded in 1978, and owned since 2009 by Chip and Dani Petersen. It has a 46-foot dive boat.

You'll pay US$100 to $145 including marine reserve fee for a two-tank dive trip to the Caye Caulker Marine Reserve or to Hol Chan, and up to about US$265 for three-tank dive trips to Lighthouse Reef Atoll and the Blue Hole, including reserve fee. Day trips to Turneffe Atoll are less than to Lighthouse Reef.

Local half-day snorkeling trips around Caye Caulker are about US$35 per person, while full-day snorkel trips to Hol Chan are around US$65 to $100 including US$10 reserve fee and, usually, lunch. Land tours for cave tubing or to visit Altun Ha Maya site start at around US$70 per person.

Caye Caulker also is home to a growing scene of other water and windsports, including paddleboarding and windsurfing and of course fishing.

Among the well-established snorkel and land tour operators are the following:

Anglers Abroad (Sea Dreams Hotel, 501-226-0602, www.anglersabroad.com) does half-day fishing trips for around US$220 and full-day for around US$350, including guide, boat and lunch.

Blackhawk Sailing (501-607-0323, www.blackhawksailingtours.com). Sailing tours on a 32-ft. sailboat for snorkeling and sightseeing at Hol Chan and around Caulker. Also offers sunset trips.

Caveman Snorkeling Tours (Front St. at Av. Hicaco, 501-505-0345, www.cavemansnorkelingtours.com). Snorkeling tours to the Caulker Marine Reserve and to Hol Chan.

Raggamuffin Tours (501-226-0348, www.raffamuffintours.com) has local sailing trips a 56-foot ketch, plus a three-day, two-night island-hopping sailing trip to Dangriga, with stopovers for camping on Rendezvous Caye and also a stay at Ragga Caye. The trip goes for US$400 per person.

Stressless Eco Friendly Tours (Calle del Sol, 501-624-6064, www.stresslessecofriendlytours.com) has popular snorkeling tours to the Caulker Marine Reserve and to Hol Chan.

Tsunami Adventures (501-226-0462, www.tsunamiadventures.com) offers snorkel and mainland tours.

Caye Caulker Lodging

This is not a complete list of island hotels, but these are among our favorites in all price ranges. They are arranged by location, either north or south of Main Street and the main "front pier" where some water taxi boats arrive, and then (roughly) by price range, from most to least expensive.

The price level for lodging on Caulker is as follows:

Inexpensive: Under US$75
Moderate: US$75-$150
Expensive: US$151-$300
Very Expensive: Over US$300

Prices are for a double room in high season (usually late November to Easter). Rates, which do not include taxes, service charges or meals (except in some cases breakfast), may be higher during holiday periods, especially Christmas and New Years. If specific prices are mentioned, they are plus 9% hotel tax and in some cases a service charge, usually 10%.

Lodging is listed alphabetically within each section.

North of the Main Front Pier:

Caye Caulker Condos. Front St. (P.O. Box 52, Caye Caulker), 501-226-0072, www.cayecaulkercondos.com. Want a suite with a full kitchen to prepare some of your own meals? Try these reasonably priced condo apartments not far from the Split. Each of the eight cozy units, on the west side of Front Street, has a private verandah facing the water, less than 100 feet away; those on the second floor have the better views. There's a small pool, too. All the units have A/C, tile floors, satellite TV and wi-fi. Bikes are free. **Moderate.**

Caye Caulker Plaza Hotel, Av. Langosta and Calle del Sol (P.O. Box 3, Caye Caulker), 501-226-0780, www.cayecaulkerplazahotel.com. This modern 30-room, concrete hotel has a central location in the middle of the village. It's about a 5-minute walk to either the sea or the lagoon. While not on the water, you do have sea and lagoon views from the fourth-level roof-top deck. Rooms are clean, with mini-fridge, cable TV and really cold air-conditioning. **Moderate.**

CayeReef Condos, Front St., Caye Caulker, 501-226-0381, www.cayereef.com. CayeReef Condos offers Caulker's version of upscale accommodations. The six condo apartments are on Front Street not far from the Split, with a small swimming pool at the front, hidden behind a wall. You can book either a two-bedroom entire unit or just one of the bedrooms. All units are fully air-conditioned, with tile floors, custom kitchens, private verandas with sea views (second and third floors), free wi-fi and cable TV. The units have Belizean art on the walls and flat-screen TVs. There are great views of the reef from the fourth floor roof top patio, where there is a rooftop whirlpool. Rates vary by the floor level – the higher the floor the higher the rate. **Expensive.**

De Real Macaw, Front St., Caye Caulker, 501-226-0459, www.derealmacaw.biz. This friendly American-owned lodging, on the west side of Front Street but still close enough to catch the breezes, has a variety of accommodations -- rooms, a beach house, cabañas and a two-bedroom condo. More-expensive units have A/C. Some units have minimum stay requirements. **Inexpensive to Moderate.**

Iguana Reef Inn, Middle St. next to soccer field (P.O. Box 31, Caye Caulker), 501-226-0213, www.iguanareefinn.com. This is the Ritz-Carlton of Caye Caulker. Sort of. The suites have air-conditioning, Belizean furniture, comfortable beds and local artwork. A swimming pool was added in 2006, and there's a nice bar with some 20 brands of rum. Considering the size and amenities of the 11 suites, the rates are reasonable, and they include continental breakfast and complimentary kayaks and bikes. There's also a penthouse suite. If there's a downside, it is that the hotel is on the backside of the island and not on the Caribbean, though the plus of that is you have a view of sunsets over the lagoon. The hotel has set up a seahorse sanctuary at the back of the property – very cool. **Expensive to Very Expensive.**

Sandy Lane Guesthouse and Cabañas, Chapoose and Langosta Sts., Caye Caulker, 501-226-0117. This longtime budget favorite has nine rooms, starting under US$25, some with private baths and some with shared baths, and four basic cabañas. Rates are a bargain. (It's worth the small extra charge to upgrade to a room with bath.) There is a grill and picnic table outside. **Inexpensive.**

Sea Dreams Hotel, Front St. near the Split, Caye Caulker, 501-226-0602, www.seadreamsbelize.com. This is a great spot for anglers or just those who want to enjoy a relaxing stay at a well-run place. The "lobby" is sand with a large tree in the middle of it. Sea Dreams, located off Front Street on the west side, near the Split, has a variety of accommodations, including five courtyard rooms, three two-bedroom apartments, a penthouse and a cabaña, a bungalow and a house. All have A/C, cable TV and wi-fi; larger units have full kitchens. Sea Dreams has a roof-top terrace with panoramic views, plus a pier/dock on the lagoon side. Rates include breakfast. Owner Haywood Curry is known as an excellent fly fisherman. Co-owner Heidi Curry helped found Caulker's first high school. **Moderate to Expensive.**

Yocamatsu, Chapoose St., Caye Caulker, 501-615-2653, www.yobelize.com. Small B&B with three rooms in the center of the island. **Moderate.**

Yuma's House, Beachfront just north of public pier, Caye Caulker, 501-206-0019, www.yumashousebelize.com. For less than US$20 you can grab a bunk bed at this hostel on the beach. Formerly it was the very laidback Tina's; now it is less laidback, with no children under 15, a zero drugs policy, no guests that aren't registered can enter the property, quiet time after 11 p.m. and other rules that are strictly enforced. A few private rooms are available. Though the hostel dorms are basic, you're right on the water, and the price and location mean this place is usually packed with young people. Reservations are a good idea – see the Yuma's for info on reservations and house rules. **Inexpensive.**

South of the Main Front Pier:
Barefoot Beach Belize. Beachfront, south of the public pier, Caye Caulker, 501-226-0205, www.barefootbeachbelize.com. Formerly the Seaview Guest House, the current owners have turned this little seafront place into one of the more popular spots on Caulker. There are a total of 17 rooms, including seven budget rooms in "The Huts." Don't confuse this place with the similarly named Barefoot Caribe. **Moderate.**

Colinda Cabañas, Beachfront, south of the public pier, Caye Caulker, 501-226-0383, www.colindacabanas.com. Colinda Cabañas (the owners are named Colin and Linda) enjoys a great reputation and many repeat guests. Located away from the main part of the village toward the south end of the island, it has three beachfront suites, two second-row suites, five bright blue and yellow cabañas and a two-bedroom house on the breezy seaside of the island with a fine view of the reef. Some units have A/C. You can lounge on hammocks or swim from the 175-foot private pier with thatch palapa. Complimentary bikes, kayaks and snorkeling gear. Wi-fi is free but the signal isn't strong in some rooms. No credit cards but accepts Paypal for deposits with the balance on arrival in cash. **Moderate to Expensive.**

Maxhapan Cabañas, 55 Av. Pueblo Nuevo, Caye Caulker, 501-226-0118. This little spot is in the center of the village and not on the water, but it's very popular because it's neat and clean, a good value and well run by the on-site owners. Set in a small, sandy and shady garden, there are rooms in a two-story cabaña and in a one-level building. They have tile floors and a veranda with hammocks. Complimentary bikes and snorkel gear. **Inexpensive to Moderate.**

OASI, Front St., Caye Caulker, 501-226-0384, www.oasi-holidaysbelize.com. Located about 5 minutes south of the main public pier, in a quieter area, OASI has four lovely rental apartments with air conditioning, wi-fi, cable TV, fully furnished kitchens and verandahs with hammocks. It is set in tropical grounds, with a fountain, barbecue grill and small bar for guests, Il Baretta, which serves real Italian espresso, wine and drinks. Complimentary bikes. Rates are a good value. Get the top floor apartment if you can. Recommended. **Moderate.**

Seaside Cabanas, Main St., beachfront (P.O. Box 39, Caye Caulker), 501-226-0498, www.seasidecabanas.com. This seafront hotel, with 17 rooms plus a seafront suite, is a high-profile spot near the village's main front pier. You're just a short walk from many of the island's restaurants, bars and shops. Painted a mustard color, with a combination of tropical thatch and concrete constructions, the Seaside buildings are in a U-shape around a pool. Una Mas is the bar. Several of the rooms have private rooftop terraces for sunning or watching the sea in privacy. Rooms have phones, free wi-fi and some have fridges. **Moderate.**

Tree Tops, Beachfront, (P.O. Box 29, Caye Caulker), 501-226-0240, www.treetopsbelize.com. Set back a little from the water, Tree Tops is run by Austrian-born Doris Creasy. All rooms have air-conditioning available, cable TV and a fridge. There are four regular rooms and two third-floor suites, Sunset and Sunrise, which have king-size beds and private balconies with views of the sea.

Rates stay the same year-round. A small courtyard is a great place to read or just lounge in a hammock. The guest rooms are clean as a pin, the entire place is meticulously maintained, and the owner is usually helpful Recommended. **Moderate.**

Pancho's Villas, Pasero St., (P.O. Box 80, Caye Caulker), 501-226-0304, www.panchosvillasbelize.com. Pancho's Villas has six rooms and three one-bedroom suites in a yellow three-story concrete building. All units have air-conditioning and ceiling fans, cable TV, wi-fi, fridge and microwave. The seafront is a short walk away. **Moderate.**

Weezie's Ocean Front Hotel and Garden Cottages, Playa Asuncion, Caye Caulker, 501-226-0603 or in the U.S., www.weeziescayecaulker.com. Near the southern tip of the island, this newish spot has rocketed to the top of social media listings. It has 12 suites, loft studio apartment and a room in the tropically concrete hotel on the sea, plus three cabañas in a garden on a residential street a couple of blocks away. There are a total of three swimming pools and a pier topped off with a thatch palapa. In this area, you'll probably want a bike to get to the main part of the village, and they're available for rent here at US$25 a week. Recommended. **Moderate to Expensive.**

Caye Caulker Vacation Rentals

For small vacation rental house on Caulker, expect to pay around US$350 to $1,000 a week, or US$75 to $200 a night. Rentals incur the 9% hotel tax.

Caye Caulker Accommodations. (P.O. Box 88, Caye Caulker), 501-226-0382, www.cayecaulkeraccommodations.com. This company manages more than two dozen houses and other rental units (some listings shared with other firms) on the island. Several have pools.

Caye Caulker Rentals. Front St., Caye Caulker, 501-226-0029; www.cayecaulkerrentals.com. This rental agency has some two dozen houses for rent.

The international companies **AirBnB** (www.airbnb.com) and **Vacation Rentals By Owner** (www.vrbo.com) also offer vacation rentals on Caye Caulker.

Dining on Caye Caulker

Caye Caulker has more than 30 restaurants, mostly small spots with a few tables and sand or wood floors, where you can get a tasty meal for a few dollars. A few are more upmarket. Some don't accept credit cards.

With the increasing popularity of Caye Caulker, there has been a boom in the restaurant business on the island over the past two or three years. More than a dozen new eateries have opened. Locals also operate "pop up" restaurants – just a grill where they prepare fresh fish or chicken for you at modest prices.

Note that some restaurants close during the slow September-October period or at the whim of the owner. Opening times and days may vary seasonally

The price level for restaurants on Caye Caulker is as follows:
Inexpensive: Under US$7
Moderate: US$8-$19

Expensive: US$20-$39
Very Expensive: Over US$40
Prices don't include tips or alcoholic drinks. If not otherwise stated, the price range is for one person for dinner.

Restaurants here are listed alphabetically.

Ana's Alladin Cuisine. Beachfront, near the Split, Caye Caulker, 501-660-1550. Alladins serves tasty, authentic Middle Eastern dishes such as kebabs, falafel, hummus and baba ghanoush at modest prices. **Inexpensive to Moderate.**

Amor y Café, Front St., Caye Caulker. Amor y Café is good place for breakfast, along with love and coffee. Open for breakfast daily. **Inexpensive to Moderate.**

Blue Beard French Restaurant, Playa Asuncion at the Split, Caye Caulker, 501-633-2234. This spot handy to the Split bills itself as a "French steakhouse." New in 2017, the owners are French, but the food in more international. The beef filet is excellent. Open for breakfast, lunch and dinner Wednesday to Sunday. **Moderate.**

Crepes & Dreams, Front St. at Av. Hicaco, Caye Caulker, 501-670-4870. Who would have thought you could get authentic savory and sweet crepes on Caye Caulker? Crepes & Dreams' Canadian owners pull it off. There are banana crepes, coconut curry crepes, spinach crepes, nutella crepes, breakfast crepes, dessert crepes and others, plus Eggs Benedict. Open for breakfast and brunch Wednesday to Monday. **Moderate.**

Caribbean Colors Art Café, Front St., Caye Caulker, 501-668-7205; www.caribbean-colors.com. Come for the art by Lee Vanderwalker. Stay for the coffee, omelet and banana pancakes. Serves breakfast and lunch. Closed Thursday. **Inexpensive to Moderate.**

Chef Juan's Kitchen & Pastries, 54 Crocodile St., Caye Caulker, 501-629-8009. New in 2016, off the beaten path in an alley near the Split, Chef Juan and wife have won a big following for low-priced, delicious seafood (lobster here is a deal), chicken and other dishes. Get the key lime pie for dessert. The seating is outdoors and limited. Open for breakfast, lunch and dinner daily except Friday. **Inexpensive to Moderate.**

Glenda's, Back St., Caye Caulker, 501-226-0148. Come to this old-school spot for a cinnamon roll, johnnycake and fresh-squeezed orange juice for breakfast, and come back at lunch for rice and beans. Open for breakfast and lunch Monday to Saturday. No credit cards. **Inexpensive.**

Hibiscus Restaurant, Middle St., Caye Caulker, 501-626-4911. Formerly Habanero's, this is still Caye Caulker's take on upscale dining. Everything tastes better with frozen mojitos. Dinner only. **Expensive.**

Il Pellicano Cucina Italian Restaurant, 49 Pasero St., Caye Caulker, 501-226-0660. Authentic Italian food prepared by Italians. Open for dinner. **Expensive.**

Pasta Per Caso Anna & Armando, Av. Hicaco, Caye Caulker, 501-602-6670. It's always seemed odd to us that visitors to a tropical island would choose Italian food for dinner, but in the case of Pasta Per Caso, we can understand it. The chef, from Milan, here does fresh pasta with light and tasty sauces, usually just a couple of dishes each evening for you to choose between. Desserts are good. Open for dinner. Closed Sunday-Tuesday. Make reservations. **Expensive.**

Roses Grill & Bar, Calle del Sol, Caye Caulker, 501-206-0407. This "open air" restaurant under a large thatch palapa is one of the best-known spots on the island, and the tables are often packed. However, some think Roses is a victim of its own popularity and that it's not as good as it once was. The specialty is seafood, and it's all fresh. Dinner daily, open for breakfast and lunch during high season. **Moderate to Expensive.**

Syd's, Middle St., Caye Caulker, south of public pier, 501-600-9481. Locals often recommend Syd's, one of the old-time places on the island. It serves Belizean and Mexican faves like beans and rice, stew chicken, garnaches, tostadas along with lobster and conch, when in season, at prices lower than you'll pay at many other eateries. Breakfast, lunch and dinner daily. **Moderate.**

Wish Willy Bar & Grill, on a side street off Front St, near the Split, across from Frenchie's. At Wish Willy you eat in the back yard of the owner, Maurice. He tells you what's on the menu today. It may be fresh fish, lamb or chicken. In most cases, the prices are low, and the rum drinks cost less here than almost anywhere else on the island. You may have to share a table with other guests, and the service is sometimes slow. **Moderate.**

The Split at Caye Caulker

WHERE TO PARTY

For Belikin and booze, the **Lazy Lizard** at the Split is probably the most popular bar on the island. Its slogan is "A sunny place for shady people." For music, dancing and a good time, check out **Barrier Reef Sports Bar & Grill**, beachfront near the water taxi piers. This busy bar has good food, too. **I&I Reggae Bar,** on Traveler's Palm Street, a funky joint with rope swings and hammocks instead of chairs, blows reggae nightly. In back is a tree house.

Photo by Simon Dannhauer/Shutterstock

MOVING TO BELIZE

Options for Living in Belize

There are three basic options for those wishing to live or retire in Belize or to spend extended periods of time in the country. Each has advantages and disadvantages.

TOURIST PERMIT

This is the easiest, cheapest way to live in the country for a while, and it requires no long-term commitment. The procedure is simple: You get a 30-day entry free (via a passport stamp) when you arrive in the country by air, land or sea. After 30 days, you can go to an immigration office (or police station in remote areas) and renew the tourist card monthly for US$25 a month for up to six months, and then US$50 a month after that. After six months, generally you also must register as an alien. Citizens of the U.S., European Community, the U.K., Canada, Australia, New Zealand, Mexico, Costa Rica, Guatemala, Colombia, CARICOM member states and many other countries get a tourist card without having to apply in advance for a tourist visa. Nationals of some 75 other countries must apply in advance for a tourist visa, and there is a fee. See the Belize Tourism Board web site, www.travelbelize.org for details.

As a tourist permit holder, you can enjoy Belize without a long-term commitment. You can buy or rent property, but you cannot work for pay. In theory, when you renew your tourist permit, you are supposed to be able to prove that you have sufficient resources, set at US$60 a day (a credit card usually suffices), to stay in Belize, but this requirement is not usually enforced.

Of course, there is no guarantee that you will be able to renew your tourist status indefinitely, as rules and conditions can change, as you have no official residency status. If you fail to renew your permit in a timely way, or if you overstay your allotted time, technically you are in violation of Belize law and can be deported or even jailed. As a practical matter, if you can offer a good reason why you failed to follow the law, and are very friendly to Immigration officers, you'll probably be let off with a short lecture from the official, and perhaps a fine. However, some people who overstay their tourist cards *are* sent packing.

QUALIFIED RETIRED PERSON STATUS

The Qualified Retired Persons Incentive Act passed by the Belize legislature in 1999 is managed by the Belize Tourism Board. The program is designed to attract more retirees to Belize. The program has attracted considerable interest and a number of applications. However, the Belize Tourism Board hasn't publicly stated how many applications it has received in total and how many have been approved. Interest in the program appears to be fairly high, but because of the income requirement, inability to work for pay in Belize, lack of official true residency status and other factors, the actual number of retirees under the program in Belize is as yet relatively small and far fewer than are in programs in Costa Rica, Panama, Mexico and elsewhere. For several years, the BTB has said it was reviewing the program to see how it can be improved, but so far no significant changes have been made.

For those who can show the required monthly income from investments or pensions, this program offers benefits of living in Belize and tax-free entry of the retiree's household goods and a car, boat and even an airplane. This program also eliminates some of the bureaucratic delays built into the permanent residency program. The BTB guarantees action on an application in no more than three months, but we have heard of qualified retirees getting approval for this program in only a few weeks.

Who qualifies? Anyone at least 45 years old from anywhere in the world can qualify for the program. A person who qualifies can also include his or her dependents in the program. Dependents include spouses and children under the age of 18. However, it also can include children under the age of 23 if enrolled in a university.

Main benefits: Besides prompt approval of residency for qualifying applicants, import duties and fees for household goods and a late-model vehicle, airplane and boat are waived.

Duty-free import of personal household effects: Qualified Retired Persons under the program can qualify for duty and tax exemptions on new and used personal and household effects admitted as such by the Belize Tourism Board. A list of all items with corresponding values that will be imported must be submitted with the application. A one-year period is granted for the importation of personal and household effects.

Duty-free import of a vehicle, aircraft and/or boat:

Motor Vehicle: Applicants are encouraged to import new motor vehicles under the program, but the vehicle must be no more than three years old. (Occasional exceptions may be made in the case of an older vehicle with low mileage, but this would be decided on a case-by-case basis.) A Qualified Retired Person may also buy a vehicle duty-free in country.

Light Aircraft: A Qualified Retired Person is entitled to import a light aircraft less than 17,000 kg. A Qualified Retired Person is required to have a valid Private Pilot license to fly in Belize. This license can be obtained by passing the requirements set by the Civil Aviation. However, if the participant has a valid pilot's license, that license only has to be validated by Civil Aviation Department in Belize.

Boat: Any vessel that is used for personal purposes and for pleasure will be accepted under this program. If for whatever reason a Qualified Retired Person decides to sell, give away, lease, or otherwise dispose of the approved means of transportation or personal effects to any person or entity within Belize, all duties and taxes must be paid to the proper authorities.

The Belize Tourism Board states: "Qualified Retired Persons must note that only after three years and upon proof that the transportation that was previously imported to Belize was adequately disposed off, will another concession be granted to import another mode of transportation."

Income Requirement: To be designated a Qualified Retired Person under the program, the applicant must have a monthly income of at least US$2,000. A couple does *not* need to show US$4,000 a month – just US$2,000, as the applicant is normally an individual and the applicant's spouse is a dependent under the program. The income rules for Qualified Retired Persons are, like many things in Belize, a little confusing. On first reading, it looks like the income must derive from a pension or annuity that has been generated outside of Belize. The rules do not specifically say so, but according to Belize Tourism Board officials U.S. Social Security income can be included as part of this pension requirement. Pension and annuity information then has to be substantiated by a Certified Public Accountant, along with two bank references from the company providing the pension or annuity. These substantiations may not be required if your pension and/or annuity is from a Fortune 500 company. Several retirees have said that they were able to include other forms of income, including investment income, in the US$2,000 figure, if supported by a CPA's statement that the income would continue indefinitely. In this latter case, the US$2,000 a month income (US$24,000 a year) can be substantiated by showing records from a bank or other financial institution in Belize that the retiree has deposited the necessary money.

Other Documents and Procedures:

Background check: All applications are subject to a background check by the Ministry of National Security.

Application: Applications for the program must be made to the Belize Tourism Board in Belize City and include the following:

Birth certificate: A certified copy of a certificate for the applicant and each dependent.

Marriage certificate, if applicable.

Passport: Color copies of complete passport (including all blank pages) of applicant and all dependents that have been certified by a Notary Public. The copies must have the passport number, name of principal, number of pages and the seal or stamp of the Notary Public.

Proof of income: The current QRP information states that there are two ways to prove that your income is sufficient:

1) An official statement from a bank or financial institution certifying that the applicant is the recipient of a pension or annuity of a minimum of US$2,000 per month.

2) A financial statement from a financial institution, bank, credit union, or building society in Belize certifying that the applicant's investment will generate the sum of a minimum of US$2,000 per month or the equivalent of US$24,000 per year.

Medical examination: Applicant and all dependents should undergo a complete medical examination including an AIDS test. A copy of the medical certificate(s) must be attached to the application.

Photos: Four front and four-side passport size photographs that have been taken recently of applicant and dependents.

The application form for the Qualified Retired Persons program is available for download from the Belize Tourism Board at www.belizetourismboard.org (visit www.belizetourismboard.org/programs-events/retirement-program/#1490202032346-1e76d79c-10c0. There is a non-refundable application fee of US$150. Upon acceptance, there is an Applicant Program fee of US$1,000 US$200 for a QRP membership card, plus US$750 for each dependent (including spouse). Thus, the application fee and member cost for the QRP program total US$1,350 for an individual or US$2,100 for a couple. There is an additional fee of US$750 for each qualifying dependent child.

Renewals of QRP must be made annually. There is a US$25 fee for renewal. Each year, you must demonstrate that you have deposited US$24,000 in a Belize bank and converted the money into Belize dollars and also that you have lived in Belize for at least 30 consecutive days in the past year.

For information on the program, contact: Belize Tourism Board, P.O. Box 325, 64 Regent St., Belize City, Belize, Central America, 501-227-2420 or 800-624-0686, fax 501-227-2423, www.belizetourismboard.org/programs-events/retirement-program/. If you have questions or problems, try contacting the Program Officer for QRP at the BTB.

In 2010, the Belize government introduced a new program, the **Diaspora Retirement Incentive Program,** directed to Belizeans who wish to return to Belize. Is is open to Belize citizens who have lived outside Belize for a minimum of 10 consecutive years. The benefits include the importation of personal/household effects, a personal vehicle and the tools of one's trade free of all import duties.

Typical Belizean home in rural area

OFFICIAL PERMANENT RESIDENT

Application requirements and most benefits are similar to those of the Retired Persons Incentive Act, but there are some important differences. The application process itself and the supporting documents needed are similar to those for the QRP, although the applications are processed by different governmental departments.

Here are the main differences: As an official Permanent Resident, you have two major advantages over a participant in the QRP program. First, you do not have to deposit annually any particular sum in a bank in Belize. However, you do have to show financial resources sufficient to obtain residency status. Second, as a Permanent Resident, you can work for pay in Belize. You also enjoy some advantages as a resident rather than a "long-term visitor" as you are considered in QRP status. As a permanent resident, you can vote in some local (not national) Belize elections.

You must live in Belize for one full year before you can apply for regular Permanent Residency. During this period, you cannot leave the country for more than 14 days. Even a short, two-hour visit to Chetumal counts as one day's absence. Note, however, that the Immigration and Nationality Department sometimes interprets this requirement only as meaning that you cannot leave the country for 14 or more CONSECUTIVE days. Yes, this is a little confusing; this is Belize.

Documents Needed for Permanent Residency Application

Here are the documents you must have to apply for Permanent Residency (photocopies of original documents must be submitted along with the original documents). The exact forms required may vary depending on the official with whom you deal and are subject to change:

Application form.

Copies of all pages of passport.

Evidence, such as passport pages with immigration stamps, that you have been in the country for one year.

Police record from Belize within past six months and from last country of residence, for yourself and all members of your family over the age of 16 who also wish to apply for Permanent Residence.

Statement of financial stability – this can be in the form of a recent bank statement.

If applicable, proof of employment or self-employment (letter from employer or Certificate of Business Registration if self-employed).

Evidence you have acquired property in Belize if you are claiming that you have – but owning property in Belize is NOT required to obtain permanent residency.

Certificate of health including HIV, venereal disease and tuberculosis tests for you and all members of your family – these tests must be conducted in Belize.

Two passport-size photos of yourself and all members of your family,

Original or certified copy of birth certificates of all applicants.

Marriage certificate (if applicable).

Income tax form.

After approval, you have up to one year to bring in household effects duty-free, on a one-time basis. However, the duty-free exemption does not apply to a vehicle, boat and airplane, as it does for the Qualified Retired Persons program.

It is somewhat expensive to apply for regular permanent residency.

Application fees for Permanent Residency vary by nationality, ranging from

US$250 to $5,000. For U.S. nationals, the fee currently (fees may change) is US$1,000 per person; for citizens of most British Commonwealth countries, the fee is US$750; for citizens of CARICOM countries, the fee is US$250; for citizens of other Central American countries, Mexico and the Dominican Republic, the fee is US$375; for citizens of EU countries, the fee is US$1,500. There is also, upon approval, a fee of US$150. In addition, if you use an "expediter" in Belize to help you with the paperwork, which is NOT required, you'll likely pay a fee of around US$1,500, plus several hundred dollars in travel and photocopying fees and taxes. Note that these fees are per-person, not per-application, as is the case for the Qualified Retired Persons program. For example, an American married couple applying for Permanent Residency would pay US$2,000 with the application and US$300 for residency stamps after approval. Residency cards are no longer provided -- instead, your passport is stamped.

You apply to Belize Immigration and Nationality Services rather than through the Belize Tourism Board. For information and application form, contact: Department of Immigration and Nationality Services, Attn: Permanent Residence Services, Mountain View Blvd., Belmopan City, Belize, Central America, 501-828-5247, www.ins.gov.bz, email pr.belize@ins.gov.bz. Besides the Immigration Department main office in Belmopan, there are regional offices in Corozal Town, Orange Walk Town, Belize City, San Pedro, Benque Viejo (border), Dangriga, Big Creek and Punta Gorda.

The Permanent Residency application form is available in PDF from www.ins.gov.bz/images/Oldforms/APPLICATIONFORPERMANENTRESIDENCE_1.PDF.

It is wise to go in person to Immigration in Belmopan to apply for Permanent Residency. Applicants usually find that several trips are necessary, to check on the progress of the application and to keep it moving. Again, being friendly and showing respect to Belizean officials is vital. Getting angry with any delays will probably be counter-productive.

Time for approval of a Permanent Residency application varies. Some find that the process goes fairly quickly, taking only a few months. Others say it took up to a year, or longer, for approval.

Pros and Cons
Each option has pluses and minuses. The main advantages and disadvantages are as follows:

Tourist Permit
Pros: No commitment, no financial requirement, flexibility, little red tape.

Cons: No tax advantages, no official status, inconvenience of having to go in person to extend, possibility rules may change, can't work for pay in Belize.

Qualified Retired Persons Incentive Program
Pros: Quick approval, application through Belize Tourism Board rather than Immigration Department, some residency-style rights (except voting), tax-free entry of household effects, car, boat and airplane, only have to live in country for one month a year.

Cons: Must deposit US$24,000 a year in a Belize bank, somewhat costly application process, can't work for pay in Belize, must be 45 or over.

Official Permanent Residency

Pros: Full residency rights (except voting in national elections), can work for pay, open to anyone regardless of age, tax-free entry of household effects.

Cons: Year-long residency in Belize before applying, more red tape, costly application process, and some people are turned down for minor details; you can bring in household goods but NOT a car, boat or airplane free of duty.

For more information, get in touch with the Belize Tourism Board (www.belizetourismboard.org/programs-events/retirement-program/), Beltraide (www.belizeinvest.org.bz) or the Belize Immigration Department (www.ins.gov.bz).

Other Programs

The controversial **Economic Citizenship** program, under which foreigners were able to buy a Belize passport and residency rights for a fee of US$25,000 to $50,000, was discontinued in 2002. Some dated information on the internet still suggests this program is in effect. If you need a second passport, you might looks at investment/passport programs in St. Kitts and some other Caribbean countries.

Belize Citizenship

In addition to the programs discussed above, regular **citizenship** in Belize is a possibility for those living in Belize over a long period. To acquire citizenship, applicants must have residency status for a minimum of five years. Applicants for citizenship need to provide essentially the same supporting documentation as those applying for Permanent Residency. Applicants also must demonstrate knowledge of Belizean history. Note that for citizenship residency purposes, stays in the Belize under the Qualified Retired Persons program currently do NOT qualify, although there have been discussions about changing this. To become a citizen, you would have to give up QRP status (perhaps having to pay back the duties you escaped under QRP), apply for Permanent Residency and begin the five-year residency from scratch.

Caution: Rules and regulations and the interpretation of them change frequently in Belize. Do NOT assume that this information is the last word on any matter pertaining to entering or staying in Belize.

This is worth repeating: CAUTION: RULES IN BELIZE CHANGE FREQUENTLY. What is true today may not be true tomorrow. Do not assume that everything you are told will apply for you.

On the road in Belize

Getting Your Stuff to Belize

If you decide to move to Belize, you have several options, including driving down with your household goods and other possessions or shipping them by sea or land. This chapter covers the mechanics of moving, including bringing pets.

Driving to Belize

Caution: Due to the drug cartel violence in Mexico, especially in border areas, many people who in previous years would have considered driving to Belize now are reluctant to do so. Those who do drive may try to convoy with other drivers or hire a Belizean who has made the trip frequently and knows the safest and best routes.

The drive from Brownsville, Texas, the nearest entry point in the U.S. to Belize, is about 1,250 to 1,500 miles, depending on the route you take. It usually takes three to four days to drive, although it can be done faster. Total non-stop driving time is around 28 to 35 hours, depending on conditions, your driving speed and other factors.

The fastest route from Brownsville/Matamoros is via Tampico, Tuxpan, Veracruz, Villahermosa and Chetumal. From the border, take Mexico national route 101 to highway 180. Just north of Veracruz, take 150D (a toll road) to Villahermosa. (Alternatively you can stay on highway 180). At Villahermosa, take route 186 for 360 miles to the Belize border (the last 5 miles may be signed as route 307). The toll roads are expensive, around US$10 for each 100 miles, but you can make 70 mph on them, much faster than on the regular roads.

Driving in Mexico can be confusing, as road through towns and elsewhere are often poorly signed. In general, avoid going through the town centers *(Centro),* as you can easily get lost and the hotels are more expensive. To enter Mexico (and later, Belize) by car, you need the original plus two copies of your passport, valid driver's license, vehicle registration card, original vehicle title, or if your vehicle is not paid for, a notarized letter of permission from the lien holder. Besides paying the Mexico tourist entry fee of 533 pesos (about US$ at current exchange rates, which vary daily), which allows entry for up to six months, you have to provide a credit card in lieu of posting a cash bond to guarantee that you will bring the car back out of Mexico. Your credit card (Master Card, Visa, American Express, Diners, which must be in the name of the driver) will be charged US$22.

Upon arrival at the Belize-Mexico border, if you are not returning to the U.S., you must have the Mexican temporary entry permit canceled at Mexican customs. If entering Mexico by car as a tourist, as a resident of the U.S. or Canada you can bring in such personal items as luggage, binoculars, laptop computer, TV, camping equipment, up to three liters of alcohol and fishing equipment. Do NOT even think about bringing in a gun, as you will find yourself in serious trouble. If you are transporting goods of a value of US$1,000 or more and/or are going through Mexico to Belize to stay permanently, you are supposed to use the services of a customs broker at the U.S.-Mexico border and get trans-migratory status, which costs money in fees and, some say, in bribes to Mexican federal officers along the way. A broker at the U.S.-Mexico border will cost you about US$150 to $200. Unless you plan to stay in Belize, it is best just to enter Mexico as a tourist and not go the trans-mig route.

Except on toll roads, driving after dark in Mexico is not advised. You may be stopped frequently for inspections. You should exchange enough U.S. dollars to get you through Mexico, as U.S. dollars are not widely accepted, or are accepted at a low rate of exchange. The exchange rate for U.S. dollars in late 2015 was around 16.5 pesos to the dollar. Gasoline stations in Mexico sometimes do not accept credit cards.

Mexican auto insurance is required; liability costs from around US$75 for five days. It is now recommended that you get at least US$300,000 in third-party liability coverage. Collision insurance coverage can add to the cost, depending on the value of your vehicle. Insurance for a month or two, or even six months, is not much more than for a few days.

Here are typical quotes for 7 days and six months:

Extended coverage including US$300,000 third-party liability for nearly new vehicle valued at US$20,000: US$120 to $135

Six months: US$400 to $415

You MUST have Mexican auto insurance. Your U.S. or Canadian insurance is NOT valid in Mexico (or Belize.)

Sanborn's (800-222-0158; www.sanbornsinsurance.com) is a well-known source of information on travel in Mexico and for Mexican auto insurance, although their insurance tends to be more expensive than insurance from most other companies. Other companies include International Insurance Group (www.sb.iigins.com), which offers insurance through Grupo Nacional and ACE

Seguros.

Do a Google search for other companies selling Mexican auto insurance, some of which can be purchased on-line in advance. One such is Mexican Auto Insurance (www.mexicanautoinsurance.com). Some U.S.-based insurance companies including GEICO and Progressive offer links to a Mexican insurance provider, with small discounts available for their U.S. or Canadian policyholders.

Sanborn maps, and in fact most maps to Mexico, may not be completely accurate. The *Guia Roji* (Red Guide) maps to Mexico are probably the best available, although ITMB maps also are good. A website with all types of helpful information on Mexico is www.mexconnect.com.

On arrival at the Mexico-Belize border, you again need your original title (no photocopies) for your vehicle, or, if you do not own it free and clear, a notarized statement from the lien holder that you have permission to take the car out of the U.S. You also have to buy Belize auto insurance, which is required by law in Belize. There are brokers at the border. Three months of insurance should cost about US$60 to $100, or one month or less about US$35. The cost may be higher depending on the coverage you get. Crossing the border you probably will have to have your car sprayed to kill hitchhiking bugs — the fee is around US$5.

Assuming that you are entering as a tourist, you should get free entry of your vehicles for 90 days, with no duty required. (However, we have heard of a number of exceptions to this statement.) Your car information is entered on your passport so you cannot sell it in Belize. You must leave the country with the vehicle.

If you plan to stay in Belize and keep your vehicle there, you have to pay import duty and tax. The rate varies by number of cylinders and type of vehicle, but it runs about 20% to nearly 80% of book value. *(For more information, see below.)* Some say that if you want a lower appraisal of value of the vehicle, have it appraised in Belize City. You can have a customs officer drive with you to Belize City for around US$20. However, others claim that appraisals are lower at the border.

If you bring your vehicle in as a tourist and do not pay import duty, and then later decide you want to keep the vehicle in Belize, you may be hit with a fine of US$250 or more in addition to import duty. So, if you are pretty sure you want to keep the vehicle in Belize, it's usually best to go ahead and pay the import duty when you first enter Belize.

For another perspective, to give you an idea of what you may face, here's a detailed post on driving from Mission, Texas, (near McAllen) to Belize from the Expat Exchange forum (www.expatexchange.com). The spelling and punctuation mostly have been left as is:

Here's the route: Driving Direction from Mission, Texas, to the Belize border. Now for those of you who have not done this, it is not that bad!! I have done this trip six times down and back. I have never paid or been asked to pay a police officer. There are Federal Police checkpoints and there are military checkpoints. Both are polite and most of the time no one speaks English. Use that to your advantage. Even if you do [speak Spanish] don't act like you do. If they can't talk to you they just look at your paperwork and send you on your way. This year I drove down and back and was never searched in Mexico or for that matter even at the US border station.

Now what I have done here is detailed the route to the mile. We zeroed the trip odometer at the Mexico border station. My passenger wrote down details at every turn. Now that won't mean our reading will be exact but they should be close. Oh do yourself a favor and cash at least US$1500 into pesos!!!!!!

Exit the Mexico border station. Zero your odometer and relax. You have 1519 miles and two nights in Mexico. I will give you two options to make this trip. One puts you south of Mexico City in Puebla the first night, and 80 miles from Belize the second night. This is the way I run the route. I will drive both nights one hour in the dark. I will give you options for the first night in Querétaro, and the second night in Villahermosa. This route brings you to the Belize border around 2 pm and you spend the night in Corozal.

Exit the border merge to the left, 90 Reynosa Drive 3.9 miles turn right on Hwy 40 to Monterey.

18.8 miles to a checkpoint you must go thru it.

27.2 miles merge right onto the Hwy 40 cuota (toll road) to Monterey.

56.4 miles enter a tollbooth (210 pesos).

108 miles come to a small town, pay attention to where you are going. Mostly stay straight and on the main drag. Follow sign to Monterey.

114 miles enter another toll. (44pesos)

116.2 merge right to Saltillo still Hwy 40

127.8 miles another toll both

134.8 stay straight towards Saltillo Cuota

148.7 Another toll for the by pass around Monterey.

158.2 miles Merge right onto cuota again?? Pay another toll (66 pesos)

181.1 yes another toll BUT you don't go thru this one. Exit to Saltillo just before it. When in doubt follow signs to Saltillo (Cuota).

Just before you get over by Saltillo we screwed up and missed a turn. Day dreaming this area was mountains and very pretty. If you see a huge orange building you missed it also. Look for the signs 57 south to San Luis Potosi and Matehuala. Hope I spell these correct.

We needed gas and there was a nice spot at mile 207.

226 toll booth (50 pesos) Plenty of gas stations after this one.

346 exit left on the San Luis Potosi cuota. This is the bypass around Matehuala.

There is plenty of gas station along this area.

350 miles tollbooth for the by pass cuota around Matehuala

452 miles merge left towards Mexico City, Querétaro.

466 miles a tollbooth.

473 The cuota splits stay left towards Querétaro. Now here is where you must decide! Do I push thru to Puebla or stay in Querétaro. There is n where that I have found to stay in between. And you will not get to Puebla until 8:30 pm It should be around 5:00 pm now. Your choice!! If you choose to go on to Puebla follow these. If you stay in Querétaro follow 57 thru town it is not bad. You will find a Best Western on your right just south of town.

568 miles exit right real quickly it splits go right. Splits again go left. This is tricky and it happens fast but there are signs. Follow sign for the cuota to San Juan Del Rio, and Mexico City. This is the bypass around Querétaro. If you miss this don't worry I went thru last year it was easy. In fact that is how I found the Best Western you can stay at.

580 miles is another tollbooth (40 pesos)

592 miles stay left the bypass reconnects to Hwy 57 south to San Juan Del Rio and Mexico City.

620 miles another toll (70 pesos)

656 miles - you are south of San Juan Del Rio, This gets a little confusing and happens fast. Look for signs, Pachuca and Puebla. This is a bypass around Mexico City. DO NOT MISS THIS!!! Split to the right! Take the second split to the right. It is label 75D Pachuca, Puebla. You then pull up to a tollbooth but at this one you just take a ticket, and pay at the other end. Also you have now fuel here until mile 740. If you need fuel do it before this exit.

760 miles you come to the tollbooth it will be dark now. Give them your ticket it was 565 pesos for us. But we were towing a trailer. We can only guess the toll for you would be half that. Now they are working on the road for the next few miles until you tie back into the main road from Mexico City to Puebla.

763 mile the road splits stay left and this road is bumpy slow down.

766 miles toll booth for a crappy road. 777 miles you will see a McDonald's.

778 miles you will see a "one" Hotel a big tower on your left.

780 miles you will see the Fiesta Inn and a Holiday in right next to each other. Stay at one of these. Next morning get up early leave at six if you can. You have a mountainous decent this morning. And then some bumpy roads.

794 miles tollbooth (55 pesos).

840 miles tollbooth and there is a volcano on your left. It had snow on the peak in January, early Feb. Hang on and take your time for awhile. You will be going down hill for the next few hours. It is steep and you go thru tunnels. Don't ride your brakes!!!

877 miles another toll (24 pesos) 895 toll booth (85 pesos) 966 toll booth (177 pesos)

1031 toll booth (155 pesos) 1069 tollbooth (17 pesos)

1076 exit right to Villahermosa Stop at the stop sign. Turn right?

1081 miles the road splits stay left to Villahermosa

1095 Inspection station, we got waved thru.

1111 miles another toll, wow imagine that.

1166 miles you have now been in some traffic for a little while. You passed the Walmart distribution center. You cross this bridge with a sign that says welcome to Villahermosa!!! Pay attention the road splits just over this bridge. Take the left split!

The best direction thru Villahermosa is to follow the main flow of traffic. Towards the airport. I always make it.

1168 under a bridge

1170 Lake on the right

1171 over a cool bridge

I think this is where it turns into Hwy 186 to Escarsega

Sign that says 11 Km to the Airport just over the bridge

Now we left Puebla at 7:00am and we are passing the Hilton south of the Villahermosa Airport at 2:30pm. We're 1177 miles into Mexico.

If you stayed in Querétaro you will be later and should stay here for you second night. Go past the Hilton, it is on your left. Two miles in front of you is a RETURNO! Circle back and spend the night.

1181 miles another tollbooth (20 pesos)

1200 miles switches from divided highway to two-lane road for the rest of your trip. The road in actually real good except for a small area here and there. But they are working on them.

1260 miles tollbooth (20 pesos)

1354 miles you are entering Escarsega take the split to the left. Burger King will be on your right. Just after that a couple hundred yards turn right towards Chetumal. You go right thru the middle of town. Looks rough but it is not. Nice Mayan statue in town.

Now somewhere after this is will get dark and sometimes there is a checkpoint at the far edge of Escarsega. The next part is very easy just follow the road to mile 1448. You have past the Becon Mayan ruins by a couple miles. You will have past the ECO Village on your left. You can stay there also. You will come to a Hotel just before the town of Xjupil. Can't miss it. DEBLIZ HOTEL on your right. Nice little place and they are always there.

Spend the night. You might even want to check Becon out. They are cool ruins. You are about 80 miles from Belize. Sleep in if you want.

Next morning head to Chetumal and at mile 1511 exit right to Chetumal.

1515 miles is the last Mexico gas station. Fill up if you have not.

1518 miles exit right up and over a bridge. Once you reach the border pull over to the right you will see a small both for immigration. They will take your tourist card. Then if you have a vehicle permit listen carefully. If you are not driving that vehicle back look to the left find the Banjercio and cancel your vehicle permit. If you are returning with the same vehicle you can wait until you get back to the US/MX boarder to cancel it. Once you have done that travel over the bridge into Belize.

Your Vehicle in Belize

Because Belize is lightly populated and fairly spread out, it's very useful to have a car or truck in Belize. A four-wheel drive is ideal, due to the many unpaved secondary and tertiary roads, which can get very bad during the rainy season. Many people consider a small four-wheel drive truck, such as Toyota Hi-Lux, as the perfect vehicle for Belize. Import duties are 10% on trucks or vans (not SUVs, which are taxed at the higher auto rates), plus GST of 12.5%. It is relatively inexpensive to buy new -- US$24,000 to $30,000+ including duty. It gets good mileage, which is important when fuel is above US$5 a gallon. The Toyota is a rugged vehicle that holds up well to tough conditions in Belize. Even better is to get a diesel-engine version, as diesel fuel costs about one-third less in Belize than gasoline, and diesel engines usually last almost forever. Other small cars and trucks are popular in Belize, including Suzuki, Mitsubishi and the smaller American models such as compact SUVs. With Belize's British heritage, the Land Rover also is popular, especially older models such as Defender, although these are expensive. However, many Belizeans drive old, large U.S. cars that were brought into Belize before the price of gas went up to its present high levels.

Most of the new car dealers in Belize are located in Belize City, with a couple in Belmopan and Spanish Lookout. Among the brands available new are Ford, Toyota, Suzuki, Kia, Land Rover, Jeep, Hyundai, Dodge, Nissan and Mitsubishi. Some Chinese brands are available in Belmopan or Spanish Lookout. Other car brands are in Chetumal, Mexico.

If you live on an island, you probably will not need a car. Smaller islands do not have any roads or vehicles. Caye Caulker has only a few emergency vehicles.

Ambergris Caye has too many vehicles for its small size and limited road system and is currently limiting the import of more vehicles to the island. On Ambergris, Caulker and other islands a golf cart is a useful way to get around. You can expect to pay around US$2,000-$4,000 for a used golf cart in Belize. Maintenance tends to be costly due to the salt air. Replacing the six batteries alone costs US$300 or more. A gas cart, rather than an electric cart, is the way to go.

Liability insurance is mandatory in Belize. If you don't have it and are stopped at a road check, common in Belize, you are likely going to be arrested and will spend at least a little time in jail. Happily, auto insurance in Belize is fairly inexpensive. You likely won't pay more than US$200 to $300 a year. Your U.S. or other driver's license is good for up to three months in Belize. After that, you are supposed to get a Belize license. You must be 18 to get a driver's license in Belize. You can obtain a driver's license in Belize City or in larger towns for a fee of US$10. You will have to provide a doctor's statement that you are in good health.

Getting Your Household Goods to Belize

What to Bring: Foreign residents in Belize are split on how much to bring to Belize. Some see a savings in bringing everything you may need to Belize, especially if you have a duty exemption on household goods as an approved permanent resident or as a participant in the Qualified Retired Persons program. On the other hand, many who have moved to Belize say it's best to bring as little as possible with you. After all, you won't need a lot of clothes. You can buy furniture cheaply in Belize, and you can find appliances and other household goods either in Belize City or in Chetumal, Mexico. Amazon.com and other companies will ship books, CDs, and other items, but international shipping charges are high. Many living in Belize use a shipping and courier service, such as Belizean Easy Shopper/Sidasheari, you have your Amazon or other products shipped to a warehouse in Miami or elsewhere, and then it is shipped on to Belize, after the shipments are consolidated. Air freight rates from the U.S. are in the range of US$2.50 a pound; ocean shipping rates are by the cubic feet – for example, a 10 cubic foot package is US$70. You may want to store most of your household goods in a storage facility back home. Then, after you've been in Belize for a while, on a trip back home you can get items you decide you really need.

Items you probably will want to bring to Belize if you are setting up housekeeping, as these are hard to find or expensive in Belize, or will be expensive to ship later:

- good-quality sheets and towels
- high-quality mattresses
- good dishes
- high-quality pots and pans, silverware and other kitchenware
- hobby equipment
- specialized hand and power tools
- fishing and diving gear
- top-end electronics
- computers, laptops, tablets

• smartphones
• books

Shipping Options

You can ship bulky items by sea or overland. Small items can be shipped via the postal system or an airfreight service. You can drive your vehicle down through Mexico or ship it by sea.

Ocean Freight

Sending goods such as furniture, household supplies and personal possessions in a 20-foot container from Miami is likely to cost you about US$2,400-$3,000, not including import duties, insurance, customs broker fees or storage fees. A 40-foot container may cost you US$4,000-$5,500, or more, by the time you get it to your home in Belize, again not including extra fees and duties.

Cars and trucks can also be shipped via ocean freight. Companies like Transporter Auto Services (800-799-3329, www.moveglobalnow.com) specialize in shipping vehicles, either in high cube containers or Roll-On/Roll-Off, but other companies also will accept vehicles. Normally you can pack your vehicle with personal goods.

Hyde Shipping is the most used and recommended shipping company serving Belize. It offers freight sailings from Port Everglades near Ft. Lauderdale and Miami to Belize City, at least once a week and sometimes twice a week. Hyde also provides service to Roatán, Honduras, Puerto Morelos, Mexico, and Grand Cayman. Both 20-ft. and 40-ft. containers are available, either dry or climate controlled. Contact Hyde in Florida at 10025 NW 116th Way, Suite 2, Medley, FL 33178, 305-913-4933; www.hydeshipping.com. Hyde's agency in Belize is **Caribbean Shipping Agency** (501-227-7396).

Other Options for Smaller Shipments

A few companies offer door-to-door shipment of LCL (Less Than Container Load) items between the U.S. and Belize. One is **Belize Freight** (832-764-7239 in the U.S., 501-223-2746 in Belize, www.belizefreight.com). Belize Freight ships monthly by sea from its warehouse in Houston. It picks up by truck from about a dozen different cities in the U.S., from the New York/New Jersey area to Texas, on a rotating pick-up schedule, and delivers to most cities, towns and villages in Belize. The company provides an "all-inclusive" quote based on the size and weight of the item or items shipped, including pick-up and delivery door-to-door, custom brokerage fees, customs duty and taxes and other charges. It's not cheap, but it's convenient. If you don't need door-to-door service, you can ship your items to Belize Freight's Houston warehouse (3340B Greens Rd., Suite #450, Houston, TX 77032) and pick up the item in Belize City. Storage also is available.

Mail and Express Freight

Small items can be shipped to Belize by air or surface postal mail, which is fairly dependable and not too expensive, or by a fast but expensive airfreight service such as **FedEx, UPS** or **DHL Express**. A 10-pound package might cost from around US$100 to $300, depending on the airfreight company and the type of service.

Sidasheari International, also known as **Belize Easy Shopper** (954-374-

8475) ships weekly from Miami via air freight and ocean. Rates start at US$10 for packages under 4 pounds for air freight and ocean freight packages of under 2 cubic feet for US$30. Package consolidation is automatic for three or more items and costs US$2.50 per item.

Companies such as **MyUS** (www.myus.com) provide a turnkey purchasing, package consolidation and shipping service. You pay a membership fee, get a U.S. address and then do your shopping at Amazon.com, eBay, Walmart or other U.S. companies. You have the store send your items to your MyUS mailing address. Then MyUS consolidates your packages into one shipment. MyUS then ships to Belize via FedEx, DHL Express or UPS. Shipping from the U.S. to Belize for a consolidated package weighing 20 pounds ranges from about US$100 to more than US$265, with delivery in from one to 14 days.

Preparing Items for Shipment
When shipping individual packages to Belize, new items require an invoice and used items require a packing list. A packing list is simply a list of the items enclosed in the package with their reasonable resale values. You need to insert one copy of the invoice or packing list into an envelope and tape it to the outside of the package, and mail or fax one copy of it to the freight company in advance of your shipment.

For shipping vehicles, you'll need the original title (or if there is a lien on the vehicle a notarized letter from the lienholder authorizing shipment), the VIN, license plate number, notarized power of attorney to ship the vehicle, addresses and phone numbers in the U.S. and Belize and full payment of all fees in advance.

Customs Brokers
Customs brokers in Belize can be very helpful in smoothing the way and in getting materials quickly released from customs. They will meet your goods when they arrive in Belize, fill out the paper work and have the goods forwarded to their final destination in Belize.

If your shipment is valued at more than US$1,500, to ship to Belize it is required that you work with a licensed customs broker in Belize. Plus, it will make your life a lot easier if you have a local customs broker working for you.

There are about 65 members of the **Customs Brokers Association of Belize** (www.customsbrokers.bz). Be sure to check references. Here are some brokers who have received recommendations from folks shipping to Belize:

Billy Valdes, Valdez Global, 160 N. Front St. (P.O. Box 4), Belize City, 501-227-7436 or 501-610-1180, email lizzvaldes@yahoo.com

Joseph Hamilton, Belize City, 501-227-1453

Milin Gomez, Belize City, 501-610-4569, email mily@btl.net

Calbert Reynolds, Belize City, 501-227-0381

Storage in Belize
What do you do with your goods after you get them to Belize, if your home isn't ready for occupancy? Freight companies usually will store your shipped items in their warehouse, for a fee of around US$12.5 cents per cubic foot per week.

This can add up; storage of a half-container would cost nearly US$700 a month

Storage facilities in Belize, other than those owned by the government or freight companies, are few and far between. One is **Cayo Self Storage** (501-651-0865, www.cayoselfstorage.com). This company also provides commercial and residential moving services. Another is **Placencia Mini Storage** (501-665-0800, www.placenciaministorages.com), with monthly storage rates from US$10 to $100, although this business is currently for sale.

A storage facility on Ambergris Caye is **Grumpy & Happy's Belize Mini Storage**, which offers an 8-feet wide, 12-feet deep, and 10-feet high container for US$150 a month, plus 12.5% tax. Larger spaces, up to 20 feet deep, are also available. Golf cart storage and boat storage are offered. Contact Grumpy & Happy at 501-226-3420, www.belizestorage.com.

Moving with Pets

In most cases, dogs and cats can be brought into Belize without quarantine.

Bringing a pet into the country falls under live animal importation and is regulated by the **Belize Agricultural Health Authority (BAHA).** Dogs and cats are allowed to enter the country provided that owners have a valid import permit, international veterinary certificate, valid rabies vaccination certificate and inspection by quarantine officer at the port of entry. Owners must get a certificate from a veterinarian at the owner's home country. The vet examination must take place within 14 days before arrival in Belize, and the certificate must state that the animal is in good health, is free from infectious diseases and has been vaccinated for rabies not less than one month and no more than one year prior to departure for Belize.

Kittens and puppies under three months of age that can't be vaccinated for rabies can be brought in but must be confined at the owner's home in Belize until they are three months old, at which time they must be vaccinated and then confined at home an additional 30 days.

The dog or cat must be inspected at the port of entry. Those coming from countries considered of risk (for example, pets from South America where there is the risk of screwworm) need to undergo veterinary inspection. There is an additional fee for veterinary inspection.

You can apply for an import permit for your cat or dog from BAHA. Permit application forms are available for download at the BAHA website at www.baha.org.bz. Return the completed form to Permit Unit of BAHA. You can send the permit application by email to bahasps@btl.net or fax 501-824-3773 or 501-824-4889.

The date of arrival must be specified. There is a US$25 entry and inspection fee, payable in U.S. or Belize dollars at the port of entry. Approved permits are faxed to applicant at a cost of an additional US$12.50 to be paid at the point of entry. If you don't follow this application process, you could be subject to a violation fine on top of the regular admission and inspection fees. In addition, any pet arriving without a valid permit or without a valid rabies vaccination may be confined at the owner's expense until the vaccination is valid.

For other pets or farm animals, such as ferrets or birds, check with BAHA for the current regulations. An import permit likely will be required. You can

download the permit application from the BAHA website
For more information, contact BAHA:
Belize Agricultural Health Authority (BAHA)
Corner Forest Drive and Hummingbird Highway
(P.O. Box 169)
Belmopan City, Belize
501-822-1378
www.baha.org.bz

Vets in Belize
More information about pets in Belize may be available from vets in Belize, including the following:
Animal Medical Centre, 1 Dr. Michael DeShield Lane, Belama Phase II, Belize City, 501-223-3781, www.animalmedicalcentre.net
Paws Veterinary Clinic, 1 Joseph Andrews Dr., San Ignacio, Cayo, 501-621-5377, www.pawsveterinaryclinicbze.com.
Note that while there are more than 20 practicing vets in Belize, most focus on large farm animals and do not care for dogs, cats and other small pets. A list of registered veterinary surgeons, as veterinarians are called in Belize, is available at the Veterinary Surgeons Board of Belize at www.veterinarysurgeonbelize.org.

Mennonite horse and buggy in Belize   Photo: Grigory Kubatyan/Shutterstock

Transporting Pets to and in Belize
Small dogs and cats can usually be carried in the cabin of scheduled commercial airlines. The kennel must fit under the seat. Reservations in advance are required, to assure that no more than a certain number, typically five to seven, animals are on a flight. A vet's certificate that the animal is in good health usually

must be provided, with the certificate done typically within 10 days prior to the date of travel.

American, Delta and United are some of the airlines flying into Belize that ship pets and allow them as checked luggage, with some restrictions. Pets are transported in the pressurized cargo hold. The kennel must be large enough for the animal to turn around in. Pets may not be accepted by the airline as checked luggage if the forecast temperature is too hot or too cold – typically above 85 or 90 degrees F. or below 45 degrees F. – at any point on the air itinerary; in some cases, the airline may accept a letter from a vet stating that the animal can stand temperatures above or below these points.

Some airlines have restrictions on which breeds can be checked as luggage. American and Delta, for example, do not permit "pug nosed" dogs such as Boston Terriers, Bulldogs or Boxers. These airlines also prohibit Burmese, Persian, Himalayan and Exotic Shorthair cats in the cargo hold.

Charges vary. American, for example, charges US$200 for a checked pet, and US$125 for a pet accompanying the passenger in the cabin. United charges $125 for an accompanying dog, cat, rabbit or bird and US$239 to US$709, depending on weight, for checked pets.

Contact the airline in advance to be sure you are following all its rules for pet travel; otherwise, you may be denied boarding.

Service animals generally are exempt from these rules and charges.

Yes, There Can Be Import Duty on Pets: You will not be charged Belize import duty on pets that accompany you on your flight. However, if you ship your pets separately, you will be charged an import duty based on a combination of the freight charges and the value of the animal, plus sales tax. The duty plus sales tax rate is about 50%. Check with Belize Customs to determine the amount of duty.

In-Country Transport of Pets: In Belize, both Maya Island and Tropic Air will carry your pet in its kennel. Tropic Air currently charges you for three seats for the pet, plus your own ticket. Maya Island Air currently charges you only for one seat for your pet, plus your town ticket. You must notify the airlines in advance that you are transporting a pet. To San Pedro and Caye Caulker, the water taxis allow pets to be carried like luggage, in kennels. The exception is legitimate service animals.

You can drive through Mexico with your pets. Some cargo services also transport animals.

Will Your Pet Adapt to Belize? Not all pets adapt well to Belize's subtropical climate. Mange and venereal disease are endemic. Snakebites and scorpion or bee stings can be dangerous or fatal to your pet. Rabies occasionally shows up in rural areas, vectored by vampire bats and other wild things. However, most dogs and cats seem to adapt satisfactorily to the climate and conditions in Belize.

Belizean Attitudes Toward Pets: Belizeans generally do not have the same view of pets as do Americans. They rarely allow dogs in the house, for example. Dogs are used more as watchdogs than as companions. You don't see that many cats kept as pets in Belize, except by expats. In some areas, feral cats are a problem, hunting birds and other wildlife. In rural areas, often you will see a number of wild animals including howler and spider monkeys and the smaller wild cats kept as pets (even though generally this is prohibited by law.

Belizean kids   Photo: Shutterstock

APPENDIXES

Appendix A: Belize National Parks

Around 26% of Belize's land is protected in government-owned national parks, monuments and reserves. There are also some quasi-official privately managed reserves.

Several types of protected areas are included in this section, including:

• **National parks,** which are afforded the highest level of protection, generally are not logged, but there are exceptions. National parks in Belize are managed under the National Park Systems Act of 1981, with the ministerial responsibility currently held by the Ministry of Forests, Fisheries & Sustainable Development. Management is usually in coordination with a local non-profit group or NGO. A few private holdings are located within national parks.

• **National monuments,** which are similar to national parks but usually smaller, recognize a specific geographic site, such as the Blue Hole. They are sometimes referred to as natural monuments.

• **Forest reserves** are protected areas but may be logged. These reserves may have pockets of private ownership.

• **Wildlife sanctuaries and preserves** are established to protect certain types of wildlife, such as jaguars or black howler monkeys. Some are managed by non-profit organizations or NGOs such as the Belize Audubon Society, and a few are on private land.

• **Marine reserves** are protected areas in the Caribbean and other waters off Belize. Fishing is prohibited in some parts of these reserves, and a user's fee is levied for visitors.

• **Archeological reserves** open to the public total 5,695 acres or about 9 square miles of area.

• **Private reserves** typically are owned and managed by non-profit organizations or, in some cases, private companies, in coordination with the Belize government. Several listed here are proposed reserves but are not yet officially recognized.

The following listing is alphabetical.

Actun Tunichil Muknal National Monument, Cayo District: Off Mile 52 of the George Price Highway, near Teakettle village, Actun Tunichil Muknal ("Cave of the Crystal Sepulcher") was rediscovered in 1989. ATM is a 455-acre (three-quarter square mile) national monument within Tapir Mountain Nature Reserve. The Maya used ATM from around 250 to 900 CE for ritual purposes, including human sacrifice. Dr. Jaime Awe, a Belizean who now heads the Belize Institute of Archeology, was the first archeologist to explore ATM, in the early 1990s. The fee to visit the site is US$15, but you cannot visit ATM on your own – you need to go with an accredited guide. Tours are offered from San Ignacio, Belmopan, Belize City and elsewhere.

Aguacaliente Wildlife Sanctuary, Toledo District: This 5,470-acre (eight and a half square mile) sanctuary in Laguna village in rural Toledo about 13 miles from PG has three freshwater lagoons and two hot springs.

Aguas Turbias National Park, Orange Walk District: This is an 8,750-acre (14 square mile) park established on the Belize-Mexico-Guatemala border in 1994.

Bacalar Chico National Park and Marine Reserve, Ambergris Caye, Belize District: Established in the 1990s, Bacalar Chico encompasses 12,640 acres of land on North Ambergris Caye (mostly public lands, some privately owned) along with 15,530 acres of government-owned marine territory. Bacalar Chico covers a total of about 44 square miles of land and sea. The park has a number of habitats, including swamps, grasslands and tropical forests including a semi-deciduous forest and a rare littoral, or beach, forest. The park is home to all of Belize's wild cats, including jaguars and pumas, along with manatees and crocodiles. The park includes the largest nesting areas in Belize for green sea turtles and loggerhead turtles, and one of the largest nesting areas in the country for hawksbill turtles. Nine Maya sites are in the park. Bacalar Chico is most easily accessible by boat from San Pedro Town. There is a small visitor center at the park. Mexico Rocks, a popular snorkeling spot, is now a part of Bacalar Chico. Park fee US$10.

BFREE (Belize Foundation for Research & Environmental Education), Toledo District: This is a private field station on a 1,153-acre (nearly 2 square miles) private reserve six miles inside the Bladen Nature Reserve from the Southern Highway. BFREE has a campground, dorm and three cabins for volunteers. On site is a 112-foot-tall galvanized steel observation tower. Day tours are offered to visitors. It has been proposed as an official private reserve.

Billy Barquedier National Park, Stann Creek District: This is a 1,640-acre park (two and a half square miles) off the Hummingbird Highway (technically the Stann Creek District Highway in this area). One entrance is off Mile 17 of the Hummingbird (miles are counted from Dangriga north). A short hike takes you to a waterfall. Park entrance fee is US$4.

Bird Sanctuaries, Belize, Orange Walk and Toledo Districts: There are seven areas, mostly cayes, totaling only 15 acres that are officially bird sanctuaries. These include Man of War Caye, Monkey Caye, Little Guana Caye, Bird Caye, Los Salones and Doubloon Bank.

Bladen Reserve, Toledo District: At nearly 100,000 acres (156 square miles) in Stann Creek and Toledo Districts, Bladen Reserve (sometimes called Swasey Bladen Reserve) is one of the largest reserves in Belize. It is a key link between Cockscomb Basin Wildlife Sanctuary in the north and the Columbia River Forest Reserve in the west and south. It also connects with the Chiquibul National Forest and Chiquibul National Park to the northwest, providing a large area for endangered species. Among the creatures found in the reserve are jaguars, Baird's tapirs, spider monkeys, howler monkeys, river otters, white-lipped and collared peccaries, great curassows, crested guans and scarlet macaws. There are at least 93 species of mammals, 337 species of birds and 92 species of reptiles and amphibians in the reserve. It is managed through a partnership between the Belize government and the Ya'aché Conservation Trust. It is most easily accessible via the Southern Highway.

Blue Hole National Monument, Lighthouse Reef Atoll, off Belize District: Blue Hole Natural Monument and the Lighthouse Reef Atoll are located 55 miles east of Belize City. The Great Blue Hole of water, 1,000 feet across, is set in a ring of corals. It is approximately 450 feet deep, the world's largest oceanic blue hole. It is believed that Belize's Blue Hole became a kind of submerged cenote (a karst-eroded sinkhole resulting from the collapse of limestone bedrock) about 12,000 years ago. Divers in the Blue Hole can see stalactites, dripstone sheets and columns at the southern rim of the Blue Hole. Jacques Cousteau brought the Blue Hole to the attention of the world in 1971 through his television series. In 1996, the Blue Home National Monument, as part of the Belize Barrier Reef and atoll system, became a UNESCO World Heritage Site. Several PADI dive operators visit it out of San Pedro, Caye Caulker, Hopkins and Belize City, along with a couple of live aboard dive ships. Because of its depth, the Blue Hole is for experienced divers only. Over the years, several divers have died in accidents at the Blue Hole. Snorkelers also can accompany dive boats to the Blue Hole and snorkel its surface waters. In fact, the Blue Hole is best appreciated from the air, and Belize airplane and helicopter charters, including Maya Island Air and Astrum Helicopters and tour operators such as Tsunami Adventures in Caye Caulker do Blue Hole flights. Park fee US$30 plus US$10 for Half Moon Caye National Monument.

Boden Creek Ecological Preserve, Toledo District: This is a private, 12,876-acre (20 square mile) reserve. In 2011, it became a REDD (Reducing Emissions from Deforestation and Forest Degradation) project and claims to be the first Verified Carbon Standard (VCS) validated project in the Western Hemisphere. The owners initially are seeking to sell, through Forest Carbon Offsets LLC, project manager, a minimum of 115,000 Verified Carbon Units. The Boden Creek Ecological Preserve, whose actual owners are undisclosed, formerly was leased to the controversial Belize Lodge & Expeditions *(see Jaguars in the Wild Belize chapter)* a collection of four lodges whose managing director allegedly allowed one caged jaguar at one lodge near Indian Creek to die from starvation. Another had to be rescued and was saved by the Belize Zoo.

Burden Canal Nature Reserve, Belize District: This reserve encompasses more than 5,200 acres (eight square miles) of mangrove backswamps of the Belize River and Haulover Creek between Belize City and Gales Point. It is home to many birds, including kingfishers, herons, white ibis and egrets. The American crocodile is also present. Near Gales Point are nesting grounds for endangered turtles. The waterway continues south from near Belize City to the Sibun River to the Northern Lagoon near Gales Point. At the southern end of the Northern Lagoon a winding creek leads to Manatee Lagoon, a prime spot for seeing West Indian Manatees. At present there is no formal visitor center for Burden Canal Nature Reserve. Tour operators or guides in Belize City and Gales Point can guide you in the reserve.

Caye Caulker Marine Reserve, Caye Caulker, Belize District: Declared a marine reserve in 1998, this 61-square mile protected area includes the portion of the Belize Barrier Reef that runs parallel to the island along with the turtle grass lagoon adjacent to the Caye Caulker Forest Reserve.

Caye Caulker North Point Sanctuary, Caye Caulker, Belize District: This is a 100-acre reserve established in 1998 at the north end of Caye Caulker above the Split. It consists mostly of mangrove forest.

Chiquibul Forest Reserve, Cayo District: The Chiquibul Forest Reserve in the Maya Mountains is the largest of the protected areas of Belize, totaling 147,000 acres or about 230 square miles. The reserve has lowland tropical broad-leafed rain forest. The Chiquibul Reserve is part of the 13.3 million acre Maya Forest in Belize, Guatemala and Mexico, the second-largest rainforest in the Americas. The Maya Forest as a whole has at least 375 plant species found nowhere else on earth. The Chiquibul Reserve is home to a huge variety of fauna and flora, from jaguars, pumas, tapirs, black howler monkeys, Morelet's crocodiles and scarlet macaws to the fungi found nowhere else. Inside the reserve is the Las Cuevas Research Station. *(See the Western Belize section for more information.)*

Chiquibul National Park, Cayo District: This is Belize's largest national park, with an area of 414 square miles. Within the park is Caracol Archeological Reserve, Belize's largest Maya site. *(See Caracol in the Western Belize section and also in the Maya and Other Archeological Sites section above.)* The 230-square-mile Chiquibul Forest Reserve adjoins *(see above)* Chiquibul National Park. Originally the park was part of the forest reserve, but in 1991 the part of the reserve that did not have active logging concessions was made into a national park. Chiquibul National Park, which is on the Guatemala border, contains the eastern slopes of the Maya Mountains. Doyle's Delight, at 3,688 feet the highest mountain in Belize, lies within the park. The park also includes part of the Chiquibul Cave System, the longest cave system in Central America and likely in the Western Hemisphere. There is tremendous natural diversity in the park, the full extent of which has yet to be explored. In the park are jaguars, jaguarundis, margay cats, ocelots, Baird's tapirs, spider monkeys, kinkajous, many species of bats and other mammals. Among the park's many birds are oscellated turkeys, king vultures, motmots, toucans and the largest breeding population of scarlet macaws in Belize. It is not known for certain how many types of trees and plants are in the park; in 1993, a team from the Missouri Botanical Garden collected more than 130 plant species previously unreported in Belize, with three species not previously known in Central America. Most of the forest is broadleaf wet tropical rainforest. Chiquibul National Park and Caracol can be visited by road from San Ignacio and from jungle lodges in the Mountain Pine Ridge. Admission to Caracol is US$10.

Cockscomb Basin Wildlife Preserve, Stann Creek District: This wildlife preserve, covering some 154 square miles in Stann Creek District to the west of Hopkins and Dangriga, was established in 1990 as the world's first jaguar sanctuary. This part of Belize was settled by the Maya as early as 10000 BCE, but the first modern exploration of the area was not conducted until 1888-89 by expeditions from Britain. Most of the forest in Cockscomb (the name derives from one of the Cockscomb Mountains range that resembles the comb of a rooster) is tropical moist broadleaf rainforest. An average of about 100 inches of rain falls in the preserve annually. Victoria Peak, the second-highest mountain in Belize after Doyle's Delight, is in the preserve. The Belize Audubon Society manages the Cockscomb Basin Wildlife Preserve. There is a campground, dorm and private cabins near the visitor center, located about 6 miles from Maya Center on the Southern Highway. Admission to Cockscomb is US$5.

Columbia River Forest Reserve, Toledo District: This forest reserve is located three to four hours by foot north of the Mopan Maya village of San Jose, and about the same time from the Kekchi villages of San Pedro Columbia and San Miguel. It covers an area of 103,000 acres or 161 square miles. A primary feature of this reserve is the Little Quartz Ridge, a length of mountain ridges that rise about to about 3,200 feet. To enter the Columbia River Forest Reserve a permit is required from the Forestry Department, and a guide is needed. The only trails are old logging roads. Much of the reserve gets more than 100 inches of rain annually.

Community Baboon Sanctuary, Bermudian Landing, Belize District: This sanctuary a community organization of around 200 members in seven villages who banded together in 1985 to protect black howler monkeys, called baboons by local people. The effort was successful, and there are now about 3,000 monkeys in the sanctuary. There is a small visitor center and museum in the village of Bermudian Landing, with guides to take you into per of the sanctuary, which altogether covers about 20 square miles of mostly privately owned land. In Bermudian Landing and nearby are several lodges and hotels. Admission is US$7.

Corozal Bay Wildlife Sanctuary, Corozal District: Corozal Bay Wildlife Sanctuary (was established in 1998 to protect the West Indian manatee and the fisheries of Corozal Bay. This sanctuary covers approximately 178,000 acres (278 square miles) of Corozal Bay and the lagoon on the west side of Ambergris Caye. The sanctuary is managed by the Belize Forestry Department in coordination with the Sarteneja Alliance for Conservation and Development. This sanctuary connects with Sanctuario del Manati (Manatee Sanctuary) in Mexico and with the Belize Barrier Reef system through Bacalar Chico Marine Reserve and National Park, North Ambergris Caye. The Corozal Bay Wildlife Sanctuary can be accessed from Corozal Town, Chunox, Copper Bank and Sarteneja villages, Ambergris Caye and Caye Caulker. Sarteneja, with a population of more than 2,500, is considered the largest fishing village in Belize. Sarteneja fishermen harvest lobster, conch and several fish species including stone bass, snapper and barracuda from the sanctuary and surrounding areas.

Crooked Tree Wildlife Sanctuary, Crooked Tree, Belize District: Crooked Tree Wildlife Sanctuary, designated as the first wildlife sanctuary in Belize, in 1984, encompasses 16,400 acres (about 26 square miles) of lagoons, creeks, swamps, savannah and broadleaf forest. It is located around Crooked Tree village, midway between Belize City and Orange Walk Town. Crooked Tree, the oldest Creole village in Belize and probably the first inland European settlement in the country, was named after the bent and crooked appearance of the cashew tree. The sanctuary is one of the best birding spots in Belize, especially during the dry season (February to late May), when birds from all over central and northern Belize flock to the large lagoons around Crooked Tree. Jabiru storks nest there from November to April or May. The sanctuary is managed by the Belize Audubon Society. There is a visitor center at the end of the causeway that connects the village to the Philip Goldson Highway, and lodging is available at lodges in the sanctuary. Admission US$5.

Deep River Forest Reserve, Toledo District: This 67,200-acre (105 square mile) forest reserve on both the west and east sides of the Southern Highway connects with Payne's Creek National Park on the Caribbean Sea just south of Monkey River village.

Five Blues Lakes National Park, Hummingbird Highway, Cayo and Stann Creek districts: This national park, on the border between Cayo and Stann Creek districts off Mile 52 of the Hummingbird Highway, has an area of 4,200 acres (six and a half square miles) with one lake said to have five shades of blue water. This national park is unusual in that it is managed by the residents of a single village, St. Margaret's. It is also mysterious in that in July 2006, quite suddenly over a period of just a few days, much of the lake water drained into the limestone. A year or so later the lake refilled. Then, in 2012, the lake drained again. Later it partially refilled once more. Today, the park gets relatively few visitors and on our last tour the park office was closed. Homestays are available in St. Margaret's village, and there are upscale jungle lodges not too far away, including Sleeping Giant Rainforest Lodge and Ian Anderson's Caves Branch Lodge. Admission of US$5 can be paid to a park ranger if one can be found.

Fireburn Private Reserve, Corozal District: Fireburn Reserve is a 1,818-acre (3 square miles) private reserve on the east of Shipstern Lagoon managed by Wildtracks, an NGO based in Sarteneja and headed by Paul and Zoe Walker. The Walkers were recognized in 2013 by the Belize Audubon Society for their conservation work.

Freshwater Creek Forest Reserve, Corozal and Orange Walk Districts: This is a private 33,400-acre (52 square mile) reserve managed by Corozal Sustainable Future Initiative (CSFI), formerly the Shipstern Nature Reserve, an international NGO. The adjoining Honey Camp National Park is being managed by CSFI for sustainable forestry.

Gales Point Wildlife Sanctuary, Belize District: This 14 square-mile sanctuary near Gales Point village covers two lagoons with sizeable West Indian manatee populations plus a coastal plain.

Gallon Jug Estates Private Reserve, Orange Walk District: Gallon Jug Estates is a 130,000-acre (203 square mile) privately owned reserve that was once part of the vast Belize Estate and Produce Company's holdings in Belize. Although some of the details are shaded in history, in the mid-1980s Barry Bowen, a seventh-generation Belizean inherited his father's bottling business in Belize City. He built it into a successful Belize conglomerate run on the profits of Belikin beer brewing, Coca-Coca bottling and Crystal water. Also, he owned or otherwise controlled nearly 700,000 acres of land in Orange Walk District.

Bowen reportedly planned to cut the remaining timber in the Orange Walk tracts as fuel for a wood-burning electric power station. However, Bowen ran into problems and reportedly to avoid foreclosure he entered into a purchase agreement with Coca-Cola Foods and a partnership of Houston investor-oilman Paul Howell and banker-developer Walter Mischer. Malcolm Barnebey, a former U.S. ambassador to Belize, worked as a consultant to Howell and Mischer. The two investors, through Barnebey, were said to have paid US$6 million for some 100,000 acres and a 60% option on an additional 550,000 acres. This was a bargain price of under US$15 an acre. About 30% of the parcel went to Houston-based Coca-Cola Foods, which planned to grow oranges on at least 25,000 acres for its Minute Maid orange juice brand. This was a hedge, in frost-free Belize, against losses of citrus trees due to periodic cold weather in Florida. (Minute Maid had suffered severely in the winter of 1983.) Mischer and Howell got 30% of the land, and Bowen retained about 40%.

Unfortunately for Coca-Coca and the entrepreneurs, international conservationists got wind of the plan to clear large areas of tropical forest. They threatened protests and boycotts of Coca-Cola. A loose coalition of conservationists, including the U.S. national Audubon Society, the Massachusetts and Belize Audubon societies, New York Zoological Society, Nature Conservancy, World Wildlife Fund and World Resources Institute, joined together to fight the land development deal. Coca-Cola backed down, put plans for citrus growing in Belize on hold and Coke donated a large tract of the land for a nature reserve. Barry Bowen divested himself of another large tract. Combined, the land became Programme for Belize's Rio Bravo Conservation and Management Area, consisting of more than 260,000 acres, the largest private nature reserve in Belize.

Bowen retained an adjoining 130,000-acre tract, plus the 3,000-acre Gallon Jug Estate farm (mainly producing cacao, coffee and cattle) and what would become Chan Chich Lodge. Sir Barry Bowen was killed in a plane crash in San Pedro in 2010. Gallon Jug Estates and the lodge are now owned by Bowen family members.

Glover's Reef Marine Reserve, Glover's Atoll, off Stann Creek District: Glover's Reef Marine Reserve was established as a national protected area in 1993. It covers 86,650 acres or 135 square miles of the marine area of Glover's Atoll, a main nursery and feeding area for finfish, lobster and conch. It is managed by the Fisheries Department of the Belize Ministry of Agriculture and Fisheries. In 1996 it was designated as one of the seven parts of the Belize Barrier Reef Reserve System, a UNESCO World Heritage Site. The Wildlife Conservation Society, a conservation group that dates back to 1895, has a research station in the reserve on Middle Caye. The Society has pioneered the use of drone airplanes to monitor the marine reserve. About 670 acres of the reserve is a wilderness area closed to visitors, and 3,800 acres are closed to fishing seasonally from December to February, with part of this section, a grouper spawning area, closed to fishing permanently. Visitors to the reserve pay a user's fee of US$30 weekly.

Gladden Spit and Silk Cayes Marine Reserve, off Stann Creek District: This protected marine reserve of about 26,000 acres (40 square miles) has long been known as a place where whale sharks congregate in the late spring during spawning of grouper and mutton snapper. The reserve has a number of pristine small cayes including North Silk, Middle Silk and South Silk south of Gladden entrance near Queen Caye. Since 2003, when the government established the reserve, it has been divided into a general use zone, a no-take zone around the Silk Cayes, a conch restoration zone and a whale shark and reef fish spawning aggregation conservation zone. Park fee is US$10.

Golden Stream Corridor Private Reserve, Toledo District: This is 24-square mile private reserve in Toledo District north of Punta Gorda.

Gra Gra Lagoon National Park, Stann Creek District: Located just south of Dangriga, the 3,000-acre (four and a half square mile) Gra Gra Lagoon National Park consists mostly of a mangrove lagoon.

Guanacaste National Park, Belmopan, Cayo District: This pocket national park at the edge of Belmopan City is only 50 acres in size, paling in comparison to Costa Rica's 80,000-acre park of the same name. Established in 1990, Belize's little park was named after a single large guanacaste tree. Despite its small size, it has decent birding and 2 miles of trails along the Belize River. The Belize Audubon Society manages it. Daytime admission fee for non-Belizeans is US$2.50.

Half Moon Caye Natural Monument, Lighthouse Reef Atoll, off Belize District: This was the first nature reserve to be officially established in Belize, in 1981. It was originally named as a bird sanctuary in British Honduras in 1924. Today, Half Moon Caye in Lighthouse Atoll is a breeding ground for a large colony of red-footed boobies, a nesting area for loggerhead, hawksbill and green turtles, all endangered, and home of the rare leaf-toed gecko and Allison's anole lizard. Off the caye is Half Moon Caye Wall, one of Belize's top dive sites. There's a lighthouse and campground on the caye, and visitors to the caye are charged a US$10 per day user fee. An additional park fee of US$30 is charge to visit the Blue Hole.

Hidden Valley Inn Private Reserve, Cayo District: Hidden Valley Inn is in a private nature reserve set on 7,200 acres (11 square acres) at around 2,000 feet elevation in the Mountain Pine Ridge. Formerly owned by Julian "Bull" Headley, a Florida lumberman, who moved to British Honduras in the mid-1960s, it is now the property of members of a prominent Belize City family, the Roes, who are involved in a number of businesses in Belize including hotels, tobacco and car dealerships. The private reserve has a wealth of fauna and flora – 239 confirmed species of vertebrates, including all five of Belize's wild cats, rare birds such as the orange breasted falcon, stygian owl, black and white hawk and solitary eagle and more than 80 species of orchids. The reserve has numerous waterfalls and hiking trails, open only by those staying at the lodge.

Hol Chan Marine Reserve, off Ambergris Caye, Belize District: Hol Chan ("Little Channel" in Maya, referring to a narrow channel through the Belize Barrier Reef) is a 4,450-acre (seven square mile) marine reserve about four miles south of Ambergris Caye, is Belize's most visited dive and snorkeling area. It is the oldest marine reserve in Belize, established in 1987. No fishing is allowed in part of the zone, and no commercial fishing is permitted in another zone, so the size and variety of fish species have increased in recent years. More than 160 species of fish have been recorded in the reserve, including large schools of jacks, groupers, snappers and barracuda, along with 40 types of coral, three species of sea turtles, nurse sharks, spotted eagle rays and stingrays, and three marine mammals, the West Indian manatee and two species of porpoises. The reserve can be visited by from San Pedro and Caye Caulker. It also gets visitors from cruise ships in port in Belize City. Visitors can enjoy the novelty of snorkeling with large numbers of nurse sharks and stingrays. While accidents are rare, at times, especially during windy periods, the wave energy through the narrow channel is strong, and several people have died from drowning or cardiovascular events. Mostly recently, in early 2016, an American tourist drowned while snorkeling in Hol Chan. A Hol Chan visitor center is in San Pedro Town. Two- to three-hour snorkel trips to the reserve from San Pedro cost around US$45 per person, not including equipment rental if needed, usually US$10 for mask, snorkel and fins, or the park fee of US$10. Rates from Caye Caulker are similar, although the snorkel trips usually last an hour or two longer and often include an additional snorkel stop.

Honey Camp National Park, Orange Walk and Corozal District: Honey Camp National Park, created in 2001, consists of 3,150 acres (5 square miles) of forested area adjoining Freshwater Creek Forest Reserve. The two areas provide an important biological corridor in Northern Belize. Both areas are co-managed by Corozal Sustainable Future Initiative, an NGO.

Laughing Bird Caye National Park, off Placencia, Stann Creek District: Named after the colonies of laughing gulls that once lived on this 2-acre island (most have now moved on to a nearby caye, replaced by pelicans). Laughing Bird Caye, declared a national park in 1991, is 11 miles off Placencia, about half way to the Great Barrier Reef. The marine part of the park totals around 10,120 acres (16 square miles). There is excellent snorkeling around the caye, and good diving, although the fish and other sea life are perhaps better than the coral. Six-hour snorkeling trips to Laughing Bird from Placencia are around US$75 per person including gear, lunch and US$10 park fee.

Laughing Falcon Reserve, Toledo District: This is a 11,000-acre (17 square mile) private tract just north of Punta Gorda, anchored by the deluxe Belcampo Lodge. It is operated by San Diego, Calif.-based investor Todd Robinson and artisan food-and-agrotourism entrepreneur Anya Fernald.

Machaca Forest Reserve, Toledo District: This is a 3,100-acre (5 square mile) government forest reserve in Toledo established in 1998.

Mango Creek Forest Reserve, Stann Creek and Toledo districts: This 30,000-acre (47 square mile) government forest reserve, which is in two segments west of Placencia, was established in 1989.

Maya Mountain Forest Reserve, Stann Creek District: This is a 41,000-acre (64 square mile) reserve.

Mayflower Bocawina National Park, Stann Creek District: Established in 2001, Mayflower Bocawina covers 11 square miles west of the Southern Highway near Dangriga and Hopkins. The park has three Maya sites, still under excavation and three beautiful waterfalls, which are a fairly short but arduous hike from the entrance. Within the park is a private jungle lodge, Bocawina Rainforest Resort, with the longest zipline in Belize. This lodge formerly was Momma Noots Eco Resort. There's a small visitor entrance at the entrance to the park, about 5 miles off the Southern Highway. Park admission is US$5.

Monkey Bay Wildlife Sanctuary, Belize District: This is a private, non-profit education, conservation and training center. The main campus is a 1,060-acre (two and a half square mile) reserve on the George Price Highway near the Belize Zoo. Monkey Bay solicits students for study abroad programs and also offers internships and seeks volunteers. Visitors can stay (and pay) for lodging in a campground, dorm or private rooms in cabins and can also get meals at the sanctuary.

Mountain Pine Ridge Forest Reserve, Cayo District: Originally designated as a reserve by British Honduras in 1944 to protect and manage the native pine forests, the forest reserve today, after parts of the original reserve were redistributed to other reserves and parks, covers about 106,000 acres (166 square miles). Parts of the reserve have been leased to private interests. Most of the reserve is massive granite rock, uplifted in the Jurassic period, making this one of the oldest parts of Central America. The western side of the reserve is limestone. Underlying soils are sandy, with areas of red clay similar to those found in Georgia and Alabama. The reserve's dominant tree, is the Honduras pine, a variant of the Caribbean pine (*Pinus caribaea* var. *Hondurensis)* that gives the reserve an uncharacteristic appearance compared with surrounding areas. Over recent decades an infestation of

Southern pine bark beetle has killed large numbers of the pines. However, they are regenerating naturally and through a replanting program. The reserve also has large areas of broadleaf forest. The elevation of the reserve ranges from about 1,300 to 2,300 feet, with the highest point being Baldy Beacon at 3,336 feet. The higher elevations enjoy a somewhat cooler climate than lowland areas of Belize, with temperatures sometimes dropping into the 40s F. in winter. All of Belize's five wild cats have been found in the forest reserve, along with tapirs and Morelet's crocodiles. There are four jungle lodges in the reserve (one is at present closed and for sale). Some logging activities continue here, along with occasional military operations by Belize Defence Forces and the United States Army. The reserve is very light populated, with only worker compounds at the jungle lodges and a small group at Douglas De Silva forest station. One main road, unpaved, through the reserve is the route to the Chiquibul and Caracol Maya site, and the reserve is crisscrossed by old dirt logging trails, good more mountain biking and hiking. Among the attractions in the reserve are the Rio Frio cave, Rio On pools, 1,000 Foot Falls, Big Rock Falls and the three main lodges, Blancaneaux Lodge, Hidden Valley Inn and Gaia Riverlodge. Hunting has been prohibited in the forest reserve since 1978, although illegal poaching and the collection of xate palms by Guatemalans who cross the long, porous border of the reserve is an ongoing problem. You can visit the Mountain Pine Ridge on tours from San Ignacio and Belmopan and by private car. Entrance to the reserve is controlled via a guarded gate on the Mountain Pine Ridge Road, but as noted the border with Guatemala is porous, and from time to time bandits have crossed over to rob visitors to the reserve. In 2014 a Belize police constable was killed.

Noj Kaax Meen Elijio Panti National Park, Cayo District: Elijio Panti National Park was established in 2001. The 13,000-acre (20-square mile) park honors the Guatemalan-born Maya natural healer who died in 1996 at age 103. The official park entrance is near San Antonio village off the Cristo Rey Road. The dirt paths in the park are passable by car only in the dry season. At other times, you must travel by foot or on horseback. In the park is Ka'am Be'en cave and Sact'aj waterfall. The park is now co-managed by the Belize government and the Belmopan-based Belize Development Foundation, which took over from the original co-manager, the Itzamna Society based in San Antonio. Itzamna was the original force behind the establishment of the park. So far, there is only very limited development of the park infrastructure.

Paynes Creek National Park, Toledo District: This 37,800-acre (59 square miles) national park stretches along the Monkey River in northern Toledo District. The park has many howler monkeys and at least four Maya sites, as yet mostly unexplored. It is managed, in cooperation with the Government of Belize, by the Toledo Institute for Development and Environment (TIDE), which also co-manages Port Honduras Marine Reserve and TIDE Protected Private Reserves in Toledo District.

Peccary Hills National Park, Belize District: This 10,740-acre (17 square mile) national park, established in 2007, is only 20 miles west of Belize City, near Gracie Rock village, the Sibun River and Northern Lagoon. At least one tour operator offers ATV tours in this park, which has caves and waterfalls.

Port Honduras Marine Reserve, off Toledo District: The 100,000-acre (156 square miles) marine reserve is in the Gulf of Honduras off Toledo District. It has nearly 140 small mangrove cayes and is home to a number of endangered or threatened species including the West Indian manatee, goliath grouper, hammerhead shark and hawksbill, green and loggerhead turtles. Seven jungle rivers flow into the marine reserve. Although fishing is permitted in most of the reserve, long lines, gill nets and beach traps are prohibited. The four Snakes Cayes, named for the boas that once lived on the islands, are located in the reserve. The southwest side of West Snake Caye has nice coral beach with white sand, good for swimming. Toledo Institute for Development and Environment (TIDE) co-manages it with the Government of Belize. Park fees US$5 per day.

Rio Bravo Conservation and Management Area (Programme for Belize), Orange Walk District: This protected area of 260,000 acres (406 square miles) is the largest mainland conservation area in Belize. It was established in 1989 by Belize City-based Programme for Belize, a nonprofit Belizean organization, with a purchase of about 104,000 acres from Barry Bowen's Gallon Jug Agroindustries. Coca-Cola had planned to grow citrus on part of the land. After an international effort by conservationist, Coke was persuaded to abandon its citrus plans and donate 94,000 acres to Programme for Belize. Additional acreage was purchased from other private landowners. In Rio Bravo are the large La Milpa Maya site and two field stations with accommodations for students and other visitors, Hillbank and La Milpa. The habitat includes upland forests, marshes, savannah and lagoons, notably the New River Lagoon. More than 370 bird species have been identified in the management area, along with more than 70 mammal species and 230 different tree species. Visitors can reach the area by car from Orange Walk Town.

Runaway Creek Private Reserve, Belize District: Runaway Creek is a 6,000-acre (9 square mile) private reserve in the karst hills, with a number of caves with Maya artifacts. It is owned by the Foundation for Wildlife Conservation headed by Dr. Gil Boese, the founder of Birds Without Borders.

Sapodilla Cayes Marine Reserve, off Toledo District: This 48- square mile marine reserve about 45 miles off Punta Gorda, established in 1996, is Belizean territory, but both Guatemala and Honduras have laid claim to parts of the area. Two of the cayes in the reserve, Hunting and Lime, have especially beautiful beaches. The reserve is administered by the Fisheries Department. Park fees are US$10 per day or US$25 per week.

Sarstoon-Temash National Park, Toledo District: This is the southernmost national park in Belize, located south of Punta Gorda on the Guatemala border. It consists of about 42,000 acres (66 square miles) of mangrove forest, wetlands and broadleaf jungle. Unfortunately, in late 2014, an oil company, US Capital Energy, began drilling for oil in the national park, after earlier being granted rights to do so by the Belize government over the opposition of local people. To date, no oil has been found.

Shipstern Conservation and Management Area, Corozal District: This 21,500-acre (34 square mile) protected area is in northeastern Corozal District near the Shipstern Lagoon system. It is owned and managed by Corozal Sustainable Future Initiative (CSFI), a Belize NGO financed in part by a group of European zoos that also co-manages Honey Camp Lagoon National Park and

Freshwater Creek Reserve. Formerly called Shipstern Nature Reserve, the conservation area dates to 1990. It was formed from a parcel of land owned in the 1980s by a British butterfly enthusiast, Clive Farrell, who developed a butterfly farm near Sarteneja village that later failed. Today, a few butterflies are kept at the Shipstern visitor center for tourism purposes. The reserve is home to all five species of Belize's wild cats, both of Belize's peccary species, more than 300 species of birds (some from the Yucatán seen in Belize only at Shipstern), 300 species of butterflies of which about 30 are seen in Belize only at Shipstern and about 80 species of reptiles and amphibians. There is a visitor center about three miles from Sarteneja. Admission is US$5, which includes a short guided tour of the botanical trail and old butterfly facility. Sarteneja and Shipstern can be reached by bus from Orange Walk Town, by car from Corozal Town or Orange Walk Town and by boat from San Pedro or Corozal Town. Tropic Air in the past has offered a stop-on-demand service at Sarteneja airstrip on its San Pedro-Corozal Town route – check to see if this is still an option when you are in Belize.

Sibun Forest Reserve, Cayo District: The 81,000-acre (127 square mile) Sibun Forest Reserve, first established in 1959, is part of a series of large reserves, sanctuaries and national parks stretching from Cayo District down through Stann Creek and Toledo districts altogether comprising more than 1.3 million acres of land, larger than the Great Smoky Mountains National Park in the United States. This provides an important corridor for wildlife in Belize, especially for large mammals such as jaguars and pumas.

Sittee River Forest Reserve, Stann Creek District: This 147-square mile forest reserve off the Hummingbird Highway is home to Davis Falls.

Slate Creek Preserve, Cayo District: A group of local landowners and lodge owners have set aside 3,000 acres (4½ square miles) of land in the Vega valley off the Chiquibul Road, bordering the Mountain Pine Ridge. The purpose is to protect the plants, animal and watershed of the valley. At present, Slate Creek is closed to the public.

Southwater Caye Marine Reserve, off Dangriga, Stann Creek District: Southwater Caye (also sometimes called South Water Caye) at 118,000 acres (184 square miles) is the largest marine reserve in Belize. This reserve, along with Gladden Spit Silk Cayes Marine Reserve, Laughing Bird Caye National Park and Sapodilla Cayes Marine Reserve, comprise the Southern Barrier Reef Complex, one of the areas with the highest biodiversity in the region. Among the cayes here are Southwater, which has one of the most beautiful beaches in Belize and three dive/fishing lodges, Carrie Bowe Caye, which has a Smithsonian Institution research station, Man-of-War Caye, a nesting site for the brown booby and the Pelican Cayes, with their deep, clear lagoons encircled by steep, lush coral ridges and coral reefs. This reserve is managed by the Belize Fisheries Department. Visitors to this marine reserve need a permit, which can be obtained from the Fisheries Department in Belize City or at the ranger station at Twin Cayes. Tour operators and lodges also can provide permits. Permits cost US$5 per day or US$15 for up to 10 days.

Spanish Creek Rainforest Reserve, Belize District: This is a 2,000-acre (3 square mile) nature reserve and organic farm near Rancho Dolores. It has 75 acres of bamboo and organic fruit orchards.

Spanish Creek Wildlife Sanctuary, in Belize District: This is a 5,985-acre (9 square miles) wildlife sanctuary adjoining the Spanish Creek Rainforest Reserve.

Spawning Aggregation Zones, Belize and Toledo Districts: These 11 marine spawning zones, mostly off Belize District, total 19,850 acres (31 square miles) of the Caribbean Sea.

St. Herman's Blue Hole National Park, Hummingbird Highway, Cayo District: This is a 575-acre (1 square mile) park on the Hummingbird Highway. It contains the inland Blue Hole and two cave systems, St. Herman's and Crystal Cave. It is managed by the Belize Audubon Society. Admission is US$4.

Swallow Caye Reserve, Belize District: Located about 19 miles southwest of Caye Caulker and 28 miles south of Ambergris Caye, the 9,000-acre (14 square miles) Swallow Caye Reserve is dedicated to the West Indian manatee, many of which live in this reserve. You can do tours from Belize City, Caulker or San Pedro. Park fee is US$5.

Tapir Mountain Nature Reserve, Belmopan Area, Cayo District: The 6,500-acre (10 square mile) Tapir Mountain Nature Reserve, managed by the Belize Audubon Society, is home to Actun Tunichil Muknal. Access is via a road south from Black Man Eddy village off the George Price Highway. The dirt road leads to the park warden's quarters. Permission to enter the reserve for scientific or educational purposes must be obtained from the management. Except for guided tours of ATM tourists are not permitted in this reserve.

Thousand Foot Falls National Monument, Cayo District: This national monument, sometimes referred to as Hidden Valley Falls, in the Mountain Pine Ridge is said to be the highest waterfall in Central America. Visitors to it, however, are usually less than awed, as all they see from the visitor area is a part of a thin trickle of water many hundreds of yards away. Admission is US$2, and there's a small picnic area and a shop for buying snacks.

TIDE Private Protected Reserves, Toledo District. Toledo Institute for Development and Environment (TIDE) manages more than 20,000 acres (31 square miles) of private lands in Toledo as forest and nature reserves. It contains areas of undisturbed virgin rainforest. Ya'axché Conservation Trust, partnering with the Government of Belize, has day-to-day management responsibility. Only researchers with valid permits issued by the Forest Department and student groups are permitted within the boundaries of the reserve. Tourists are not permitted in the reserve.

Vaca Forest Reserve, Cayo District: This 35,000-acre (55 square mile) forest reserve was established in 1991.

Victoria Peak National Monument, Stann Creek District: Victoria Peak in the Cockscomb Mountains is the second-highest mountain peak in Belize, at 3,675 feet, after Doyle's Delight in the Maya Mountains. The peak, which on a clear day can be seen from the coast, was first climbed by Europeans in 1888. Belize declared it a national monument in 1998. A trail to the peak is usually open during the dry season, February to May. Getting to the peak and back, a 32-mile rough roundtrip trek from Cockscomb Basin Wildlife Sanctuary park headquarters and visitor center, usually takes three days. The monument is managed by the Belize Audubon Society.

LAN SLUDER

Appendix B: Recommended Reading

Many of these books are available from Amazon.com, either as new books or through their used-book sellers system. Many are also available as ebooks for Kindle (Amazon), Nook (Barnes & Noble), iBooks (Apple) or other formats. Also, try ABE (www.abebooks.com) for out-of-print books. In the case of books published by Cubola, a Belize publishing company, visit www.cubola.com. Note that the publication dates given are usually those for the original edition, except in the case of travel guidebooks, where the most recent edition publication date is provided.

Archaeology
Awe, Jaime. *Maya Cities, Sacred Caves,* Cubola Productions, 2005, 104 pp. A guide to 10 noted Maya sites in Belize, by the director of Belize's Institute of Archaeology.

Coe, Michael D. *The Maya,* Thames and Hudson, 7th ed., 2005, 224 pp. Originally published in 1993, this is the best general introduction to the subject.

Coe, William R. *Tikal, A Handbook of the Ancient Maya Ruins,* University Museum at the University of Pennsylvania, 1967. Useful when touring Tikal.

Ferguson, William M. and Adams, R.E.W. Mesoamerica's Ancient Cities: Aerial Views of Pre-Columbian Ruins in Mexico, Guatemala, Belize and Honduras, University Press of Colorado, rev. ed., 2000, 272 pp.

Foster, Byron, Ed. *Warlords and Maize Men, A Guide to the Maya Sites of Belize,* Cubola Productions, Belize, 1992, 82 pp. The first popular guide focused entirely on Maya sites in Belize, by the late Dr. Foster (he was murdered at his farm in western Belize.) Maps, color photos.

Garber, James F., ed. The Ancient Maya of the Belize Valley: Half a Century of Archeological Research, University of Florida Press, 2003, 448 pp.

Guderjan, Thomas H. *Ancient Maya Traders of Ambergris Caye,* Cubola Productions, 1993, 40 pp.

-- The Nature of an Ancient Maya City: Resources, Interaction, and Power at Blue Creek, Belize, University of Alabama Press, 2007, 244 pp.

Hammond, Norman, Ed. *Cuello: An Early Maya Community in Belize,* Cambridge University Press, 1991 (hardcover), 2009 (paper). 284 pp.

Harrison, Peter D. Pulltrouser Swamp: Ancient Maya Habitat, Agriculture and Settlement, University of Utah Press, 2000, 294 pp.

Henderson, John S. *The World of the Ancient Maya,* Cornell University Press, 1981, 271 pp.

Kelly, Joyce. *An Archaeological Guide to Northern Central America: Belize, Guatemala, Honduras, and El Salvador,* University of Oklahoma Press, rev. ed. 1996, 352 pp. Includes coverage of many smaller sites. Photographs by Jerry Kelly.

McMillon, Bill. *The Archeology Handbook: A Field Manual and Resource Guide,* Wiley, 1991, 259 pp. Not specific to Belize, but provides the amateur archeologist or volunteer with information on excavation techniques, tools, methods, etc.

Montgomery, John. Tikal: An Illustrated History of the Ancient Maya Capital, Hippocrene Books, 2001, 275 pp.

Sharer, Robert and Traxler, Loa. *The Ancient Maya,* Stanford University Press, 6th ed. 2005, 931 pp. A classic in the field, this is the most comprehensive work on the Maya.

Thompson, J. Eric S. The Maya of Belize: Historical Chapters Since Columbus, Cubola Productions.

Boating

Calder, Nigel. *The Cruising Guide to the Northwest Caribbean,* McGraw-Hill, 2nd ed., 1991, 272 pp. Navigational and anchorage information on the Caribbean Coast of Mexico, Belize, Guatemala and Honduras. Unfortunately this has not been recently updated.

Copeland, Liza. *Comfortable Cruising Around North and Central America,* Romany Enterprises, 2001, 312 pp. Several chapters on cruising the Caribbean Coast of Central America, including Belize.

Rauscher, Freya. *Cruising Guide to Belize and Mexico's Caribbean Coast,* Windmill Hill Books, 3rd ed., 2007, 312 pp. with 117 charts and 185 photos. Comprehensive cruising guide, the best available to this region, from Isla Mujeres in Mexico to the Rio Dulce in Guatemala. Includes large charts of Belize's coast and Mexico's Caribbean Coast.

NOAA-28004 *Nautical Chart of Caribbean Sea, Northwest Part,* 1:1300,000 scale, undated. Includes Belize.

Waterproof Chart # 4, Caribbean and Gulf of Mexico.

Cookbooks

Aponte-Jolly, Minvera (ed.), *Aaah ... Belizean Rum Recipes,* Cubola Productions, 2003, 152 pp. If you like more than a rum and tonic or a rum and Coke.

Arvigo, Rosita, *Food of the Gods, Vegetarian Cooking in Belize,* Cubola Productions, 2010, 158 pp. Guide to Belizean vegetarian cooking by the noted natural healer who moved to Cayo.

Burns, E. L. What's Cooking in the Belizean Kitchen, Angelus Press, 74 pp.

de Langan, Tracey Brown. *Mmmm ... a Taste of Belizean Cooking,* Cubola Productions, 2003, 142 pp. Chefs from leading Belizean restaurants contributed to this cookbook.

Nord, Alice, Martinez, Myrna and Shrine, Kaaren. *Cooking Belize,* self-published, c. 1995, 126 pp.

Belize Hospital Auxiliary Cookbook, Angelus Press, 126 pp.

Belizeous Cuisine, Delicious Belizean Recipes, by Los Angeles Belizean Educational Network (LABEN), 1997, 102 pp.

To Catch a Cook, by South Ambergris Caye Neighborhood Watch, self published, 2009

Silly Bug & Bittle Recipes, Crooked Tree Village Creative Women's Group, self-published, 100 pp.

U Toucan Cook Belize Cookbook, self-published, 126 pp.

Fiction, Drama and Poetry

Auxillou, Ray. *Blue Hole,* self-published, date unknown, 479 pp. A collection of tales about mercenaries, drug runners and adventure. Other books in the same vein by Auxillou include *Belize Secret Service, Belize Connection* and *The Belize Vortex.*

Crone, Andrew. *Chameleon War,* Booksurge Publishing, 2008, 244 pp. You'll want to wash your hands after you read this garbage.

Coxe, George Harmon. *With Intent to Kill,* Knopf, 1964, 180 pp. Action/adventure.

Edgell, Zee. *Beka Lamb,* Heinemann, 1982, 192 pp. Classic novel about ordinary life in British Honduras.

— *In Times Like These,* Heinemann, 320 pp. English-educated Belizean returns home.

— *The Festival of San Joaquin,* Heinemann, 1997, 155 pp. Explores domestic violence in Belize.

Ellis, Zoila. *On Heroes, Lizards and Passion, Seven Belizean Short Stories,* Cubola Productions, 1994, 130 pp. "White Christmas an' Pink Jungle" is one of seven deliciously Belizean stories, from a distinguished Belizean/Garifuna writer.

Esquivel, Cathy. *Under the Shade,* Angelus Press, 192 pp. Tales of the drug trade.

Godfrey, Glenn D. *The Sinners' Bossanova,* Cubola Books, 1987, 269 pp. Action/adventure.

Hagerthy, Tim, and Parham, Mary Gomoz, Eds. *If Di Pin Neva Bin, Folktales and Legends of Belize,* Cubola Productions, 128 pp.

Hernandez, Felicia. *Those Ridiculous Years,* 64 pp. Short stories about Garifuna life.

Heusner, Karla. *Food for Thought, Chronicles of Belize,* Cubola Productions, 2004, 207 pp. Collection of weekly newspaper columns by a Belizean journalist who now lives in the U.S.

Koerner, Nancy R. *Belize Survivor: Darker Side of Paradise,* NK Marketing, 2007, 300 pp. A novel, based on a true story, of a young woman who comes to Belize, lives in the bush and gets more than she bargained for.

Lindo, Louis. *Tales of the Belizean Woods,* Cubola Productions, 82 pp. Short stories set in backabush Belize.

McKay, Claudia. *Twist of Lime, A Lynn Evans Mystery,* New Victoria Publishers, 1997, 188 pp. Mystery featuring lesbian newspaper reporter on Maya dig in Belize.

Miller, Carlos Ledson. *Belize, A Novel,* Xlibris Corp., 1999, 402 pp. Fast-paced saga of father and sons over four decades, beginning with Hurricane Hattie in 1961.

Miller, Harold R. *The Belize File,* Taylor-Dth Publishing, 2008, 372 pp. An ex-DEA agent turned private eye is hired to find a friend's daughter, missing on her honeymoon in Belize.

Mueller, William Behr. *Operation Belize,* CreateSpace, 2008, 358 pp. The U.S. Secretary of State is kidnapped in Belize, and American Special Forces attempt a rescue.

Patrick, William. *The Five Lost Days,* Pearhouse Press, 2008, 336 pp. A documentary filmmaker travels to the Maya Mountains of Belize to get footage of a Maya healer.

Phillips, Michael, Ed. *Of Words, an Anthology of Belizean Poetry,* Cubola Productions, 1997, 104 pp. A collection of poems by more than three dozen Belizean poets.

-- *Ping Wing Juk Me, Six Belizean Plays,* Cubola Productions, 2004, 120 pp. A collection of plays by George Gabb, Carol Fonseca Galvez, Evan X. Hyde, Glady Stuart, Shirley Warde and Colville Young.

-- *Snapshots of Belize, an Anthology of Belizean Short Fiction,* Cubola Productions, 2004, 122 pp. A collection of short stories by seven Belizean writers.

Portis, Charles, *The Dog of the South,* Knopf, 1979, 246 pp. Hilarious, offbeat road trip tale set mostly in Mexico and Belize City in the late 1970s, by the author of *True Grit.* Republished in a paperback edition by The Overlook Press.

Rimmer, Stephen. *The Way to Go: Four Men & Three Women Sailing from Florida to Cozumel & Belize – A Story of Sex, Lust & Drug Trafficking, with a New Kind of Morality about Sinning of All Kinds!,* IUniverse, 2000, 428 pp. This novel is an example of the downside of the new print-on-demand technology.

Ruiz Puga, David Nicolas. *Old Benque,* Cubola Productions, 160 pp. Short stories in Spanish.

Stray, P.J. *The Danger on Lighthouse Reef,* Silver Burdett Press, 1997, 144 pp. Children's mystery story.

Theroux, Paul. *The Mosquito Coast,* Houghton-Mifflin, 1982. Obsessed American drags his family to Central America. Actually set in Honduras, not Belize, but the movie of the same name was filmed in Belize.

Vasquez, Ian. *In the Heat,* St. Martin's Minotaur, 2008, 245 pp. Caribbean Noir mystery set in Belize City and Cayo, by a talented new Belizean writer who now lives in Florida. *In the Heat* in 2009 won the Shamus Award for best first novel from the Private Eye Writers of America.

-- *Lonesome Point,* Minotaur Books, St. Martin's Press, 2009, 263 pp. Vasquez's second novel is set in Florida, with flashbacks to Belize.

Westlake, Donald. *High Adventure,* Mysterious Press, 1985. Dope, dummies and deliverance in Belize, by popular adventure writer.

Wilentz, Gay. *Memories, Dreams and Nightmares, Vol. 1, a Short Story Anthology by Belizean Women Writers,* Cubola Productions, 2004, 164 pp. Collection of stories by 13 Belizean female writers.

-- Memories, Dreams and Nightmares, Vol. 2, a Short Story Anthology by Belizean Women Writers, Cubola Productions, 2005, 124 pp. The second volume.

Young, Colville. *Pataki Full,* Cubola Productions, 120 pp. Collection of short stories by noted Belizean writer and scholar.

ZooDoc. *War Star Rising: Legend of Toucan Moon,* Star Publish, 2008, 216 pp. Young adult novel about a Maya princess at Xunantunich who speaks out against human sacrifice.

Guidebooks/Travel Guides

Egerton, Alex, Harding, Paul and Schechter, Daniel C., *Lonely Planet Belize,*

6th ed., Lonely Planet Guides, 2016, 320 pp. An improvement over previous *LP Belize* guides.

Eltringham, Peter. *Belize, The Rough Guide,* Rough Guides, 2014, 400 pp. Thoroughly researched guide by knowledgeable writer who spent many years in Belize and Guatemala. Peter Eltringham passed away in 2008. Updated by various Rough Guide authors, but this 2014 edition is somewhat out-of-date.

Girma, Lebawit Lily, *Moon Belize,* Moon Handbooks, 2017, 432 pp. Good, up-to-date guide that builds partly on the work of Joshua Berman, who formerly did the *Moon Belize* guides.

Glassman, Paul. *Belize Guide,* Open Road Publishing, 12th ed. 2006, 295 pp. Glassman was a pioneering guidebook author to destinations in Central America, including Costa Rica, Nicaragua and Belize. A Kindle edition was released in 2012 and another 2014.

Greenspan, Eliot. *Frommer's Belize,* Wiley Publishing, 2011, 352 pp. Useful guide though now badly dated.

Harvard Student Agencies, *Let's Go Guatemala & Belize: The Student Travel Guide,* Let's Go, 2009, 304 pp. Budget-oriented guide researched by intrepid Harvard students. Now out of print, however.

Insight Guides Belize, Insight Guides, 5th. ed., 2015, 341 pp. Excellent photos and good general background on the country; weak on hotels and restaurants.

Jones-Burgess, Kate, *Explorer's Guide Belize,* Explorer's Great Destinations, Countryman Press, 2010, 368 pp. One of our very favorite guides ever written to Belize – too bad it hasn't been updated and reprinted.

King, Emory. *Driver's Guide to Beautiful Belize,* Tropical Books, 2007, 40 pp. Mile-by-mile guide to most roads in Belize. Not updated since Emory King's death and currently out of print.

Lougheed, Vivien. *Adventure Guide to Belize,* Hunter Publishing, 6th edition, 2006, 555 pp. Tons of good information by the author of *Central America by Chickenbus.* Unfortunately, now out of print and very dated.

-- *Belize Pocket Adventures,* Pocket Adventures, 2009, 316 pp. Shorter version of Lougheed's early book for Hunter Publishing. Also available in a Kindle edition.

Mahler, Richard. *Adventures in Nature Belize,* Avalon, 1999, 362 pp. A guidebook that focuses on nature travel in Belize. This was a good idea that was canned by Avalon. Someone should do the concept again, as this guide is now badly out-of-date.

Middleton, Ned. *Diving Belize,* Aqua Quest Diving, 1998, 128 pp. Better than Lonely Planet's dive guide though an update is needed.

Morris, Charlie. *Open Road's The Best of Belize,* Open Road, 3rd ed. 2013, 248 pp. Guidebook series claims to cut to the chase and give only what's best at the destinations. Not up-to-date.

Rock, Tim. *Lonely Planet Diving & Snorkeling Belize,* 4th. edition, Lonely Planet, 2007, 144 pp. Improved from earlier editions, but overlooks some dive and snorkel sites.

Sluder, Lan and Lambert-Sluder, Rose. *Fodor's Belize: with a Sidetrip to Guatemala,* Fodor's Travel, 7th ed., 2017, 320 pp. Lan Sluder has been doing the *Fodor's* guides to Belize, with coverage of parts of Guatemala, for 20 years. Sluder did the first and all subsequent *Fodor's Belize* guidebooks until this edition and before that did the Belize portion of *Fodor's Belize and Guatemala.* Rose Lambert-Sluder, who has been traveling to Belize since she was three years old, co-authored this new edition.

Sluder, Lan, *Best Belize Hotels and Restaurants,* Equator, 2016, 160 pp. This book (also an ebook) reviews and rates the best hotels and restaurants in Belize.

—*Lan Sluder's Guide to the Cayes, Coast and Beaches of Belize,* Equator, 2016, 316 pp. Covers all of the cayes plus coastal areas of Belize in detail.

— *Lan Sluder's Guide to Belize,* Equator, 2016, 490 pp. One of the most complete, detailed and up-to-date guidebooks to the country.

— *Lan Sluder's Guide to Mainland Belize,* Equator, 2016, 367 pp. Covers all of mainland Belize, plus the Tikal area of Guatemala. Replaces an earlier edition.

— *San Pedro Cool, Guide to Ambergris Caye, Belize,* Equator, 2002, updated as an ebook in 2009, 201 pp. Comprehensive guide to Ambergris Caye, with short section on Caye Caulker and other islands.

History and Culture

Balboni, Barbara. *Taking Stock: Belize at 25 Years of Independence,* Cubola Productions, 2007, 343 pp. Noted Belizeans take a look at what Belize has achieved in its first 25 years of independence.

Barry, Tom with Vernon, Dylan. *Inside Belize,* Resource Center Press, 2nd. ed., 1995, 181 pp. Useful but now somewhat dated overview of history, politics, media, education, economy and the environment.

Bolland, O. Nigel, *Colonialism and Resistance in Belize, Essays in Historical Sociology,* Cubola Productions, 2003, 228 pp. Examines colonialism in the country over three centuries.

Bulmer-Thomas, Barbara, and Bulmer-Thomas, Victor, *The Economic History of Belize,* Cubola Productions, 2012, 214 pp. An economic history of Belize from the 17th century to after independence.

Burdon, Sir John Alder (ed.). *Archives of British Honduras* (3 vols.), Sifton Praed, 1931-35. This controversial history of British Honduras by Sir John Burdon, a governor of the colony, helped create and perpetuate myths about British colonialism and "benign" slavery in Belize that continued to influence historians for decades.

Burnworth, Joe. *No Safe Harbor: The Tragedy of the Dive Ship Wave Dancer,* Emmis Books, 2005, 256 pp. The story of the 21 people who died on the Wave Dancer live-aboard in Hurricane Iris in October 2001.

Cayetano, E. Roy. *The People's Garifuna Dictionary,* Angelus Press, 82 pp. Work in progress —a dictionary of the Garifuna language.

Cayetano, Sebastian. Garifuna History, Language & Culture of Belize, Central America & the Caribbean, Angelus Press, 170 pp.

Crosbie, Paul, editor-in-chief; Herrera, Yvette; Manzanares, Myrna; Woods, Silvana; Crosbie, Cynthia; and Decker, Ken, eds. *Kriol-Inglish Dikshineri English-Kriol Dictionary,* Belize Kriol Project, 2007, 465 pp. First comprehensive dictionary to the Belize Kriol language.

Dobson, Narda. *A History of Belize,* Longman Caribbean, 1973, 362 pp. History from Early Maya period to 1970.

Foster, Byron. *The Baymen's Legacy,* Cubola Productions, 2nd. ed., 1992, 83 pp. A history of Belize City.

— *Heart Drum,* Cubola Productions, 60 pp. A look at dagu and other aspects of Garifuna life.

Henderson, Peta. *Rising Up: Life Stories of Belizean Women,* Sister Vision Press, 1998, 302 pp.

Kane, William and Stanton, John. A Jesuit in Belize: The Life and Adventures of Father Buck Stanton in Nineteenth Century Central America, CreateSpace, 2008, 422 pp.

King, Emory. *Diary of St. George's Caye,* Tropical Books, 32 pp.

— *The Great Story of Belize,* Volume 1, Tropical Books, 1999, 53 pp. The first in what was to be a four-volume set, this volume covers the history of Belize from 1511 when the first Europeans arrive until 1798, when the Baymen won the battle of St. George's Caye.

— *The Great Story of Belize,* Volume 2, Tropical Books, 1999, 87 pp. Volume 2 tells the history of Belize from 1800 to 1850, the period which shaped Belize's history for generations to come.

— 1798 *The Road to Glory,* Tropical Books, 1991, 348 pp. Fictionalized and somewhat glorified account of the Battle of St. George Caye.

Koop, Gerhard S. *Pioneer Years In Belize,* Angelus Press, 144 pp. History of the Mennonites in Mexico and Belize.

Leslie, Robert, Ed. *A History of Belize: Nation in the Making,* Cubola Productions, rev. ed., 1995, 125 pp. First published in 1983, this history of Belize is written for Belize schoolchildren.

McClaurin, Irma. *Women of Belize: Gender and Change in Central America,* Rutgers University Press, 1996, 232 pp. Three women describe their experiences in Belize.

Merrill, Tim. *Guyana and Belize Country Studies,* Federal Research Division, Library of Congress, 2nd. ed.,1993, 408 pp. One in the Area Handbook series sponsored by the U.S. Army; nevertheless, the historical, cultural and economic information is first rate.

Peedle, Ian. *Belize, A Guide to the People, Politics and Culture,* Interlink Books, 1999, 100 pp. Tries to cover everything in a small volume, and fails.

Setzekorn, William David. *Belize, Formerly British Honduras,* Ohio University Press, 1981, 300 pp. A profile of Belize's folklore, history, culture, economics and geography.

Shoman, Assad. *Thirteen Chapters of a History of Belize,* Angelus Press, 1994, 4th. printing 2000, 297 pp. Somewhat left-wing interpretation of Belize history, by a prominent Belizean intellectual and politician.

Simmons, Donald C. Jr. *Confederate Settlements in British Honduras,* McFarland & Co., 2001, 176 pp. Discusses ex-Confederates who settled in Belize after the U.S. Civil War.

Smith, Godfrey P., *George Price: A Life Revealed,* Ian Randle Publishers, 2011, 358 pp. Godfrey Smith is an attorney and PUP politician, so this is not exactly an unbiased biography of the "father of Belize," but it is well written and goes a long way to explain why the late George Price was so beloved in Belize.

Sutherland, Anne. *The Making of Belize, Globalization in the Margins,* Bergin & Garvey, 1998, 202 pp. An American university professor with long family ties to Belize looks at "postmodern" Belize.

Thomson, P. A. B. *Belize, A Concise History,* MacMillan Caribbean, 2005, 192 pp.

Twigg, Arthur. *Understanding Belize: A Historical Guide,* Harbour, 2006, 240 pp. Arthur Twigg is the editor of a Canadian book magazine.

Waddell, D.A.G. *British Honduras, A Historical and Contemporary Survey,* Greenwood Press, 1961, reprinted 1981, 151 pp. An academic history.

Wilk, Richard R. Household Ecology: Economic Change and Domestic Life Among the Kekchi Maya in Belize, Northern Illinois University Press, 1997, 280 pp.

Young, Colville. *Creole Proverbs of Belize,* Cubola Productions, 44 pp.

Maya Atlas: The Struggle to Preserve Maya Land in Southern Belize, compiled by the Maya People of Southern Belize, Toledo Maya Cultural Council, 1997.

Living in Belize

Day-Wilson, Victoria *Moon Living Abroad in Belize,* Avalon Travel Publishing, 2012, 328 pp. It is what it is.

Dhillon, Bob, and Langan, Fred, *Business and Retirement Guide to Belize: The Last Virgin Paradise,* Dundurn, 2011, 128 pp. Short book, short on illustrations, maps and information.

Gallo, Roger. *Escape from America,* Manhattan Loft Publishing, 1997, 352 pp. Devoted to living/retiring abroad. Includes chapters on Belize. Roger Gallo later established the EscapeArtist.com website, based in Panama where he lived.

Golson, Barry and Golson, Thia. *Retirement Without Borders,* Scribner's, 2008, 432 pp. Looks at retirement options in a number of countries around the world. Lan Sluder contributed the chapter on Belize.

Gray, Bill and Gray, Claire (pseudonyms). *Belize Retirement Guide,* Preview Publishing, 4th ed., 1999, 140 pp. Guide to "living in a tropical paradise for $450 a month." Somehow, we kinda doubt it.

Koerner, Nancy R., *Belize Survivor: The Darker Side of Paradise,* NKD Marketing, 2007, 300 pp. Personal memoir of being abused in a relationship in Belize. Not so much about Belize as about the author.

King, Emory. *"Hey, Dad, This Is Belize,"* Tropical Books, Belize, 4th printing, 114 pp. Collection of vignettes about Belize and Belizeans. Originally appeared in the Belize Times and other publications.

— *How to Visit, Invest or Retire in Belize,* Tropical Books, 1989, 32 pp. Early booklet on the subject.

— *"I Spent It All In Belize,"* Tropical Books, 194 pp. More sketches of Belizean life. Emory King was a genius at picking book titles.

Marsh, Sonia, *Freeways to Flip-Flops, A Family's Year of Gutsy Living on a Tropical Island,* Gutsy Publications, 2012, 328 pp. A breezy memoir of a family moving from Southern California to Belize and trying to make a life on Ambergris Caye. It wasn't long before the author picked up and left.

Peham, Helga. *Escaping the Rat Race – Freedom in Paradise,* World Audience, 2007, 344 pp. A series of interviews with expats and others in Belize, by a woman who lived in Corozal. Also available in a Kindle edition.

Roebuck, G., *Moving to Belize, Not for Me!* CreateSpace, 2014, 102 pp. Thin little book. Everyone is entitled to an opinion.

Salisbury, Christina and Salisbury, Kirby. *Treehouse Perspectives: Living High on Little,* Mill City Press, 2009, 324 pp. Memoir of a couple's 36 years living in a treehouse in Toledo.

Sluder, Lan. *Living Abroad in Belize,* Avalon, 2005, 367 pp. Comprehensive guide to living, retiring, working, and investing in Belize.

— *Adapter Kit: Belize,* Avalon, 2001, 261 pp. The predecessor edition of *Living Abroad in Belize.* Still in the libraries of many expats and hotel owners in Belize.

— *Easy Belize: How to Live, Retire, Work and Invest in Belize, the English Speaking, Frost Free Paradise on the Caribbean Coast,* Equator, originally published in 2010, fully revised and expanded 2nd edition, 2016, 459 pp. This is the new edition of the best-selling book and ebook on living or retiring in Belize. Available from Amazon.com as a paperback and in a Kindle edition and also available from bookstores worldwide.

Memoirs

Conroy, Richard Timothy. *Our Man in Belize,* St. Martin's, 1997, 324 pp. Fascinating, highly readable memoir of life in former British Honduras in the late 1950s and early 60s. We love this book!

DeMarks, Dean Fortune. *The Tourist: Who's Too Dangerous for Belize,* BookSurge Publishing, 2009, 354 pp. Semi-literate account of why Belize is such a terrible place, by a would-be Placencia real estate developer who was deported from the country.

Fry, Joan. *How to Cook a Tapir: A Memoir of Belize,* University of Nebraska Press, 2009, 294 pp. Fascinating recollections of a young American woman's experiences in Toledo in the early 1960s.

King, Emory. *The Little World of Danny Vasquez,* Tropical Books, 1989, 134 pp. Emory King's presentation of his father-in-law's memoirs.

Natural History

Ames, Oakes and Correll, Donovan Stewart. *Orchids of Guatemala and Belize,* Dover Publications, 1985, 779 pp. with 204 black-and-white illustrations. Republication of Chicago Natural History Museum 1953 field guide and 1965 supplement. Exhaustive, covering 527 species.

Arvigo, Rosita and Balick, Michael. *Rainforest Remedies, One Hundred Healing Herbs of Belize,* Lotus Press, 1993, 221 pp. Guide to traditional Mayan/Belizean herbal remedies.

Arvigo, Rosita with Epstein, Nadine and Yaquinto, Marilyn. *Sastun, My Apprenticeship with a Maya Healer,* HarperSanFrancisco, 1994,190 pp. Story of Arvigo's time with Don Elijio Panti.

Arvigo, Rosita with Epstein, Nadine. Rainforest Home Remedies: The Maya Way to Heal Your Body and Replenish Your Soul, HarperOne, 2001, 240 pp.

Barcott, Bruce. *The Last Flight of the Scarlet Macaw: One Woman's Fight to*

Save the World's Most Beautiful Bird, Random House, 2008 hard cover, 2009 paper, 336 pp. Remarkable, gripping story of Sharon Matola's fight against the Chalillo dam.

Beletsky, Les. *Travellers' Wildlife Guide, Belize and Northern Guatemala,* Travellers' Wildlife Guides, 2010, 477 pp. Lavishly color-illustrated guide, oriented to the amateur, to the most commonly spotted mammals, birds, amphibians, reptiles, fish and corals.

Belize Bird Guide, Rainforest Productions, 2012. A 14-page laminated pamphlet to help you identify common birds in Belize.

Campbell, Jonathan A. *Amphibians and Reptiles of Northern Guatemala, the Yucatán, and Belize,* University of Oklahoma Press, 1998, 380 pp., with 176 color photographs. The best guide to herpetofauna of the region.

Emmons, Katherine. Cockscomb Basin Wildlife Sanctuary: Its History, Flora and Fauna for Visitors, Teachers and Scientists, Community Conservation Consultants, 1996. Definitive on the subject.

Frenz, Bert, *A Birders Guide to Belize,* American Birding Association, 2012, 374 pp. The newest and one of the most useful books on birding in Belize. It has a detailed guide to the locations where you're likely to see specific birds. However, for bird identification you'll need Lee Jones' *Birds of Belize (see below).*

Greenfield, David W. and Thomerson, Jamie E. *Fishes of the Continental Waters of Belize,* University Press of Florida, 1997, 311 pp. Comprehensive guide, with black-and-white illustrations.

Edwards, Ernest Preston, illustrated by Butler, E.M. *A Field Guide to the Birds of Mexico and Adjacent Areas: Belize, Guatemala, and El Salvador,* University of Texas Press, 1998, 288 pp. This is used by many local guides in Belize.

Harris, Kate. *Trees of Belize,* self-published, 2009, 120 pp. Handy guide to common and notable trees of Belize, with color photos of most of them.

Horwich, Robert H. *A Belizean Rain Forest,* Orang-utan Press, 1990, 420 pp. A look at the Community Baboon Sanctuary and the northern forests of Belize.

Jones, H. Lee and Gardner, Dana. *Birds of Belize,* University of Texas Press, 2004, 445 pp. The gold standard of Belize bird books. A must for any birder traveling to Belize.

Keesmaat, Irene, *A Rainbow of Colors, A Guide to the Flowers of Belize,* Cubola, 2011, 30 pp. Short booklet on some popular flowers of Belize.

Koeppel, Dan, *Banana, The Fate of the Fruit That Changed the World,* Hudson Street Press, 2008, 281 pp. Fascinating story of how the banana became the most popular fruit in the world. Sections of this book are on banana production in British Honduras/Belize.

LaBastille, A. *Birds of the Mayas,* West of the Winds Publications, 1993.

Lee, Julian. A Field Guide to the Amphibians and Reptiles of the Maya World: The Lowlands of Mexico, Northern Guatemala and Belize, Cornell University Press, 2000, 488 pp.

Matola, Sharon. *Birds of Belize, A Field Handbook,* Belize Zoo, 28 pp.

Meyer, John R. and Foster, Carol Farneti. *A Guide to the Frogs and Toads of Belize,* Krieger Publishing, 1996.

Miller, Carolyn M. and Miller, Bruce W. *Exploring the Tropical Forest at Chan Chich Lodge Belize,* Wildlife Conservation Society, 2nd. ed., 1994, 51 pp.

Peterson, Roger Tory and Chalif, Edward L. *A Field Guide to Mexican Birds: Mexico, Guatemala, Belize, El Salvador,* Peterson Field Guides/Houghton-Mifflin, 1999. The birder's pal, though it lacks Spanish names of birds.

Rabinowitz, Alan. *Jaguar,* Arbor House, 1986, 368 pp. Fascinating story of effort to establish the Cockscomb Preserve.

Reichling, Steven B. *Tarantulas of Belize,* Krieger Publishing Co., 2003, 148 pp. Everything you never wanted to know about tarantulas in Belize.

Sayers, Brendan, and Adams, Brett, *A Guide to the Orchids of Belize,* Cubola, 2009, 152 pp. Not as thorough as some orchid guides but certainly sufficient for the layperson.

Stafford, Peter J. and Meyer, John R. *A Guide to the Reptiles of Belize,* Academic Press, 1999, 356 pp.

Stevens, Kate. *Jungle Walk.* Birds and animals of Belize, with many illustrations

Woods, R.L., Reid, S.T. and Reid, A.M. *The Field Guide to Ambergris Caye.* Near exhaustive study of the island and surrounding sea.

Wright, Charles. *Land in British Honduras: A Report of the British Honduras Land Use Survey Team,* Her Majesty's Stationery Office, 1959, 327 pp. What began as a soils survey by Toledo resident Charles Wright became a detailed analysis of farming practices and land use in mid-twentieth century British Honduras.

Snakes of Belize, Belize Audubon Society, 55 pp. Short guide to the snakes you probably won't see in Belize.

Survivalist and Sustainable Living

Gehring, Abigail R. (ed.). *Back to Basics: A Complete Guide to Traditional Skills,* Skyhorse Publishing, 2008, 456 pp. This book, written by experts in various fields, gives you the tools and skills you need to live in a sustainable away in Belize or anywhere.

Rawles, James Wesley. *How to Survive the End of the World as We Know It, Tactics, Techniques, and Technologies for Uncertain Times,* Plume Books, 2009, 316 pp. The author, a former U.S. intelligence officer, is an expert on family preparedness, including food and fuel storage, self-defense, gardening for sustainability and other subjects.

The Good, David. *Totally Crazy, Easy Florida Gardening: The Secret to Growing Piles of Food in the Sunshine State,* CreateSpace, 2015, 112 pp. Florida's climate is somewhat similar to Belize's, so you'll find this short, to-the-point book on gardening in semi-tropical areas of value.

Wiseman, John "Lofty." *SAS Survival Handbook for Any Climate in Any Situation,* Collins, 2009, 576 pp. Written by a 26-year veteran of the British Special Air Service, this information-packed guide covers everything from basic survival needs to campcraft, first aid and disaster survival.

Tales of Travel

Canby, Peter. *Heart of the Sky, Travels Among the Maya,* HarperCollins, 1992, 368 pp. Modern classic on the modern Maya.

Chaplin, Gordon. *The Fever Coast Log*, Simon & Schuster, 1992, 229 pp. Couple sets sail aboard the Lord Jim to sail the Caribbean Coast. You know it's all going to end badly.

Faber, Carol and Perlow, Paula. *2 Jamericans Travel to San Pedro, Belize*, Trafford Publishing, 2006, 136 pp. Little book on the experiences of two women vacationing in San Pedro.

Davis, Richard Harding. *Three Gringos in Venezuela and Central America*, Harper & Brothers, 1896. Early travelogue begins in British Honduras.

Heistand, Emily. The Very Rich Hours: Travel in Orkney, Belize, the Everglades and Greece, Beacon Press, 1992, 236 pp.

Janson, Thor. Belize, *Land of the Free by the Carib Sea*, Bowen & Bowen, 2000, 96 pp. Published in Belize, this book has wonderful photos of the country and the people.

Huxley, Aldous. *Beyond the Mexique Bay*, Greenwood, 1975. First published in 1934, this book by the author of *Brave New World* holds the record for the most-quoted comment on British Honduras: "... if the world had any ends, British Honduras would surely be one of them."

Pride, Nigel. *A Butterfly Sings to Pacaya*, Constable. A 1970s trip through Mexico, Belize and Guatemala.

Roberts, Orlando W. *Voyages and Excursions on the East Coast and in the Interior of Central America*, University of Florida Press, reprint 1965 (originally published in 1827).

Sluder, Lan, *Rambles Around Belize*, 2005-2012. Short ebooks, published annually, on travels around Belize.

Stratman, Steve. *Belize to Guatemala: a nine-day adventure guide*, The Artful Nomad Company, 2006, 60 pp. The author narrates a short trip from Caye Caulker via San Ignacio to Flores and Tikal, Guatemala.

Straughan, Robert P. *Adventure in Belize*, A.S. Barnes & Co., 1975, 215 pp. Explorations in Belize, by a pet store and tropical fish store owner.

Stephens, John L. *Incidents of Travel in Central America, Chiapas and Yucatan*, Harper and Brothers, 1841. The great classic of early Central American travel books.

Wright, Ronald. *Time Among the Maya: Travels in Belize, Guatemala and Mexico*, Grove Press, 2000, 464 pages. Travel diary in impressionistic style.

Maps and Atlases

Ambergris Caye Belize Dive Map & Reef Creatures Guide, Franko Maps, 2011. Laminated fish card.

Atlas of Belize, Cubola Productions, 20th ed., 1995, 32 pp. with 11 maps and 80 photographs. Prepared for use in schools.

Belize Atolls Dive Map & Reef Creatures Guide, Franko Maps, 2013. A small map of the atolls is on one side and an identification guide to fishes around the atolls is on the other. Laminated. Useful aid for divers and snorkelers.

Belize National Geographic Adventure Map, National Geographic Maps, 2009. Helpful, but with some errors.

Belize Traveller's Map, ITMB, 2005. The best general road map of Belize, although it is now somewhat out of date. Scale 1:250,000.

British Ordnance Survey, Topographical Map of Belize, 1991. Two sheets, with maps of Belize City and towns on reverse. 1:250,000-scale. Out of print.

British Ordnance Survey, Area Topographical Maps, various dates, 1970s-1990s. Country is divided into 44 sections, each 1:50,000-scale. Most are out of print.

Insight Fleximap Belize, American Map, 2003. Sturdy and water-resistant but not fully up-to-date.

Laminated Belize Map, Borsch, 2012. German cartography company produced this handy, durable map. Scale 1:500,000. Would have been nice if the scale were a little larger. In English, Spanish, French and Italian.

Wall Map of Belize, Cubola Productions. This large 36 x 58 inch color map of Belize is suitable for hanging on your wall. Scale is 1:250,000. It is updated fairly often. However, it is expensive, near US$60 including shipping. Cubola also publishes several other Belize maps.

Appendix C: Belize Attorneys

The following list of attorneys practicing in Belize was provided by the United States Embassy in Belize. Neither the Embassy nor the author assumes any responsibility for the professional ability of the individuals or firms listed here. Names are listed alphabetically, and the order in which they appear has no other significance. The information in the list on professional credentials, areas of expertise and language ability are provided directly by the lawyers. You may receive additional information about the individuals by contacting the Belize Bar Association at 501-227-2785.

ARGUELLES, EMIL of ARGUELLES & COMPANY LLC, 35 New Road, Belize. Born July 4, 1972, Belize. Graduated from Marquette University, B.A.; U.W.I., LL.B.; Norman Manley Law School, C.L.E. Trust & Estate Practitioner (TEP). Admitted to Belize Bar in 1998. Appointed Speaker of House of Representatives in 2008. Corresponds in English. Corporate, Tax, Intellectual Property, Real Estate and General Practice. Can provide translator/reporter/stenographer/notary. Will take cases outside Belize City. Office Phone: 501-223-0088, 223-0858. Fax: 223-6403. Cell Phone: 610-2961. Email: info@belizelawyer.com/ Website: www.belizelawyer.com. Personal Email: belizelawyer@hotmail.com

ARNOLD, ELLIS R. LL.B. (Hons) CLE 52 Albert Street, Belize City, Belize. Graduated from the Norman Manley Law School, C.L.E.; University of the West Indies LL.B. in 1977. Admitted to Belize Bar in 1983. Corresponds in English. General Practice and criminal matters. Notary Public. Will take cases outside of Belize City. Office phone 501-227-0810; 227-1106; Fax: 227-1119; Cell: 610-1276 E-mail: ellisarnold@hotmail.com

BARROW, DYLAN, of the LAW OFFICES OF RAYMOND H. BARROW, 121 Albert Street, Belize City, Belize. Born January 24, 1950, Belize. Graduated from U.W.I. C.L.E. Admitted to Belize Bar in 1985. Corresponds in English. General Practice and Criminal Matters. Can provide translator / reporter / stenographer / notary. Office Phone: 501-227-2912. Fax: 227-1270.

BRADLEY, JR., LEO, 90A New Road, Belize City, Belize. Born December 31, 1967, Belize. Graduated from St. Thomas University, B.A. U.W.I., LLB. Norman Manley Law School, C.L.E. Admitted to Belize Bar in 1998. Corresponds in English and Spanish. General Practice and Criminal Matters. Can provide translator / reporter / stenographer / notary. Office Phone: 501-223-3014

CHEBAT, MICHELLE of SHOMAN, CHEBAT, & ASSOC., 53 Barrack Road, Belize City, Belize. Born January 27, 1964, Belize City, Belize. Graduated from U.W.I., C.L.E. Admitted to Belize Bar in 1988. Corresponds in English and Spanish. General Practice with specialty in commercial / corporate / offshore. Can provide translator / reporter / stenographer / notary. Will take cases outside Belize

City. Office Phone: 223-4160 / 223-4161 Fax: 223-4222. Email: attorney@btl.net www.shomanchebat.com

COURTENAY, S.C., DEREK of W. H. COURTENAY & CO., 1876 Hutson Street, Belize City, Belize. Corresponds in English and Spanish. Commercial and General Practice. Can provide notary. Office Phone: 501-223-5701; 224-4248. Fax: 223-9962. Email: derek@courtenaylaw.com

COURTENAY, S.C., DENISE of W. H. COURTENAY & CO., 1876 Hutson Street, Belize City, Belize. Corresponds in English and Spanish. Commercial and General Practice. Can provide notary. Office Phone: 501-223-5701; 224-4248. Fax: 223-9962. Email: denise@courtenaylaw.com

COURTENAY, JEREMY of W. H. COURTENAY & CO., 1876 Hutson Street, Belize City, Belize. Corresponds in English. Commercial and General Practice. Office Phone: 501-223-5701; 224-4248. Fax: 223-9962. Email: jeremy@courtenaylaw.com

RETREAGE, VANESSA of W. H. COURTENAY & CO., 1876 Hutson Street, Belize City, Belize. Corresponds in English. Commercial and General Practice. Office Phone: 223-5701; 224-4248. Fax: 223-9962. Email: vanessa@courtenaylaw.com

LINDO, DEAN R. of LINDO'S LAW FIRM, 7 Church Street, (P.O. Box 558, Belize City, Belize. Born September 4, 1932, Belize. Graduated from Wesley College. NYU, BSc and LL.M. University of Durham, England, LL.B. (Hons.). Gray's Inn. Admitted to the Belize Bar in 1964. Corresponds in English and Spanish. General Practice. Can Provide translator / reporter / stenographer / notary. Will take cases outside Belize City. Office Phone: (501) 227-7388 Fax: (501) 2275168 Home Phone: 224-4217 Email: linlaw@btl.net

LUMOR, FRED of MUSA & BALDERAMOS, 3750 University Blvd Edem Place, P.O. Box 2577, Belize City, Belize. Born November 17, 1952, Ghana. Graduated from Rivers State in Nigeria, LL.B. (Hons.) Ministry of Justice 4.5 years. Corresponds in English. General Practice. Can provide translator / reporter / stenographer / notary. Will take cases outside Belize City. Office Phone: 501-223-6024 Fax: 501-223-6001. Email: flumor_co@yahoo.com

MARIN, MAGALI G. , 99 Albert Street, P.O. Box 617, Belize City, Belize. Born November 18, 1971, Belize City. Graduated from University of Oklahoma, B.A. U.W.I., LL.B. Norman Manley Law School, C.L.E. Admitted to the Belize Bar in 1997. Corresponds in English and Spanish. General Practice. Can provide translator / reporter / stenographer / notary. Will take cases outside Belize City. Office Phone: 501-227-5280 Fax: 501-227-5278. Email: attorneys@barrowandwilliams.com Website: www.barrowandwilliams.com

MARSHALLECK, E. ANDREW of BARROW & COMPANY, 23 Regent Street, Belize City, Belize. Born July 23, 1969, Kingston, Jamaica. Graduated from Regis College, BA. U.W.I., LL.B. Norman Manley Law School, C.L.E. Admitted to Belize Bar in 1996. Corresponds in English. General Practice. Can provide translator / reporter / stenographer / notary. Will take cases outside Belize City. Office Phone: 223-5900/ 223-5903/ 22-35908 Fax: 223-5913 Email barrowco@btl.net

MOORE, ANTOINETTE of the LAW OFFICES OF ANTOINETTE MOORE, Cassian Nunez Street, Dangriga Town, Stann Creek District. Born June 3, 1955, Brooklyn, New York. Graduated from Lawrence University, B.A. Loyola University of Chicago, J.D. Norman Manley Law School, C.L.E. Admitted to Belize Bar in 1996. Temporary member of Belize Supreme Court. Corresponds in English and some Spanish. General Practice and Criminal Matters. Can provide translator, reporter, stenographer and notary. Will take cases outside Belize City. Office Phone: 522-2457 Fax: 522-2457 Email: moorelaw@btl.net

MUSA-POTT, SAMIRA Suite 308 Marina Towers, Newtown Barracks Belize City, Belize. Born April 29, 1971, Belize City, Belize. Graduated from Florida Int'l University, B.A. U.W.I., LL.B. Norman Manley Law School, C.L.E. Admitted to Belize Bar in 1996. Corresponds in English and some Spanish. General Practice. Can provide translator / reporter / stenographer / notary. Will take cases outside Belize City. Office Phone: (501) 223-2238 35924 Fax: (501) 223-2360 Email: smusapott@btl.net

SABIDO, OSCAR A. of OSCAR A. SABIDO & CO., #5 New Road, Belize City, Belize. Born January 7, 1949, San Ignacio Town. Graduated from U.W.I., LL.B. Norman Manley Law School, C.L.E. Admitted to Belize Bar in 1979. Corresponds in English and fluent Spanish. General Practice and Criminal Matters. Can provide translator / reporter / stenographer / notary. Will take cases outside Belize City. Office Phone: 223-5803 Fax: 223-5839. Home Phone: 227-2901 Email: oasabido@btl.net

SOOKNANDAN, LUTCHMAN of SOOKNANDAN'S LAW FIRM, 3 Barrack Road, Belize City, Belize. Born March 21, 1948, Guyana. Graduated from U.W.I., LL.B., C.L.E. Admitted to Belize Bar in 1986. Corresponds in English. General Practice and Criminal Matters. Office Phone: 223-2469. Home phone: 223-2625 Fax: 223-5164 Email: lsooknan@btl.net

TWIST, OSWALD H. of the BELIZE LEGAL AID CENTER, 16 Bishop Street, Belize City, Belize. Born June 9, 1959, Belize. Graduated from U.W.I., LL.B. Norman Manley Law School, C.L.E. Admitted to Belize Bar in 1996. Corresponds in English. General Practice and Criminal Matters. Can provide translator / reporter / stenographer / notary. Office Phone/Fax: 227-5781 BELMOPAN OFFICE: Phone: 822-1475 Fax: 822-1476 Home Phone: 802-3471

WILLIAMS, RODWELL of BARROW & WILLIAMS, 99 Albert Street,

Belize City, Belize. Born September 29, 1956, Belize City, Belize. Graduated with B.A., LL.B., C.L.E. Admitted to Belize Bar in 1985. Corresponds in English. General Practice. Can provide translator / reporter / stenographer / notary. Will take cases outside Belize City. Office Phone: 227-5280. Fax: 227-5278 Email: attorneys@barrowandwilliams.com Website: www.barrowandwilliams.com

YOUNG, MICHAEL CLARENCE EDWARD of YOUNG'S LAW FIRM, 28 Regent Street, Belize City, Belize. Born January 7, 1955, Southhampton, England. Graduated from U.W.I., LL.B. Norman Manley Law School, (Hons) C.L.E. Admitted to Belize Bar in 1977. Solicitor of the Supreme Court of Belize. Corresponds in English. General Practice. Office Phone: 227-7406 / 72408 / 72544 Fax: 227-5157 Home Phone: 223-2519 Email: services@younglaw.bz Website: www.younglaw.bz

LOIS YOUNG BARROW & COMPANY 120 A New Road, PO Box 565, Belize City, Belize Tel: 501-223-5924 Email loisblaw@btl.net

Appendix D: Belize Websites

Here are some of our favorite web sites about Belize, In addition to these, search Facebook for pages on Belize. Several are devoted to expats in Belize.

Destination and General Websites
www.agreport.bz Excellent information on farming and ranching in Belize.

www.ambergriscaye.com Impressive site with massive amount of material about Ambergris Caye. Good links to other sites, including most hotels, dive shops, real estate firms and other businesses on the island. Active message board.

www.sanpedrosun.com News about Ambergris Caye by its leading weekly newspaper

www.corozal.com Pretty good information about Corozal District, provided by students of Corozal Community College. A sister site, www.corozal.bz, has business listings and information.

www.hopkinsbelize.com Information on Hopkins village.

www.placencia.com Good tourist information on the Placencia peninsula from the BTIA.

www.destinationsbelize.com All kinds of news and information about Placencia.

www.cayecaulkervacation.com Official site of Belize Tourism Information Association in Caulker.

www.puntagordabelize.com The official web site of the town of Punta Gorda.

www.belmopanbelize.com Information on Belize's capital city.

www.belizefirst.com On-line magazine about Belize (Lan Sluder, editor and publisher) with dozens of articles on travel, life and retirement in Belize.

www.belize.gov.bz Official site of the Government of Belize – not always up-to-date, unfortunately.

www.belizeinvest.org.bz Site of Beltraide, which is charged with attracting business investment to Belize.

www.belizenet.com Well-done site on Belize travel and other information, by folks who provide a lot of web design services in Belize. Associated with an active message board, Belize Forums at www.belizeforum.com.

www.channel5belize.com This Belize City TV station provides definitive and reliable sources of news on Belize. The weekday evening news broadcast is provided in transcript form and also in video.

www.7newsbelize.com Another good Belize City TV station with video and transcripts of the news broadcasts.

www.belizenews.com This site has links to most newspapers, TV and radio stations, magazines and other media in Belize.

www.stonetreerecords.com Stonetree has been making Belize music since 1995.

www.cubola.com Site of publisher of books and maps on Belize.

www.travelbelize.org or www.belizetourismboard.org Recently revised versions of the official site of the Belize Tourism Board, with tons of information on hotels and sightseeing.

www.fodors.com Some guidebooks authored or co-authored by Lan Sluder, including *Fodor's Belize, Fodor's The Carolinas and Georgia,* and *InFocus Great Smoky Mountains National Park* are published by this Random House division, and parts of these books are available on-line.

www.belizeembassy.gov Official site of the U.S. Embassy in Belize.

www.expatexchange.com This site has a fairly active forum section on moving to and living in Belize.

www.internationalliving.com This for-profit company runs articles regularly and sells reports on Belize. There's a lot of useful information, but it is laced with commercial plugs.

Belize Blogs

http://belizebus.wordpress.com Excellent site with up-to-date information on bus, water taxi, air and other transportation options in Belize.

www.tacogirl.com Perhaps the best of all the personal blogs about Belize. Covers the country although mostly focused on Ambergris Caye, where the author lives.

http://winjama.blogspot.com Run by a man who moved to Corozal, this very helpful blog focuses on living in Belize.

http://tropicat.wordpress.com This blog is about living in the Belize bush.

http://bubbasbirdblog.blogspot.com Elbert Greer's blog on birding in Belize.

http://barnaclesbelize.blogspot.com Great Belize photos on this blog by "Barnacle Bill Taylor" in Maya Beach.

http://moonracerfarmbelize.blogspot.com A young couple, Marge and Tom, with a small lodge in Cayo near the Mountain Pine Ridge blog on living and running a lodge in a somewhat off-the-beaten-path part of Belize.

http://www.caribbean-colors.blogspot.com Lee Vanderwalker blogs about her life and art, especially on Caye Caulker.

About Lan Sluder

Lan Sluder is an old Belize hand, having been reporting on and writing about Belize since 1991. The author of more than 15 books and ebooks on Belize, Sluder has advised many people on the pros and cons of a new life in Belize. He also has helped thousands of travelers plan the vacation of a lifetime in this little English-speaking country on the Caribbean Coast of Central America.

Among Lan Sluder's Belize books, besides this one, are *Easy Belize, Fodor's Belize, Lan Sluder's Guide to Belize, Lan Sluder's Guide to thee Beaches, Cayes and Coast of Belize, Lan Sluder's Guide to Mainland Belize, Best Hotels and Restaurants in Belize, Living Abroad in Belize, Adapter Kit: Belize* and *San Pedro Cool.* Sluder is also founder, editor and publisher of *Belize First Magazine* – a web edition is at www.belizefirst.com.

In addition to his books on Belize, Sluder has authored three books on Asheville and the North Carolina mountains, including *Amazing Asheville, Asheville Relocation, Retirement and Visitor Guide* and *Moving to the Mountains.* He wrote *Frommer's Best Beach Vacations: Carolinas and Georgia* and co-authors *Fodor's The Carolinas & Georgia.* In addition, he has written books on the game of bridge, on classic Rolls-Royce and Bentley motorcars and on 25 of the most fascinating private eyes in books, film and television.

A former business newspaper editor and reporter in New Orleans, where he won a number of New Orleans Press Club awards, Sluder has contributed articles on travel, retirement and business subjects to publications around the world, including *The New York Times, Chicago Tribune, Miami Herald, Where to Retire, Globe and Mail, St. Petersburg Times, Bangkok Post, The Tico Times, Newsday* and *Caribbean Travel & Life.* In addition, he also authored the travel guides *InFocus Great Smoky Mountains National Park* and *Frommer's Best Beach Vacations: Carolinas and Georgia* and co-authored several editions of *Fodor's The*

Carolinas & Georgia.

When not in Belize or traveling elsewhere, Sluder lives on a mountain farm near Asheville, N.C. Questions, complaints and rants to Lan Sluder can be sent to him at lansluder@gmail.com.

Rose Lambert-Sluder, who shot most of the photos for this book and who has contributed to other books on Belize, including co-authoring the most recent *Fodor's Belize*, earned a Master of Fine Arts degree in creative writing at the University of Oregon, where she was a Graduate Teaching Fellow. She is pursuing a career as a fiction writer.

Goodbye to All That?

Remember, it never snows in Belize!

CPSIA information can be obtained
at www.ICGtesting.com
Printed in the USA
BVHW031015150323
660492BV00003B/54